Building Strategic Capabiliti

Firms in emerging markets are becoming leading global players despite operating in challenging home country environments, but little is known about how they build their capabilities. By analyzing multiple companies operating across over a dozen emerging markets in Asia, Latin America, Africa and Europe, the authors identify the specific challenges faced by emerging market firms to become internationally competitive. Furthermore, they provide actionable solutions to upgrading capabilities, sustaining competitive advantage, and achieving multinational status, all while operating in emerging economies. Featuring contributions from eminent business scholars from across the globe, this timely volume provides a valuable tool for academics and practitioners, managers and consultants, especially those involved with emerging market firms working to grow and succeed globally.

Alvaro Cuervo-Cazurra is Professor of International Business and Strategy at Northeastern University, a fellow of the Academy of International Business, and co-editor of *Global Strategy Journal*.

William Newburry is Chair of the Department of International Business and the Ryder Eminent Scholar of Global Business at Florida International University and a fellow of the Academy of International Business.

Seung Ho Park is President's Chair Professor of strategy and international business and Director of Nanyang Center for Emerging Markets at Nanyang Technological University and a Fellow of the Academy of International Business.

Building Strategic Capabilities in Emerging Markets

Edited by

Alvaro Cuervo-Cazurra
Northeastern University

William Newburry
Florida International University

Seung Ho Park
Nanyang Technological University

CAMBRIDGE
UNIVERSITY PRESS

University Printing House, Cambridge CB2 8BS, United Kingdom

One Liberty Plaza, 20th Floor, New York, NY 10006, USA

477 Williamstown Road, Port Melbourne, VIC 3207, Australia

314–321, 3rd Floor, Plot 3, Splendor Forum, Jasola District Centre,
New Delhi – 110025, India

79 Anson Road, #06–04/06, Singapore 079906

Cambridge University Press is part of the University of Cambridge.

It furthers the University's mission by disseminating knowledge in the pursuit of
education, learning, and research at the highest international levels of excellence.

www.cambridge.org
Information on this title: www.cambridge.org/9781108474375
DOI: 10.1017/9781108565240

© Cambridge University Press 2020

First published 2020

A catalogue record for this publication is available from the British Library.

ISBN 978-1-108-47437-5 Hardback
ISBN 978-1-108-46425-3 Paperback

Contents

List of Figures   *page* vii
List of Tables   viii
Notes on the Contributors   xi
Preface   xxi

1 Building Strategic Capabilities in Emerging Economies   1
   ALVARO CUERVO-CAZURRA, WILLIAM NEWBURRY,
   AND SEUNG HO PARK

2 Upgrading Capabilities in Emerging Markets: Imitation,
   Integration, Incorporation, and Internal Development   11
   ALVARO CUERVO-CAZURRA AND STEPHANIE LU WANG

3 Building Strategic Capabilities in Chinese Companies:
   Developing Global Competitive Advantage   39
   MOHAN SONG, WILLIAM NEWBURRY, AND SEUNG
   HO PARK

4 Strategic Capabilities of Emerging Indian Multinational
   Enterprises   71
   SUBHASHISH GUPTA, P. D. JOSE, AND ASHOK THAMPY

5 The Capabilities of South African Multinational
   Enterprises in Wider Africa   101
   HELENA BARNARD AND CHRISTIAN NEDU OSAKWE

6 Five Cases on Strategic Capabilities of Russian Firms 124
   NATALIA GUSEVA

7 Strategic Capabilities of Polish Firms   155
   MARIOLA CISZEWSKA-MLINARIČ AND KRZYSZTOF OBŁÓJ

8 Emerging Market Multinationals: The Case of
   Kazakhstan   186
   VENKAT SUBRAMANIAN AND ALMIRA ABILOVA

 9 Internationalization Capabilities of Argentine Firms   207
    MICHEL HERMANS AND DIEGO FINCHELSTEIN

10 Building Strategic Capabilities in Brazilian Firms   235
    MARIA TEREZA LEME FLEURY, CYNTIA VILASBOAS
    CALIXTO, CLÁUDIA SOFIA FRIAS PINTO, AND AFONSO
    FLEURY

11 Building Strategic Capabilities in Chilean Companies:
    Developing a Global Competitive Advantage   258
    SANTIAGO MINGO AND FRANCISCA SINN

12 Strategic Capabilities of Colombian Firms   286
    MARIA ALEJANDRA GONZALEZ-PEREZ, ANA MARIA
    GOMEZ-TRUJILLO, EVA CRISTINA MANOTAS, CAMILO
    PÉREZ-RESTREPO, MARIA TERESA URIBE-JARAMILLO,
    JUAN VELEZ-OCAMPO, AND VERÓNICA DUQUE-RUIZ

13 Capabilities of Mexican Exporters and Multinational
    Corporations   309
    MIGUEL A. MONTOYA AND GERARDO VELASCO

14 Building Strategic Capabilities in Emerging Market
    Firms: The Case of Peru   337
    ARMANDO BORDA REYES AND CARLOS CORDOVA CHEA

15 Examining Strategic Capabilities Across Emerging
    Markets and Their Firms   359
    ALVARO CUERVO-CAZURRA, WILLIAM NEWBURRY,
    AND SEUNG HO PARK

    Bibliography   383
    Index   412

Figures

2.1 Stock of outward foreign direct investment from
    advanced and emerging economies   *page* 14
2.2 Stock of outward foreign direct investment from
    advanced and emerging economies as a percentage of world
    total   16
2.3 Capability upgrading as a dynamic process evolving with
    firm development stages   29
2.4 Capability upgrading as a dynamic process evolving with
    home country development stages   36
3.1 China's GDP, 1978–2018   40
3.2 China's FDI net outflow, 1978–2018   41
3.3 China's FDI net inflow, 1978–2018   42
3.4 China's GDP per capita, 1978–2018   45
4.1 India's FDI outflows, 2000–2017   72
6.1 Gazprom Marketing & Trading, a subsidiary of the
    Gazprom group   139
7.1 Exports of goods and services from Poland, 1990–2016   162
7.2 Stock of outward FDI from Poland, 1990–2016   162
8.1 Net foreign assets in Kazakhstan, 1993–2016   189
10.1 Evolution of Brazil's outward and inward FDI   237
11.1 Chile's outward FDI flows, 2000–2016   261
11.2 Chile's outward FDI stock, 2000–2016   261
11.3 Chile's outward FDI stock as a percentage of total outward
     FDI stock from top fifteen developing countries, 2015   262
12.1 Colombia's outward FDI, 1994 –2018   288
13.1 Mexico's FDI stock abroad, by country, 2012   313
15.1 Relative identification of strategic capabilities   361
15.2 Strategic capabilities by value chain segment   364
15.3 Summary of strategic capability levels   380

Tables

2.1 Fifty largest publicly traded firms from emerging
   markets, ranked by revenue   *page* 17
2.2 One hundred emerging market challengers: firms
   from emerging markets that may become global leaders
   in their industries   19
2.3 Largest foreign investors from emerging economies,
   ranked by foreign assets   21
2.4 Stereotypical conditions of emerging countries and
   their likely effect on the behavior of emerging market firms
   at home and abroad   27
3.1 Data relating to the internationalization of the Chinese
   economy, 2009–2018   47
3.2 Percentage of total merchandise exports from China to
   low- and middle-income economies and to high-income
   economies   48
3.3 Data collection matrix for the selection of Chinese
   firms as case studies   48
3.4 Capabilities of Chinese firms studied   68
4.1 Indian companies included in the study   74
4.2 Facts about India, 2018   75
4.3 Checklist of capabilities for Indian companies   76
4.4 Summary of capabilities of Indian firms studied   97
4.5 Capabilities of Indian firms studied and modes of acquisition   98
5.1 South African economy: selected indicators, 2017   103
5.2 Inward FDI stock, 2000–2016: South Africa and comparable
   economies on the continent   104
5.3 Outward FDI flow, 2000–2016: South Africa and
   comparable economies on the continent   105
5.4 Capabilities that South African multinationals use to operate
   in wider Africa   110
5.5 Capabilities of South African firms studied   121
6.1 Inward and outward flows of FDI in Russia   127

6.2 Top ten Russian multinationals by foreign assets, 2017   128
6.3 Main recipients of Russian outward FDI   129
6.4 Characteristics of Russian firms studied   132
6.5 Russian company and interviewee descriptions   134
6.6 Russian company profiles and financial data   135
6.7 Strategic capabilities identified in domestic and multinational
     Russian companies   150
6.8 Comparison of the Russian firms studied, by strategic
     capabilities   152
7.1 GDP, international trade, and FDI trends in Poland,
     1990–2017   158
7.2 Institutional characteristics of Poland's economic and
     political system   160
7.3 Data collection matrix for the selection of Polish firms as case
     studies   163
7.4 Key characteristics of Polish firms studied   164
7.5 Capabilities of Polish firms studied   181
7.6 Strategic capabilities of Polish firms studied   182
8.1 Socioeconomic indicators in Kazakhstan, 2016–2018   187
8.2 Data collection matrix for the selection of Kazakhstani firms
     as case studies   190
9.1 Argentina: key economic indicators, 1992–2017   210
9.2 Data collection matrix for the selection of Argentinean firms
     as case studies   212
9.3 Argentinean company profiles and financial information,
     2017   213
9.4 Capabilities of Argentinean firms studied   232
10.1 Data collection matrix for the selection of Brazilian firms as
     case studies   238
10.2 Strategic capabilities of Brazilian firms studied   254
10.3 Major international activities and major strategic capabilities
     and challenges among Brazilian firms studied   255
11.1 Chile: country fact sheet – annual data, 2018   259
11.2 Data collection matrix for the selection of Chilean firms as
     case studies   263
11.3 Selected data for Chilean firms studied   264
11.4 Capabilities of Chilean firms studied   281
12.1 Colombia: macroeconomic data, 2012–2018   287
12.2 Data collection matrix for the selection of Colombian firms as
     case studies   290
12.3 Colombian company profiles and financial data   291
12.4 Capabilities of Colombian firms studied   306

13.1 Mexico: country profile   310
13.2 Mexican FDI stock abroad by geographical destination   312
13.3 Data collection matrix for the selection of Mexican firms as
        case studies   316
13.4 Financial summary of Mexican firms studied   317
13.5 Resources and capabilities of Mexican firms studied   332
14.1 Peru: country profile   338
14.2 Data collection matrix for the selection of Peruvian firms as
        case studies   339
14.3 Resources and capabilities of Peruvian firms studied   356
15.1 Breakout of capabilities by industry   366
15.2 Breakout of capabilities by multinationality   371
15.3 Breakout of capabilities by country   376

Notes on the Contributors

Almira Abilova is a PhD candidate in Marketing at the Rotterdam School of Management, Erasmus University. Her research focuses on marketing strategy and consumer responses to global technological advancement. She has worked as a research associate in the Graduate School of Business at Nazarbayev University, Kazakhstan.

Helena Barnard is a professor at the Gordon Institute of Business Science at the University of Pretoria, South Africa. Her research interests are in how knowledge (and with it technology, organizational practices, and innovation) moves between more and less developed countries, particularly in Africa. She researches both organizational mechanisms (notably emerging multinationals and internet-enabled businesses) and individual mechanisms such as scientific collaborations, doctoral training, and the diaspora. Her research has appeared in the *Journal of Management*, *Journal of International Business Studies*, *Research Policy*, and *Journal of World Business*. She is the 2017–2020 Vice President for Administration of the Academy of International Business, an area editor for the *Journal of International Business Policy*, and the deputy editor in charge of Africa for *Management and Organizational Review*.

Armando Borda Reyes is an assistant professor, director of the International MBA, and head of the Graduate Student Exchange Office in the Graduate School of Business at ESAN University, Peru. His areas of interest are international business, strategic management, and entrepreneurship. His work has been published in the *Journal of World Business*, *Journal of International Business Studies*, and *Journal of Business Research*. He is a member of the Academy of International Business and the Academy of Management.

Mariola Ciszewska-Mlinarič is a dean of the College of Management and an associate professor of Strategic and International Management at Kozminski University, Poland, and has been a visiting professor at universities in France, Austria, and Slovenia. Her research interests include the theory of strategy and the internationalization process, focusing on emerging market firms, decision-making processes, and the role of distance in international expansion. She is a consultant in enterprise growth strategies and in the implementation of performance management systems in the chemical and energy industries and for nonprofit organizations. In 2017 she was awarded a medal for special merit in education by Poland's Minister of National Education. She has published in the *Journal of Business Research, Business History, Journal for East European Management Studies*, and *European Journal of International Management*.

Carlos Cordova Chea is a PhD student at Alliance Manchester Business School, University of Manchester, and an instructor at ESAN Graduate School of Business, ESAN University, Peru. His research interests lie at the intersection of international business, emerging markets, and strategic management. He has coauthored articles published in *Multinational Business Review, Advanced Series in Management*, and *Emerald Emerging Markets Case Studies*, and has presented at the conference of the Academy of International Business Latin America and the Caribbean chapter.

Alvaro Cuervo-Cazurra is a professor of Global Strategy at Northeastern University, a fellow of the Academy of International Business, and coeditor of *Global Strategy Journal*. He studies the internationalization of firms, particularly emerging market multinationals; capability upgrading, focusing on technological capabilities; and governance issues, particularly corruption in international business.

Verónica Duque-Ruiz is Chief Procurement Officer at Prodenvases, the Colombian branch of the multinational Comeca Group. She has worked in international trade and international procurement for various firms and has coauthored two book chapters on the internationalization of emerging market firms.

Diego Finchelstein is an assistant professor at San Andrés University, Argentina, and a researcher at the Argentine national research agency, CONICET. His main areas of expertise are the relation between institutions, state actors, and internationalization and the evolution of business groups in Latin America. His research has been published in the *Journal of World Business, Desarrollo Económico*, and *Multinational Business Review*. He is a member of the Emerging Markets Research Network and is on the academic advisory board of the Emerging Market Institute,

Cornell University. He is also on the executive board of the Latin America and Caribbean chapter of the Academy of International Business.

Afonso Fleury created the interdepartmental area of Work, Technology, and Organization at the University of São Paulo, Brazil, where he also served as Head of the Production Engineering Department. His research projects have addressed such issues as work organization, technology management, and industrial and technology policies in industries including aeronautics, automobiles, capital goods, computing and information, digital games, machine tools, footwear, software, telecommunications, and textiles/apparel. His research in international business and international operations management looks at the impact of digital transformation on the international production networks of both developed and emerging country firms. He is associate editor of *Operations Management Research* and is on the editorial boards of the *Journal of International Management* and *Journal of Manufacturing Technology Management*.

Maria Tereza Leme Fleury is a professor of International Management at the Getulio Vargas Foundation (FGV) and the University of São Paulo (USP), Brazil. She was Dean of the School of Business Administration at FGV (2008–2015) and is currently its Director, having also served as Dean of the School of Economy, Administration, and Accountancy at USP. She has been a research fellow at the Institute of Manufacturing at Cambridge University, UK; at the Institute of Development Studies, University of Sussex, UK; and at the Institute for Development Economics, Japan; and a visiting professor at ESSEC, France. She is a fellow of the Academy of International Business and served as its Vice President Program (2019 Program Chair). She is member of the board of IE Business School, Spain, and has served on the boards of several international universities. Her work has been published in *Journal of International Business*, *Journal of World Business*, *Journal of Business Research*, and *Journal of International Management*.

Cláudia Sofia Frias Pinto is an assistant professor at the University of the West of Santa Catarina, Brazil, and a researcher at the Center for International Business Studies and at GlobAdvantage, the Center of Research on International Business and Strategy at the Politechnic Institute of Leiria, Portugal. Her research focuses on international business in emerging markets, particularly the influence of local contexts on the strategies and operations of emerging market multinationals.

Ana Maria Gomez-Trujillo is an assistant professor in the International Business Department at CEIPA Business School, Colombia. Her research and teaching interests include the internationalization and sustainability of companies from emerging markets. She has authored several journal articles and coauthored book chapters on the internationalization of emerging market firms, and she has presented her research at eight international academic conferences.

Maria Alejandra Gonzalez-Perez is a professor of Management at EAFIT University, Colombia. She was Vice-President of Administration at the Academy of International Business (AIB), 2015– 2018, and is the regional Chapter Chair for its Latin America and the Caribbean chapter, 2018–2021. She is a member of the World Government Summit global council for the UN's Sustainable Development Goal Number 1 (End Poverty) and a research partner at the Center for Emerging Market Studies. She is Area Editor of the journal *Cross-Cultural and Strategic Management*; Associate Editor of UNCTAD's *Transnational Corporations*; and Editor-in-Chief of the emerging market journal *AD-minister*. She has published sixteen books, over sixty peer-reviewed papers, and several book chapters in the areas of internationalization of emerging market firms, sustainability, corporate social responsibility, and international migration.

Subhashish Gupta is a professor of Economics at the Indian Institute of Management Bangalore (IIMB), India. His research interests are in industrial organization (regulation, antitrust, economics of organizations), international business with a focus on Southeast Asia, and telecommunications. He has served as a consultant to the World Bank, the Asian Development Bank, the Energy Research Institute, the government of India, the Competition Commission of India, the All India Council for Technical Education, and 24/7 Customer, a business process outsourcing firm. He teaches managerial economics, game theory, industrial organization, regulation, and advanced microeconomics to MBA, executive education, and PhD students. He has served as Chair of the Economics department and Admissions Chair at IIMB.

Natalia Guseva is a professor at the School of Business and Management, and the Academic Director of the Doing Business in Russia program, at the National Research University Higher School of Economics, Russia. She has published more than 115 research works, including refereed articles and books. Her major research interests are modern management trends, organizational capabilities, cross-cultural management, foreign professionals, and negotiations in a cross-cultural context. She was nominated for a Best Teacher award in 2019, 2018, 2015, and 2014. She has served as a senior expert for the World Bank and for the European Business Club in Moscow. She was a visiting research professor at the School of Business and Public Management, George Washington University, USA, and a lecturer at the School of Business at Buckinghamshire College, Brunel University, UK. She is a member of the Association of International Business, the Association of North America Higher Education International, USA, and the French–Russian Cercle Kondratieff, France.

Michel Hermans is an assistant professor at IAE Business School, Austral University, Argentina. His research focuses on how firm internationalization affects employees and how strategic human resources management contributes to the development of organizational capabilities that allow firms to compete in the global business context. His work has been published in the *Journal of International Business Studies*, *Research in Personnel and Human Resources Management*, and *Harvard Business Review* (Latin America edition). He has been a visiting instructor at business schools in Brazil, Ecuador, and Mexico, and was the Host Chair for the Annual Meeting of the Academy of International Business Latin America and the Caribbean chapter in Buenos Aires.

P. D. Jose is a professor of Strategy at the Indian Institute of Management Bangalore (IIMB), India. He currently chairs IIMB's Digital Learning Initiatives, particularly through Massive Online Open Courses. He teaches courses on competition and strategy, business and sustainability, and learning from corporate failures. His research interests include strategy formulation and implementation, crisis management and organizational renewal, corporate sustainability, and corporate social responsibility management. He has held visiting positions at universities in India, the UK, and Sweden. He has also been a consultant for several private- and public-sector organizations, government agencies, state governments, and international organizations.

Eva Cristina Manotas is an associate professor at the National University of Colombia at Medellín. She was a researcher with the university's Applied Statistics Research Group, 2004–2008. She is currently a member of the Economy and Environmental Research Group at the National University and of the Management in Colombia Research Group at EAFIT University, Colombia. She has worked as a researcher with REDAIRE and the Epidemiological Research Center at the

University of Antioquia, her research contributing to the reduction of air and noise pollution in the metropolitan area of the Aburra Valley. Her research areas are international entrepreneurship, business internationalization, the survival of small and medium-sized enterprises, reliability analysis, multivariable data analysis, geostatistics, sampling, forecasts, and time series.

Santiago Mingo is an associate professor in the School of Business at Adolfo Ibáñez University, Chile, where he teaches business strategy, global strategy, and international business. His research explores how the institutional and business environment affects corporate strategy, global strategy, and entrepreneurial activity. Most of his work focuses on emerging markets. He has published in such journals as *Management Science, Administrative Science Quarterly, Journal of International Business Studies, Journal of Management, Industrial and Corporate Change,* and *Journal of World Business,* and has presented his research at numerous conferences and universities around the world. He is associate editor of the *Journal of Business Research* and serves on several journal editorial boards. He is currently affiliated with the Nanyang Centre for Emerging Markets, Singapore.

Miguel A. Montoya is a professor at Tecnológico de Monterrey, Mexico, where he teaches courses in International Economics and International Business. He is a member of the National Council for Technology and Science (CONACYT-Mexico), the Economic Council of Business Association (COPARMEX-Mexico), the Academy of International Business, and the Academy of Management. He has published academic journal articles and book chapters and has participated in academic conferences. He has been a visiting professor at the University of South Carolina, USA; ESAN University, Peru; the University of San Francisco de Quito, Ecuador; the Ortega y Gasset Institute, Spain; and the Bordeaux School of Business and Montpellier Business School, France. His areas of interest are multinational companies and business at the bottom of the pyramid.

William Newburry is Chair of the Department of International Business and the Ryder Eminent Scholar of Global Business at Florida International University, USA, a fellow of the Academy of International Business, and a nonresident senior research fellow at the Nanyang Business School Center for Emerging Market Studies. He is an associate editor of *AIB Insights* and series editor for *Research in Global Strategic Management.* He was Chapter Chair of the Academy of International Business Latin America and the Caribbean chapter,

2012–2018. His research focuses on how multinational corporations relate to subsidiaries and local stakeholders when they invest abroad, with an emphasis on reputation in emerging markets. He coauthored *Emerging Market Multinationals: Managing Operational Challenges for Sustained International Growth* (2016), has coedited four books, and has published more than forty journal articles and more than twenty book chapters. He serves on the senior advisory board of *Review of International Business and Strategy* and on several journal editorial boards.

Krzysztof Obłój is a professor of Strategic and International Management at Kozminski University, Poland, and former President of the European International Business Academy. He has lectured in the US, Europe, and China. He serves as Chair of the Department of Strategic Management at Kozminski University and of the School of Management at the University of Warsaw, Poland. His research interests include strategic and international management and entrepreneurship in emerging economies. He has published papers in *Entrepreneurship: Theory and Practice, Journal of Management Studies, International Human Resource Management Journal, Business History, Journal of Organizational Change Management, European Management Journal,* and several Polish journals. He is the author of *Passion and Discipline of Strategy* (Palgrave, 2013). He has an extensive experience as a consultant, corporate speaker, and supervisory board member for many companies in Poland and elsewhere. He was an advisor to the President of Poland, 2012–2015.

Christian Nedu Osakwe is a research associate of the Gordon Institute of Business Science, University of Pretoria, South Africa. He has reviewed for journals such as *Marketing Intelligence and Planning, Journal of Marketing Management, European Journal of Marketing,* and *International Journal of Bank Marketing*. One of his research interests is identifying and understanding the marketing or business capabilities of an enterprise, with a particular focus on emerging economies in Africa. His publications include journal articles, conference papers, and a book chapter.

Seung Ho Park is President's Chair Professor of Strategy and International Business and Director of Nanyang Center for Emerging Markets at Nanyang Technological University, Singapore. He was the founding president of the Samsung Economic Research Institute China and Skolkovo-EY Institute for Emerging Market Studies. His coauthored books on emerging markets include the award-winning *Rough Diamonds: Four Traits of Successful Breakout Enterprises in BRIC Countries* (2013, with Nan Zhou and Gerardo R. Ungson; Jossey-Bass), *Scaling the*

Tail: Managing Profitable Growth in Emerging Markets (2015, with Gerardo R. Ungson and Andrew Cosgrove; Palgrave Macmillan), *Managing Emerging Multinationals: Solving International Challenges* (2016, with Alvaro Cuervo-Cazurra and William Newburry; Cambridge University Press), and *ASEAN Champions: Emerging Stalwarts in Regional Integration* (2017, with Gerardo R. Ungson and Jamil Paolo S. Francisco; Cambridge University Press). He is a fellow of the Academy of International Business. His research focuses on sustained-high-performance organizations, emerging market multinationals, and growth strategies for multinational and local companies in emerging markets.

Camilo Pérez-Restrepo is a professor in the Business School at EAFIT University, Colombia, and serves as Coordinator of its Asia Pacific Studies Center. He is currently the Managing Editor of the online journal *Mundo Asia Pacifico*. He has served as a researcher for the Pacific Economic Cooperation Council in Singapore, and as a consultant for private-sector organizations and the government of Colombia. His research areas include trade policy, foreign direct investment, and regional economic integration between Asia and Latin America.

Francisca Sinn is an associate professor in the School of Business at Adolfo Ibáñez University, Chile, where she is also Head of the Strategy Unit and Director of the Family Business Center. She is the country leader and a former global board member of the Successful Transgenerational Entrepreneurship Practices Project, a global applied research initiative that explores the entrepreneurial process within business families and generates solutions that have immediate application for family leaders. She was coeditor and coauthor of the books *Strategy Today and Forever* and *Women and Entrepreneurial Activity in Chile* (published by the Global Entrepreneurship Monitor). She has published articles in such journals as *Journal of Consumer Research* and *Journal of Business Research*. She has been a consultant for many Chilean firms and advises business families.

Mohan Song is a doctoral candidate at Florida International University, USA. Her research interests focus on international business and strategy, specifically in the areas of country and corporate reputation and dynamic capabilities in emerging markets. She has published three articles and two book chapters in the fields of management and hospitality management and has presented papers at several conferences in the management and international business fields.

Venkat Subramanian is an associate dean and an associate professor of Strategy in the Graduate School of Business at Nazarbayev University, Kazakhstan. He has held faculty appointments at the University of Hong Kong and at Vlerick Business School, Belgium. He was a research fellow in Strategy and International Management at Catholic University of Leuven, Belgium, and a research associate in Strategy and Finance at INSEAD, France. He was also a visiting scholar at the Fuqua School of Business, Duke University, USA. He has published in academic and practitioner journals, and in the business press, on strategy and international business and on competition in emerging markets.

Ashok Thampy is a professor of Finance and Accounting at the Indian Institute of Management Bangalore (IIMB), India. His teaching and research interests are in corporate finance, banking, and the internationalization of firms. He has held visiting positions at the Department of Economics at Santa Clara University, USA, and the School of Business, Economics and Law at the University of Gothenburg, Sweden. He is the Editor of the *IIMB Management Review*, a journal with a focus on emerging markets.

Maria Teresa Uribe-Jaramillo is Head of the International Relations Office at EAFIT University, Colombia, where she has also worked as a researcher at the Asia Pacific Studies Center. She is a political scientist and international negotiator for EAFIT University and the EM Strasbourg Business School, France. She has served as an advisor to the Ministry of Foreign Affairs of Colombia and to various companies in Colombia and Mexico, and as a consultant for institutions including the Inter-American Development Bank and the Konrad Adenauer Foundation.

Gerardo Velasco is Director of Postgraduate Courses in the School of Engineering at Tecnológico de Monterrey, Mexico, where he has also worked in regional development studies. He has been the Regional Coordinator of the Center for Studies for the Preparation and Socio-economic Evaluation of Projects, a trust set up by BANOBRAS, where he was responsible for coordinating the evaluation of more than 165 investment projects. He has served as director of Tecnológico de Monterrey's Finance Academy and is on the councils of the Glaucoma Institute, the Strategy and Specialized Consulting Group Mexico, and the Economic and Social Council for the Competitiveness of the State of Jalisco.

Juan Velez-Ocampo is an assistant professor in the Management Department at Antioquia University, Colombia, where he also serves as Academic Coordinator for the MBA program. His research and teaching interests include the impact of globalization in emerging economies, the international expansion and performance of multinational enterprises from emerging economies, the interlinks between internationalization and corporate reputation, and the institutionally based view of strategy. He has authored more than ten journal articles and presented his research at more than twenty international academic conferences.

Cyntia Vilasboas Calixto is a lecturer at the Getulio Vargas Foundation, Brazil, and a researcher at the foundation's Center for International Business Studies. Her research interests relate to international business, business models, and multinational enterprises' political connections. She is a Program Chair of the Academy of International Business Latin America and the Caribbean chapter, 2019–2022, and is on the board of the Teaching International Business Special Interest Group of the Academy of International Business.

Stephanie Lu Wang is an assistant professor in the Department of Management and Entrepreneurship, Kelley School of Business, Indiana University, USA. Her work lies at the intersection of international business and strategic management. She studies the processes of capability upgrading, internationalization, and multinational management. She is particularly interested in the rise of emerging market multinationals. She has won awards including the FIU Emerging Scholar Award from the International Management Division at the Academy of Management Annual Meeting, 2018, and the inaugural *Journal of World Business* Best Phenomenon-Based Article Award, 2018. She serves on the editorial boards of the *Journal of International Business Studies*, *Journal of World Business*, and *Global Strategy Journal*. She is a research fellow at the Nanyang Centre for Emerging Markets, Singapore.

Preface

In the book you are now reading, you will discover suggestions on how to upgrade the strategic capabilities of firms in emerging economies. Some emerging market firms are in the process of becoming leading competitors in the global economy. False perceptions that these firms were only good enough to operate in their home countries – protected by their governments and providing, at best, export products that relied on inexpensive labor – are quickly being replaced by the realization that some are becoming credible competitors, if not global leaders, in their industries. Many researchers have studied emerging market multinationals, marveling at their technological advances and marketing prowess. Yet these multinationals are only a tiny minority of firms in emerging economies: the ones that have been successful at upgrading their capabilities and expanding abroad. Many other firms are in the process of improving; some will become leading multinationals in the future. This book analyzes such firms and identifies the methods they use to build their competitiveness to international levels.

This study of the ways in which emerging market firms build their strategic capabilities is important not only because this process is the foundation of later international expansion, but more fundamentally because the focus of this research varies from the approaches commonly used in analyzing firms in advanced economies. In emerging markets, firms cannot rely on sophisticated and well-functioning infrastructure such as that underlying many of the advantages provided to companies in advanced economies. As a result, emerging market firms have to use methods to upgrade their capabilities that differ from the methods used by firms in advanced economies. This is the understanding that we provide in this book: how to upgrade a firm's competitive capabilities in spite of the unsupportive context in the typical emerging market.

We present a detailed analyses of the processes that have enabled emerging market firms to upgrade their capabilities by studying how firms in twelve emerging countries have achieved this. We researched firms with a wide diversity of characteristics, in terms of their industry of operation (high-tech, low-tech, and service) and level of internationalization (purely domestic, exporter, or multinational). These analyses were conducted by local experts possessing contextual understanding of the subtleties of the countries and firms studied, who gathered contextual data and interviewed top managers of the participating firms.

This book is a collaborative venture that could not have become a reality without the effort of thirty-four scholars from nineteen institutions. The initial idea came from a research project conducted in association with the network of scholars associated with the Nanyang Centre for Emerging Markets (CEM), Singapore. CEM is a platform that facilitates the development of knowledge on emerging markets through a global network of leading researchers, thinkers, institutions, and corporations. In 2016, this volume's coeditors collaborated on the volume titled *Emerging Market Multinationals: Solving Operational Challenges in Internationalization* (Cambridge University Press). The present book builds on and connects with other books on emerging market multinationals written by the coeditors. For example, Alvaro Cuervo-Cazurra coedited *Mexican Multinationals: How to Build Multinationals in Emerging Markets* (2018, with Miguel Montoya) and *Understanding Multinationals from Emerging Markets* (2014, with Ravi Ramamurti; both Cambridge University Press) and edited *State-Owned Multinationals: Governments in Global Business* (2018, Palgrave). William Newburry coedited *International Business in Latin America: Innovation, Geography, and Internationalization* (2016, with Maria Alejandra Gonzalez-Perez; Palgrave) and *Contemporary Influences on International Business in Latin America: Environmental, Firm and Individual-Level Factors* (2019, with Leonardo Liberman and Moacir de Miranda Oliveira Jr.; Palgrave). Seung Ho Park co-wrote the books *ASEAN Champions: Emerging Stalwarts in Regional Integration* (2017, with Gerardo R. Ungson and Jamil Paolo S. Francisco; Cambridge University Press), *Scaling the Tail: Managing Profitable Growth in Emerging Markets* (2015, with Gerardo R. Ungson and Andrew Cosgrove; Palgrave), and *Rough Diamonds: The Four Traits of Successful Breakout Firms in BRIC Countries* (2013, with Nan Zhou and Gerardo R. Ungson; Jossey-Bass).

The three coeditors identified the theme for this book and invited local experts from a variety of emerging markets, all part of CEM's global research network, to join this intellectual enterprise: Helena Barnard and Christian Nedu Osakwe from the University of Pretoria, South Africa; Subhashish Gupta, P. D. Jose, and Ashok Thampy from the Indian Institute of Management Bangalore, India; Venkat Subramanian and Almira Abilova from Nazarbayev University, Kazakhstan; Santiago Mingo and Francisca Sinn from Adolfo Ibáñez University, Chile; Miguel Angel Montoya and Gerardo Velasco from Tecnológico de Monterrey, Mexico; Maria Alejandra Gonzalez-Perez, Camilo Pérez Restrepo, and Maria Teresa Uribe-Jaramillo from EAFIT University, Colombia; Verónica Duque-Ruiz of Prodenvases, Colombia; Ana Maria Gomez-Trujillo from CEIPA Business School, Colombia; Eva Cristina

Manotas from the National University of Colombia at Medellín; Juan Velez-Ocampo from Antioquia University, Colombia; Amanda Borda Reyes and Carlos Cordova Chea from ESAN University, Peru; Michel Hermans from Austral University, Argentina; Maria Tereza Leme Fleury and Afonso Fleury from the University of São Paulo, Brazil; Cláudia Sofia Frias Pinto from the University of the West of Santa Catarina, Brazil; Cynthia Vilasboas Calixto from the Getulio Vargas Foundation, Brazil; Mariola Ciszewska-Mlinarič and Krzysztof Obłój from Kozminski University, Poland; and Natalia Guseva from the National Research University Higher School of Economics, Russia. The research team also included Stephanie Wang from Indiana University, USA, and Mohan Song from Florida International University, USA.

It required almost three years of conference calls, gatherings, and workshops to advance this large-scale global collaboration. The editors worked with the research team to develop the framework used to guide field studies and data-gathering in each country. The local experts used the framework to select the target firms and gather the information necessary to understand the process of capability development. The team reviewed and shared the preliminary findings in panel sessions at the Academy of Management and the Academy of International Business. It has been a long and challenging process, but we were able to pull it through thanks to strong commitment from everyone in the team and with the help of the Nanyang Centre for Emerging Markets, Singapore.

Besides the participating authors, we need to thank other individuals who supported this project through the various stages of the entire process. Valerie Appleby at Cambridge University Press provided excellent guidance on how to position and improve the manuscript. Ji Hong and Roxy Luo at China Europe International Business School (CEIBS) did a great job managing the global coordination of the project. We also benefited from institutional support at CEIBS, Nanyang Business School, Florida International University, and Northeastern University and its Center for Emerging Markets. Of course, our loved ones stood by us providing moral support to help us complete the book. We thank each of them with all our hearts.

1 Building Strategic Capabilities in Emerging Economies

Alvaro Cuervo-Cazurra, William Newburry, and Seung Ho Park

Emerging market firms are becoming an increasingly influential component of the global economy, impressing managers and academics alike. Many are becoming large multinationals dominating their industries and creating new competition against long-time incumbents from advanced economies. Several studies have examined the phenomenon of emerging market multi-nationals, praising their virtues and competitive capabilities and describing their internationalization processes (Cuervo-Cazurra & Ramamurti, 2014; Demirbag & Yaprak, 2015; Guillén & García-Canal, 2012; Park, Zhou & Ungson, 2013; Peng, 2002; Ramamurti & Singh, 2009; Sauvant, 2009). Others have identified the challenges these firms face in their internationalization (e.g. Cuervo-Cazurra, Newburry & Park, 2016).

However, before these firms became multinationals, they needed to upgrade their capabilities to become internationally competitive at home and abroad. Surprisingly little attention has been devoted to the way this happens across multiple countries (an exception being Williamson et al., 2013). Most studies have instead focused on single-company cases of leading firms, such as the Chinese platform Alibaba (Clark, 2016; Erisman, 2015); the Brazilian airplane manufacturer Embraer (Rodegen, 2009); the Chinese software firms Alibaba, Xiaomi, and Tencent (Tse, 2015); the Chinese white goods firm Haier (Fischer & Lago, 2013; Hu & Hao, 2017; Yi & Ye, 2013); the Mexican cement producer Cemex (Fuentes-Berain, 2007; Lessard & Lucea, 2009); and the Chinese telecommunication equipment manufacturer Huawei (Yang, 2015; Tian & Wu, 2015).

In this book, we complement these studies by providing a better understanding of how firms manage the twin challenges of upgrading capabilities to international levels while operating in the challenging conditions of emerging economies. Much of the competitive advantage of a multinational comes not from supportive factors in the home country but from the ability to learn from multiple countries (Bartlett & Ghoshal, 1989; Doz, Santos & Williamson, 2001), obtain technology from advanced countries (Luo & Tung, 2007), to arbitrage differences across countries (Kogut, 1985;

Ghemawat, 2001), and to benefit from the economies of scale that global operations facilitate (Yip, 2000). However, before firms become multinationals, they need to achieve the level of competitiveness that enables them to compete across countries and the resources to deal with the costs of doing business abroad (Hymer, 1960/1976). Emerging market firms must also deal with the challenges of operating in emerging economies (Grosse & Meyer, 2019), such as those in which a large proportion of the population has low income (Prahalad, 2004) and in which there are underdeveloped institutions with limited promarket infrastructure (Khanna & Palepu, 2010).

Thus conditions in the country of operation become central to our understanding of the processes by which emerging market firms upgrade their capabilities. Instead of discussing one type of capability and how firms from a variety of countries deal with that capability (as in Williamson et al., 2013), we focus on analyzing how firms from various emerging markets have dealt with some of the challenges of succeeding in their own countries and managed to upgrade their capabilities both at home and in their international operations. The book's focus is on providing contextually relevant analyses and recommendations based on studies of multiple companies across a wide range of emerging markets.

The overarching message of the book is that the development of capabilities to international levels can best be understood by examining the conditions present in the countries in which firms operate. Our approach extends the traditional structure–conduct–performance paradigm of industrial economics (Bain, 1956), in which the structure of competition in the industry determines the strategies of firms and the level of their success. We expand this model by including the context of the country in the causality chain, so that it becomes context–structure–conduct–performance. We explain how conditions in the country influence the competitive strategies that firms use to upgrade their capabilities and thus, eventually improve their performance.

The context and conditions present in a country include many dimensions. In this book we group them into two broad categories: institutions, which comprise the set of rules and norms that facilitate interactions and transactions among economic actors (North, 1991); and endowments, which are the factors and resources that can become inputs for the productive systems of companies (Penrose, 1959). Emerging economies are typically characterized by the underdevelopment of institutions (Khanna & Palepu, 2010), in the form of relatively less supportive and sophisticated laws and regulations and weaker judicial systems that result in lower protection of contracts and intellectual property. These factors discourage investment in the development of advanced capabilities. Such countries are also characterized by the underdevelopment of endowments, populations with relatively low levels of education and income, and unsophisticated innovation systems and weak capital markets. These factors tend to limit investment in capability development.

Thus we tackle the challenge of explaining how companies in emerging economies manage to develop competitive capabilities to international levels despite the underdevelopment of systems and resources in the home countries in which they operate. To do so, we conduct a country-by-country analysis in which we study a variety of companies in terms of the type of industry in which they function (low-tech, high-tech, or service) and also in terms of their internationalization (purely domestic, exporter, or multinational). This provides insights into processes of capability development that have broad applicability and can be easily generalized to firms in other countries. Our research methodology is explained in the next section. In the chapter's final section, we summarize our process for accomplishing our research aims and explain the structure of the book.

1.1 Research Methodology

In this project, we systematically examine the various strategic capabilities that are likely to help emerging market firms achieve success. This includes identifying capabilities that will be most beneficial to these firms in their future advancement, revealing actions and processes that facilitate the development and honing of sophisticated capabilities, and uncovering strategies that enable firms to reduce disadvantages. To accomplish this, we pursued the following steps.

First, we realized that the complexities of studying a phenomenon that requires in-depth local knowledge demanded a team of researchers from around the globe. We believe that this necessity for local knowledge is a major reason why so many emerging market studies are based on a single country or very few countries. To enable global comparisons, we developed a network of research partners from some of the top universities in twelve emerging markets that were part of the global research network of Nanyang Business School's Centre for Emerging Markets. Our selected team included researchers from Asia (China, India and Kazakhastan), Africa (South Africa), Europe (Russia, and Poland), and Latin America (Argentina, Brazil, Chile, Colombia, Mexico, and Peru). These researchers brought with them knowledge along with significant local contacts, either known to them individually or facilitated on the basis of the prestige of their universities. This enabled access to CEOs and top company managers whose input we needed in order to truly understand our study phenomenon.

Table 1.1 *Data collection matrix*

		Firm category		
		Purely domestic	Exporter	Multinational
Industry type	High-tech			
	Low-tech			
	Service			

Second, we asked research partners in the twelve countries to identify and collect information on company cases, each corresponding to a different cell out of the nine total cells within our data collection matrix, shown in Table 1.1. This matrix records both the industry in which a company operates (low-tech, high-tech, or service) and the degree of internationalization of a firm (purely domestic, exports, or multinational). From preliminary discussions, we realized that firms representing all nine cells might not be available in all markets due to industry differences and other variations in the local economies. Additionally, in many cases, purely domestic firms might not yet have developed the capacity to adequately evaluate the strategic nature of their capabilities at an international level. Our goal was, nonetheless, to collect enough data across these two dimensions to obtain a good cross-section of firms to compare.

Third, while we expected the case study examinations to be exploratory in nature given the widely varying conditions across the emerging markets and our nascent understanding of the phenomena, we also aimed to achieve some degree of comparability across the cases. To aid in this regard, we identified several potential capabilities, listed in Table 1.2, that were shown by prior research to be associated with firm success. This list was not meant to be exhaustive, as different capabilities may be needed in different markets, but rather to provide a starting point for our examinations and to allow comparison among firms and countries.

Fourth, we also developed a series of general questions to guide researchers in their interviews. We did not necessarily advocate that the researchers pose the questions in a standard manner, but rather that they engage the interviewees in a conversation, first asking them to describe their business and what capabilities they felt had best aided them in achieving success. The questions were then used to guide the interview as topics naturally came up, or to fill in gaps not covered by the interviewee. These questions were sent to the interviewees in advance, along with a cover letter describing the project, so that they could be adequately prepared for the interviews. These were conducted in person and

Table 1.2 *Potential strategic capabilities*

Major capability category	Subcategories
Obtaining resources	Resource identification
	Ability to purchase inputs
	Ability to develop resources internally
Product/service capabilities	Product manufacture
	Research and development
	Local product adaptation
Operations and management	Production management
	Supply chain management
	Hard skills
	Soft skills
	Entrepreneurship
	Cross-cultural management
Marketing	General sales capabilities
	Understanding local customer needs
Managing the external environment	Political capabilities
	Relationship capabilities
	Adjusting to poor infrastructure

generally lasted from sixty to ninety minutes. The questions investigated the following aspects of various potential capabilities and resources.

1) To what extent are these resources critical to the company when operating in its home market? In other emerging countries? In advanced economies?
2) To what degree does the company possess this particular capability in comparison to its domestic, host country, or global competitors?
3) If a company lacks a critical strategic capability, how can it obtain that capability in the home and host countries?
4) To what extent is each capability important across different stages of the internationalization process: the entry stage (e.g., during country selection, entry mode selection, or establishment of a foreign subsidiary) or the operations stage (e.g., during local operations, integration of a subsidiary with the broader multinational, or expansion of operations)?
5) How does the firm's degree of internationalization impact the importance of particular strategic capabilities?
6) To what extent does the firm's industry impact the importance of particular strategic capabilities?
7) How does the firm's target customer base impact the importance of particular strategic capabilities?

We realized that organizing such a large network of researchers in twelve countries required special attention to ensure consistency, even with the common tools guiding the data collection described above. To help ensure this, we held a forum for all the authors to attend at the China-Europe International Business School in Shanghai, China, early in the process of collecting data to discuss preliminary data collection efforts in order to identify specific issues that might have developed. This was useful in ensuring a common methodology. We supplemented this in-person meeting with multiple videoconferencing calls to address ongoing issues.

At the meeting in Shanghai, we also established a common format for the chapters along with shared elements that we planned to include in each chapter, including a presentation of the breakout for each country based on the Table 1.1 framework and a similar breakout of which capabilities were described as strategic for each company, building on Table 1.2. We did not dictate a rigid chapter format given the unique nature of each of the country environments we were examining, but we focused on achieving enough commonality in essential elements to ensure comparability across the countries. The book's three editors reviewed each chapter and provided feedback to the authors several times to ensure the best possible consistency of presentation throughout the book.

Information was collected from seventy-two companies in our twelve study countries. They are listed by country, along with their industry types and levels of multinationality, in Table 1.3.

1.2   Organization of the Book

The next chapter (Chapter 2) provides a theoretical overview of the academic literature related to the development of strategic capabilities among emerging market firms. It presents a four-I framework of mechanisms that emerging market firms have used in their capability development: imitation, integration, incorporation, and internal development. The chapter highlights how the relative usage of these four mechanisms varies depending on the development stages of both emerging market firms and their host countries.

Each of the next twelve chapters (Chapters 3 through 14) examines how firms upgrade capabilities in each individual country. The chapters are organized by region and written by local experts.

Among emerging Asian countries we have included chapters on China, by Mohan Song, William Newburry, and Seung Ho Park; India, by Subhashish Gupta, P. D. Jose, and Ashok Thampy; and Kazakhstan, by Venkat Subramanian and Almira Abilova.

Table 1.3 *Companies studied*

Country	Company	Industry type	Multinationality
Argentina	Grupo Mirgor	high-tech	domestic
	Bodega Lagarde	low-tech	exporter
	Arcor	low-tech	multinational
	San Miguel	low-tech	multinational
	Grupo Bagó	high-tech	multinational
	Grupo ASSA	service	multinational
	Globant	service	multinational
Brazil	Dr.Consulta	service	domestic
	Grendene	low-tech	exporter
	WEG	high-tech	multinational
	Fanem	high-tech	multinational
	Stefanini	service	multinational
	Integration	service	multinational
Chile	BeitGroup	low-tech	domestic
	Kunstmann	low-tech	exporter
	Casas del Toqui	low-tech	exporter
	ALTO	high-tech	multinational
	Forus	high-tech/service	multinational
	Derco	service	multinational
	eClass	service	multinational
China	AVIC	high-tech	multinational
	Advantech	high-tech	multinational
	ShangGong Group	high-tech	multinational
	Higer	high-tech	exporter
	Chervon	low-tech	multinational
	Siwei-Johnson	low-tech	multinational
	Baby First	low-tech	exporter
	Sanpower	service	multinational
Colombia	Grupo Bios	high-tech	domestic
	Mattelsa	low-tech	domestic
	Haceb	high-tech	exporter
	Sempertex	low-tech	exporter
	New Stetic	low-tech	exporter
	Brainz	service	exporter
	Colcafé	low-tech	multinational
India	Gokaldas Exports	low-tech	exporter
	Tata Consultancy Services	service	multinational
	Biocon	high-tech	multinational
	Titan Company Ltd.	low-tech	multinational
Kazakhstan	Air Astana	service	domestic
	Tsesna	low-tech	exporter
	Kamaz	high-tech	multinational
	Sportmaster	service	multinational
	Sberbank	service	multinational

Table 1.3 (*cont.*)

Country	Company	Industry type	Multinationality
Mexico	Interlub	high-tech	exporter
	Belticos	low-tech	exporter
	Vidanta	service	exporter
	Neoris	high-tech	multinational
	Farmacias Similares	service	multinational
	KidZania	service	multinational
	Elektra	service	multinational
Peru	Deltron	low-tech	domestic
	Cantol	low-tech	exporter
	Resemin Group	high-tech	multinational
	Alicorp	low-tech	multinational
	Yobel	low-tech	multinational
	Lolimsa	service	multinational
Poland	Kooptech	high-tech	exporter
	Granna	low-tech	exporter
	Prochem	service	exporter
	Aplisens	high-tech	multinational
	Nowy Styl Group	low-tech	multinational
	Audioteka	service	multinational
Russia	SIBUR	high-tech	domestic
	Gazprom M&T	high-tech	domestic
	ByTerg	high-tech	domestic
	Ecolab	high-tech	multinational
	Swilar	service	multinational
South Africa	Standard Bank Group	service	multinational
	Nedbank Group	service	multinational
	Clover Industries	low-tech	multinational
	Tiger Brands	low-tech	multinational

Our chapter on South Africa was prepared by Helena Barnard and Christian Nedu Osakwe.

The chapters on emerging Europe cover Russia, written by Natalia Guseva; and Poland, by Mariola Ciszewska-Mlinarič and Krzysztof Obłój.

We covered six countries in the emerging Americas: Argentina, written by Michel Hermans and Diego Finchelstein; Brazil, by Maria Tereza Leme Fleury, Cyntia Vilasboas Calixto, Cláudia Sofia Frias Pinto, and Afonso Fleury; Chile, by Santiago Mingo and Francisca Sinn; Colombia, by Maria Alejandra Gonzalez-Perez, Ana Maria Gomez-Trujillo, Eva Cristina Manotas, Camilo Pérez-Restrepo, Maria Teresa Uribe-Jaramillo, Juan Velez-Ocampo, and Verónica Duque-Ruiz; Mexico, by Miguel

A. Montoya and Gerard Velasco; and Peru, by Armando Borda and Carlos Cordova Chea.

Each of these chapters provides insights into the ways in which the specific characteristics of the particular country have influenced the development of companies and their strategic capabilities, while also examining the common elements we have already mentioned to enable us to make comparisons within each country, across industries, and across multiple countries.

Stemming from the evidence gathered through the seventy-two interviews conducted in the twelve study countries, the final chapter (Chapter 15) integrates the findings of the cases. It first presents a summary of which capabilities were identified by the most companies as being strategic in their development. It then breaks down which companies were most prominent based on industry (low-tech, high-tech, and service), degree of firm internationalization (purely domestic, exporter, and multinational), and country of evaluation. The chapter integrates examples from the various chapters to illustrates the capabilities that were found to be most strategic and proposes some reasons why this is the case.

Looking at some of our most prominent results, understanding local customer needs was the strategic capability that was most strongly identified by the emerging market firm leaders in our study. It was perceived as highly important across industries and levels of multinationality, although there was some interesting variation across countries. In particular, this capability was universally identified as important across all of the six Latin American countries in the study. The second most strongly identified strategic capability, relationship capabilities, was also shown to be commonly identified across industries and levels of multinationality. However, an unusually low score in China was notable, and seemed contrary to findings presented in prior literature. The result may reflect the rising level of development of Chinese firms, leading the country to focus on the internal development of technical capabilities, such that relationships may be less important.

Beyond these first two capabilities, we begin to see much more variation in capability identification. For example, we found that general sales capabilities were more highly identified as important in low-tech and service industries and among multinationals. Similarly, local product/ service adaptation was identified by these same two industries and by both multinationals and exporters. By contrast, research and development capabilities were highly associated with high-tech industries, where competition may be based on differentiation as opposed to low cost. Supply chain management was identified more frequently among low-tech firms and purely domestic firms. These results and many more are presented throughout the book.

Overall, the book makes significant contributions that will be useful both to academic researchers and to practitioners. Most research by academics on emerging markets in general, and on emerging market strategic capabilities in particular, focuses on only one country, often China, or a small set of countries, to draw conclusions about emerging markets in general. By examining a varied set of emerging market countries across five continents, we are able to add needed depth to the study of emerging market multinationals. We present information on both consistent patterns and significant differences across these markets, along with variations at the industry level and across levels of multinationality. Thus we are able to provide a more nuanced understanding of these firms than is contained in much of the existing academic literature.

For practitioners, the research is particularly valuable in presenting practical advice on the development of strategic capabilities – advice that can be tailored to their country, their industry, and their firm's level of multinationality. This should be useful to companies operating in their home countries but also to multinationals operating across different host countries in terms of understanding the capabilities that drive local competitive dynamics.

2 Upgrading Capabilities in Emerging Markets

Imitation, Integration, Incorporation, and Internal Development

Alvaro Cuervo-Cazurra and Stephanie Lu Wang

2.1 Introduction

Firms based in emerging markets are increasingly able to compete with market leaders in the global arena.[1] The rise of these emerging market multinationals challenges the notion that firms can compete abroad only after their home countries reach a high level of economic development.[2] Although governments in emerging markets occasionally support internationalization,[3] in most cases, firms have achieved global leadership with little or no help from their home governments.

It is important to note that there is large variation in the level of competitiveness of firms from emerging markets. Although emerging market multinationals have received most of the attention, they are only a minority. The vast majority of emerging market firms only operate locally. Thus, it is particularly intriguing to understand how firms from emerging markets upgrade their capabilities.[4] In addition, analyzing the diversity in levels of competitiveness among emerging market firms may help us understand the influence of the home country on the strategy of firms better.[5] In advanced economies, firms can benefit from a supportive environment – in terms of financial markets, human capital, innovation systems, and regulatory frameworks – that facilitates upgrading their ability to compete at international levels.[6] As emerging economies provide few of these favorable environmental conditions, emerging market firms may adopt different methods to upgrade capabilities. Indeed, in emerging markets, access to capital, skilled workers,[7] and reliable infrastructure is often challenging, as is intellectual property protection,[8] while other regulatory frameworks may be biased toward firms with strong links to local politicians.[9]

This chapter explores the range of methods used by companies in emerging economies to upgrade their capabilities, revealing how conditions in the underdeveloped support environment influence the selection and usage of firms' approaches to capability upgrading. We propose that emerging market firms use a combination of four upgrading methods (imitation, integration, incorporation, and internal development),[10] contingent upon the development stages of their home countries and upon their own stages of development. More importantly, we emphasize that the use of the four-I upgrading methods evolve over time because the feasibility and effectiveness of each mechanism change as the firm transforms from a laggard to a leader, and as the home market evolves from an underdeveloped into a more advanced economy.[11]

Thus *imitation*, as a speedy way to catch up, is used more intensively when emerging market firms are far away from the international competitiveness frontier. Next, the *integration* of capabilities from alliance partners plays an essential role as companies seek to learn the subtleties of process technology and establish partnerships with foreign firms. *Incorporation* of tacit knowledge occurs when emerging market firms seek to acquire individual technology or firms in advanced economies is more likely to be adopted. Finally, *internal development* becomes the most prevalent method used by emerging market firms as they reach and in some cases surpass the technological frontier. In summary, emerging market firms, in decreasing proportions over time, use imitation, integration, incorporation, and finally, internal development to upgrade capabilities.

Section 2.2 outlines the transformation of emerging market firms into global leaders, briefly reviews the conditions of emerging markets, and explores how these affect the upgrading of capabilities to international levels. The bulk of the chapter explains the use of imitation, integration, incorporation, and internal development by emerging market firms for capability upgrading. We then discuss the dynamics of the application of these methods as emerging market firms move toward the international frontier.

2.2   Global Leaders from Emerging Markets

An increasing number of firms from emerging markets now compete in the global arena.[12] These firms challenge our traditional foreign direct investment (FDI) models, which generally assume that countries can generate multinationals only after reaching a mid-level of economic development.[13] Yet many firms from emerging markets reach multinational status while the development of their home countries lags.[14]

The investment development path model[15] argues that the inward and outward FDI flows of countries would follow a transformation sequence aligned to their level of development. The model proposes that a country with low development level will attract inward FDI, due to advantageous conditions in factor markets, such as abundant natural resources and a large, low-cost (even if unskilled) labor pool. As the country develops, its emerging middle class expects local products with better quality, attracting more inward FDI that also seeks to benefit from increasingly skilled yet still inexpensive labor. Once the country develops to the middle-income level, the model predicts outward FDI from domestic companies that can offer products of sufficient quality to market externally, and that can generate financial surpluses. Meanwhile, inward FDI slows as domestic factor costs increase. As the country develops, its increasingly supportive infrastructure and the more demanding requirements of customers move its firms toward international competitiveness levels. Eventually, its firms may reach the international frontier of competitiveness and invest in other countries. Higher factor costs reduce the attractiveness of recently advanced countries as production sites and shift the focus of their outward FDI toward capturing new markets and capabilities.

The appearance of emerging market multinationals in recent times challenges this traditional explanation of the evolution of foreign direct investment being aligned to the development of a national economy. Many companies based in emerging markets have expanded abroad much earlier, given the level of development of their home country, than the traditional FDI model would predict. Moreover, some have become not only multinationals but also credible threats to the dominance of multinationals from more advanced economies.

Trends in foreign direct investment stocks and flows illustrate this rapid and impressive global expansion of firms from emerging economies. Using data on foreign direct investment compiled by the United Nations Conference on Trade and Development (UNCTAD), Figure 2.1 illustrates the rapid and essential transformation of the foreign investment world.[16] We have separated countries into two groups based on the classification of countries by the International Monetary Fund.[17] The stock of outward foreign direct investment started accumulating rapidly from advanced economies in the 1980s and has dominated ever since. Emerging market economies only began to accumulate significant stocks of outward FDI in the 2000s. Their outward FDI increased in the 2010s, although levels remain well below the level of advanced

Figure 2.1 Stock of outward foreign direct investment from advanced and emerging economies

Source: Created using information from UNCTAD (2019)

economies. The result is a rapid reduction in the dominance of foreign investment from advanced economies, decreased from nearly all FDI stock to slightly over 80 percent of the world total, as illustrated in Figure 2.2.

Aggregate outward FDI figures do not reveal which firms from emerging markets have become the world's leading competitors. For this, we rely on other sources, such as the list of the largest publicly traded firms compiled by Fortune.[18] This list ranks companies by their revenues and includes only publicly listed firms, thus excluding many of the large and important privately held firms and some of the crucial business groups that tend to dominate many economies.[19] Nevertheless, the list provides an initial approximation for understanding which firms from emerging economies are reaching the scale that can help them eventually challenge advanced economy competitors. Table 2.1 lists the fifty largest publicly traded firms from emerging markets. Chinese firms dominate the Fortune list. Many of these have relied on rapid economic growth and their home country becoming the world's second largest economy to achieve significant revenue levels, although some are minor competitors outside China. In contrast, many firms based in smaller emerging economies are significant foreign investors, and have acquired the sophisticated capabilities needed to succeed across borders because they have been unable to rely only on their home market to grow their revenue levels.

Another perspective on leading firms from emerging economies appears in the list published by the Boston Consulting Group (BCG) of "Global Challengers": firms from emerging economies that are poised to become dominant global players.[20] Since 2006, the consulting company has identified companies it believes will challenge firms from advanced economies for global leadership. It revises the list periodically by removing those companies that it considers have already become global competitors and including new names that will do so in the future. Table 2.2 lists one hundred firms that the BCG suggested in 2018 were on the verge of dominating their industries. Unlike the Fortune ranking, this list shows a wide diversity of firms in terms of country of origin and primary industry.

Finally, UNCTAD identifies the largest multinationals, "transnationals" in their parlance, by ranking firms in terms of foreign assets.[21] Table 2.3 shows this ranking. The original UNCTAD list included firms from countries considered as developed, such as Hong Kong, South Korea, Singapore, and Taiwan, which we have excluded here to permit comparison with the other lists shown in this chapter.

The few emerging market firms that have become industry leaders reflect the role of capability upgrading. Many of these firms are little known outside their industries because they have tended to operate in

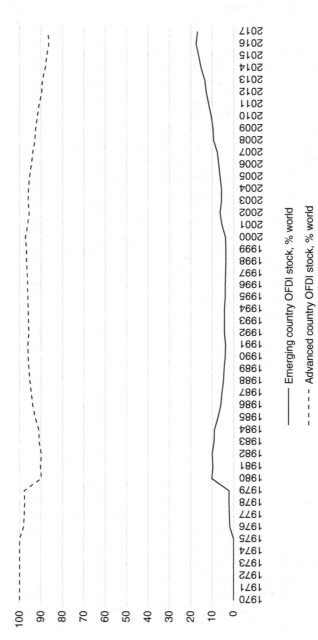

Figure 2.2 Stock of outward foreign direct investment from advanced and emerging economies as a percentage of world total

Source: Created using information from UNCTAD (2019)

Table 2.1 *Fifty largest publicly traded firms from emerging markets, ranked by revenue*

	Rank in Fortune 500	Company	Country	Revenues, USD million
1	2	State Grid	China	348,903
2	3	Sinopec Group	China	326,953
3	4	China National Petroleum	China	326,008
4	23	China State Construction Engineering	China	156,071
5	26	Industrial & Commercial Bank of China	China	153,021
6	29	Ping An Insurance	China	144,197
7	31	China Construction Bank	China	138,594
8	36	SAIC Motor	China	128,819
9	40	Agricultural Bank of China	China	122,366
10	42	China Life Insurance	China	120,224
11	46	Bank of China	China	115,423
12	49	Gazprom	Russia	111,983
13	53	China Mobile Communications	China	110,159
14	56	China Railway Engineering Group	China	102,767
15	58	China Railway Construction	China	100,855

	Rank in Fortune 500	Company	Country	Revenues, USD million
26	107	Pemex	Mexico	73,850
27	109	China Minmetals	China	72,997
28	110	China Southern Power Grid	China	72,787
29	111	Amer International Group	China	72,766
30	113	China Post Group	China	72,197
31	115	Rosneft Oil	Russia	72,028
32	117	People's Insurance Company of China	China	71,579
33	122	China Oil and Foodstuffs Corporation	China	69,669
34	124	Beijing Automotive Group	China	69,591
35	125	China First Automobile Works Group	China	69,524
36	132	Tewoo Group	China	66,577
37	133	Itau Unibanco Holding	Brazil	66,287
38	137	Indian Oil	India	65,916
39	140	China North Industries Group	China	64,646
40	141	China Telecommunications	China	63,974

Table 2.1 (*cont.*)

Rank in Fortune 500	Company	Country	Revenues, USD million	Rank in Fortune 500	Company	Country	Revenues, USD million
16 63	Lukoil	Russia	93,897	41 148	Reliance Industries	India	62,304
17 65	Dongfeng Motor	China	93,294	42 149	CITIC Group	China	61,316
18 72	Huawei Investment & Holding	China	89,311	43 161	Aviation Industry Corporation of China	China	59,263
19 73	Petrobras	Brazil	88,827	44 162	China Baowu Steel Group	China	59,255
20 86	China Resources	China	82,184	45 163	PTT	Thailand	58,819
21 87	China National Offshore Oil	China	81,482	46 166	Banco Bradesco	Brazil	58,062
22 91	China Communications Construction	China	79,417	47 167	ChemChina	China	57,989
23 96	Pacific Construction Group	China	77,205	48 168	Bank of Communications	China	57,711
24 98	Sinochem Group	China	76,765	49 175	Banco do Brasil	Brazil	55,269
25 101	China Energy Investment	China	75,522	50 180	América Móvil	Mexico	54,006

Source: Created using information from Fortune (2019).

Table 2.2 *One hundred emerging market challengers: firms from emerging markets that may become global leaders in their industries*

AirAsia (Malaysia)	Embraer (Brazil)	Jollibee Foods (Philippines)	Sasol (South Africa)
Alfa (Mexico)	Emirates Global Aluminium (United Arab Emirates)	Koc Holding (Turkey)	Sinochem (China)
Alicorp (Peru)	Etihad Airways (United Arab Emirates)	Larsen & Toubro (India)	Sinohydro (China)
Almarai (Saudi Arabia)	Etisalat (United Arab Emirates)	LATAM (Chile)	Sun Pharmaceuticals (India)
Alpargatas (Brazil)	EuroChem (Russia)	LC Waikiki (Turkey)	Tech Mahindra (India)
Apollo Tyres (India)	Falabella (Chile)	Lukoil (Russia)	Tenaris (Argentina)
Arca Continental (Mexico)	FEMSA (Mexico)	Lupin (India)	ThaiBev (Thailand)
Aspen Pharmacare (South Africa)	Fuyao Glass Industry Group (China)	Mahindra & Mahindra (India)	Thai Union Group (Thailand)
Aviation industry Corporation of China (China)	Geely (China)	Mercadolibre (Argentina)	Tianqi Lithium Corporation (China)
Axiata Group Berhad (Malaysia)	Gerdau (Brazil)	Mexichem (Mexico)	Trina Solar (China)
Ayala Corporation (Philippines)	Godrej Consumer Products (India)	Midea Group (China)	Turkish Airlines (Turkey)
Bajaj Auto (India)	Golden Agri-Resources (Indonesia)	Mindray (China)	Unionpay (China)
Bharti Airtel (India)	Goldwind (China)	Motherson Sumi Systems (India)	Universal Robina (Philippines)
BRF (Brazil)	GRUMA (Mexico)	MTN (South Africa)	UPL (India)
BYD (China)	Grupo Empresarial Antioqueno (Colombia)	Natura (Brazil)	Vedanta Resources (India)
Charoen Pokphand Foods (Thailand)	Grupo Gloria (Peru)	OCP Group (Morocco)	Vina Concha y Toro (Chile)
ChemChina (China)	Grupo Mexico (Mexico)	OPPO Electronics (China)	Votorantim (Brazil)
China National Offshore Oil Co. (China)	Haier (China)	Pegasus Airlines (Turkey)	Wanxiang (China)

Table 2.2 (*cont.*)

China Railway Construction Corp. (China)	IHH Healthcare (Malaysia)	PetroChina (China)	WEG (Brazil)
Cielo (Brazi)	Indofood (Indonesia)	Petronas (Malaysia)	Weichai Power(China)
CITIC Group (China)	Indorama Ventures (Thailand)	PTT (Thailand)	Wipro (India)
Dangote Cement (Nigeria)	Infosys (India)	Qatar Airways (Qatar)	Xiaomi (China)
Discovery (South Africa)	Iochpe-Maxion (Brazil)	Reliance Industries (India)	Yildiz Holding (Turkey)
Dr. Reddy's Laboratories (India)	Jain Irrigation Systems (India)	Sabanci Holding (Turkey)	Zhengzhou Yutong Bus (China)
Elsewedy Electric (Egypt)	JinkoSolar (China)	Safaricom (Kenya)	Zoomlion (China)

Source: Created using information from Meyer et al. (2018).

Table 2.3 *Largest foreign investors from emerging economies, ranked by foreign assets*

Corporation	Home economy	Industry	Foreign assets, USD million	Total assets, USD million	Foreign sales, USD million	Total sales, USD million
China COSCO Shipping Corp Ltd	China	Transport and storage	84,419	109,044	22,800	34,668
China National Offshore Oil Corp (CNOOC)	China	Mining, quarrying, and petroleum	67,282	173,408	21,348	81,482
State Grid Corporation of China	China	Electricity, gas, and water	60,000	585,299	45,003	343,796
China National Chemical Corporation (ChemChina)	China	Chemicals and allied products	56,241	121,444	32,788	59,226
Tencent Holdings Limited	China	Computer and data processing	51,012	85,236	1,183	35,178
China Minmetals Corp (CMC)	China	Metals and metal products	42,790	131,338	17,308	72,997
Tata Motors Ltd	India	Motor vehicles	42,146	50,844	36,577	45,820
América Móvil SAB de CV	Mexico	Telecommunications	37,581	75,331	39,344	54,022
Vale SA	Brazil	Mining, quarrying, and petroleum	37,369	99,042	30,060	34,015
Petronas – Petroliam Nasional Bhd	Malaysia	Mining, quarrying, and petroleum	37,213	148,209	36,968	51,996
China State Construction Engineering Corp Ltd (CSCEC)	China	Construction	36,583	238,338	12,577	155,961
Naspers Ltd	South Africa	Telecommunications	30,091	35,344	3,115	6,058

Table 2.3 (*cont.*)

Corporation	Home economy	Industry	Foreign assets, USD million	Total assets, USD million	Foreign sales, USD million	Total sales, USD million
Legend Holdings Corporation	China	Computer equipment	27,165	61,828	40,141	56,299
Cemex S.A.B. de C.V.	Mexico	Stone, clay, glass, and concrete products	24,934	28,769	10,477	13,649
Fosun International Limited	China	Metals and metal products	23,882	82,027	6,965	13,024
Lukoil OAO	Russian Federation	Petroleum refining and related industries	22,922	90,325	83,552	101,721
China National Petroleum Corp (CNPC)	China	Mining, quarrying, and petroleum	22,447	629,846	9,187	346,260
Sinochem Group	China	Mining, quarrying, and petroleum	20,724	64,110	59,319	76,763
Lenovo Group Ltd	China	Computer equipment	19,626	28,496	33,993	45,576
Oil and Natural Gas Corp Ltd	India	Mining, quarrying, and petroleum	19,289	70,621	1,616	56,187
Ooredoo QSC	Qatar	Telecommunications	19,257	24,610	6,853	8,993
Midea Group Co Ltd	China	Electric equipment	17,701	38,126	15,458	35,793
Etisalat – Emirates Telecom Corp.	United Arab Emirates	Telecommunications	17,629	34,931	5,321	14,068
Genting Bhd	Malaysia	Hotels and restaurants	17,287	23,130	2,984	4,655
JBS SA	Brazil	Food & beverages	17,206	32,812	38,810	51,801
DP World Limited	United Arab Emirates	Transport and storage	16,957	23,113	1,445	4,729
Fomento Economico Mexicano SAB	Mexico	Food & beverages	16,930	29,831	8,407	24,348

Company	Country	Industry				
Sasol Limited	South Africa	Chemicals and allied products	16,671	30,514	6,647	12,675
Sinopec - China Petrochemical Corporation	China	Petroleum refining and related industries	16,448	346,784	90,557	355,140
MTN Group Ltd	South Africa	Telecommunications	16,357	19,788	6,780	9,975
Huawei Technologies Co, Ltd	China	Communications equipment	15,527	77,637	44,169	89,309
Abu Dhabi National Energy Co PJSC (TAQA)	United Arab Emirates	Electricity, gas, and water	14,585	28,055	2,603	4,542
China Three Gorges Corp	China	Electricity, gas, and water	14,333	107,706	2,697	13,316
YTL Corporation Bhd	Malaysia	Construction	14,309	17,398	2,493	3,436
Shougang Group	China	Metals and metal products	14,285	76,957	1,100	27,489
China Molybdenum Co Ltd	China	Mining, quarrying and petroleum	13,554	15,034	2,665	3,573
Qingdao Haier Co Ltd	China	Household appliances	13,183	24,141	9,949	23,562
Axiata Group Bhd	Malaysia	Telecommunications	12,851	17,275	3,808	5,674
Sabic – Saudi Basic Industries Corp.	Saudi Arabia	Chemicals and allied products	12,431	85,988	32,385	39,938
Cofco Corp	China	Food & beverages	11,943	82,797	7,139	71,388
Infosys Limited	India	Computer and data processing	11,942	12,259	10,592	10,938
China Mobile Limited	China	Telecommunications	11,694	233,885	5,705	114,104
Hindalco Industries Ltd	India	Metals and metal products	11,502	22,657	14,167	17,963
Sime Darby Bhd	Malaysia	Wholesale durable goods	11,491	15,767	6,153	7,252
Steinhoff International Holdings Ltd	South Africa	Retail trade	11,199	20,667	15,118	20,761
Ternium SA	Argentina	Metals and metal products	10,913	12,123	7,384	9,700
China Electronics Corporation (CEC)	China	Electronic components	10,827	40,400	8,573	31,990

Table 2.3 (*cont.*)

Corporation	Home economy	Industry	Foreign assets, USD million	Total assets, USD million	Foreign sales, USD million	Total sales, USD million
China Communications Construction Company Ltd	China	Construction	10,658	130,560	16,454	71,433
San Miguel Corp	Philippines	Food & beverages	10,322	27,671	1,991	16,386
Petroleo Brasileiro SA	Brazil	Mining, quarrying, and petroleum	10,160	251,008	6,364	88,913
Grupo Bimbo SAB de CV	Mexico	Food & beverages	10,067	13,140	9,367	14,146
China General Nuclear Power	China	Electricity, gas, and water	9,761	97,610	2,515	12,576
Gazprom JSC	Russian Federation	Mining, quarrying, and petroleum	9,457	315,220	76,828	112,163
Sonatrach	Algeria	Mining, quarrying, and petroleum	9,180	91,801	38,784	41,922
Bharti Airtel Limited	India	Telecommunications	9,116	38,450	3,379	12,981
Tata Steel Ltd	India	Metals and metal products	9,077	32,186	11,804	20,632
Mobile Telecommunications Company KSC (Zain)	Kuwait	Telecommunications	8,917	10,042	2,302	3,392
BRF S.A.	Brazil	Food & beverages	8,666	13,653	4,437	10,490
Empresas COPEC SA	Chile	Wholesale petroleum and fuels	8,581	22,174	9,685	20,353
Cencosud S.A.	Chile	Retail trade	8,534	16,307	9,237	16,115
Mediclinic International PLC	South Africa	Health care services	8,352	8,933	2,624	3,803
Banpu Public Company Limited	Thailand	Mining, quarrying, and petroleum	8,154	8,206	2,677	2,874

Alfa, S.A.B. de C.V.	Mexico	Metals and metal products	8,124	18,195	9,531	16,795
Gerdau SA	Brazil	Metals and metal products	7,978	15,185	7,355	11,571
Mexichem SAB de CV	Mexico	Rubber and miscellaneous plastic products	7,811	9,759	4,620	5,828
Dalian Wanda Group	China	Construction	7,530	107,568	5,046	33,641
Grupo Mexico, S.A. de C.V.	Mexico	Mining, quarrying, and petroleum	7,194	26,553	6,125	9,786
SACI Falabella	Chile	Retail trade	6,925	23,376	5,271	13,762

Source: Created using information from UNCTAD (2019b).

business-to-business industries or to purchase foreign brands to facilitate their internationalization. Among the global leaders from emerging economies that have joined the largest firms in their industries are the Thai seafood firm Thai Union, Mexican bakery goods company Bimbo, Brazilian orange juice producer Citrosuco, Argentinean seamless tubes manufacturer Tenaris, Chilean copper miner Codelco, Brazilian iron ore miner Vale, and Chinese telecommunication equipment Huawei.

Many emerging market firms have purchased beloved legacy brands from advanced economies to facilitate the upgrading of their marketing and technological capabilities and to ease their international expansion in advanced economies. These include the Brazilian investment fund 3G Capital, which purchased the US fast-food firm Burger King, the Canadian fast-food chain Tim Hortons, and the US packaged food companies Heinz and Kraft; the Chinese appliance maker Haier, which acquired the US division GE Appliances; the Turkish food conglomerate Yildiz Holding, which purchased the US (originally Belgian) chocolate brand Godiva Chocolate; the Chinese automobile producer Geely, which acquired the Swedish car firm Volvo from its US parent Ford; the Indian conglomerate Tata, which purchased a multiplicity of firms from advanced economies, including leading British car producers Jaguar and Land Rover and the British tea firm Tetley; or the investment fund Qatar Holdings, which bought the British retailer Harrods. Purchasing legacy brands from advanced countries does facilitate the upgrading of capabilities, although firms from emerging markets have access to a large variety of methods, which evolve with the competitiveness of the firm, as we explain in the remainder of this chapter.

2.3   Upgrading Capabilities in Emerging Markets

A key challenge for any firm is to continuously upgrade its capabilities to stay ahead of competitors and satisfy customers better. In the case of emerging market firms, the choice of methods to upgrade capabilities is influenced by the level of underdevelopment of their home countries.[22] Table 2.4 summarizes the stereotypical view of the conditions of emerging countries and their predicted impact on the behavior of emerging market firms at home and abroad.[23] The four conditions discussed reflect the four underlying disciplines of economics, political science, sociology, and economic geography.

The underdevelopment in home country conditions tends to impede the upgrading of capabilities by emerging market firms. These companies cannot rely on a supporting infrastructure and environment that is typical of advanced economies, and that enables their firms to specialize and focus on a narrow set of activities and competencies, relying on external

Table 2.4 *Stereotypical conditions of emerging countries and their likely effect on the behavior of emerging market firms at home and abroad*

Country dimension	Conditions of emerging countries compared to advanced nations	Impact of country conditions on the behavior of emerging market firms at home	Impact of country conditions on the behavior of emerging market firms abroad
Economic	Less sophisticated innovation systems Underdeveloped capital markets Fewer and less developed suppliers	Firms upgrade technology by absorbing foreign technology via license and through alliances with foreign companies in the home country Firms generate efficiency innovations that take into account lower capital availability (i.e. they are more capital-efficient) Firms internalize more suppliers of inputs (i.e. they are more vertically integrated)	Firms are more likely to establish alliances and/or acquire firms in advanced economies to upgrade technology Firms quote in foreign financial markets to access larger and more sophisticated sources of capital
Politico–regulatory	Poorer governance/worse regulation More uncertainty/higher volatility Fewer rights and freedoms	Firms become resilient to the uncertainty and volatility of the political system Firms become accustomed to poorer governance and regulation and to governments that are more unpredictable Firms internalize more transactions (i.e. they become business groups)	Firms enter into more and different countries using their higher flexibility and ability to internalize transactions and operate in difficult environments Firms tend to have higher levels of control in their foreign operations

Table 2.4 (*cont.*)

Country dimension	Conditions of emerging countries compared to advanced nations	Impact of country conditions on the behavior of emerging market firms at home	Impact of country conditions on the behavior of emerging market firms abroad
Social	Lower education Lower health Lower income Younger population Higher outward economic migration	Firms generate consumer innovations that take into account differing needs (e.g. extreme poverty), lack of complementary assets in the country (e.g. unavailable finance), or lack of complementary assets in consumers (e.g. lack of access to electricity) Emerging market firms generate efficiency-enhancing innovations that take into account the lower quality of labor (e.g. lower education)	Firms internationalize not only in emerging countries but also in advanced economies to take advantage of larger markets that pay more for efficiency-enhancing innovations Firms internationalize into countries that are different from the country of origin but have a large home-country immigrant community
Geographic	Worse infrastructure	Firms invest in the creation of supporting infrastructure that is missing in the country (e.g. schools, hospitals, roads) Firms generate resilient innovations (e.g. sturdy packaging, tough products) that take into account infrastructure constraints (e.g. unreliable electricity flow)	Firms are more likely to establish operations abroad that rely less on the infrastructure Firms enter advanced economies bringing resilient innovations that address extreme conditions

Source: Adapted from Cuervo-Cazurra (2012).

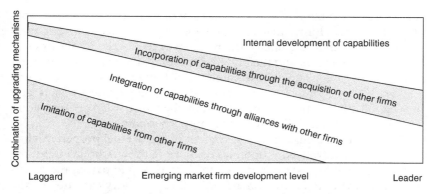

Figure 2.3 Capability upgrading as a dynamic process evolving with firm development stages
Source: Adapted from Wang (2014)

providers for most complementary activities. Moreover, a lower level of development also limits the competitiveness of firms from emerging markets, as they are not exposed to competitive forces and sophisticated demands from consumers that force them to innovate and upgrade. The outcome of this is that firms from emerging economies must turn to a wide range of methods they can use to improve their capabilities. The use of these methods varies with firms' relative levels of competitiveness.

Specifically, we propose that the frequency in the use of methods evolves with the level of competitiveness of the emerging market firm. Those firms that are laggards in capability upgrading are more likely to use imitation intensively as they can rely on the capability of others to quickly improve their standing. As they upgrade, they move toward using the integration of capabilities via alliances to obtain more sophisticated process knowledge. The continued upgrading leads them to use the incorporation of capabilities via acquisitions as they obtain tacit knowledge and technology. Once they become leaders, they use internal development more intensively to reach and push the technological frontier. Figure 2.3 illustrates these processes, which we discuss in more detail in the next part of the chapter.

2.3.1 Imitation

Imitation is often the first method emerging market companies use to upgrade capabilities. Firms from emerging economies improve their capabilities by analyzing what firms closer to the technological frontier are doing, and copying their practices.[24] Staying abreast of how their competitors gain the preference of customers requires gathering competitor intelligence. Firms analyze the characteristics of their own products and processes and benchmark them against the offers and activities of competitors to understand their relative standing. In the case of emerging market firms, the protection of intellectual property rights tends to be weaker. Hence, companies can often directly copy the products and services of other firms and benefit from their discovery or innovation with little regard for their intellectual property rights, given the inherent weakness in the defense and enforcement of intellectual property rights. Firms based in advanced economies cannot use this method without the fear of litigation for patent or design infringement and paying the penalties. Thus, the underdevelopment of the home country can support the upgrading of capabilities in emerging market firms, by facilitating imitation of the innovations and products of other companies. This process can help the firm replicate the products of other firms, thus upgrading their capabilities to the level of creating copies of products for their home markets that are superior to those they were previously manufacturing.

This process of imitation can go beyond the mere copying of other products, and lead to further learning and capability development. Emerging market firms can reverse engineer products to understand how they function and search for ways in which they can replace the most expensive components with locally produced ones that are simpler, yet serve the same function. This can help the firm lower product cost and thus the price, providing an advantage over its competitors. This method enables the firm to go beyond the mere imitation of products from other firms, and move toward initial product innovation as their engineers seek to understand the products and tweak them in ways that facilitate cost reductions and improve the price competitiveness of the company. It may also defend against infringement claims.

2.3.2   Integration

The process of imitation and improvement over existing products by reconfiguring components and functions is useful for upgrading capabilities, but in the long run is limited to products the firm can reverse engineer. Improving the processes of the firm through imitation is more challenging, as it is difficult to observe the processes of competitors. Processes tend to be not only internal to the firm and not easily accessible by outsiders, but may also have a more complex nature with many interrelated activities that are not easily observable.

Thus, the next stage in upgrading capabilities may lead the emerging market firm toward integration of the capabilities of alliance partners that have sophisticated processes with the aim of learning from these firms how to improve their processes and achieve greater efficiency and effectiveness.[25] These alliances can take the form of becoming the preferred suppliers to firms that are highly sophisticated, either subsidiaries of foreign multinationals or better local companies, and aim to improve capabilities via the direct spillovers from the customers. These more sophisticated customers can train and provide the preferred suppliers with the technology and expertise needed to integrate and create high-quality parts and components that ensure the quality of the final products. This direct collaboration between supplier and customer facilitates the supplier's capability upgrading.[26] As the firm in the emerging market takes increasingly complex tasks, it receives technology from its partners. Consequently, it can evolve from a firm that can only produce parts to a firm that can produce the entire systems.

When a foreign company that is interested in entering an emerging country forms a joint venture with a local company, the emerging market firm becomes its local partner. In this situation, the emerging market firm provides access to the local market and its contacts and relationships in exchange for the integration of the superior technology and processes of the foreign company. This helps the emerging market firm learn the tacit knowledge and skills of the foreign firm and improve its production processes and ability to make sophisticated products to the level desired by consumers in foreign markets.[27] Over time the emerging market firm can integrate ideas and technologies for improving its processes and products to the point at which it can manufacture the complete products for the firm. As a result, it becomes an original equipment manufacturer that produces for the specification of the customer and adds the customers' brand name to facilitate sales abroad.

2.3.3   Incorporation

As the firm improves its products and processes with the help of alliances with domestic and foreign firms, it obtains the technologies that the partners are willing to provide to become a better supplier. However, the partners are likely to withhold the most advanced technologies and especially the product and process development capabilities from the alliance to sustain their competitive advantage and for fear of potentially creating a competitor.

Hence, the emerging market firm may have to incorporate capabilities via the acquisition of companies to gain the control and ability to force the transfer of technologies it needs to continue upgrading to more sophisticated capabilities.[28] Firms from emerging economies can benefit from the purchase and incorporation of innovations from technology providers that give them the ability to use more sophisticated innovations in exchange for the payment of royalties. This process is valuable not only because the licensed technology can come with the support of the technology provider, but also because licensed technology, as opposed to copied one, can help the firm expand abroad and avoid potential litigation in a foreign market by the providers of the technology. However, the incorporation of acquired technology in exchange for the payment of royalties has limitations in enabling the upgrading of technologies. Such technologies are self-contained, and the firm is receiving well established and easily transferable technologies that can help improve areas in which the firm is deficient. Nevertheless, the incorporation of individual technologies does not provide access to the underlying capabilities that enabled the technology suppliers to create innovations in the first place, posing a limitation to the capability upgrading of emerging market firms.

The purchase of complete firms is a mechanism that provides emerging market firms with a way to incorporate advanced capabilities needed to upgrade their competitiveness to a higher level, because it grants access to both the technologies created by the target firm as well as the capabilities that led to the creation of such technologies. The purchase of firms can be selective, with the emerging market firm acquiring divisions or plants of a competitor rather than the whole firm. These acquisitions of parts of a competitor not only reduce the premium paid but also provide access to complementary technologies and brands that the emerging market firm may value while limiting the additional assets that are not needed by the emerging market firm. The emerging market firm can access and bring back to its existing facilities the underlying production processes that help it upgrade the efficiency of its existing plants, while avoiding producing in countries with much higher costs of operations. The purchase of firms and their brands can also give the emerging market firm immediate and direct exposure to customers globally and in countries in which it would be challenging, if not prohibitively expensive, to build new brands from scratch. In addition to the brand, the emerging market firm can acquire capabilities to manage the relationships with the customers and understand how to sell to more demanding consumers. All these together can help the firm upgrade its marketing and promotion knowledge.

These acquisitions do not have to be prohibitively expensive, as the emerging market firm may target firms with technology that is "good enough" and can be more easily integrated with its current operations. Some target firms may have internal problems or be near bankruptcy, enabling the emerging market firm to access their more sophisticated capabilities and resources for a low price. The integration of such

capabilities and resources into current operations can yield high returns as
the firm upgrades its operations to levels that approach the international
frontier.

2.3.4   Internal development

The use of imitation, alliances, and acquisitions can enable the firm to
reach the frontier; however, the emerging market firm cannot push the
frontier and become a leader by relying on these methods of transferring
technology and capabilities from other firms.[29] These external methods
would provide the firm with competitive parity with existing competitors.
To surpass this level, an emerging market firm needs to undertake internal development and build capabilities that are superior to those of its
competitors.

Internal development serves a variety of functions and can be useful
through the upgrading process. The use of internal development is not
limited to when the firm nears the technological frontier, however. It has
been part of the upgrading process since the beginning of the operations
of the firm as it helped it to identify the technologies that it needed to
imitate, the practices it needed to obtain via alliances, and the target
technologies and firms it required to acquire. In the initial stages of
upgrading of capabilities when the firm is far from the technological
frontier, internal development provides the ability to understand where
the firm stands in comparison to competitors and in which areas it can
upgrade its abilities quickly by imitating the products and practices of
competitors. This same process of identification and use of external
methods can be applied to the implementation of alliances for capability
upgrading, with the firm using internal development to identify how the
use of alliances can help it obtain needed technology and knowledge.
Similarly, internal development can help identify the underdeveloped
areas and target firms whose acquisition can help the firm complement
and upgrade its activities.

Internal development enables assimilation of external knowledge and
its integration with existing practices to build well-functioning internal
systems that satisfy the needs of customers better than those of its competitors. Internal development is valuable for upgrading capabilities by
facilitating the assimilation of internal knowledge and technology with the
internally generated capabilities to expand them toward the external
frontier. The internal development provides employees in the firm with
the needed capacity to absorb external technology and practices.[30] As
they improve their personnel capacities through training and learning by
doing, they can understand better how the external, sophisticated

knowledge can help them plug gaps in their knowledge and understanding of advanced technologies.

Once the emerging market firm has reached levels approaching or at the international level of best practices, internal development enables its employees to push the boundaries of knowledge and technologies by innovating and creating novel concepts and practices that are not available in other firms. It is at this point in which internal development becomes the only method that helps the emerging market firm surpass its competitors to create products and services that are superior to the offers of competitors. However, with the emerging market firm reaching and in some cases surpassing the frontier of knowledge, it may end up with the challenge of how to protect its newly developed intellectual property. The legal protection of intellectual property might help in countries in which such protection is supported, but may not in their home country, and thus the emerging market firm might find itself in a position in which it becomes the target for imitation or alliances, or even acquisition by firms from emerging countries that are laggards in technological advances. Its internally developed technologies can not only help the firm upgrade capabilities beyond the international frontier, but also facilitate the protection from imitation by ensuring a level of internal secrecy and complexity that reduces the ability of technological laggards from learning its advances.

2.4   Conclusions

Emerging market firms face the challenge of upgrading their capabilities to international levels within a relatively unsupportive institutional and economic context. Some are not yet forced to improve. However, continuous technological development and integration of their home countries within the global economy[31] exposes them to sophisticated competitors, and may soon force them to upgrade.[32] Meanwhile, many others have upgraded their capabilities, but to levels that are not internationally competitive.[33] Some firms took full advantage of the transformation of their economies to become leaders, while a few are industry leaders not only in their home country but also globally.[34]

This chapter reviewed the upgrading alternatives available to firms from emerging markets. In contrast to the traditional suggestion that is provided to firms in advanced economies of using internal development to ensure the building of a competitive advantage that is sustainable, emerging market firms have a wider variety of methods to choose from because of their varying levels of international competitiveness and the effect of the conditions of their home countries. Thus, they can start their upgrading process by imitating the products and practices of more sophisticated firms, and learn by reverse engineering advanced products. As they gain a better understanding of how to improve products, they can move to integrate capabilities from their alliance partners to enhance their processes, gaining access to the more tacit expertise of their partners. Incorporation of capabilities via acquisitions can help emerging market firms push their capabilities higher by assimilating technologies and practices that are traditional subject to secrecy. Internal development, which complements the other methods in the upgrading of capabilities, becomes the preferred method as the emerging market firm reaches the level of international competitiveness and pushes the technological frontier. Thus the recommendation on the methods to use to upgrade capabilities converge for advanced economy firms and those from emerging economies as they become global leaders.

This review thus points to an evolution of the methods used to upgrade capabilities with the level of international competitiveness achieved by the emerging market firms. Although the four methods can be used at all levels of the competitiveness, the frequency and more importantly the likelihood of helping the firm quickly achieve significant improvements in their competitiveness evolve. Imitation is the method that can have a quick and substantial impact on upgrading for those emerging market firms that are far away from the technological frontier, then integration might become the preferred method of upgrading, followed by incorporation, and finally by internal development. This sequence balances the cost of using the methods to upgrade capabilities with the benefit derived in upgrading and building a sustainable competitive advantage that leads the emerging market firms to become the global leaders in their industries.

The individual country chapters in the book provide a more detailed illustration of the role that the conditions of the home country play on the upgrading of capabilities of emerging market firms. Some of these reflect the discussion of the importance of the underdevelopment of institutions and economy, while others highlight some of the particular conditions of the country. Thus, the use of the methods varies not only with the level of upgrading of the firm, but also with the level of development of the country. Figure 2.4 illustrates this point. In the least developed countries, the underdevelopment of the country places a ceiling on the competitiveness of firms and thus on the intensity of use of the methods of capability upgrading, with most companies imitating the products of other firms and few engaging in integration, incorporation and internal development.

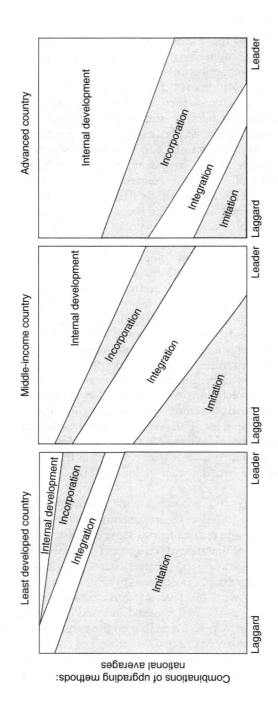

Figure 2.4 Capability upgrading as a dynamic process evolving with home country development stages
Source: Adapted from Wang (2014)

In middle-income countries companies are more sophisticated as the country has a more supportive environment, and thus the intensity in use of imitation is lower, while the utilization of integration, incorporation and especially internal development increases. Finally, in advanced economies, much of the effort at capability upgrading is centered in internal development, as commonly argued, with less focus on incorporation, integration, and especially imitation.

The above reflects the need for a better understanding of the home conditions of emerging market firms and how they affect the upgrading of capabilities. These conditions operate in a dual Janus-like fashion, with some elements supporting upgrading while others are constraining it. The concluding chapter retakes this theme in more detail and reflects on the particular lessons gained from the cross-comparison of the experience of the firms in the various emerging countries.

Notes

1. See Cuervo-Cazurra, Newburry & Park (2016), Guillén & García-Canal (2012), Khanna & Palepu (2010), Ramamurti & Singh (2009), Sauvant (2009).
2. Dunning (1981).
3. Aggarwal & Agmon (1990), Luo, Xue & Han (2010), Wang, Luo, Lu, Sun & Maksimov (2014).
4. Williamson, Ramamurti, Fleury & Fleury (2013).
5. Cuervo-Cazurra & Ramamurti (2014), Cuervo-Cazurra, Luo, Ramamurti & Ang (2018), Grosse & Meyer, 2019; Estrin, Meyer & Pelletier, 2018.
6. See Khanna & Palepu (2010) for an extensive review of differences between advanced and emerging economies.
7. Wang and Cuervo-Cazurra (2017).
8. Zhao (2006), Chitoor et al. (2009), Luo, Sun & Wang (2011).
9. Ghemawat & Khanna (1998).
10. Wang (2014).
11. Wang (2014).
12. Guillén & García-Canal (2012).
13. Dunning (1981).
14. Ramamurti (2012).
15. Dunning (1981).
16. UNCTAD (2019).
17. The list of advanced countries in IMF (2018) is: Australia, Austria, Belgium, Canada, Cyprus, Czech Republic, Denmark, Estonia, Finland, France, Germany, Greece, Hong Kong, Iceland, Ireland, Israel, Italy, Japan, Korea, Latvia, Lithuania, Luxembourg, Macao, Malta, Netherlands, New Zealand, Norway, Portugal, Puerto Rico, San Marino, Singapore, Slovak Republic, Slovenia, Spain, Sweden, Switzerland, Taiwan, United Kingdom, and

United States. We consider emerging countries to be those that are not classified as advanced.

18. Fortune (2019).
19. Colpan, Hikino & Lincoln (2010).
20. Meyer et al. (2018).
21. UNCTAD (2019b).
22. For a more detailed explanation of the impact of the underdevelopment of institutions and economies on multinationals from emerging economies, see Cuervo-Cazurra & Ramamurti (2014).
23. See Cuervo-Cazurra (2012) for a more detailed discussion.
24. Chitoor et al. (2009), Luo, Sun & Wang (2011).
25. See a review of alliances in Contractor & Lorange (1998).
26. Dyer (1996).
27. Luo & Tung (2007).
28. Luo & Tung (2007), Madhok & Keyhani (2012).
29. Barney (1989).
30. Cohen & Levinthal (1990).
31. Yergin & Stanislaw (2002).
32. Bruton (1998).
33. Kumaraswamy et al. (2012).
34. Guillén & García-Canal (2012), Khanna & Palepu (2010).

3 Building Strategic Capabilities in Chinese Companies

Developing Global Competitive Advantage

Mohan Song, William Newburry, and Seung Ho Park

3.1 Introduction

In 1949, the newly founded People's Republic of China faced poor access to natural resources, weak social capital, and severe political turbulence. Seventy years later, China is a thriving and prosperous global power. After Deng Xiaoping's reform and opening-up policy was initiated in 1978, its planned economy was relentlessly transformed into a socialist market economy. In the past three decades, China's GDP has grown at a sustained rate approaching 10 percent, soon becoming the largest emerging market and the second largest economy in the world (IMF, 2018b). By 2018, China's GDP was 92.53 trillion yuan (about US$13.608 trillion), an increase of 12.06 percent over the previous year (World Bank, 2018a) (Figure 3.1).

China is now the largest industrial nation, the largest agricultural nation, the second largest service nation, and the world's largest trading country. China's output and export volume in more than 200 product categories ranks first globally (CIA, 2018), and its economic growth has benefited from investment and export earnings. Until recently, China's foreign direct investment (FDI) inflow and outflow saw rapid growth (see Figures 3.2 and 3.3). However, despite their considerable success, Chinese companies now appear to need to build stronger capabilities to face the increasingly turbulent international trade environment.

This startling economic developmental success is a result of not only state decisions and actions but also the efforts of China's state-owned and private enterprises to compete in markets at home and abroad. The experiences of leading Chinese enterprises can serve to inform other emerging markets. This chapter offers lessons learned – from both success and failure – by eight companies.

Cuervo-Cazurra, Newburry, and Park (2016) analyzed the challenges that emerging market multinational corporations face as they invest internationally. In this chapter, the authors will explore the strategic

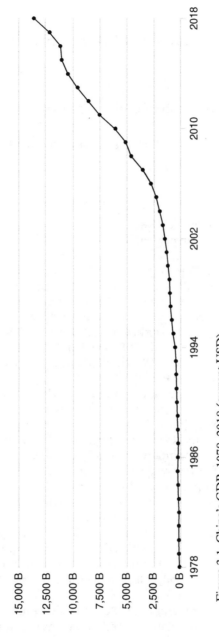

Figure 3.1 China's GDP, 1978–2018 (current USD)
Source: World Bank (2018a)

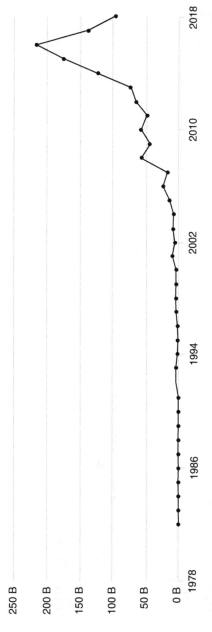

Figure 3.2 China's FDI net outflow, 1978–2018 (BoP, current USD)
Source: World Bank (2019)

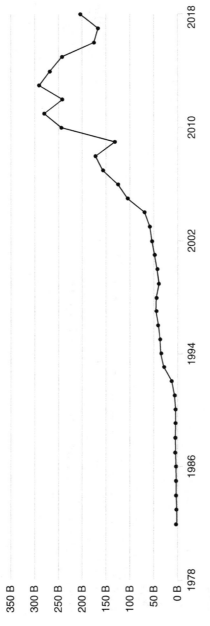

Figure 3.3 China's FDI net inflow, 1978–2018 (BoP, current USD)
Source: World Bank (2019)

capabilities that representatives of these firms have assessed as being important, as well as the challenges inherent in developing these capabilities within the context of the internationalization process for Chinese companies. Through an in-depth analysis of the challenges faced by each of eight companies in different industries with different degrees of internationalization, the authors will identify the unique sets of capabilities that helped each firm develop its sources of competitive advantage to challenge its competitors in the international arena. Competitive advantage grows out of "value a firm is able to create" (Porter, 1985), and is sustainable only when buyers are willing to pay more for such value than it costs the sellers to create and provide it (Ghemawat, 1986). These established models serve to guide the concluding discussion of each case study, which identifies the paths that different types of emerging market companies can pursue to address the challenges of internationalization.

3.2 Country Background

The People's Republic of China (PRC) in East Asia is the world's most populous country, with a population of roughly 1.4 billion, and the fourth largest country by total area (3,700,000 square miles). Rich natural resources, hard-working people, and a unique political history gave rise to the Chinese nation's strong vigor and vitality. Its culture spans nearly 4,000 continuous years. China was regarded as an agricultural country in 1949, and its population had endured long-term wars, a fluctuating economy, and many natural, political, and economic crises up until the founding of the PRC following the 1946–1949 revolution. From 1953 to 1957, the new Chinese government implemented a planned economy and, with help from the Soviet Union, began to move steadily forward.

However, the Great Leap Forward, which began in 1958, caused serious damage to the Chinese economy and led to widespread famine and death. Concurrently, Sino-Soviet relations deteriorated drastically, leading to the termination of Soviet economic assistance. After a brief recovery from 1963 to 1965, the economy became stagnant, and the nation entered its decade-long Cultural Revolution. After years of political turmoil and natural disasters, Deng Xiaoping's "reform and opening-up" policy, implemented from 1978, restarted the development of China's economy.

Economic Outlook (1978–1997)

In 1978, Deng initiated a reform policy designed to transform the Chinese economy from its planned-economy model to a mixed-economy model based on a combination of market forces with government control. The government adopted a series of administrative and policy measures in the 1980s, resulting in the establishment of special economic zones and the reform and restructuring of state-owned enterprises, among other reforms. Those measures soon enabled China to become the world's fastest-growing economy. China's GDP grew by an average of 9.8 percent from 1978 to 2007, and the population's poverty rate fell from 64 percent in the late 1970s to less than 10 percent in 2004 (Dollar, 2007). These three remarkable decades of development laid the solid economic foundation required for the internationalization of Chinese enterprises.

During this era, the Chinese state continued to encourage the development of agriculture, light manufacturing, and foreign trade, but shifted its attention to exports. From 1979 to 1981, nominal exports grew at an average annual rate of 29 percent. The initial export emphasis was on textile products and light manufacturing of industrial products, such as bicycles, sewing machines, and minerals. The trade deficit disappeared in 1981, and from 1982 a large surplus became the norm. At the same time, both state-owned and private companies began to raise funds independently and develop their export strategies. In 1992, Deng Xiaoping proposed continuing reform and opening-up policies. The Chinese economy continued its rapid development trajectory until the Asian financial crisis in 1997.

Economic Outlook (1998–2018)

After 1998, the Chinese government adjusted its economic growth strategy in response to the Asian financial crisis and to rising wages. It implemented a proactive fiscal policy, invested surplus funds in new technologies and new industries, and reformed or shut down a number of state-owned enterprises that had performed poorly. This resulted in the dismissal of a large number of employees of state-owned enterprises, leading to social unrest.

From 2000 onward, China's economy continued to advance, with impressive GDP growth (Figure 3.1) and GDP per capita growth (Figure 3.4). In 2001, China joined the World Trade Organization and vigorously promoted its economic development. To combat the effects of the 2008 global financial crisis, China implemented a four trillion yuan (RMB) ($600 billion) economic stimulus plan. In 2009, China ranked 29 in the Global Competitiveness Report (World Economic Forum, 2009) and ranked 132 in the Index of Economic Freedom (Heritage Foundation, 2020). China's GDP growth peaked in 2010. Statistics show that with the growth of GDP, China's comprehensive competitiveness is increasing, and China's business environment is also improving.

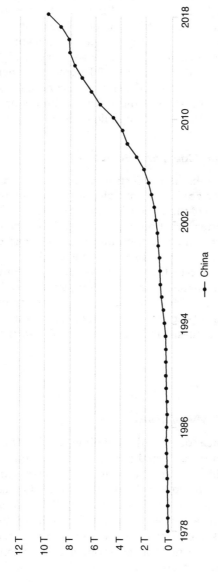

Figure 3.4 China's GDP per capita, 1978–2018 (current USD)
Source: World Bank (2019)

In 2013, President Xi Jinping proposed the "One Belt, One Road" policy (later known in English simply as "Belt and Road"), which, by leading the development of logistics and other infrastructure in order to facilitate international trade, encourages Chinese companies to internationalize process (see Table 3.1). China's exports and outward foreign direct investment (OFDI) have since experienced significant growth. By 2016, around 70 percent of merchandise exports were to high-income economies (see Table 3.2). The remaining 30 percent of merchandise exports were to low-income and middle-income economies, with one-third of these going to East Asia and the Pacific. The major target for China's OFDI is commercially viable technology (Ramaswamy, 2012).

3.3   Methodology and Company Selection

To answer the question: "What kinds of strategic capabilities do Chinese firms possess?", this study applies a multiple case study method. Two criteria guided the selection of the case companies (Table 3.3). First, they include manufacturing industries, both high-tech and low-tech, and service industries. Second, they include both multinationals and exporters. Our analysis was based on both primary and secondary data: the research team conducted in-depth face-to-face interviews (60 to 90 minutes) with one to three CEOs or top managers in each company in 2017, supplemented by public data from websites, financial reports, and other publications. In the following subsections of the chapter, an introduction of each case is followed by analysis and discussion of the firm's strategic capabilities.

3.4   Case Analysis

AVIC: High-Tech Multinational

Founded in 1979 and headquartered in Beijing, AVIC International Holding Corporation is a state-owned aerospace and defense company group. In 2008, it went through a restructuring and consolidation of two corporations, China Aviation Industry Corporation I and China National Aero-Technology Import & Export Corporation. AVIC owns about 100 subsidiaries, of which thirty are listed, and of which eight are listed overseas. With more than 450,000 employees around the world, AVIC engages in the business of international aviation, electronic components, trade and logistics, retail and consumer goods, real estate and hotel management, electronics, and resource development sectors worldwide. AVIC centers on aviation and provides a full range of services to

Table 3.1 *Data relating to the internationalization of the Chinese economy, 2009–2018*

Indicator Name	2009	2010	2011	2012	2013	2014	2015	2016	2017	2018
GDP (billion current USD)	5,102	6,087	7,552	8,532	9,570	10,439	11,016	11,138	12,143	13,608
Exports of goods and services (billion current USD)	1,250	1,604	2,009	2,175	2,356	2,463	2,360	2,198	2,429	2,651
High-technology exports (billion current USD)	310	406	457	506	560	559	550	496	504	n/a
GDP growth (annual %)	9.40	10.64	9.54	7.86	7.76	7.30	6.90	6.70	6.90	6.60
Foreign direct investment, net inflows (% of GDP)	2.56	3.99	3.70	2.82	3.03	2.56	2.19	1.56	1.37	1.50
Foreign direct investment, net outflows (% of GDP)	0.86	0.95	0.64	0.76	0.76	1.17	1.58	1.93	0.83	0.71
Agricultural raw materials exports (% of merchandise exports)	0.45	0.46	0.53	0.46	0.44	0.45	0.40	0.42	0.41	n/a
Transport services (% of commercial service exports)	19.38	29.35	17.76	19.40	18.29	17.54	17.84	16.33	17.64	18.24
Insurance and financial services (% of commercial service exports)	1.61	2.62	1.93	2.60	3.49	4.17	3.38	3.49	3.54	3.56
ICT service exports (% of service exports, BoP)	6.29	8.91	6.92	8.06	8.26	9.21	11.29	12.20	12.66	n/a
Manufacturing exports (% of merchandise exports)	93.57	93.55	93.30	93.93	94.02	93.99	94.37	93.75	93.60	n/a

Source: World Bank (2019)

Table 3.2 *Percentage of total merchandise exports from China to low- and middle-income economies and to high-income economies*

Middle East and North Africa	2.76
South Asia	4.58
East Asia and Pacific	10.44
Latin America and Caribbean	4.61
Sub-Saharan Africa	3.20
Europe and Central Asia	4.03
High-income economies	70.17

Source: World Bank (2016)

Table 3.3 *Data collection matrix for the selection of Chinese firms as case studies*

		Firm category	
		Multinational	Exporter
Industry type	High-tech	AVIC Advantech ShangGong Group	Higer
	Low-tech	Chervon Siwei-Johnson	Baby First
	Service	Sanpower	

customers, from research and development to operations management, manufacturing, and financing (Bloomberg, 2018a).

Previously, we also held huge real estate, mineral, and forest, etc. Based on the lead and recommendation of the parent company, the AVIC group, we are backing away from those business sectors. Therefore, we currently focus on four segments: aviation, electronic components, international trade, and the modern service industry, like retail and property management, especially those that put aviation as the first category. (AVIC International executive)

AVIC passed through three phases in its internationalization process. The first was going out to get to know the market, which was completed in the 1980s. The second was setting offices in local areas to deeply understand local markets. The third phase is localization: AVIC is in the early stage of this phase. AVIC hopes to take root in the global market and make more local investments. Because AVIC is a state-owned enterprise, its actions needed to take into account the policy-oriented goals of its parent company rather than being primarily driven by market-oriented factors. This is one of the disadvantages the company has faced in its internationalization efforts.

However, there are very few things we [AVIC] can do because we have to follow the lead of our parent company. ... We just implement our policy. (AVIC International executive)

The advantage of being a state-owned enterprise is that it has access to rich resources that help AVIC access different markets. In the early stage of its internationalization, the pace of AVIC's expansion was too fast, leading to many failures. The company did not do a good job of resource identification and usage, resulting in wasted resources.

To learn from its early stage of expansion, AVIC reviewed its process of large-scale development and reflected on what the company had done well and what had failed. AVIC has worked hard to reverse the situation. The company has realigned its strategic distribution, transformed its basic business, and invested in innovations in different industries. At the same time, the company also realizes that it is still lacking many key capabilities. For example, AVIC had tended to enter an area because of attractive resources within it. However, the company was at those times not well prepared and not capable of dealing with problems that may occur in an unfamiliar industry, which resulted in failure.

AVIC had an opportunity to acquire a significant portion of the KHD company, an engineering firm primarily operating in the global cement industry, an industry new to AVIC. The acquisition was proposed by one of AVIC's subsidiaries, and AVIC's headquarters lacked professional judgment at the time. The leaders did not know whether they should enter the industry and rashly believed in the subsidiary's plan. However, the subsidiary lacked post-acquisition management resources and skills.

This somehow tells the story of failure on the management side of the entire process. On the AVIC side, there might be some problems in managing the subsidiaries. The problem is not only because of the SOP [standard operating procedure] of how the proposal should be [carried out] and how it can be signed off, but also the subsidiary may not be following the way it [the procedure] is supposed to be [carried out]. (AVIC International executive)

After the acquisition, the company was in a chaotic situation. When AVIC looked back and reflected on the transaction process, they saw several reasons for the failure. First, this hasty decision was made in a rapid growth period, in which the expansion was blind. Second, AVIC bought KHD at its peak, and then the whole industry declined. These market changes were unexpected. Third, AVIC was not familiar with the local market in Germany, where KHD was headquartered, notably its high labor costs. Their efforts to build relationships with local trade unions resulted in misunderstandings and conflicts in the operation. Fourth, at time of writing AVIC was still seeking a reliable leader for KHD. They had been trying to use local people, but there were trust issues with locals that created significant difficulties.

In the process of the company's development, and having gone through both successful and failed ventures, AVIC gradually built up a unique capability: a capacity for reflection. AVIC now often asks, "Although we have all kinds of resources in hand, can we identify these resources and make rational use of them?"

One of the demonstrations of our resources advantage is the constant process of reidentifying not only the resources we have, but also identifying what resources can do for us, and that they can help us access different things. Because the same resource can work differently at different times, we constantly look back on the same thing and think of what we can do at this time by using the resources that we have. (AVIC International executive)

The point is that the same resource may play different roles at different times. To help it grow, AVIC continues to reflect on what has been done with these resources, whether resources have been used effectively previously, and what these resources can do at present. AVIC's reflective philosophy has been widely accepted and adopted by all levels of managers. While reflecting on the overall understanding of industry trends, the company also prepares for monthly and quarterly meetings, as well as actively adjusting their strategies. AVIC also suggests that companies that are going global should think twice before they act. First, they should consider what position they have in the domestic market and whether they should go outside it. If a company is not ready, they should not move blindly.

As a lesson for other Chinese firms that want to go global, the AVIC case reveals that companies need to judge their positions in the domestic market and measure whether they are capable of moving outwards. Nowadays, it is relatively easy to go international because of supportive policies and globalization tendencies in the environment. However, management subsequently may be very difficult and lots of firms have failed post-acquisition due to not being well prepared. Therefore, companies need to be sure to do the right thing at the right time and place and be careful not to make decisions rashly. What is more, leaders need to constantly reflect on their own strategy and what they can do to make better use of resources (Anseel et al., 2009).

Chervon: Low-Tech Multinational

Chervon, headquartered in Nanjing, Jiangsu Province, is one of the top ten leading companies in the global power tool industry. It provides tools, such as hand-held power tools and stationary bench tools, and equipment, such as laser and electronic equipment and outdoor power equipment. It is also a total-solution provider. Its own brands include Ego, Devon, Hammerhead, and X-Tron, complemented by established global brands acquired by the firm such as Flex and Skil. Today, the company has thousands of employees around the world.

The president of Chervon, Longquan Pan, and the other two founders left a state-owned trading company and established their own company, Chervon. Chervon started as a trading company with borrowed money. In about 1999, Chervon realized that it had to move to a higher level, so it switched from a trading company to a manufacturing company. At this time, Chervon started as an original equipment manufacturer (OEM) business, making products to specifications provided by buyers. Because the company has always respected the production of high-quality products, it built its reputation by cooperating with world-renowned companies. At that time, the world's largest retailers were looking for partners in China to develop their own brands, providing Chervon with promising opportunities to enter this market as an OEM. Chervon seized the opportunity to provide high-quality products and services, thus enhancing its global reputation and status. This business has helped Chervon become one of the top ten suppliers in the world and a leading global innovator in the power tool and outdoor power equipment industries.

Chervon caught the earliest part [of OEM in the industry in China]. At that time, we had the opportunity to work with Sears, a very old brand, and Craftsman, the owned brand in that store, and the typical private label [brand for Sears]. We also had the chance to work with The Home Depot, which has a private label. We also worked with Lowe's and Menards. We also had the chance to work with CTR [Canadian Tire]; it's the largest retailer for construction materials in Canada. Besides North America, we also had a similar customer structure in Europe, with the largest retailers there as well. This business helps us reach another level because very soon we will become one of the top ten manufacturers in the world. (Chervon executive)

In the company's history of more than twenty years, Chervon has actively managed several distinct business units. The power tool business unit, established in 1993, is the largest unit in Chervon and operates a full-fledged value chain, incorporating research and development (R&D), sourcing, manufacturing, testing, marketing, sales and distribution, and after-sales service and solutions. The company has product research and testing centers in mainland China, Hong Kong, North America, and Europe (Bloomberg, 2018b). It offers handheld tools, bench tops, garden and laser tools, angle grinders, hammers, drills, circular saws, woodworking tools, etc.

From 2007 to 2008, Chervon began to actively promote its own brand, Devon, starting from the Chinese market and gradually promoting it overseas. This brand was developed from zero, and it helped Chervon to take its first step into the brand business.

If we want to expand the Devon brand overseas, especially to mature markets like Europe or North America, it's very difficult because it is a new Chinese brand with no reputation. (Chervon executive)

Because promotion in overseas markets is different from promotion in China, the company was willing to acquire some historic manufacturing brands in order to expand the company's global influence. In 2013, Chervon acquired Flex, a very old, well-valued, and highly professional and durable German brand, from Bosch. In addition, it acquired the European and North American business Skil, another well-known brand in the industry. With these brands, the company was able to develop its own product lines to provide truly professional products for the European and North American markets.

Right after we acquired Flex, we had another opportunity, which contributed about one-third of our company's brand, which is our new adventure in the North American market. We actually launched the Ego brand. This brand is a pure, new brand as well, but it's very innovative. We are offering the most powerful battery-driven OP [outdoor power] products to replace the gas-driven OP products. Even with this new brand [Ego], [which] nobody knows, but with new cutting-edge technology and very good performance of the product, we will very soon occupy the market. (Chervon executive)

In the process of external expansion, facing different cultures, rather than sending Chinese managers abroad, Chervon hired local managers so that local people could manage themselves. Nowadays, Chervon has its own brands and has the ability and possibility to sell in mainstream markets, such as the European and North American markets. In the process of further expanding their overseas market share, the company used cutting-edge technology and superb skills to occupy these markets, and at the same time built bargaining power so it could smoothly promote its own brands.

This is a general introduction to the development of our company over the course of 20 years. It basically progressed from a trading company to a lower manufacturer. Gradually, we grew to a higher level, and then we focused more on our own brands. China's power tool industry began with the replication of overseas products. Most of them are imitations, and we don't want to be one. (Chervon executive)

Throughout the transition from OEM to original design manufacturer (ODM), Chervon not only developed strong R&D and product development capabilities but also set high standards for product quality and established its own R&D team. The R&D team is working to constantly improve its capabilities. For example, when the team cooperates with a big foreign design team, it is good at learning.

We work with renowned design companies to help us develop products directly. . . . and when we work with pioneers or opinion leaders, we learn from how they work. We even learn how to observe users and how they use tools. We learn how to brainstorm ideas, how to generate ideas, how to filter out better ideas, test ideas in different ways, and then define products. (Chervon executive)

In addition, Chervon has rich customer relations resources. The company attempts to understand customers as much as possible. It understands market needs and maintains a close interaction with customers, from sales to operations. For example, Chervon asks its designers to be as close to the market as possible and truly understand customer needs. Chervon constantly senses changes in the market, and has gradually established the ability to conduct market research by continually communicating with customers, getting feedback, finding problems, and improving products. The process is consistent with the "sense, seize and reconfigure" model used in dynamic capabilities research (Teece, 2007). Additionally, Chervon keeps up with new technologies and seeks theoretical and technical support from university academics. After learning from foreign design teams and collecting customer feedback, Chervon gradually established a local R&D team to further expand research and development capabilities.

In sum, Chervon sytematically expanded its geographic scope and the technological sophistication of its products in its global businesses, resulting in a corresponding increase in its global reputation. It started with an OEM business model. After accumulating sufficient capital, Chervon moved to acquire international firms with strong brands to increase its market reach, global influence, and reputation. As Chervon gained experience in global sales and marketing, it developed an internal R&D

team and moved to an ODM business model, in which it now designs and makes its own products.

Sanpower: Service Multinational

Sanpower Group, founded in 1993, is a multinational conglomerate that engages in the businesses of department stores, 3C (computer, communications, and consumer electronics) product chains, internet and supply chain services, financial services, and smart data. It owns more than 100 subsidiaries, a number of listed companies, and key privately held global enterprises. In 2016, Sanpower Group's annual gross sales reached RMB 130 billion.

The company did not have a clear strategy before setting up a focus on three segments: "new healthcare, new consumption, and new finance." When assessing potential acquisitions, Sanpower reviewed the assets that the target company owned and considered the degree to which it could reinvigorate and add value to the company after purchase. If these conditions looked good, Sanpower could consider buying the company and changing its structure. Sanpower acquired House of Fraser in 2014 for £155 million ($259 million). There were two reasons to acquire House of Fraser. First, Sanpower planned to reduce finance costs.

The reason why we acquired the company is we find we can reduce the finance cost because they have a senior debt and the interest rate is around 9 percent [which was causing the company to lose money]. However, through refinancing, we can reduce the cost to 4.5 [percent], which means we can reduce half of the costs to around 15 million pounds a year, which is a significant amount of money, you know. (Sanpower executive)

Second, Sanpower hoped to transfer the House of Fraser business model to China to improve existing retail in China.

Another reason is we find that the Chinese retail business model needs to be changed. We find the Western business model in retail more [developed] than [the typical one in China, and] we want to transfer [this model] to China. (Sanpower executive)

Sanpower's plan was to bring the concept of scenario shopping to China. If Shopping Mall A offers customers a unique experience, it will attract consumers. Consumers enter Shopping Mall A no longer just to buy one thing, but to share happy times with their families.

After acquiring House of Fraser, I was thinking about how to improve current retail and make current segmentation in retail stronger and stronger. Then, we formed our strategy in retail: control channel, control contents, and control scenarios. "Scenarios" means we need some scenarios to try to be unique. Because when you do some searching, Chinese retail will find many department stores and shopping malls, and in the near future, there will be more and more shopping malls open. However, you will find all the products' brands in the shopping malls are similar. Why does the consumer go to A, not to B? We should give the reason for the customer, so we want to have some unique scenarios in our mall. (Sanpower executive)

In 2015, Sanpower acquired Hamleys, a 258-year-old toy retailer in the UK, to enrich the scenario concept.

If you can make your clients stay in the mall more time, then you can sell other products – not only toys – to customers. That's the unique scenario we want to create to attract the customer. (Sanpower executive)

Like other internationalized Chinese companies, Sanpower encountered post-acquisition challenges. After acquiring House of Fraser and Hamleys, Sanpower believed that the focus should be not on integration but on synergy. House of Fraser kept its existing management team in the United Kingdom. Sanpower empowered managers to do what they needed and provided them with resources to build an ecosystem within Sanpower. In order to achieve this synergy, Sanpower has its own seven elements as a supporting methodology.

First, we set up a 3-to-five-year schedule strategy for those companies, so in this way, we will manage them. However, we will not become involved very deeply in their daily operation. Second is the budget. We will help them to form their yearly budget. After we agree to the budget, we let them do what they want. Third is double-ten. We call it double-ten. Ten goes for operation and ten goes for management. The first ten goes for operation, for example, like revenue, gross margin, or profit. The second ten goes for management, like setting up the IT system, or organization. Fourth is an organization, which means setting up organizations and recruiting people – the core management. They can be approved by the group level, the Sanpower group level. The fifth is authorization. The Sanpower group chairman will authorize the chairman or CEO of the portfolio company to do something. We have a list of what they can do and what they need to [obtain] authorization or approv[al for]. That's the authorization. The sixth is performance evaluation. That means the core management KPI [key performance indicators] will be set up by the group at the end of this year. The group will evaluate the performance of the core management of the portfolio company. The last one is branding. In branding, we have a comprehensive branding strategy. That means the branding strategy will be led by the group. Also, we will consider their own special considerations. (Sanpower executive)

Sanpower offers a wide range of products and services. In order to manage its businesses in such a way as to create synergy, it also uses these seven elements to manage portfolio companies or subsidiaries to satisfy its corporate diversification strategy (Rumelt, 1982). The head office's finance department, audit department, legal department, etc., help the strategy team to manage these companies as well. Throughout the operation, Sanpower gives advice but does not make any final decisions.

Sanpower tried to transfer the House of Fraser operating system from the UK to China, but due to factors such as culture, geography, and consumer habits, the process of transfer was more difficult than Sanpower expected. Perhaps this is because of differences between the retail industry and other industries; the retail industry is fragmented, with substantially different operating practices in different locations, which led to difficulties in the transfer process. However, Sanpower did not consider transferring the UK senior management to China. This was because these people may be familiar with the consumer habits of UK consumers, but may not be able to adapt to Chinese consumer's consumption habits. Sanpower's intention was to transfer business models and hire local managers in China.

In terms of improvement and suggestions to other Chinese firms, first, Sanpower would recommend establishing a more comprehensive plan to motivate and retain talent at acquired firms (as in the case of House of Fraser). This is because people, the core of a company, are often afraid that their positions and status may be under threat when their firms are acquired, particularly by foreign firms from unfamiliar countries. This may lead key people to leave, decreasing the value of an acquisition.

You may read some reports that the core management team resigned from HOF UK. I think it is more or less related to the incentive plan. (Sanpower executive)

Second, the management team has to be localized if the company is planning to transfer the business model to China. The UK team would not understand the Chinese market and customers; although they might provide resources and external advice, the final decisions would need to be made by the local management team. Third, employees who have overseas work experience are a necessity for a company doing business in foreign countries. Fourth, it is important for a Chinese company to build financial credit in the world financial market. Once a company has successfully completed an international acquisition, it has already begun the process of building its own credit, which enables future acquisitions. Therefore, mergers and acquisitions represent a very important strategy for the company's internationalization, particularly for emerging market firms that have accumulated capital to a certain level and are eager to gain global influence. Recently, financial control policy has been very strict in

China. However, companies can negotiate with the government as long as the mergers and acquisitions are likely to be beneficial to the Chinese people.

Siwei-Johnson: Low-Tech Multinational

Siwei-Johnson was established in 1997 and is one of China's leading automobile manufacturers. It produces sixty-six different models of special purpose vehicle, such as armored cash transit vehicles and ambulances. It grew out of a Chinese and British joint venture enterprise. From 2003 to 2007, the Beijing-based firm Siwei bought stocks from the British firm Johnson, which eventually resulted in Siwei-Johnson, a wholly owned Chinese multinational company headquartered in Beijing. In 2009, Siwei-Johnson acquired a company in Germany that produced ambulances. The goal of Siwei-Johnson has been to take advantage of low labor costs and the capital market in China and acquire and expand the business in five to seven categories. Today, the company's core business is modified vehicles such as armored cash transit vans, dangerous goods transport vehicles, emergency rescue vehicles, and ambulances.

The process of integrating two companies, Siwei and Johnson, faced some cultural differences and failures of unification in operations. The problems were mainly focused on the transfer of power between China and the UK. Because the parent company was in a developing country and had no reputation, brand, or known history outside of China, the difficulties it faced can be imagined. Therefore, Siwei headquarters focused on job allocation between the UK and China.

What we are doing is distributing labor between the UK and China offices. For example, the UK side is mostly in charge of branding, sales, services, and customer service after sales, and also new technologies' R&D. On the China side, the responsibilities are for engineering design and for manufacturing, as well as trading that export to the third country with the entire assembled car. (Siwei-Johnson executive)

The company pursued some efforts to make the acquisition and post-acquisition processes smoother. It has downplayed the status of Siwei, recognizing and fully respecting the value of the Johnson company.

Especially the people, the [Johnson] team leaders, they cannot be replaced. They are a very popular brand, actually. They own 80 percent of the UK market and more than 40 percent of the European market. They are a really strong brand, and they are strong for a reason. As a parent company, we need to respect them. (Siwei-Johnson executive)

Siwei encountered some challenges in the process of transferring advanced technology to China, due to the nature of the small-scale customization industry. Eventually, Siwei found an effective method in the global market that can be applied to the industry. Siwei sends Chinese engineers to the UK to study technologies and invites British engineers and teams to come to China to understand the market. Training for these positions usually takes more than five years. At the same time, Siwei trains at each stage in the supply chain, instead of simply applying quality control at the final stage. Siwei's goal is to transfer manufacturing operations to China and minimize dependence on the UK side because China's labor costs are lower. Specifically, Siwei-Johnson is attempting to complete 80 percent of production in China and 20 percent of assembly in the UK. In addition to assembly, the UK is still responsible for sales and design, because the sales and design teams need to work closely together. Moreover, the UK side is also responsible for R&D and controls the operation of the international supply chain. After calculating labor costs in the two countries, Siwei decided to increase its core competitiveness by transferring labor from the UK to China and reducing labor costs. Thus Siwei-Johnson has not only advanced technology and good-quality products but also has lower labor costs. For further cost control, Siwei has also studied how to use machinery instead of labor to standardize output and increase efficiency.

In its organizational management, Siwei always follows the principle of "locals managing locals." Siwei downplays its Chinese headquarters and seeks to use the brand advantage of Johnson to continue to compete in the global market. Using the Johnson brand name is also beneficial for maintaining a good relationship between headquarters and subsidiaries, as it demonstrates an understanding of the subsidiary's contribution to the overall organization. In the process of expansion, Siwei-Johnson has shown deep understanding of how to leverage its advantages and avoid disadvantages, in both acquisition and post-acquisition processes. In the future, Siwei plans to imitate the IKEA model, which is to produce standardized components and ship them for local assembly according to local needs. In the process of expansion, Siwei always seeks out talented employees with a global vision, such talent being the only guarantee for achieving Siwei-Johnson's goals.

Advantech: High-Tech Multinational

Founded in 1983 and headquartered in Taipei, Taiwan, Advantech is the number-one worldwide industrial PC provider with a 34 percent market share, providing trusted, innovative products, services, and solutions, such as Internet of Things intelligent systems. Since its beginning, Advantech was soberly aware that Taiwan's market is very small, and it needed to go global. The company has chosen a market segment that other big companies did not like or did not pay too much attention to. This segment has a high profit margin, which has allowed the company to survive and develop in the global market.

At that time, the industry computer market was very small, I would say less than 0.1 percent of the PC market, so all the big companies like Lenovo, HP, and IBM moved into the mainstream. The PC grew very fast, but in the end, you see everyone suffered, and no one made money. You utilize all the resources, people, and capital, but you only make little money. This gave us the opportunity to work on the niche market, like IPC [industry PCs]. (Advantech executive)

Advantech set up a San Francisco office in 1987 and offices in Beijing, Paris, and Milan in 1992–3. The firm entered mainland China in 1992, and soon the mainland was not only a sales market but also a source of resources for labor and engineering. In 2003, Advantech decided to make a base in China and officially named it Greater China region. Success in the Chinese market was the company's foundation for success from the year 2000.

At that time, China's economic development was very slow. Now, it has totally changed, and we are lucky. We also enjoy the growth of the China market. I was in Beijing for ten years, and I started to think about how to make China a very important market. . . . In 2003, we announced Greater China as our formal name, which was a kind of strategy, so we started to establish R&D in different cities in China. In a way, at least, this allowed us to promote the brand in China. (Advantech executive)

Advantech also entered other emerging markets, including India, Brazil, Russia, Malaysia, and Vietnam. These markets are still developing slowly, with relatively low sales, but Advantech has confidence in their prospects and hopes they will become the next China. Therefore, Advantech plans to continue to invest in those markets.

In 1994 and 1995, Advantech founded Advantech Germany, Advantech Singapore, and Advantech Hungary, which accelerated the process of global expansion. The company's global sales revenue was USD 1.6 billion in 2018. Greater China accounted for 31 percent of this total, North America 30 percent, Europe 19 percent, and the rest of Asia 14 percent, with the remaining 8 percent broadly distributed. Advantech offers comprehensive system integration, hardware, software, customer-centric design services, embedded systems, automation products, and global logistics support. Advantech cooperates closely with its partners to help provide complete solutions for a wide array of applications across a diverse range of industries. In terms of products, Advantech is a global leader in industrial computers, including systems for subways, high-speed railways, firewalls, network systems, and smart retailing. It divides sales into industrial markets. Each segment has an independent sales team. Sales teams focus on the vertical market and introduce the company's products to their target customers in a simple way.

Looking back, Advantech emphasized several factors that made its internationalization successful. First, Advantech continually focuses on innovation, adapting to change and adjusting strategies according to different markets, whether such changes are in industry trends or business models.

I think nowadays the key is differentiation in every company. First, because we are based in Taiwan. In Taiwan in general, I think we have good engineers, and we have a good education system. Because we lack resources, we are forced to develop our capabilities in innovation. In Taiwan, we are quite innovative, actually. The second thing is, I think it depends on the founders. This is because all the founders are coming from HP. HP focuses on innovation, and we learned all the capabilities of innovation from HP. Because of these kinds of characteristics driving the founders, the company has become very innovative. (Advantech executive)

Second, Advantech decided to become international once it was established. In the process of globalization, the company has overcome a series of difficulties. For example, how could the company find talented people who can speak different local languages and also speak English? To solve this problem, Advantech started to expand the market from a place where many engineers were educated, the USA. At the same time, Advantech established its own sales channel. This sales channel is also a learning organization. Because emerging market countries are relatively lacking in technologies, the company can use the advanced management experience the company has learned in European and American markets to teach customers in emerging markets such as India.

Third, Advantech firmly established its own brand, because it always has believed that only a brand can generate good profits. In order to establish a brand, brand promotion activities have been ongoing for decades to increase customer loyalty. The company also holds a "solution day" every year. This is a technical seminar in which everyone discusses the future development trends of the industry. This annual meeting also helps with brand and reputation.

This company has thirty-five years of history, and it has a strong culture. The heads of the various branches regularly return to the headquarters to work for a period of time and to experience the culture. The company firmly believes that culture is the foundation for attracting and retaining talent. Because of the company's globalization strategy, it is not limited to using Taiwanese or Chinese people, but employs people from all over the world. At the same time, it has created an informal and relaxed corporate culture with no hierarchy. This is the root of its success in innovation.

Baby First: Low-Tech Exporter

Baby First was founded in 1998 and has a twenty-year history in manufacturing child car seats. The company started with low-cost exports. The company's strategy was clear: to produce cheap products and sell them to small and medium-sized brands. Because the company's product quality is based on international standards, and it was the only manufacturer in China that passed the European Economic Union standard ECE R44/04, it was able to enter the European market, its first international market entry, before other Chinese companies.

In Europe, Germany was the most important market for Baby First. It then expanded from Germany to other northern European countries, to Italy and to Eastern Europe, and then gradually expanded to the Americas, Australia, and Africa. Not only has the company met the European standard, but it also passed the USA's standard FMVSS213 and Australia's AS/NA 2011 and became one of the largest manufacturers in China. Because Baby First produces good-quality products at a cheap price, it is now able to export to more than fifty countries.

Beginning in 2001, the situation changed. Previously, when Baby First competed with European brands, it had a price advantage. However, when many other Chinese manufacturers joined the competition at a cheaper price, the competitiveness of Baby First in Europe decreased significantly. The company needed to begin focusing on the Chinese domestic market to generate more sales. In 2008, the company realized that its strategy needed to be changed in response to the global financial crisis and the impact of this on China's RMB currency. On the one hand, the company strengthened its domestic sales team and tried to increase the domestic sales ratio. Moreover, the company not only did OEM but also started to do ODM, targeting the mid-to-high-end market. Furthermore, it set up an office in Shanghai to establish itself and market the brand. In the process of building the brand, the company encountered many difficulties. Because ODM and branding are completely different from Baby First's previous OEM business, different organizations and different people were needed to open the mid-to-high-end market. Therefore, Baby First decided to become the distributor of two famous brands from Korea (Boyong) and the UK (Britax), taking advantage of their sales and distribution channels and brand influence.

I tried to get help. We are the only distributor for Boyong in the China market. We started this in 2008 because the product Boyong sells. We don't need to educate the market. By this, we could also get into the main channel in China at that time. Otherwise, for car seats only, it is difficult to put our products in stores or in better stores. In 2010, we also became the distributor of Britax, which is a leading brand globally, for car seats. (Baby First executive)

Looking back, Baby First emphasized several factors that were important in its internationalization. First, products that meet international standards help the company compete with others in the market. Therefore, as an emerging market firm, the priority was to focus on the product's quality. Second, a company leader needs to know the future direction of the industry and must pay attention to the preferences of consumers. This refers to the people who pay the money, that is, the parents in this industry. Leaders also must pay attention to the development of the Internet and how it affects consumer behavior. Nowadays, people are used to shopping online. Companies need to adjust their strategies and focus more on e-commerce. Company leaders must also observe the development of new technologies and make their products more intelligent, an approach Baby First is using in aiming to protect children when traveling.

Maybe in 10 years, nobody will drive a car. The key point is that there may not be a product called "car seat." However, we still have a need to protect kids during travel. Maybe something will come out completely new, but we will not call it a car. People still need to travel, and when people are traveling, the kids need to be protected. Maybe we can do such a kind of service. That should be done step by step. First, we need to make all our products smart. At least they can connect our products to smartphones or cars or other things that may be coming soon. (Baby First executive)

Third, in the process of internationalization, the company needs access to reliable talent. Baby First has struggled with this problem. In China, it has a very good sales team that manages a good supply chain and IT system to achieve effective information management. However, it lacks reliable professional management talent to assist the company overseas. At the time of writing, this problem had not been solved.

Higer: High-Tech Exporter

Higer Bus, a Chinese bus manufacturer and a subsidiary of King Long Bus, was founded in 1998 and is headquartered in Suzhou. Higer is one of the leading exporters of buses and coaches. Higer produces buses (coaches, city buses, new energy buses, school buses, and minibuses) and light-duty vehicles. It began exporting in 2003. The first market that Higer targeted was the Middle East and Africa, and then they slowly expanded to Southeast Asia, South America, and Europe. In 2007, Higer and the Swedish vehicle manufacturer Scania reached a strategic alliance to create the brand Scania-Higer. In this cooperation, Scania taught Higer the importance of standardizing production and how to improve product quality, while Higer guaranteed production capacity for Scania. This cooperation also laid a solid foundation for the development of Higer in Europe. In 2015, Higer's sales revenue reached RMB 11.7 billion, and it became the fastest-growing company in China's bus industry.

Higer has shown strong adaptability in the process of internationalization and has been able to adjust quickly to environmental changes. This adaptability has developed as a result of the diversity of demand in the Chinese market. Because China has a vast territory and different road conditions, the transport situation is very complicated. Higer's ability to respond flexibly in this market has given it confidence to face the different requirements of other markets and the ability to design different products for different customers.

Service is another of Higer's competitive advantages, with quick responses to customer requests. Higer's products have strong cost performance compared to other firms, although not the highest quality. However, the low price of a Higer bus coupled with a good after-sales service team make it attractive in comparison with competitors. Moreover, all exported Higer products are mature products that have been tested in the Chinese market for more than three years, so that Higer can ensure that all parts are good.

Higer has always been committed to maintaining good relations with governments, both in China and abroad, because many orders come from governments. Maintaining good relationships has ensured that Higer can compete fairly with other competitors in foreign markets. Higer has also nurtured relations with the Chinese government and state-owned enterprises that carry out infrastructure construction abroad, because they have both demand and purchasing power.

The choice of distribution channels is also important.

I take Saudi Arabia as an example. The Saudi market is the largest market in the world, importing more than 200 million US dollars of Chinese buses every year. Initially, when Higer entered the market, it was smaller than the first brands in the market of King Long and Yutong. Higer focused on finding good dealers, and then it conducted a market survey and found that the M brand bus is different from other buses. Higer ensured that customers needed this product. In the first year, Higer sold about 50 buses to this market. King Long and Yutong's sales volume of 200–300 per year was not reached. In the second year, Higer sold 150 buses, only a little bit less than Yutong and Jinlong. In the third year, Higer sold about 400 buses and ranked first in the market. The most important thing is that we first choose the right distributors and provide high-quality products. (Higer executive)

In the process of internationalization, Higer has also encountered many challenges, which may give some inspiration to other Chinese companies that want to go global. The first problem was the technical barrier. Higer needed its technology and qualifications to be recognized by local markets, and many certificates were required. At the same time, Higer also needed to increase investment in research and development capabilities. Second, the quality of Higer needs to be improved to enhance its reputation. The Higer brand has not been recognized by most international markets. When entering each new market, it has encountered many difficulties because its brand is not well known. Third, Higer needs strong financial support to ensure the smooth completion of large orders. Fourth, Higer is a state-owned enterprise, and it takes longer to approve every single decision than in a private enterprise. Fifth, Higer still lacks talent and has a lot to improve on in terms of talent localization. Sixth, Higer's main competitors are in China, where everyone has similar advantages. When everyone is competing in the same market globally, they need to sit down and negotiate to achieve a win–win situation instead of vicious competition.

ShangGong Group: High-Tech Multinational

ShangGong Group (SGG) is a mixed-ownership company headquartered in Shanghai. It is listed on the Shanghai Stock Exchange and was the first listed company in China's sewing-machine industry. It has more than thirty branches and subsidiaries, including fifteen overseas. Originally, the company was called Shanghai Industrial Sewing Machine Factory, and its factory was built in 1965. It was a successful state-owned company with brands such as Butterfly, Flying Man, and Bee. It was listed in the Shanghai Stock Market in 1993 and absorbed funding from the capital market. It cooperated with the Japanese firm JUKI by purchasing one of the company's product lines.

We purchased a big process line from JUKI for about 200,000,000 RMB. We [did not have strong bargaining power] about our formal terms, and we at least got limited technology from this line where only one type of machine can be put into its process. Meantime, we cooperated closely with JUKI, and merged sales [channels] for both brands [ShangGong and JUKI] only in China. (President of SGG)

The company was renamed ShangGong in 1997. In 2005, it merged with an office equipment company, Shanghai SMPIC Co., and the new firm took the name ShangGong Group (SGG). The industrial sewing equipment produced by SGG has been widely applied to different industries, such as traditional clothing, automotive, aerospace, and new materials. The company's major clients include LV, Gucci, Hermes, Boss, and Armani in traditional clothing, bags, suitcases and leather shoes; Mercedes-Benz, Audi, BMW, and GM in automotive interior processing; and Boeing, Airbus, and COMAC in airplane products. In responding to "going out" policies in China, in 2005, SGG acquired Dürkopp Adler AG, a German sewing-equipment manufacturing company more than 150 years old, through one of its wholly owned subsidiaries and became international. SGG went through a tough process in this acquisition. First, SGG suffered because of replacement in the top leadership. Then it suffered financial problems.

And nobody can lead this project, because our former chairman suffered from serious cancer. He asked for a new chairman, but unfortunately, this guy just came to the company and he didn't know the details of the negotiation. Then the project stopped. When I came, I tried to negotiate with them in English. We restarted our cooperation. Finally, within 3 months, we reached and signed an agreement in Shanghai. But at that time, it was difficult to fulfill all conditions, especially one continuing condition [which] was [that] the new ShangGong should finance the target company €9,000,000 of working capital. Unfortunately, both companies [were having financial difficulties], so no bank agreed to loan to us. I did a very hard job for six months to solve this problem ... That was a difficult time for me because there were not so many Chinese enterprises going abroad and cooperating with companies in developed countries. Even the currency management department didn't know how to issue credits. (President of SGG)

Fortunately, the acquisition was made after SGG raised funds from the stock market. Dürkopp Adler AG has been run very well after the acquisition. SGG was able to apply Dürkopp Adler AG's technology to production in China and combine this with cheaper labor. Having gained experience in the Dürkopp Adler AG case, SGG has continued to build its reputation in Europe, and Dürkopp Adler AG has made good profits. In 2013, after several rounds of negotiations, SGG acquired PFAFF, the largest sewing-equipment company in Europe and Dürkopp Adler AG's major competitor, thus laying a solid foundation for leading the sewing industry. Six months later, SGG acquired KSL, a small company that uses machine robots to make sewing applications. SGG believes that technology will be the future in this industry. After several successful acquisitions, SGG was able to bring their technology and brands from Europe to Asia and establish better sales channels with European brands. On the other hand, SGG was able to introduce its own brands and products to Europe after its reputation had been established. SGG then increased its capital in H. Stoll AG. & Co. KG. and became stronger in the airplane industry, after different manufacturers began using its machines to produce different parts of the airplane.

Looking back, SGG emphasized several factors that have been important in its internationalization. First, SGG has been able to acquire leading European companies in the sewing industry, which has greatly reduced its chances of being aggressively competed against in the European market. Second, SGG believes that leading technology and innovation assist companies in staying competitive. It strongly encourages and supports R&D and hopes to build a harmonious research and development environment among the different acquired companies and add synergy value to SGG group. Third, in terms of how to deal with post-acquisition issues, SGG firmly believes in not changing the foreign company's culture, as long as everyone in the acquired company agrees to the same goals and shares the same vision.

Conclusion

This chapter examined eight Chinese companies at varying levels of internationalization. Every company has unique characteristics. However, discussion with our interviewees to identify their companies' strengths, weaknesses, opportunities, and challenges revealed both commonalities and differences among these companies. We believe these aspects will provide insights and inspiration to other Chinese companies and many companies in other emerging markets. While all companies in our China sample relied on a wide range of capabilities to be successful, Table 3.4 summarizes the major capabilities that were identified in each of the companies studied as being strategic to their development based on standard categories used in characterizing each of the countries examined within this book.

Examining broader trends among our sample companies, some of the leading companies interviewed by the team began at the low end of a market, and moved upward to gradually become global leaders. This reflects the dissatisfaction of Chinese companies with the "world factory" role, and their desire to migrate from low-end markets to higher-margin and international markets. For example, Chervon started as an OEM company and gradually accumulated the resources needed to acquire international firms, build its own R&D team, and upgrade to an ODM company. Baby First focused on low-cost exports, pursuing its very clear strategy to produce inexpensive products for small brands. As they evolved, these Chinese companies made merger and acquisition (M&A) choices that were rationally linked to their strategies. For example, Siwei-Johnson became an international firm by acquiring companies in directly related fields and by aligning its management practices to the international context (i.e. having local people manage locals).

The need for rational management also applies to state-owned companies. For example, access to rich resources and financial support enabled state-owned companies such as AVIC, lacking experience in strategic decision making in the international arena, to invest outbound. As a consequence of their failures, AVIC gained what they refer to as "reflection capability." The company can now look back to make more cautious decisions regarding internationalization.

Riding the wave of reform and opening up, many Chinese companies sensed and seized new opportunities and developed to become international players. In the process of enterprise growth, some companies, such as Chervon and Advantech, focused on establishing their own brands. To gain the core competencies needed to strengthen their own brands, they have moved to acquire well-known foreign companies and learned from the international experiences of other firms. Yet other companies, such as Siwei-Johnson, seek to compete in global markets by exploiting the global influence and brands of the companies they have acquired. In any case, all in our sample are aware that to take the internationalization path, they need to be stronger in their respective industries. Some pursued M&A, while others (such as Baby First) gained global influence as the largest distributor for large foreign companies. Companies that faced difficulty (e.g. AVIC and Sanpower) mentioned a unique ability: reflection. Reflection is a cognitive process used to improve performance by learning from past experience after feedback (Anseel et al., 2009). Both firms brought the feedback mechanism into wider organizational use.

Chinese companies have significant factor advantages such as cheap labor resources, which help reduce costs, especially in labor-intensive processes in low-tech companies. Labor cost advantages enabled Siwei-Johnson to shift its production (80 percent of work) back to China and leave assembly (20 percent of work) in the Europe market. Chinese companies have always been at the world's leading level among emerging market firms in terms of product production capacity and process manufacturing. In addition, many Chinese companies have capital advantages, especially state-owned enterprises that rely on the government's strong financial platform to take the lead in international mergers and

Table 3.4 *Capabilities of Chinese firms studied*

Capability category	Subcategories	AVIC	Chervon	Sanpower	Siwei	Advantech	Baby First	Higer	ShangGong Group
Obtaining resources	Resource identification	✓							
	Ability to purchase product inputs	✓		✓	✓			✓	✓
	Ability to develop resources internally				✓			✓	✓
Product/service capabilities	Product manufacture						✓	✓	✓
	Research & development		✓		✓	✓	✓	✓	
	Local product adaptation		✓	✓	✓			✓	
Operations and management	Production management				✓			✓	
	Supply chain management				✓		✓	✓	
	Hard skills								
	Soft skills								
	Entrepreneurship		✓		✓				
	Cross-cultural management	✓	✓						
Marketing	General sales capabilities		✓				✓	✓	✓
	Understanding the market and local customer needs		✓			✓	✓	✓	
Managing external environment	Political and negotiating capabilities	✓					✓	✓	✓
	Relationship capabilities							✓	
	Adjusting to poor infrastructure	✓							
	Knowledge about the national context	✓						✓	

acquisitions. However, many Chinese companies have realized that to improve their core competitiveness, they must increase their R&D capabilities and avoid imitating products. Therefore, some have increased their R&D investment, kept up with new technologies, and are close to their markets, producing products that meet market needs.

However, in the internationalization process, due mainly to cultural differences between Chinese and Western countries, Chinese companies still encounter many post-M&A challenges, and some subsidiaries that they acquired failed to provide the expected value. Also, companies all face the lack of talent needed for international expansion. Many companies face difficult issues such as whether to send trusted Chinese employees to manage foreign companies or, instead, to let local people manage locals. Furthermore, few Chinese companies have the professional talent to exploit international markets. Many business leaders now realize that only with access to scarce talent will they succeed in certain M&A plans and agreements in the international market. Another gap faced by some Chinese companies is that many have weak brand capabilities or no international brand. This gap will make it difficult for an unknown company from an emerging market to enter and compete in an international market. While building a brand cannot be done overnight, we see that many companies realize this problem and are working hard toward brand building. We hope to see more Chinese brands competing on the international stage in the next ten to twenty years.

Returning to the main theme of this chapter, we now analyze how these Chinese firms built their capabilities. State-owned enterprises in China have greater access to resources than private enterprises. Thus the two enterprise types pursue different strategies. Most private enterprises started with an OEM business model, using cheap Chinese labor to produce goods to a customer's specification. We refer to this stage as "reserve resources." At this stage, most companies focus on export, which is the basic level of internationalization (as for Higer & Baby First). After acquiring an adequate level of surplus resources, private companies with sufficient funds, solid client relationships, and experienced management teams may be able to move to the next level and acquire overseas firms. These acquired firms can potentially bring Chinese private firms a better reputation, advanced technologies, strong branding, broader markets, and a mature supply chain. Facing China's strict financial controls, private firms are more cautious in M&A transactions and try to go international through "purchase," which we view as the second stage of internationalization. At this stage, private companies (e.g. Chervon and Siwei-Johnson) and state-owned companies such as AVIC are passionate about "purchase" through international M&A. Because state-owned companies face fewer obstacles in accessing resources and restrictions in financial control, transaction failure due to a lack of rigorous preliminary research is more likely to occur (Zhang et al., 2011; Zhang & He, 2014). After these two stages, most Chinese companies become international or multinational.

Recently, more companies have become aware of the gradual disappearance of the advantages of China acting as a "world factory." Chinese wages are increasing as the economy grows and the workforce becomes more educated. More foreign companies are shifting their factories to Southeast Asian countries such as Vietnam and the Philippines. Chinese companies urgently need to shift from labor-intensive industries to those in which their competitive advantages create value. Thus, after expansion through M&A, low-tech companies such as Chervon and Siwei-Johnson started building their own R&D teams and transferring and deploying technologies from their acquired firms. At the same time, high-tech companies such as Advantech and ShangGong Group have invested heavily in R&D rather than relying on technology from developed countries. We consider this stage "self-improvement." Chinese firms that have achieved this third stage have upgraded their capabilities and are poised at the entry gate to globalization.

4   Strategic Capabilities of Emerging Indian Multinational Enterprises

Subhashish Gupta, P. D. Jose, and Ashok Thampy

4.1   Introduction

India is the world's fifth largest economy (in USD terms[1]) and the third largest in purchasing power parity terms. Economic growth has averaged about 7 percent since the 1990s, when the country liberalized its economy. The International Monetary Fund forecast for 2019 was 7 percent growth. India is one the fastest-growing countries in the world, possibly the fastest among large countries. Its business landscape is well developed and it has a large number of firms specializing in a wide variety of manufacturing and service activities. It is often viewed as a successor to China, yet another country with a large and growing middle class, offering its huge domestic market to businesses around the world. It is also seen as a possible alternative to China for low-cost manufacturing as Chinese wages become more expensive. In contrast to most advanced countries, India has a relatively young population and, given the failure of its attempts at population control, is going to stay young for some time to come. In contrast, China's one-child policy implies premature aging. Thus the prognosis for India looks quite optimistic.

The phenomenon of Indian multinational enterprises is far from new. India's history of business relationships with its Asian neighbors, the Middle East, and Africa goes back several centuries. While the British occupation of India slowed down manufacturing and trading activities by indigenous businesses, many eventually overcame their disadvantages to emerge as domestic powerhouses. By 1947, India was the tenth largest producer of manufactured goods in the world.[2] Business houses such as Tata, Birlas, Walchand Hirachand, and Shriram developed their manufacturing and entrepreneurial capabilities. The economy was liberalized somewhat in 1975 and more fully in 1991, in response to a balance-of-payments crisis. The manufacturing sector remains highly regulated, particularly with respect to labor laws.[3]

A number of Indian firms, growing with its developing economy, now operate in other countries around the world. Forays by Indian entrepreneurs into other countries' markets in the last century are exemplified by the textile mills and engineering units set up in Indonesia and Kenya respectively in the late 1950s. These were perhaps the first instances of large outward foreign investments by an Indian firm. In 1976, Lakshmi Mittal set up Arcelor Mittal's first steel mill in Indonesia; by 2010 it was world's largest steelmaker, with manufacturing units in sixteen countries. Other recent examples of Indian multinationals making their presence felt have been Tata Motors' acquisition of Jaguar-Land Rover and Daewoo, the latter giving it access to markets in Korea and China. Ranbaxy, Dr. Reddy's Laboratories, Biocon, and Aurobindo Pharma are among the world's largest pharmaceutical companies. Asian Paints has manufacturing spread over twenty-four countries, while Essel Propack is the world's largest manufacturer of toothpaste tubes and Bharat Forge is among the largest forging companies in the world. The skills of Indian information technology (IT) service companies such as Tata Consultancy Services (TCS), Cognizant, Infosys, and HCL are well known.

From a mere 25 million USD in 1990, foreign direct investment (FDI) outflows in the form of equity, loans, and guaranteed issue reached a peak of 46.6 billion USD in 2011–12 and stood at USD 11.33 billion in 2017–18. Manufacturing has attracted the largest share of outward FDI historically, though the trend has begun to change. Russia was the largest recipient of outward FDI from India in 2001–2 but has been replaced by other countries in the Asia-Pacific region. Figure 4.1 shows FDI outflows from India between 2000 and 2017.

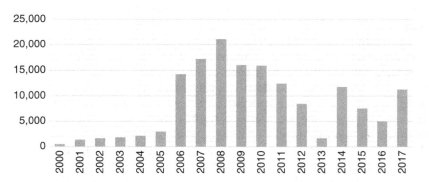

Figure 4.1 India's FDI outflows, 2000–2017 (million USD at current prices)
Source: UNCTAD 2019

The scope of outward FDI from India varies widely, in terms of industry type, destination, and scale. Traditionally, the largest export sectors from India are petroleum refining, gems, pharmaceuticals, textiles, and IT services. The pattern of FDI outflows also reflects the size distribution of Indian firms. Petroleum refining requires scale – it should be no surprise that Reliance is the largest Indian firm appearing on Forbes World's Largest Public Companies 2019 at number 71. Firms working with gems and textiles are typically small in scale, and no Indian firm in these sectors appear on the list. Tata Consultancy Services (TCS) is at 374 and Sun Pharma is at 1,606. A number of banks and state-owned companies precede these firms: Housing and Finance Development Corporation (HDFC) is at 209 and the Oil and Natural Gas Corporation is at 220. This does not necessarily reflect any internationalization of their operations. Thite et al. (2016) propose a transnationality index, which places Tata Steel on top with an index of 60, compared with its position in the Forbes list at 552. Overall, there are fifty-five Indian firms in the Forbes list, compared with the predominance of US, Chinese, and Japanese firms; this is indicative of the relative development of the Indian economy.

The relative paucity of Indian firms in the list and their low ranks reveal the imperatives that drive their strategic choices in terms of globalization. These are consistent with the experiences of the businesses we interviewed. Most Indian firms depend on the large domestic market for growth, and some will soon face the choice of what to do when they outgrow it. They can rely on low production costs and the quality of Indian human resources as sources of competitive advantage in the international arena. Indian firms make extensive use of partners and joint ventures to garner strategic capabilities, such as technology, human resources, or market knowledge. In their early years, some expanded into neighboring countries, perhaps comforted by "psychic distance."[4] Some, however, did not. The Indian multinational enterprises (MNEs) that have sought international growth follow diverse paths, as their motivations and capabilities are dissimilar. This realization drove the choice of firms we selected for further examination. We focused on four Indian firms: Gokaldas Exports (textiles), Tata Consultancy Services (IT), Biocon (pharmaceuticals), and Titan Company Limited (watches). Some company details are shown in Table 4.1.

India is a lower-middle-income country, as classified by the World Bank, and a democracy. Some basic facts on India are given in Table 4.2. The liberalization process that began in the 1990s focused on making the economy more market- and service-oriented, expanding the role of private and foreign investment, removing regulatory barriers for industry, removing the state from business decisions, and facilitating international flows of goods and capital. However, large state-owned enterprises

Table 4.1 *Indian companies included in the study*

Company	Gokaldas Exports	TCS/TCSiON* (Tata Group)	Biocon	Titan Company Ltd. (Tata Group)
Industry	textiles	software	pharmaceuticals	watches and jewelry
Ownership	private sector (unlisted)	private sector (listed)	private sector (listed)	private sector (listed)
Established in	1978	1968	1978	1984
Revenues (USD)	145 million	20.9 billion	729 million	2.5 billion
Employees	25,000	400,875	10,300	7,600
Global footprint	30 countries	Japan, Latin America, UK, Ireland, Africa	subsidiaries: Biocon Pharma US, Biocon Biologics UK, Biocon SDN BHD, Malaysia, and Biocon SA, Switzerland	30+ countries

* TCSiON is a subsidiary of TCS. Standalone numbers for it are not available.

Table 4.2 *Facts about India, 2018*

Population	1.366 billion
Surface area (km^2)	3287263
Population density (per km^2)	455.4
Gross domestic product (GDP, million USD)	2,259,642
GDP growth rate	7.1%
GDP per capita (USD)	1,706
Gross value added: agriculture	17.4%
Gross value added: industry	28.8%
Gross value added: services	53.8%
Employment in agriculture	41.6%
Employment in industry	23.9%
Employment in services	34.5%
Exports (million USD)	216,913
Imports (million USD)	337,414
Exchange rate (rupees to USD)	63.9

Source: UN, http://data.un.org/en/iso/in.html.

(SOEs) such as the State Bank of India (SBI) and the Oil and Natural Gas Corporation continue to dominate their respective industries. The number of SOEs has dwindled, and some, including Air India and telecom operator BSNL, struggle to earn profits. Private-sector banks, such as ICICI and HDFC Bank, have grown rapidly and are more profitable than SBI.

Indian MNEs first ventured abroad during the stifling era of the "license raj" (1947–1990): the bureaucratic system of licenses and regulations that had to be worked through in order to launch and run a business in India. After liberalization, some firms, facing increased competition in domestic markets, looked overseas for new markets, while others searched for resources. After coming to terms with the competition in these new markets, some began to acquire high-tech capabilities: for example, Tata Motors' acquisition of Jaguar-Land Rover, Arcelor Mittal's acquisition of Corus, and Biocon's acquisitions in pharmaceuticals. Others, such as TCS, concentrated entirely on foreign markets from their inception. They relied on their cost advantages and the quality of their human capital to provide solutions to North American firms. The state's emphasis on higher education enabled India to produce a large number of skilled professionals, some of whom migrated to the USA and other advanced economies. This accounts for the significant presence of Indian managers, academics, and health professionals around the developed world, many of whom have later returned to India to pursue new opportunities. Thus Indian firms do not lack higher-level managerial talent, and they lead in "frugal innovation." They are engaged in exporting their best practices and using their cost advantages and large domestic markets to get into other mature markets. Few Indian firms, unlike Chinese ones, actively engage in acquiring high-tech, except in technology-based industries. Thus outward FDI is relatively less transformative of Indian industry and its human resources, although inward FDI may play this role.

4.2   Interview Structure

To structure the interviews and provide a coherent framework for answers to our questions, we divided the resources and capabilities into four categories: those related to managerial skills, to competition, to financial skills, and to technical skills. Within each of these broad categories we identified a set of capabilities to investigate.[5] We aligned our choice of the capabilities that we investigated to the idiosyncrasies of India, so that our questions made sense to us and our interviewees could relate to them. We then mapped the responses to the comparison table that is a common theme across all interviews and all countries examined in this book. The checklist we used is given in Table 4.3.

Table 4.3 *Checklist of capabilities for Indian companies*

Managerial skills	Environment assessment and forecasting skills
	Speed of response to changing market conditions
	Flexibility in organizational structure
	Ability to attract and retain highly creative people
	Effective communication and control systems
	Entrepreneurial orientation
Competitive capabilities	Product strength, quality, uniqueness
	Ability to compete on prices
	Use of home country experience curve for pricing in external markets
	R&D investments
Financial resources	Required capital investments
	Ability to access capital when required
	Liquidity, available internal funds
	Degree of leverage, financial stability
Technical skills	Technical and manufacturing skills
	Level of technology used in product
	Strength of patents and processes
	Effective production and delivery schedules
	Level of coordination and integration
	Supply chain management skills

We followed up with questions related to each capability: to what degree did the firm under study possess this capability? Did it lack the critical strategic capability to obtain growth by leveraging its resources in their home or host countries? To what extent was each capability important across different stages of the internationalization process: the entry stage (e.g. during country selection, entry mode selection, or establishment of a foreign subsidiary) or the operations stage (e.g. during local operations, while integrating a subsidiary with the broader multinational, or while expanding operations)?

4.3   The Interviews

4.3.1   Gokaldas Exports

Gokaldas Exports Limited, founded in 1978, is a leading global exporter of apparel. Its operations are largely based in the state of Karnataka, with some operations in Tamil Nadu and Andhra Pradesh. The company has focused its efforts to move from jackets, its original mainstay, into high-margin products such as shirts and tops. In 2016–17, tops and shirts made up 44 percent of its revenues, followed by jackets (26 percent), trousers (19 percent), shorts (6 percent) and other items (5 percent). In the same period, the leading exporters of apparel to the USA were China (33 percent), Vietnam (13 percent), Bangladesh (6 percent), Indonesia (6 percent), and India (5 percent).[6] Gokaldas exports mostly to the US and Europe, followed by Asia. Its exports to South America and the rest of the world are comparatively negligible. Rising wages in China and reported quality problems in Bangladesh could help Indian exports. Further, policy interventions by the federal government to generate employment in the cotton textiles sector, in the form of export subsidies and other support, could be helpful. Regional governments also provide additional support. India has some additional advantages: it is the third largest cotton producing country in the world after the US and China, and the second largest cotton yarn exporter.

In 2016–17 financial year, Gokaldas had a sales revenue of INR 9.4 billion, about USD 145 million. In its early years, the company benefited from the quota-based trade in textiles under the Multi-Fibre Agreement. However, after 2004, as quota-based trade was disbanded and the garment export business became more competitive, the company has had to innovate and become efficient to remain competitive (Elbehri, Hertel, and Martin, 2003). The firm has successfully positioned itself as a one-stop shop for several of the world's most acclaimed brands and is one of the largest manufacturers and exporters of apparel in India.

Gokaldas Exports employs over 25,000 people across 23 manufacturing units, produced over 20 million garments in 2018–2019, and exports to over 30 countries. It should be noted, for context, that Gokaldas Exports operates in the larger ecosystem of the textile industry, India being one of the leading centers in the world for textiles with a market share of about 5 percent of world apparel trade.

The apparel manufacturing business is very dynamic: fashion changes rapidly and has a strong influence on the business. This necessitates the ability to assess and forecast key fashion trends. As industry trends change, it is important for the organization to quickly respond to the changes, which requires a flexible organizational structure with an entrepreneurial orientation. This may explain why most of the firms in apparel manufacturing are not very large and are owner managed. Gokaldas Exports is one of the few professionally managed and publicly listed Indian garment-manufacturing firms.

Gokaldas Exports provides several services to their customers which enable integration to the global supply chain of major global brands, and these differentiate the firm from job shops that provide custom manufacturing for specific orders. A key resource that Gokaldas Exports brings to these relationships is in-house designers who engage with designers in Europe and the United States, track and forecast fashion trends, and are aware of current trends in fabric-finishing technologies to produce different fabric effects.

Garment manufacturing is a people-intensive business, with large numbers of employees in garment production: employee costs are about 20 percent of total costs. Managing employees, and ensuring an adequate availability of employees with the requisite skill sets, are key capabilities needed to be able to deliver quality products on time. Because labor cost is a significant part of manufacturing cost, low-cost geographies such as Bangladesh are cornering a growing share of the business and it is a challenge for firms operating in India to compete only on cost. Another aspect of the business is that because garment manufacturing involves managing relations with unions and government agencies, an appreciation of the local political environment is important.

While strength in design and fabric-finishing technologies are key competences, Gokaldas Exports views manufacturing quality, efficiency, and reliability as crucial to the delivery of quality products on time to their demanding global customers, while controlling production costs.

Production planning, such as optimizing line usage based on varying batch requirements and fabric use, are core competencies that enable garment firms to optimize capacity and control costs. Industrial engineering skills in production-line optimization, while keeping different product construction complexities in mind, enables optimal use of available production capacity.

Producers purchase a significant proportion of the value of the garment, such as fabric and fittings, from third-party vendors. Efficient sourcing of raw material brings significant competitive advantage. Gokaldas Exports, being located in India, has an advantage due to knowledge of and relationships with local textile mills. This proximity to suppliers enables it to understand the technical capabilities of different vendors and to source raw material at competitive prices and with short delivery times. Of course, in the area of technical fabrics, the availability of producers in India is limited; for garments using these engineered fabrics, they are at a relative disadvantage in that the local suppliers are limited in capacity and capabilities.

As the major Gokaldas Exports customers are in the United States and Europe, transportation costs and time are important factors that customers consider before placing orders. The ability to reduce transport time to the major markets is a huge advantage in this industry, as garments must get to markets before fashion and seasons change. Gokaldas Exports does its best to reduce transportation costs and time through a mix of different modes of transport and logistic partners. While the distance to market is long, Gokaldas Exports has a cost advantage with regard to the transport of raw materials due to the availability of fabric mills within India.

Several firms in the garment industry have experienced negative publicity due to sourcing garments from factories employing children and also due to unhealthy and unsafe work environments for their employees. The negative publicity and the resulting pressure from consumers and activists have made major fashion brands give importance to the compliance of garment factories to sustainable practices and healthy work environments. As otherwise they are likely to suffer major losses in their reputation with customers due to concerns with exploitation of labor in developing countries, where most of the garment factories are located, Gokaldas Exports is very cognizant of this and ensures full compliance with the norms, such as not employing children and providing safe work environments. While this increases their cost, major global brands prefer to work with companies that are in compliance with work norms because their reputation may otherwise be at risk.

Globally, the garment retail industry was estimated to be about USD 340 billion in 2018 (Statista, 2018); the share of the largest garment retailer is only 1 percent. Thus garment retailing is highly fragmented. At the same time, while there are a very large number of garment manufacturers who work on a contract basis to provide basic garment production, there are few large firms that provide value-added services with in-house designers and quality assurance. As a result, relationships tend to be durable: it is very rare among large brands to switch entirely to new suppliers, as it takes a few years to ensure product and service quality and at the same time comply with work norm requirements. At the same time, the highly competitive garment industry means that cost increases are difficult to pass on to the customer. In such a situation, it becomes imperative for firms to operate very efficiently and to constantly explore opportunities to be efficient so as to achieve stable margins.

Summary   The garment manufacturing industry is highly competitive, with a large number of firms doing contract manufacturing with low value addition and a few large firms that provide integrated services. These services include in-house designers, fabric specialists, and capability to produce to quality specifications, without compromising on compliance with regulations. While there are countries with lower labor cost, firms such as Gokaldas Exports are able to compete effectively by bringing competencies that are not easy to replicate.

S. Ganapathi, Managing Director of Gokaldas Exports, says their strategy represents "an effective convergence of manufacturing scale, operational skills, ecosystem sophistication and power of marquee customer relationships" (Gokaldas Exports, 2018). These competencies are (1) in-house design capabilities that enable codevelopment, with major brands, of products that meet design requirements, yet can be manufactured within a target cost; (2) sourcing capabilities due to knowledge of and relationships with local textile mills; (3) manufacturing capabilities at scale; and (4) compliance with norms for workers and the environment that help to mitigate the risk of loss of reputation to the major retail garment brands.

4.3.2   TCSiON

Tata Consultancy Services (TCS), established in 1968, is a software services company and is part of the Tata Group. Its revenues in 2017 stood at INR 1179.66 billion (17,732 million USD) and its profits were INR 262.89 billion (3,951.6 million USD). Its 387,223 employees span 130 nationalities across 50 countries. Women constitute 34.7 percent of the workforce. During 2017, TCS added 11,500 non-Indian employees to its payroll. North America accounts for 54 percent of its revenues, followed by the United Kingdom at 14 percent, Europe at 12 percent, the Asia-Pacific region at 10 percent, India at 6 percent, the Middle East and

Africa at 2 percent, and Latin America at 2 percent. TCS was the first software services company established in India and the first Indian software firm to set up operations in the United States.

TCSiON is a strategic business unit of TCS, which is the largest information technology (IT) service provider in India and is among the top ten IT service providers in the world. TCS has 141 solution centers in 19 countries. TCSiON focuses on providing cloud-based IT services for manufacturing industries, mostly small and medium businesses, educational institutions, and examination boards. The last term requires some explanation. In India, states are responsible for education. Each state has a school board that sets the syllabus for all the schools under its jurisdiction and conducts state-wide examinations at the end of the tenth and twelfth years of schooling. Given the size of the population in India, individual states can have populations that dwarf those of many good-sized countries and examinations can involve a large number of candidates.

The story of TCSiON captures the development of a relatively new business unit within TCS under the broad umbrella of the Tata group. So, we will provide some insight into the globalization of TCS, and along with it, the experience of TCSiON. Along the way, we will also reflect on the advantages of belonging to the Tata group.

Consider the case of TCS's foray into China. TCS was very clear about four strategic objectives for this venture. The first looked at the role that its China operations would play in TCS's global operations. The second involved using its China operations to serve the domestic Chinese market. The third was to serve adjacent markets in Southeast Asia and East Asia, and the fourth was to provide an alternate solution center to its Indian operations. A TCS representative told us:

First of all, in both Hungary and China we started both with very clear strategy of how we could use China for our global market, how we can use China for the local market, how we can use China for the adjacent market itself, and an alternate for India. These are the four views in which we looked at China. In general, before we start looking at any country, we start looking at what is going to be the position of that country for TCS at large. . . . One of the strategies that emerged at that time was a large number of global customers that we had been servicing were moving into China as a market and we thought it was important to create a strong presence locally in order to address the global [customers' requirements in the locality]. (TCS executive)

The strategic objectives were the same for TCS's expansion into Hungary. The driving force behind the expansion into China was that many TCS's customers across the globe were setting up operations in China and TCS wanted to follow these customers to China to serve them.

TCS officials toured all the major cities: Beijing, Hong Kong, Dalian, Shenzhen, etc., spoke at length with local people, and visited multiple universities. It was important to gauge the level of talent that was available, because people are TCS's most valuable resource. Besides local talent, other factors that were considered included infrastructure, ability to hire, the degree of localization required, and the ability to create the right organizational structure. Globalization efforts by TCS could be driven by the need to serve global customers and not local ones, as was the case with their expansion into Hungary. This was quite different from the experience with Latin America, where the focus was on local customers. Thus, when TCS considers a new market for expansion, it has to think about the market segment that it will serve and the organization structure that will be required. They do an initial study, sometimes with the help of local consulting companies. After that, they have to decide on how to sell the product to the customers, global or local. In some cases, globalization efforts have been driven by the needs of customers with whom TCS has formed partnerships.

An interesting case is the development of the Saudi Arabia center in partnership with General Electric (GE). GE was already a customer of TCS and had made a commitment to develop its business in Saudi Arabia. Together the two of them decided to build an all-women delivery center, a unit of TCS where all employees had to be women. Initially the unit was designed to meet only GE's requirements, but over time it expanded to serve other customers. This assurance from GE helped TCS to build up its business in Saudi Arabia. According to a senior TCS manager,

Another good example that comes to me is the Saudi delivery center we set up with GE [General Electric] as a partner in Saudi. In any of these cases, whether it is China, Saudi, Latin America, or Hungary, we go through the initial study, in some cases we also use a local consulting company in order to do that exercise, come back, make a decision on how you are going to position this to our customers. In few scenarios it may be a joint exercise with the customer in which the operations starts with specific requirements in hand ... The Saudi all-women center is a specific example of the General Electric requirements that we wanted to fulfil.

So, TCS has used different avenues for expansion over the years. Sometimes, as above, the original impetus originated from a customer, to serve a specific need in a country where TCS did not have any operations. Over time, the business expanded beyond the needs of that customer to serve other customers. At other times, TCS entered into markets looking for specific resources or skills to serve the global market. For example, TCS started operations at Dalian to serve customers in Korea and Japan from China. TCS sometimes finds the local market attractive, as in Japan. TCS acquired Mitsubishi's IT organization and formed a joint venture with Mitsubishi. Initially this joint venture served only Mitsubishi and its subsidiaries, before moving on to other customers.

We keep evaluating multiple markets for different sets of products and services all the time. For example, as I stand today in TCS, we are looking at the South African market and how to penetrate there, and so on. But in any market that we look at, we look at specific areas. . . . Some of them include: what are the processes and the ease of doing business from a legal entity perspective? What are all the finance-related aspects that you have to keep in mind, the language-related challenges, the staffing and skilling costs, infrastructure challenges, location, ease of set-up? . . . etc. We also look at a large number of indexes in the country including the GDP, inflation, unemployment, engineering graduates who are coming out of the country on a regular basis, annual growth in the country. These are some of the things we consider before we finally make a call on whether that market is a potential market for us. (TCS executive)

Thus, TCS has two approaches to globalization. The first is to analyze different markets in different countries for possible opportunities and expand if it seems attractive. The other is to follow a customer or country, or both, because they would like TCS to start operations in that country. The first approach requires a thorough investigation of a number of issues and indices, as described in the quotation above. An example of the other kind of expansion is the Saudi Arabia case. A further example is the expansion of TCSiON in Ireland. In that case, a number of academic institutions in Ireland approached them and suggested they expand into Ireland. The Irish prime minister supported this endeavor wholeheartedly and helped catalyze the expansion.

That is another angle; in fact the iON story with respect to when we expanded in Ireland was that a set of academic institutions in Ireland came to us and said "You have a strong set of products and you have market leadership in India, why not consider Ireland as a country and we will provide all the necessary support." [We] went and met the prime minister in Ireland, he was very keen. There could be specific countries approaching us in order to leverage what we have done in India and bring it back to their country. So, we have two possible things: one is we go proactively to multiple markets, analyzing and studying each market in order to understand the market opportunities; second, some specific opportunity being given from a country to a partner or a customer. These are possible options. (TCS executive)

On the issue of filling gaps in skills or language, TCS's approach varies from country to country. The example of China may be enlightening. Initially, when TCS went to China in 1998, it found, from visiting educational institutions, that basic English-speaking skills were poor.

However, Chinese officials insisted that their students would have these basic skills within two years. Consequently, TCS felt more confident about getting workers with bilingual skills and moved into China in 2000. The other source of temporary expertise is their customers. At that time GE Medical Systems had a very large presence in China and TCS approached them for people with human resource and other skills to come and work temporarily for TCS and to put the first organizational structures in place. TCS also sends workers from India to man areas where there are skill shortages. However, after a while, the reliance on Indian expats is reduced; at present, the leadership positions in China and Japan are locals. To help foreigners understand the TCS culture, they are sent for training to India for three to six months. There is a constant exchange of personnel across the many countries in which TCS has a presence.

China is interesting . . . I remember we went to multiple colleges, just our ability to find basic English-speaking skill at that time was very poor. But China was also interesting that time because of the determination that they have to make anything happen, they said "we will make our children in the next two years mandatorily gain English speaking skills," and they actually started that. Subsequently when we started around 2000 we felt more confident that we can hire bilingual skills in China and hence we went ahead and took a firm decision to move forward. We kind of encouraged the local academic institutions to start building certain skills which are relevant for our industry. That is one angle; second, we always look at our existing customers in China: for example, GE Medical Systems had a large presence in China and we went to GE Medical Systems in Chicago and asked them to check on some people from their organization, like people from HR and others who could come into TCS and work with us for some time in order to build the initial delivery center, that is the second approach. (TCS executive)

Among the competencies that TCS values highly, we have already mentioned market assessment and forecasting skills. Other managerial skills are equally important, and it is the combination of these skills and circumstances that matter. For example, when TCS entered Hungary, it evaluated Czechoslovakia, Romania, and Poland as well. The Hungarian government was the keenest to get TCS to start operations there. Romanian skill levels were higher as was their unemployment rate, but TCS chose Hungary. The other contributing factor was that GE Lighting had acquired a Hungarian firm called Tungsram, so TCS was able to turn to them for information on business practices in Hungary. Further, the Hungarian education system was developing people with good multilingual (German) talent. Hungary's location, on the border of Germany and Austria, was an added attraction. Thus a fairly large number of factors come together to drive TCS's expansion decisions.

Let me give you an example about our Hungary operations. Czechoslovakia, Romania, Poland, and Hungary are the four countries we evaluated in Eastern Europe in order to determine where we can set up the delivery center and we finally set it up in Hungary, in Budapest. One of the primary reasons is when we actually did our initial foray, the fire in the belly of the Hungarian government in order to bring TATA and TCS into Hungary was much higher. ... In India, when we went to the Hungarian consulate asking for information, ... all of them wanted the center in Budapest. ... In fact, Romanian skill levels are much higher than Hungarian skill levels. Unemployment was very high in Romania, but we still felt Hungary was the better option for us. (TCS executive)

TCS is fairly flexible in terms of its organizational structure. As long as it feels comfortable that the new organization has the right values and the right people, the exact structure is not an issue. There are practices that are peculiar to some countries or firms. Some of these have been adopted by TCS as a whole and inducted into other countries.

For acquisitions and expansion into other countries, change management has three prongs. First, TCS does not insist on a structure, but extols the virtues of its own structure and slowly gets employees to adapt. In some cases, particular structures and practices are localized or customized for certain countries. In case of a new practice, TCS goes through an evaluation phase before it decides to incorporate it as standard practice.

In terms of competitiveness, a second important factor is the integration architecture. This is built on the primacy of local leadership, supported by a standard operating procedure that ensures integrated quality management.

There are multiple factors, but one most important factor is how do we create an integration architecture with TCS which is driven from India or headquartered in India ... The primary aspect of the integration architecture is local country leadership. ... Today the Chinese head, Latin American head, all of them are locals. That is the integral part of the architecture. Second, we have a standard operating procedure in terms of our integrated quality management system that ensures that when a global customer like ABN-AMRO consumes [TCS] services from Latin America, from Hungary, from Tokyo, or from India they do not see differential services from all of these countries. Even though culturally these services are very different in nature, we have put in an integrated quality management system in order to ensure that this is like McDonald's, which is supposed to have the same burger in Japan or India from an overall taste perspective. There can be localization to meet local requirements but there cannot be differential service quality, that is important for us. (TCS executive)

The third differentiator is the ability to put together teams from different countries and diverse skill sets to solve problems. To address the needs of an American customer, it can put together a team that comprises an

American, a Chinese national residing in China, and an Indian in India, all having different competencies. The ability to handle multicultural and multiskill backgrounds gives TCS an edge.

In terms of competitiveness, costs of employees are not a major issue; skill levels are seen as more important. Pricing also varies from country to country and depends on local conditions. There are also variations depending on the products and platforms. TCS's scale of operations allows it to exploit economies of scope and also affords greater flexibility.

Moving to financial matters, the experience of TCSiON shows the importance of being a part of TCS. Accessing finance for investment was never an issue. Further, the fact that TCS was established in fifty-five countries meant that the company could rely on established expertise and knowledge. This makes the process of globalization for a unit like TCSiON a lot smoother. Also, being a part of the Tata group, with its brand name and goodwill, is very useful, particularly in large, mature markets.

What sets TCS apart from its competitors such as Infosys, Wipro, and other Indian IT companies is that TCS is always interested in the local market. TCS has also often been the first among its competitors to enter a market. This was risky but it afforded a first-mover advantage. Moveover, TCS has been able to find the right partners, either customers or otherwise, to learn about local conditions and to partner with local academia. Finally, TCS is often the largest IT services firm in a host country. It does not have to struggle to provide services with a below-scale apparatus. Going forward, TCSiON will need new partners, but given the advantage of working under the TCS umbrella, it will be able to speed up the process of expansion. TCS may look to expand further geographically. Also, TCS does not have presence in certain sectors such as mining in Australia, which is an exciting prospect. They are trying to introduce new products and services, such as with TCSiON, to enlarge the basket of services they provide.

Summary TCSiON and TCS provide IT services. Their most important resource is skilled professionals. Using their competencies they focus on their clients. Sometimes they follow clients into certain countries, as with China and Saudi Arabia. At other times they are drawn to a country, such as Hungary, for the talent it provides, which can then be used to service other countries. Sometimes a country has a large market to service and is also a source of talent, as in the case of China. TCS tries to standardize its processes so that customers can expect the same quality of service around the world. It has used its partnerships to expand into many markets. TCSiON, as a subsidiary of TCS, can leverage on the success of

TCS to speed up its expansion. It provides TCS with new products to serve its existing customers as well as to acquire new ones.

4.3.3   Biocon Ltd.

Kiran Mazumdar Shaw founded Biocon in 1978, and its headquarters are in Bangalore. Revenues for 2016–17 were INR 40,787 million (613 million USD), of which 70 percent came from its international operations. Biocon's international subsidiaries include Biocon Pharma US, Biocon Biologics UK, Biocon SDN BHD, Malaysia, and Biocon SA, Switzerland. The firm is oriented toward international business, mainly through its focus on innovation and the discovery of new pharmaceutical products. Operating in India means relatively low production costs, while margins on overseas sales are much higher than at home.

Biocon began as a joint venture with Biocon Biochemicals of Ireland to manufacture and export enzymes for use in the beverage industry. Biocon immediately focused on exports. In 1979, it became the first Indian company to export enzymes to the United States and Europe. In 1989, Unilever acquired Biocon (Ireland), effectively making Biocon (India) a Unilever subsidiary. In the 1990s, Shaw wanted to focus Biocon toward biopharmaceuticals rather than enzymes; as that did not align with Unilever's business objectives, Unilever sold their ownership stake in Biocon to the Indian partners in 1998.

In its early phase from 1978 to 1999, the firm focused on enzymes. However, from 2000 onwards, Shaw transformed Biocon into a biopharma company. Building on its expertise in fermentation technology, Biocon became the first Indian firm to get United States Food and Drug Administration (FDA) approval for manufacturing Lovastatin (a cholesterol-reducing drug) in 2001. In 2004, Biocon became the first company globally to commercialize rh-insulin manufactured through Pichia fermentation technology. As pharmaceutical innovation in biosimilars requires strong financial resources and the ability to continue to sustain investments in product research and development over long periods, since 2009, Biocon has used partnerships to spread the financial costs and risks of product innovation in biosimilars.

Biosimilars and generics are in similar in a commercial sense, yet technically distinct. A biosimilar is a biologic, or a large molecule created out of living cells. Drug regulatory agencies review and approve biosimilars. Clinically, a biosimilar must not be meaningfully different in terms of safety and effectiveness from other approved products that serve as reference products. Biosimilars and generics have a common commercial role, in that both are marketed after the patent on the original drug expires.

Generic drugs are simple molecules that are easy to characterize and have a small, well-defined structure that makes them amenable to be synthesized with greater ease than biosimilars due to the greater complexity of biologic molecules. Biosimilars are not produced through stable chemical processes but are synthesized in living cells, which renders the process significantly more complex. This difference between biosimilars and generics makes the development of biosimilars significantly more technologically challenging, requiring capabilities in biotechnology as well as higher investments. While generic drugs require an investment in the range of 1 to 4 million US dollars per product, biosimilars require investments in the range of USD 100 million to USD 250 million. Biosimilars also take more time to get to market compared to generics, given their complex structures and the numerous studies needed to obtain regulatory approvals. A generic drug can reach the market in a period of two to three years, while it would take between seven and eight years for a biosimilar to be marketed. The difference in product characteristics and complexity between generics and biosimilars requires different capabilities for success.

Given these complexities, firms engaged in the biosimilar business require strong capabilities in human resources, technology, finance, market assessment, and the navigation of the regulatory process. An important strategy adopted by Biocon to reduce investment risk and expand capabilities is through collaboration and partnership. In 2009, Biocon signed one of the earliest partnerships in the global pharma industry for the codevelopment of biosimilars with Mylan. This collaboration resulted in the first jointly developed biosimilar product, Trastuzumab, to treat cancer, receiving approval from the United States FDA in 2017.

In 2018, Sandoz, a Novartis division and the global leader in biosimilars, entered into a global partnership with Biocon to develop, manufacture, and commercialize multiple biosimilars in immunology and oncology for patients worldwide. Under the terms of the agreement between Biocon and Sandoz, both companies share responsibility for end-to-end development, manufacturing, and global regulatory approvals for a number of products, and also have a cost- and profit-share arrangement. Worldwide commercialization responsibilities are divided, and each company's strengths are leveraged within specific geographies. Sandoz is responsible for leading commercialization in North America and the EU, while Biocon leads commercialization in the rest of the world. Biocon does enjoy certain cost advantages from its base in India. However, given the technological sophistication needed to develop biosimilars and the financial investments required to develop them, success in this business rests on critical capabilities. It is incorrect to attribute the success of Biocon only to the cost advantage offered by India. A more complete story emerges from looking at the critical resources that contribute to the success of Biocon and how the firm manages these. Human resources are key to the success of any business. In the case of biosimilars, the ability to attract and retain key scientific talent is essential. Biocon has been able to attract and retain talent trained in the leading universities and people who have gained experience working in leading multinational pharma companies. Over the years, Biocon's open culture has attracted the technological and commercial talent needed to enable the firm to grow.

Biocon has been successful in building on its early capabilities in fermentation technology to expand into active pharmaceutical ingredients and biosimilars. In its partnerships with leading biologic firms, Biocon provides both research and development (R&D) and manufacturing capabilities. Managing partnerships and convincing their partners to manufacture in India have required Biocon to develop sophisticated technologies and processes that meet global standards.

One of the key factors that enabled Biocon to succeed, particularly in the biosimilars market, is its ability to continue investing in biosimilar products despite delays and hurdles. The ability to fund the resource-intensive research programs needed to develop biosimilars without expecting quick returns has been critical to their success. Biocon has been able to fund the investment in biosimilars from its small molecules business and from less risky contract research and manufacturing activities that provide steady cash flows. This tactic, together with partnering with leading multinationals to share risks, costs, and revenues, has supported the enormous investments required to develop biosimilar products.

The pharmaceuticals and biosimilars sectors are dominated by multinationals from developed countries. It is important for firms from resource-scarce countries such as India to be able to identify niche areas for product development that are reasonably large markets. Biocon has been able to assess these market niches where the likelihood of success is reasonable and then partner with leading multinationals to pursue these opportunities by assigning geographies to the partner with better marketing and distribution capabilities in the respective markets. In the words of Kiran Majumdar Shaw, the collaboration with international firms provides a "risk-sharing platform" (Biocon, 2018).

Pharmaceuticals is a highly regulated industry with stringent norms for drug approvals and manufacturing processes. In the case of biosimilars, regulatory approvals are more drawn-out than for generics, and require large numbers of studies. Partnership with leading multinationals in developed countries has helped Biocon to meet the stringent regulatory norms and receive approvals for biosimilars and also for their manufacturing operations based in India and Malaysia.

Biocon is an early mover in forming partnerships for drug development and manufacturing. However, to successfully partner with leading firms, Biocon first had to establish its capabilities and credibility among pharma firms. Their early experience as a Unilever subsidiary helped Biocon establish a clear governance process in terms of structures, roles, and responsibilities. Today, Biocon provides technical and management quality, clear corporate governance, and an organizational structure with which multinational firms are comfortable. These factors have certainly been important in enabling the firm to develop deep partnerships with leading multinational firms.

Summary   The journey of Biocon, from being a subsidiary of a multinational firm engaged in manufacture and export of enzymes to a leading independent biopharma company, is revealing. It provides insights regarding the resources and capabilities needed to succeed in a technologically complex and financially resource-intensive business, particularly when based in a country with high capital costs. This point highlights the key resources and capabilities that have enabled Biocon to emerge as a significant player in the biosimilars market. While organizational, commercial, technological, and human resources have been important, the leadership that provided unwavering focus on building these capabilities and continuing to invest in innovation with long gestation periods has been critical to Biocon's growth.

4.3.4   Titan

Titan Company Limited, otherwise known as Titan, is part of the Tata Group. It started life in 1984 as joint venture between the Tamil Nadu Industrial Development Corporation (TIDCO) and the Tata group and was initially named Titan Watches Limited. Tamil Nadu is a large state in southern India with a sizable industrial base. Titan claims to be the "fifth largest integrated own brand manufacturer in the world" (Titan Company, n.d.). Titan produces more than 15 million units every year. It entered the European market in 1993 and then the Middle East and Asia Pacific. Its share of the watch market is around 50 percent, and it has sold 150 million pieces across 32 countries. It acquired the Swiss watch brand Favre-Leuba in 2011 and relaunched it in 2016. Besides watches, Titan sells jewelry, eyewear, and perfumes, and it has a handloom subsidiary. In 2018 Titan had an income of INR 157.42 billion (2.20 billion USD) with a profit of INR 11.62 billion (0.16 billion USD).

Titan began its operations at a time when the only watchmaker in India was Hindustan Machine Tools, a public-sector company. Titan leveraged a series of technology choices, such as moving to digital quartz technology in a market dominated by mechanical watches, and innovative marketing approaches to make a broad product variety available to the Indian market. The company's early success also owed to its decision to directly enter the retail segment through its World of Titan showrooms.

All managerial skills are important to Titan. An important characteristic of Titan is that it has worked along the entire value chain. Making watches is an art and there are a large number of components, some really small. The only watchmaker around in India when Titan started was Hindustan Machine Tools and so the expertise was not available. Titan, of course, tied up with European companies to help with technical knowledge.

We ... created a state-of-the-art manufacturing setup back then which is still a pride for us and has given us a distinct competitive advantage as well as rich knowledge about the category. It started with that, and I think we also ensured that every part of the value chain including sales, retailing, marketing, communication, after-sales service, customer engagement, customer research, etc., was all done completely by us and it was not outsourced. That was how we started this company. (Titan executive)

Soon after Titan started up, it began its first international operations in Oman. Although customers were positively predisposed toward the brand as a Tata product, market entry was very difficult, particularly getting shelf space from retailers. This made the firm realize that international markets and home markets are different, and require a different skill set to succeed. These include abilities to cope with ambiguous and uncertain situations, with a lack of market data, and with an opaque operating environment; to reach out and network with other industries and organizations; and to continuously monitor market developments. These qualities remain in demand, as Titan looks to expand globally.

Titan has a large presence in the Middle East and Southeast Asia. They have a presence in the USA and are contemplating entry into the UK and the European Union. Another market currently being evaluated is Canada. Markets such as Japan and South Korea are not on the radar right now, nor are Latin American countries. Titan had an office in London back in the 1990s, but returns were low compared to investments. Titan is positioned as a midpremium brand. This requires Titan to operate in markets that are sufficiently large to provide the required volumes. This is difficult in Europe as the market there is mostly geared to the high-end segment, which is already very crowded. Titan usually invests in branding and physical assets, so returns have to be commensurate. The largest international markets are in the Middle East and in Singapore, Vietnam, and Malaysia. The USA is the largest watch market in the world, but Titan is a recent entrant there. The other large market is China, which is very different; Titan is absent there, though it is contemplating entry. The other issue that has accelerated expansion is the advent of e-commerce. Traditionally, selling watches has been a bricks-and-mortar business: setting up distribution channels and working on branding and other related matters. It takes time and resources to be able to achieve decent sales. The spread of e-commerce has changed all that, and it is now possible to enter markets at a low cost and have access to all consumers at a low level of risk. It is also possible to gather rich information on the consumers.

Environment assessment and accurate forecasting is very important. The watch business is not as dynamic as the mobile phone industry, so quick responses are not that important. It is an old industry that developed to fulfill specific needs. Recent developments such as smart watches and wearable tech may make up to 5 percent of the market. The remainder of the market caters to timekeeping, accessorizing, and styling, and this is unlikely to change. Entrepreneurial skills are extremely important because the watch market is very competitive and making money is difficult. Titan allows more flexibility in international operations than in the home market. It also hires people who can find creative solutions to complex situations. Inflation is not much of an issue, because Titan is a midrange band and can hold its own from both sides.

You are in an environment ... that doesn't give you too much and you have to go out and create a space for yourself and do it in a profitable manner. Money is there for you, but you have to get the money back home. ... We have allowed the international business team to operate as an independent unit from the main domestic team and gave it the space and freedom to exercise flexibility, undertake experiments, and take new risks ... That has resulted in success, despite cut-throat competitions in all these markets. (Titan executive)

Titan's foundations rest on exceptional design, and its studios can produce a new style every day. Titan has its own in-house design studio and can also rely on the R&D expertise it possesses. It needs to address different segments with varying style needs at different prices across the world, for which it relies on its team's analytical skills. The competition abroad is much stronger than in India, where Titan can afford to price at a premium compared to other brands. Abroad, it has to search for extra margins or access to premium shops or showrooms through differentiated design.

In India we are in a position of strength, we are a market leader, so therefore premium pricing is very much possible. Whereas in foreign markets we are challenger brand and it is difficult for challenger brands to take premiums. We end up pricing ourselves at par in most cases. There are differentiated designs, like we have the slimmest watch in the world called the Edge; it is quite unique, and there we are able to get some premium. (Titan executive)

The margins demanded by the retailers and distributors also affect the selling price. In international markets the margins can be twice as much as in India. This increases the selling price. The retailing of watches has also changed over the years. In the past, watches would be sold by traditional family businesses owned by the same family over generations, but now they are sold in malls and by large department stores. This has increased the margin requirements in retailing and had affected prices. Because Titan's brand is not that well known in international markets it has to be flexible on pricing and spend on branding. This is a delicate balancing act and it limits the profitability of international markets. Unlike some firms, Titan is not willing to suffer losses in its international operations, which it can subsidize through its domestic operations. Most famous watch companies are based in Europe or Japan, which have small domestic markets. Consequently, they have to depend largely on the international market. Titan, which can depend on a low-income but large and growing domestic market, does not face similar pressures.

Most international brands are not manufacturers but get their watches produced in China, which can produce at a very low cost given the scale of their operations. These competitors can then command high margins because of the power of their brands. This is a fact that Titan has to battle against, but it still values highly its manufacturing ability because it allows it to stay abreast of technological changes. As far as barriers to entry are concerned, it is a more pertinent issue when it comes to India, where Titan has 65 percent market share. However, in the global market, it a comparatively new entrant and international markets are highly fragmented, with the largest brands achieving at most 14 percent market share.

The most important factors that drive competitiveness for Titan internationally are the uniqueness of its products, low selling and distribution costs, the ability to price competitively, and its R&D and new product development capabilities. The use of domestic experience as a leverage for operations in foreign markets is less important, and it is impossible to build entry barriers in international markets.

Titan's capital requirements abroad are quite low, unlike in India, where they have invested in offices, manufacturing plants, assembly units, and showrooms. In international markets Titan follows a buy-and-sell model. It sells its products through distributors who have many watch brands as clients. The distributor then negotiates with retailers to get the products displayed by the retailer. Beyond that, the only other expenses are commercial and communication costs. Showrooms and exclusive brand outlets are for high-end brands such as Rolex and Omega. So capital requirements are almost exclusively for operations in India. The margins that Titan makes from its distributors are sufficient for meeting most of its expenses abroad. Occasionally, a bit more investment is required for entering a new market. Also, no credit is extended, and distributors pay cash up front to pick up products from Titan. Operations in the Indian market are profitable enough and foreign markets are not essential.

Titan does not depend financially on the Tata group. However, it helps to be associated with the Tata brand when entering a new market. The fact that the Tatas are associated with high-value brands such as Jaguar and Land Rover also helps. Further, a lot of the employees are from the Tata group, people working with Tata Administrative Services. So Titan does depend on the Tata group for human resources but not financial resources.

Titan's operations abroad are light on both capital and assets. This is a deliberate strategy, as international markets are dynamic and unpredictable. For instance, the Middle East was a big and attractive market with oil prices at 110 USD, but with a fall in oil prices it looks less attractive. Firms that have invested heavily in that market cannot get out quickly, but Titan has that option.

The other factor is the size of the market. The Indian market is huge: 50 to 63 million units per year. You can slice it any way you want and play around with the segments and still have very large numbers. In contrast, places such as Singapore or Dubai are tiny in terms of population sizes and the market is very competitive. Of course, China and the USA are much larger markets, but the competitive challenges are very different. Any firm can go to China, pick up fancy watches and sell them under its own home label, selling along with Seiko and Titan and making much larger margins. So overall, for Titan's international operations capital requirements are not that important.

In the watch business, technical skills are also not that important. It is possible to get the manufacturing done in China and businesses can then concentrate on the commercial side of things. Titan has, though, always placed a strong emphasis on manufacturing skills. The values of the Tata group for integrity, empathy, and partnership with consumers are exhibited through the quality of manufacturing. This helps Titan distinguish itself from its competitors and helps overcome the facts that it is not a strong global brand and also not a price leader.

The other side ... is that we have invested in a large state-of-the-art manufacturing setup and that has been upgraded every time we have the opportunity. A lot of the category players, a lot of brands that exist, are not manufacturers themselves. China is manufacturing for a lot of these brands, a lot of these fashion brands, a lot of these Western brands, they are manufactured there. The Japanese brands, Casio, Seiko, etc. have their own manufacturing plants. A handful of Western brands, such as Timex for example, have their own manufacturing plants. But the rest of them all contract their manufacturing to some factory in China. There the premium is on styling and a Western-sounding name or a new phrase that endorses their brand, and so the aura of being international gets them through. That is a thing with these guys. (Titan executive)

The level of technology used and the need to stay abreast of developments is also important, particularly with the advent of smart watches. Titan is actively pursuing the production of smart watches with alliances and partnerships worldwide. Patents are not crucial, because Titan's watches are based on the quartz movement, an old technology.

Titan tailors its strategies to suit different markets. It started its foray abroad in the Middle East with a pure export model. After sales picked up, it established offices in Dubai and started pursuing other markets in the Middle East. After that it moved into Singapore and London. Usually it starts with brand building, but once sales pick up there is a period of consolidation and optimization so that the business becomes profitable. In this way, seven countries have become good cash generators for Titan. Some countries remain in the investment mode for some time, while others evolve to the maintenance mode. Still others are purely for export, with no investment in brand building. The overarching narrative is Titan's international presence, which fits nicely with its expansion based on e-commerce.

Initially Titan faced difficulties in entering international markets because India was not associated with watchmaking, then a preserve of the Swiss and the Japanese. Most early sales were to the Indian diaspora, and Titan built on this initial success to project an international aura to the brand. Their design and manufacturing facilities enable Titan to produce unique products, rather than copy others. Its manufacturing facilities impress visitors, which builds confidence in its partnerships. Consumer attitudes also change: today they are less bothered about the country of origin. They care about styling, design, features, pricing, and the quality of the product.

Summary Titan's strongest asset is its presence in the large and lucrative Indian market, of which it has 65 percent market share. From this base, Titan ventured into markets in the Middle East, which has a sizable Indian diaspora. This enabled them to expand their sales to the local population. Encouraged by this they ventured into nearby Asian markets, but they have avoided developed countries such as Europe and Japan. Titan's design and manufacturing facilities provide capacity to generate new and original designs, a strong source of competitive advantage. It has defined itself as a midrange brand, thus avoiding stiff competition at the high end as well as the low margins at the low end. It has expanded into the USA and is contemplating entry into China.

4.4   Analysis

These conclusions are based on a limited data set drawn from a select group of companies in diverse industries. The findings therefore need to be seen in the context of this limited sample.

Our study indicates that ability to develop internal resources, entrepreneurship, and ability to adjust to poor infrastructure are the most important capabilities needed by firms to develop the resources needed to internationalize their activities, with all four of the firms studied relying on these capabilities (see Table 4.4). For a developing country like India, it comes as no surprise that coping with poor infrastructure is among these essential capabilities.

At a second level, factors such as resource identification, ability to source inputs, understanding the local context, manufacturing and product adaptation, and supply chain management were critical to each firm's success abroad. Interestingly, contrary to what one would expect intuitively, political and negotiating capabilities do not appear to be as critical as expected for successful internationalization. This may be because the firms under study either had strong global partners or were able to leverage on their parent company's presence abroad.

At the sectoral level too, the differences are striking. It appears that sectors such as textiles (garment manufacturing) have a harder time in establishing an international presence compared to other sectors such as software and pharmaceuticals. In our study, the firms overcame this entry barrier by building strong customer partnerships. On the other hand, in the software sector the critical required capabilities relate to ability to develop resources internally, local customization, and cross-cultural management skills. TCSiON managed to leverage the resource base and skill sets of its parent company, which already had a significant international presence. Titan is also an interesting case in point, in that it leveraged its internal design, technology, marketing, and financial resources to venture out, initially, into markets adjacent to India.

Table 4.4 *Summary of capabilities of Indian firms studied*

Major capability category	Subcategories	Gokaldas	TCSiON	Biocon	Titan
Obtaining resources	resource identification			✓	✓
	ability to purchase product inputs	✓		✓	✓
	ability to develop resources internally	✓	✓	✓	✓
Product/service capabilities	product manufacture	✓		✓	✓
	research and development			✓	✓
	local product adaptation	✓		✓	✓
Operations and management	production management	✓	✓	✓	✓
	supply chain management	✓		✓	✓
	hard skills	✓			✓
	soft skills	✓	✓	✓	
	entrepreneurship	✓		✓	✓
	cross-cultural management			✓	✓
Marketing	general sales capabilities				✓
	understanding the market and local customer needs	✓			
Managing external environment	political and negotiating capabilities	✓			
	relationship capabilities	✓		✓	
	adjusting to poor infrastructure	✓	✓	✓	✓
	knowledge about the national context			✓	✓

Among the least important capabilities among the four firms were purchasing inputs and knowledge about the national context. Supply chain management, R&D, and soft skills are slightly more important. The rest of the capabilities lie in the middle: important for some but not for others.

At a broader level, we can look at areas that score consistently high, such as product/service capabilities and marketing. Operations management and managing the external environment are somewhat important. Interestingly, obtaining resources seems least important. It could be that India, with a large population, does not lack for labor resources, skilled or unskilled. It is also plausible that the firms have deliberately chosen to enter industries where there are plentiful resources.

Table 4.5 *Capabilities of Indian firms studied and modes of acquisition*

	Challenge	Method
Gokaldas	Market access	Capability complementing (joint ventures)
TCSiON	Market development	Capability complementing and augmenting
	Understanding local country context	(leveraging on TCS resources)
Biocon	R&D knowledge	Complementing, augmenting and developing
	Market access	new capabilities (partnership for
	Regulatory understanding	biosimilars)
		Cost sharing (joint ventures)
Titan	Sales and distribution	Augmenting capabilities

A common factor in all the cases studied was the firms' ability to arbitrage the manufacturing and labor cost differentials between the home and target markets. This was especially critical to the success of the firms in the garments and pharma sectors. As the case of Biocon indicates, the high barriers to entry in this segment of the pharma industry have implications for cash flow. Without high up-front investment in research and development, competitors may not be able to develop or copy these capabilities.

It is also interesting to examine the firms individually in terms of capabilities (see Table 4.5). Gokaldas seems to require a whole host of capabilities, possibly because it is in a highly competitive market where cost leadership and rapid response to market trends are key success factors. On the other hand, Titan, also in a very competitive market, does not seem to be as constrained. It is possible that this is the result of Titan's positioning in the middle of the market. A helping factor could be its dominance in the large domestic market. TCSiON and Biocon appear quite similar, yet are very different in terms of the resources and capabilities they value. Biocon requires large investments, strong R&D, and strong relationships and political capabilities, given its business in pharmaceuticals. TCS, on the other hand, as an IT services company, relies mainly on the skills of its employees and the relationships it builds with its partners and clients.

4.5   Conclusion

These case studies appear to indicate that the competencies required to succeed are significantly determined by the nature of the industry in which these firms operate and the prior history of internationalization by associated companies. However, it is also necessary to emphasize here that a few case examples do not allow for broad generalizations. To gain a better understanding of these issues it would be necessary to moderate for industry, size, and ownership effects. It would be also be interesting to investigate firms that are start-ups or those going through turbulent times. It will be our endeavor to explore these issues in the future.

Significantly absent from the interviews with the firms is the notion of upskilling or upgradation of Indian firms and the knock-on effects on the development of the country. Most firms emphasized that they could rely on homegrown skills, which they would complement with specific skills and technologies from abroad. Gokaldas's venture abroad led it to tighten up its processes to deliver the quality and delivery timelines expected and to improve its design capabilities. However, India has a large domestic apparel market with a large number of firms to serve it. Gokaldas can always rely on the domestic market for a large part of its revenues. There are no indications of any knowledge spillover from Gokaldas to its competitors. Similarly, Titan based its foray into international markets on its dominance of the Indian watch market. The firm used its technological and design capabilities to successfully compete in the middle range of the watch market. Again, there is no indication that its ventures abroad have resulted in significant skills upgrading. The watchmaker found international markets hard to enter and compete in because of the number of competitors at the low end and the brand value at the high end. Titan had to work very hard to improve its advertising and retailing skills.

TCS and TCSiON concentrated on external markets for their success. They had no domestic market they could depend on. However, they deployed the large number of engineers that India produces to provide low-cost, high-quality IT solutions to firms around the world. The processes that TCS developed are homegrown and these have been inducted into other countries. One significant skill gained by TCS is cross-cultural management. In this case there may have been some skill transfer among TCS and other large Indian IT firms such as Infosys, Wipro, and HCL. There is a strong ecosystem for Indian software companies with their own industry association, NASSCOM. Knowledge spillovers are prevalent, particularly in terms of market conditions and development of new technologies.

Biocon depends primarily on international markets. The most important capability it needed to move into biosimilars was the ability to navigate the regulatory process related to drugs certification, for which it relied on partners. Most other pharmaceutical companies in India produce generics, and it seems unlikely that Biocon's forays abroad have enabled skills upgrading in other Indian pharmaceuticals.

Therefore, the most pressing need for Indian firms seeking growth by venturing abroad would be in marketing skills, analysis of market, conditions and cross-cultural management. This is where the Indian government and business associations should concentrate their efforts.

Notes

1. If the size of the economy is measured in US dollars, the size can differ based on the exchange rate.
2. Tomlinson, 1993.
3. For a discussion of the issue see Besley and Burgess, 2004.
4. Thite, Wilkinson, and Budhwar (2016) provide an interesting discussion on the motives for globalization of Indian MNEs over time.
5. List adapted from Rowe et al., 1994.
6. Gokaldas Exports, 2018.

5 The Capabilities of South African Multinational Enterprises in Wider Africa

Helena Barnard and Christian Nedu Osakwe

Africa has experienced relatively consistent growth over recent decades (Fosu, 2015) and is increasingly seen as an attractive host location for multinational enterprises (MNEs), due in part to slowdowns in other emerging markets. However, MNEs and other firms operating on the African continent face many challenges, including a lack of critical infrastructure, the high volatility of local currencies, and unusually high levels of policy uncertainty (Barnard, Cuervo-Cazurra & Manning, 2017). Even under these difficult conditions, some emerging market MNEs outperform their counterparts from high-income countries in the world's least developed countries (Cuervo-Cazurra & Genc, 2008). Research is needed to understand how emerging market MNEs deal with these challenges, including how they go about upgrading their capabilities to compete successfully in their host economies.

Upgrading capabilities is generally understood to mean developing the capabilities needed to thrive in more advanced economies. However, firms operating in less developed contexts also need specific capabilities to be effective (Becker-Ritterspach & Bruche, 2012; Cuervo-Cazurra & Genc, 2008). For MNEs to succeed, they need to develop capabilities that are appropriate to specific contexts. This chapter examines how capabilities are developed when going "downstream," specifically in sub-Saharan Africa.

This study of four MNEs from South Africa – relying on insights from C-suite executives of South African headquarters and drawn from some of their subsidiaries in sub-Saharan Africa – distills three key categories of capabilities needed to operate successfully in Africa. Business acumen generally refers to abilities to understand and deal with business issues and problems in a manner that is likely to lead to a satisfactory outcome. Often taken for granted, this capability plays a big role in the success of emerging market multinationals operating in underdeveloped contexts. Embeddedness – the extent to which noneconomic institutions and environmental forces shape economic activity – determines flows of information and behaviors among the actors. Intra-MNE embeddedness refers to value-adding relationships among the parent firm and its subsidiaries. Local embedding emerged as the most critical capability revealed in this study, and the one that most often determines whether MNEs succeed or fail when they try to operate in wider Africa. Local embedding takes place via relationships between actors within the firm and other actors such as government agencies, industry partners in the value chain, etc.

Overall, the MNEs were able to upgrade their capabilities through exchanges of shared and pooled knowledge from their subsidiaries abroad as well as by learning to develop close interactions with important stakeholders in the markets they served, particularly regulators, politicians and customers. Understanding customers was key, as were efforts invested in building the local ecosystem, for example through local partnerships and/ or strategic alliances with credible organizations and other stakeholders who had long-established footprints in the host markets. Most of the capability upgrading happened as MNEs sought to improve upon their existing capabilities in key areas such as cost efficiency, distribution, and networking, and allowed them to overcome several of the institutional impediments that are familiar to those working on the subcontinent. However, some level of arrogance was also apparent, probably because the host environments were less developed than the MNEs' home environment. This meant that where MNEs needed to comprehensively engage with a host environment to develop new capabilities, they often faltered.

5.1   South Africa and the African Continent

South Africa's economy still bears the imprint of apartheid, nearly a quarter-century after its fall. The country is troubled by socioeconomic issues such as the highest income inequality in the world and high levels of unemployment, particularly among its black population (IMF, 2005). World Bank Development Indicators show that the official unemployment rate in South Africa grew from 22.4 percent in 2008 to about 29 percent in 2019 (World Bank, 2019c).

GDP per capita in South Africa continues to lag behind that of its middle-income peers. With a population of nearly 56 million people, South Africa has a per capita GDP of USD 13,200 while Brazil's and Russia's GDPs, for example, are USD 15,200 and USD 26,500 respectively (CIA, 2017). Nonetheless, post-apartheid South Africa has progressed (modestly) in key areas such as diversification of its economic base and trade liberalization (IMF, 2005, 2017). Additional statistics about the South African economy are reported in Table 5.1.

South Africa is perceived as an important inward foreign direct investment (IFDI) gateway to the sub-Saharan market (Ernst and Young,

Table 5.1 *South African economy: selected indicators, 2017*

Indicator	Measurement value
GDP per capita growth (annual %)	0.06
Exports of goods and services (% of GDP)	29.77
Imports of goods and services (% of GDP)	28.41
Government expenditure on education, total (% of GDP)	6.13
Domestic credit to private sector (% of GDP)	147.53
Lending interest rate (%)	10.38
Market capitalization of listed domestic companies (% of GDP)	352.85
Human capital index (HCI) (scale 0–1)	0.41
Fixed broadband subscriptions (per 100 people)	1.98

Source: World Bank (2017)

2014), although not all scholars agree (Alden & Schoeman, 2015). South Africa and Kenya ranked joint second in IFDI attractiveness among African countries, after Morocco (Ernst and Young, 2017). South Africa leads the continent in terms of IFDI stock holdings in continental Africa, at about USD 128.8 billion as of 2018(UNCTAD, n.d.). In 1997, the stock of South Africa's IFDI (as a share of GDP) was barely 10.8 percent. A decade later this number was about 44 percent; nearly two decades later, IFDI reached about 47 percent. Table 5.2 compares the stock of South Africa's IFDI to that held by Angola, Egypt, and Nigeria, other important FDI destinations in Africa.

Outward FDI (OFDI) flows from South Africa have fluctuated, falling from USD 1.2 billion in 1994 to USD 271 million in 2000 and then rising from USD 565 million in 2003 to USD 6.7 billion by 2013 (see Table 5.3, which again compares South Africa with Angola, Egypt, and Nigeria) (UNCTAD, n.d.). Reaching an all-time high in 2014, OFDI declined by about 25 percent in 2015 and a further 41 percent in 2016, relative to 2015 figures (UNCTAD, n.d.).

The decline since 2015 can be attributed to the country's economic slowdown, which can in turn be traced to falling commodity prices and depreciating local currency (African Development Bank et al., 2017). Nonetheless, South Africa ranks as the fifth-largest investor on the continent after the UK, US, France, and China (Ernst and Young, 2017; RMB Global Markets, 2017). South African MNEs initiated eighty-four greenfield FDI projects in 2015 and eighty-seven in 2016. The annual value of cross-border mergers and acquisitions rose from USD 559 million in 2015 to USD 5.1 billion in 2016 (UNCTAD, 2017b, annex tables 10 and 21). South Africa emerges as the African continent's undisputed leader in foreign assets

Table 5.2 Inward FDI stock, 2000–2016: South Africa and comparable economies on the continent (billions of USD)

Year	2000	2001	2002	2003	2004	2005	2006	2007	2008	2009	2010	2011	2012	2013	2014	2015	2016
South Africa	43.45	34.70	35.89	57.06	80.28	96.69	106.93	131.83	83.65	138.75	179.57	159.39	163.51	152.12	138.91	126.76	135.45
Angola	7.98	10.12	11.87	15.44	17.64	16.34	16.30	15.41	17.08	19.29	32.46	43.28	41.81	34.69	25.48	32.31	29.18
Egypt	19.96	20.47	21.11	21.35	23.51	28.88	38.93	50.50	60.00	66.71	73.10	72.61	78.64	82.89	87.49	94.31	102.32
Nigeria	23.79	25.06	27.10	29.28	31.40	26.35	31.24	37.33	45.58	54.23	60.33	69.24	76.37	81.98	86.67	89.74	94.18

Source: UNCTAD (2017a)

Table 5.3 *Outward FDI flow, 2000–2016: South Africa and comparable economies on the continent (billions of USD)*

Year	2000	2001	2002	2003	2004	2005	2006	2007	2008	2009	2010	2011	2012	2013	2014	2015	2016
South Africa	0.27	−3.2	−0.40	0.57	1.35	0.93	6.06	2.97	−3.13	1.15	−0.08	−0.26	2.99	6.65	7.67	5.74	4.47
Angola	n/a	n/a	0.10	0.10	0.78	0.22	0.19	0.91	2.57	0.01	1.34	2.09	40.89	0.92	0.89	−0.79	0.27
Egypt	0.05	0.01	0.03	0.02	0.16	0.09	0.15	0.67	1.92	0.57	1.18	0.63	0.21	0.30	0.25	0.18	0.21
Nigeria	0.17	0.09	0.17	0.17	0.26	0.02	0.32	0.88	1.06	1.54	0.92	0.82	1.54	1.24	1.61	1.44	1.31

Source: UNCTAD (2017a)

owned by developing and transition economy MNEs (UNCTAD, 2017b, annex table 24).

A joint publication by North-West University and the Columbia Center on Sustainable Investment states that the "first foreign affiliates of the top 20 [South African] MNEs were established in 1993, with numerous subsequent foreign mergers and acquisitions as well as greenfield investments" (North-West University & Columbia Center on Sustainable Investment, 2016, 2). Although South African firms had long sought to operate globally, negative perceptions of apartheid and the apartheid government limited their efforts (Barnard & Luiz, 2018). The end of apartheid marked a major shift in the evolution of South African MNEs, and they started investing abroad in much greater numbers.

Although most of South Africa's OFDI goes to European markets such as the UK (Verhoef, 2016), during the past few years many South African MNEs have invested aggressively on the continent, particularly in sub-Saharan Africa (Kiruga, 2016). Between 2007 and 2011, South African MNEs reported 1,000 new investments in 36 African nations to the South African treasury (National Treasury, Republic of South Africa, 2013).

South African MNEs have had their fair share of successes and failures on the continent. For example, MNEs such as Nando's, Telkom, Tiger Brands, Sun International, and Woolworths have found competing in different African markets extremely difficult and unprofitable (Games, 2013). As a result, these multinationals were forced to exit those markets (Ajai, 2015). Yet the African continent remains an important market for South African MNEs.

We believe that lessons learned by South African MNEs operating on the continent will help us identify those capabilities needed to successfully navigate the numerous challenges and uncertainties in African business environments. We have relied on our interviews with executives at four MNEs to help discover these capabilities.

5.2   Background on the Selected Cases

We wanted to examine South African MNEs that operate in regulated industries in order to understand upgrading in the context of formal quality standards. We can divide quality standards into two categories: technical standards that reduce uncertainty about a given technology or process, and organizationally or institutionally based standards intended to increase confidence in firms' output by assuring the credibility and legitimacy of products, typically through consensus processes among role-players (Banda, Mugwagwa, Kale & Ndomondo-Sigonda, 2016). African host countries generally have lower income levels and perhaps lower formal quality standards than does South Africa. Most South African MNEs are required to comply with at least institutionally based standards to achieve legitimacy in their host environments. After considering various options, we decided to focus on financial service and agro-processing firms.

International financial service firms are knowledge-intensive service firms that enable client participation in the global economy. To provide services that cross borders not only at the level of the individual (e.g. remittances) but also at the firm level (e.g. investment banking), they need to meet both technical standards, for example by having a functioning global clearing-house system, as well as institutional standards, for example by conforming to Basel III. As South African MNEs expand in Africa, they must operate in a context with a very large informal and "unbanked" customer base (Osei-Assibey, 2009), and thus they need to align their services to local norms and preferences.

Agro-processing firms manufacture food products and are typically highly regulated. However, African food safety performance is often weak (Kussaga, Jacxsens, Tiisekwa & Luning, 2014). Given that technical standards in South African agro-processing firms are likely to exceed those of their host countries, institutional standards are more important. The criticality of food safety often drives private firms to supplement the regulatory efforts of local institutions (Kirezieva, 2014). Indeed, because their products are perishable, it matters relatively little to South African agro-processing MNEs whether government regulations in some of the host African countries are less demanding than in their home country. Firms can lose inventory unless they have a certain level of efficiency in their operations, for example cold-chains and relatively rapid distribution systems. In addition, in agro-processing, perhaps even more than in financial services, local preferences matter.

We identified two MNEs in each of the two sectors. All of the MNEs in this study are listed on the Johannesburg Stock Exchange (JSE) and have a substantial African footprint. Unless otherwise specified, the background company information provided is from company websites and documents filed with the JSE.

Standard Bank Group

Standard Bank is a financial services provider that has operated in Africa for more than 150 years. Its core businesses are personal and business banking, and corporate and investment banking. In terms of assets, it is the largest financial services group on the continent, with an asset base of USD 149 billion and a market capitalization of USD 18 billion. It currently employs more than 54,000 people. Standard Bank appears on the Forbes Global 2000 and FT Emerging 500 lists. The overarching strategic agenda of Standard Bank in the past few years has been to expand its reach to African countries beyond its regional neighbors. Acquisitions were made in Nigeria and Kenya about a decade ago, while in 2016, Standard Bank expanded into Francophone Africa through its greenfield investments in Côte d'Ivoire. In 2016, Standard Bank had about twenty subsidiaries in Africa, plus a few beyond the continent.

Nedbank Group

Nedbank was founded in 1831, and by 2016 had a total asset base of USD 70 billion with a market capitalization of nearly USD 8.6 billion. Nedbank appears on the FT Emerging 500 corporations list. It has a client base of about 7.7 million customers and employs nearly 32,500 people. It has about 800 outlets in South Africa and the rest of Africa. In 2014, Nedbank entered a strategic alliance with a leading pan-African financial institution, Ecobank Transnational Incorporated. As a result, Nedbank now has presence in thirty-nine African countries. Between 2014 and 2016, Nedbank also bought major stakes in banks in Mozambique and Zimbabwe, both of which are perceived to be high-risk operating environments.

Clover Industries

Clover is an agribusiness company that has produced foods and dairy products since the late nineteenth century. By 2016 Clover had about 8,500 permanent employees and an asset base of over USD 360 million. Clover has a significant footprint in neighboring countries, and its primary export markets include the Democratic Republic of the Congo, Ghana, Kenya, Uganda, and Madagascar. The firm outsources some of its production and distribution to partners on the continent and has had plans for greenfield investments in Angola and Nigeria; while the Angolan expansion has taken place, investment into Nigeria went on hold due to low oil prices and the subsequent financial crisis (Clover Group, n.d.).

Tiger Brands

Tiger Brands was founded in the early 1920s and operates in the agribusiness industry as South Africa's leading provider of a wide range of packaged goods. Tiger Brands is one of South Africa's leading nonfinancial MNEs – its total assets and foreign assets in 2015 were USD 1.6 billion and USD 352 million respectively (North-West University & Columbia

Center on Sustainable Investment, 2016). Tiger Brands employs about 14,600 people. Over the past decade, the firm has sought to increase its footprint in several African markets, with mixed success to date. For example, after acquiring Dangote Flour Mills in 2012, Tiger Brands sold the company back to its original Nigerian owners only three years later. Despite the internalization challenges that Tiger Brands has faced in recent times in Africa (Business Daily, 2017), it still maintains a significant footprint on the continent. For example, it exports to more than twenty-five African countries and has subsidiaries in Central and West Africa.

5.3   Our Evidence Base

After conducting background research on prospective MNE cases and selecting the four named in the previous section, we conducted twenty-one semi-structured interviews with C-suite executives between December 2016 and September 2017 at the South African headquarters of the MNEs. Interviews lasted on average one hour and were, with the permission of interviewees, recorded and professionally transcribed. Our interviewees included the key decision makers responsible for functions such as operations, marketing, finances, and human resources. The interviews with executives were conducted at the South African headquarters of these MNEs, but the research team also paid specific attention to the views of executives at subsidiaries in other sites in Africa, including Botswana, Kenya, Nigeria, and Zimbabwe.

A condition for granting the interviews was that specific evidence should not be traceable to specific MNEs or specific subsidiaries in host locations, so the comments quoted in this chapter are not ascribed to individuals or to specific companies. Industry-specific research may well find different types of, for example, foundational business acumen capabilities.

We had attempted to elicit information about failure, but most representatives of these firms were reluctant to discuss what they did not manage to achieve. However, we were able to speak to one (previous) local partner in a related industry whose relationship with a South African MNE had failed. The assessment of this local competitor provides a useful closing to the chapter, as it highlights, in their absence, the importance of some of the capabilities discussed.

5.4   Capabilities Used by South African MNEs in Wider Africa

Three main capabilities that influence MNE success in Africa emerged from the four case studies: business acumen, intra-MNE embedding, and

Table 5.4 *Capabilities that South African multinationals use to operate in wider Africa*

Business acumen
• Foundational business acumen
• Evolving business acumen
Intra-MNE embedding
• Parent–subsidiary embedding
• Subsidiary–subsidiary embedding
Local embedding
• Regulator embedding
• Supplier embedding
• Customer embedding

local embedding. Each of these capabilities can be further subdivided. The capabilities and subcategories are listed in Table 5.4.

Business Acumen

Business acumen emerges as a key feature of the interview data, suggesting that it is an important capability for managers of South African MNEs in wider Africa. We define business acumen as the capability of corporate decision makers to take decisions that enable profitable business operations. We differentiate between two types. Foundational business acumen involves the capability to implement basic business principles, such as managing costs and ensuring profitable operations. Our evidence suggests that the upgrading of this capability took place internally to the MNE, and essentially involved constant reminders to executives about the importance of not losing sight of those quite basic but fundamental requirements.

Evolving business acumen relates to the implementation of new ways of doing business. In terms of innovation, it can be even more basic than the lowest tier of the Community Innovation Survey hierarchy – new-to-the-world, new-to-the-market and new-to-the-firm (Battisti & Stoneman, 2010). In our evidence, executives sought ways to profitably apply in the host countries what were basically requirements for doing business at home.

Business acumen is seldom theorized about, perhaps because it can be easily taken for granted by managers from or located in advanced economies. But given the complexity and underdevelopment of the African business environment, as well as the fact that South African MNEs, like most emerging market MNEs, are still in an earlier stage of their evolution (Meyer, 2014), the possession of business acumen appears to be a critical capability that should not be taken for granted. Certainly, insights gathered from senior executives both at home and in various host countries reflect business acumen as a fundamental and differentiating capability for MNEs.

Foundational Business Acumen

In Africa you can't just go and sell your products; you need to invest in more than that.   (Agribusiness: commercial executive)

This statement suggests that the business environment in Africa is so underdeveloped that specific investment is needed in capabilities that would in other contexts be seen as business basics. Foundational business acumen cannot be assumed in an environment such as Africa. One of the respondents explained: "And we try to make sure that if they make profit, we make profit," while another commented:

I need to make sure that my costs are contained; I need to make sure that I am giving good service to the customers. (Bank: South-Africa-based strategy manager)

This repeated assertion of very basic principles suggests that it is not always easy to achieve them. For example, cost control assumes unusual importance given that the cost of doing business in Africa is known to be extremely high (Eifert, Gelb & Ramachandran, 2008).

Moreover, MNEs often provide premium products (Ge, Lai & Zhu, 2015). In a low income and typically price-sensitive market, considerable attention is given to making sure that customers have reason to pay the premium:

So service becomes key and ensuring there is consistency in service. (Bank: Kenya-based operations manager)

If you take our understanding of categories, our understanding in terms of the research that we do, it is a huge competitive advantage for us; if you don't understand those dynamics you are going to have a huge problem protecting those consumers from the vultures out there! (Agribusiness: commercial executive)

In fact, branding has emerged as an important way of motivating efforts to acquire a range of foundational capabilities. Executives across different business domains mentioned different capabilities that were needed to support a (superior) brand, including quality control, distribution, and service:

We want to make sure that our brand is available because they are usually a bit more expensive than the nonbranded products, and if availability is not there then you defeat the object you know? . . . So you need to be very careful about quality, you need to be very careful about pricing, in terms of losing them to other brands ... You need to be on top of your brand and you need to be close to the consumers. (Agribusiness: South-Africa-based commercial executive)

We do a lot of monthly brand index checking and reporting and everything and month on month, year on year we have seen a massive improvement in the way they [customers] classify us. (Bank: Nigeria-based operations manager)

Evolving Business Acumen   Two types of evolving business acumen were evident from the data. The first involves developing capabilities to anticipate and respond to market trends. The second involves the increasing use of digital solutions to support the business.

Of course, meeting customer needs is foundational to running a profitable business. But unlike in the case of quality assurance or cost control, MNEs need to engage somewhat creatively in order to meet changing customer needs. Moreover, MNEs need to make sure that their offering is sophisticated enough to justify their premium pricing, but they cannot afford to overinvest in relatively low-income markets. The responses of executives suggest that an important capability is seeing the value of, and then making, the relatively small changes in business practices that allow the MNE to better serve its market:

What are the new trends? And then find something that suits our customers, given where they are – the trends and the need. (Bank: Zimbabwe-based operations manager)

We've started [...] a more unique and different experience, you know, it is like a weekend farmers' market type of feeling, where people go there for a specific experience. (Agribusiness: commercial executive)

This capability is similar to one of the subcapabilities under embedding, customer embedding. But whereas the emphasis of customer embedding is on the relationship with the customer, we define evolving business acumen in terms of sensing, and responding to, "trends" and the desire for "unique and different experiences." Such trends may originate in the host country or elsewhere; what is important is a willingness to make changes to the product offering.

We were struck by the number of times executives highlighted the importance of digital capabilities. It is noteworthy that these executives, who emphasized the importance of basic business principles such as cost management and consistent service, also mentioned quite sophisticated digital solutions:

We spend a lot of time looking at big data. [...] We have got one of the biggest databases now in Africa to pull data either from ourselves, or from secondary sources ... trying to drive efficiency, trying to drive the categories better, trying to figure out what are the opportunities in the market. (Agribusiness: commercial executive)

There are two key elements we are looking at. One is workflow solutions and the other is our customer relationship management solutions. Those are the key things that we believe will enable us to drive digitization to the limit that we want to achieve. (Bank: Nigeria-based operations manager)

The fact that we do have a corporate system – we call it the Business Online – that also is a differentiator in the market ... So whatever we have from an electronic channel is a key differentiator. (Bank: Kenya-based operations manager)

Tempting as it may be to see this as a case of "leap-frogging," the evidence suggests that leap-frogging does not take place as effortlessly as the term would suggest (Hobday, 1994; Nelson & Pack, 1999; Rock, Murphy, Rasiah, Van Seters & Managi, 2009). However, in this case it is noteworthy that digital solutions require relatively little in terms of local technical understanding. South African MNEs can acquire or develop solutions in the somewhat more sophisticated South African market, to apply with relatively little customization in other, very different countries.

The critical factor for developing and applying this capability is to balance efforts to meet quite basic business requirements with a willingness to explore the adoption and application of more cutting-edge business tools.

Intra-MNE Embedding

The notion of embeddedness and indeed "multiple embeddedness" is key to conceptualization of the MNE (Meyer, Mudambi & Narula, 2011; Rugman & Verbeke, 2001). Subsidiaries of MNEs can be embedded internally, within the MNE network (as observed by Yamin & Andersson, 2011), with the parent (Ciabuschi, Dellestrand & Martín, 2011; Nell & Ambos, 2013), or with the host country, and specifically in technical and relational networks (Andersson, Forsgren & Holm, 2002).

But while many scholars use the noun "embeddedness," we argue that a key capability relates to "embedding" as a verb – the establishment of potentially value-adding relationships. When internationalizing to lower-income countries, the development of the embedding capability is complicated by the fact that executives from the MNE may not be particularly keen to embed in a location that is less developed than at home. Embedding in a country such as Sweden intuitively appears to have greater benefits than embedding in a country such as Sudan. Evidence suggests that the "not invented here" syndrome is a negative consequence of institutionalized socialization (Burcharth & Fosfuri, 2014). Embedding into lower-income countries therefore requires the development of an alternative way of socialization, in which the benefits of mutual learning are made clear. Thus in MNEs where successful embedding has taken place, both headquarters (i.e. parents) and subsidiaries are committed to mutually supporting each other.

Our evidence suggests that South African MNEs that are successful in wider Africa have two main intra-MNE embedding capabilities. The first is parent–subsidiary embedding, where the insights from the parent are seen as relevant and helpful. Somewhat to our surprise, subsidiary–subsidiary embeddedness, even though it has been less theorized about (Zhao & Luo, 2005), was more in evidence than subsidiary–parent embedding, where the parent has appreciation for the knowledge from the subsidiary – "reverse knowledge transfer" (Ambos, Ambos & Schlegelmilch, 2006; Govindarajan & Ramamurti, 2011).

Parent–Subsidiary Embedding   The literature on technological upgrading (Hobday & Rush, 2007; Marin & Bell, 2006) has as a central assumption that firms in less developed countries can benefit from deliberate engagement with the technology of the parent. In those studies, the parent is typically an advanced MNE, and the subsidiary is located in a middle-income country. As our cases suggest, a similar process takes place when the parent is an emerging MNE from a middle-income country, and the subsidiary is located in a low-income country. Because parent company executives may well be biased in their assessment of the subsidiary's appreciation for their technology, we have relied especially here on the judgment of the subsidiary executives. They mentioned a large number of examples where they were seeking out and using knowledge from the parent:

Nigeria is the only one in the bank's group that has its own platform that is different from others, but the one from headquarters is actually more robust than what we have in Nigeria, but we take some learning from them [...] We do take from the larger group in South Africa those best practices and everything we can align across from the other countries as well [...] And we also learn from them. One area from a digitization process is robotic automation, which we sent three guys to Johannesburg. They are back now and we are going to start creating and using robots for some of our processes and everything, things we have learnt from them. (Bank: Nigeria-based operations manager)

So our company does provide a lot of support for us in that area, there are certain things that we can't get easily here, so we rely on the head office, sometimes even their own internal resources at the head office do come over to help us with certain areas. (Bank: Zimbabwe-based human resources manager)

Subsidiary–Subsidiary Embedding Executives in the subsidiaries quite frequently mentioned their learnings from other subsidiaries, and also seemed willing to share their insights. Indeed, the sense from the subsidiary managers was that they saw themselves as part of a pan-African network:

As that group started exploring going into markets to test their idea they actually came across what Mozambique did and they said, "this works." They completely changed their way of working here and adopted the Mozambique approach. (Bank: human resources manager)

So I would say we pick information from various aspects. If head office came up with something and they said "this country is doing very well," or "they have rolled out this particular aspect," then we will ask ourselves as Kenyans, "Is it something that we need to do in Kenya?" (Bank: Kenya-based operations manager)

I think about – was it two months ago? . . . the sorting team had a problem where they do some of the processing in my producing area, specifically in branch fulfilments. So we sent some guy to Swaziland for a week and they got very positive things on how we have changed the environment, we do exchange [knowledge]. (Bank: Botswana-based operations manager)

In contrast to how frequently we heard executives based in wider Africa mention new business insights coming from the parent company, few of the South Africa-based executives of the MNEs highlighted important generalized learnings that they had acquired from their subsidiaries. We suggest that this may well be the case because the subsidiaries are located in similar regions to each other. The subsidiaries saw the similarities and the value of learning from each other's countries better than the parent, located in an economically somewhat more successful country, could see the value of learning from its wider network.

Local Embedding

Local embeddedness has been defined as the degree to which the MNE has established strong ties in its host markets (Andersson, Björkman & Forsgren, 2005). Local embedding is the capability of the MNE to form close relationships with local actors in host markets. Concerning this form of capability, three key features emerge from our data: regulator embedding, supplier embedding, and customer embedding.

Regulator Embedding Regulator embedding refers to the capability of the MNE to meaningfully engage with regulatory authorities. C-suite executives repeatedly mentioned the value of having continued engagement with regulators and other government bureaucrats. Their behavior is consistent with evidence of the importance of government in less developed contexts (Wright, Filatotchev, Hoskisson & Peng, 2005) and also with evidence of the important role that MNEs can play even in policy formulation in those countries (Macher & Mayo, 2015). Moreover, many African countries still suffer high levels of policy uncertainty (Bartels, Napolitano & Tissi, 2014). To several of the C-suite executives, building successful relationships with government decision makers offers their companies a greater opportunity to successfully navigate the complexities of their host markets:

We think it is important to have good personal relationships with [government] stakeholders, so both our chief executives and other senior members in the country, we will encourage them to have good relationships with people in the presidency and the various ministries, the central bank, state-owned enterprises etc. and we will also encourage people from the broader group when they visit the country to take the time to meet with government stakeholders and establish relationships. (Bank: investment banking manager)

We have built relationships with many of those people [government officials], on a personal level even, making sure that they understand where we are going, and that they understand the complexity of our business. (Agribusiness: commercial executive)

The regulator, there is nothing I can do without them. He is so key and so important. Almost on a daily basis we've got interactions. (Bank: Zimbabwe-based operations manager)

Regulator embedding does not involve simply the forging of personal relationships, although that seems an important capability. Instead, a number of respondents argued that deeper engagement with regulators and government decision makers, mainly through industry associations, is critical to the long-term survival and growth of the industry:

If you just sit and the regulator brings out regulation that actually destroys your business, you can make a choice and say okay let's take that and make it happen. Let's find a way how we are going to massage and do things in the bank in order to accommodate this and lessen the impact. Or are you going to lead this courageously and go and tackle the regulator. Go and put a position case. Take partner firms with you etc. and sit there and say, guys, we are now destroying value, not value just to the bank but also how we impact society. (Bank: human resources manager)

Can I just say in Africa, we do get our managers to be much more involved in government politics, or not government politics, but government issues. (Agribusiness: commercial executive)

The general expectation of MNEs is that building relationships with regulators will help create a more favorable business climate that will justify the effort to engage with government officials. It is worth remembering that regulators were key in determining whether and how our MNEs could access host country markets in the first place. Thus each MNE was clearly motivated to develop specific relationships and, beyond this, a general capability to embed itself with government.

Supplier Embedding   In line with our previous definitions, we define supplier embedding as the degree to which the MNE strongly engages with suppliers and distributors in host markets. This seems to be a useful capability especially for overcoming the logistical challenges of host markets, and was therefore particularly important in the manufacturing context, although executives from finance service firms also mentioned its importance.

We have got through to market, we have got the sales force embedded, we have got our distribution and our own trucks embedded, and now we look at a factory. And that has sort of been the recipe for us, going into Africa ... So our agreement has always been wherever we are involved in Africa, that we procure whatever we can in the country as a first step – whether it is milk or diesel or packaging or whatever – and we will only use our international or South African suppliers to top up or where we can't find suitable quality in the right quantities. (Agribusiness: commercial executive)

Generally we do get a lot of our goods and raw material from South Africa, we are very dependent on South Africa, but for areas where there are opportunities to on-board local suppliers, we take that into consideration. (Bank: Botswana-based operations manager)

Further, there seemed to be a conviction that forging stronger ties with local suppliers increased the likelihood of competing successfully in host markets. Consider, for example:

So we do encourage local development [of suppliers] as an extension of our investment. .... I think for that part you need to be very close to your suppliers because you know, you don't fight these days on individual product level, you fight on the value chain level. (Agribusiness: commercial executive)

However, MNEs saw this as a "nice to have" capability, in that the MNEs repeatedly highlighted that they did not *require* local suppliers or their development, because the South African operations could provide backup. There was also very little evidence that MNEs were actively involved in developing this capability, instead profiting from it when it was in place with relatively little effort.

Customer Embedding   The importance of customer embedding in African markets emerged clearly from our interviews with C-suite executives, and it is tied in with the ability to develop novel offerings for customers (discussed in the section on evolving business acumen). The need for deeper engagement with their core customer base was repeatedly stressed. In particular, the view among the interviewees is that strong customer embedding offers an opportunity for the firm to develop customized products for clients, which can be a key differentiator in the market. Thus, interviewees emphasized:

We are not a prescriptive bank as it were. We want to understand the clients' business and then after understanding it we want to begin to develop a solution together with the client so that it is a more customized solution that answers to their problem. (Bank: Zimbabwe-based corporate banking manager)

... so because we are client-centric, we are not just developing products and just say take it, this is what we have for you and everything. We actually look at the needs of those customers and based on the needs of those customers coming up with those capabilities that will make them to be digital ... So if we want to introduce a new product and improve our processes and everything it has to be from a client's point of view. (Bank: Nigeria-based operations manager)

In all these cases, MNEs highlighted that understanding the customer was key to ensuring that the firm succeeds in meeting the needs of the customer.

When Capabilities are Not in Evidence

An interview with an East African firm that had previously partnered with a South African MNE revealed a number of capability gaps. The partnership had broken down, and the partner continued to operate successfully on its own in its home region, planning further expansion across the continent. In reflecting on the relationship with the South African MNE, the partner highlighted a number of capabilities that were absent. The following section draws entirely on the comments of the Kenya-based sales manager of this agribusiness.

The South African MNE, showing a lack of business acumen, seemed to not have understood their local customer, who noted,

But the preferences of the food in the southern part of Africa is not the same as the eastern part of Africa. So it really didn't gel in terms of the business, the business concept was right, but the product portfolio I think was wrong.

The executive contrasted the South African MNE with its own operations, arguing:

Basically it was our portfolio of products that made us have that success. Today we serve East Africa; we are present in Kenya, Tanzania, Uganda, Rwanda, Burundi, Eastern Congo, Ethiopia. So in terms of the business environment in our region, we have the know-how and the capability.

In interviews with the successful MNEs, the subsidiaries of South African MNEs were generally keen to learn from the parent. However, local partners were far less receptive to what it perceived as an arrogant approach by the MNE, even though the local partner acknowledged the technical expertise of the South African MNE:

So even when they come here, their attitude is wrong and you can't synchronize it. They are the ones – these South African corporations have this attitude that you can't trust anybody apart from yourself. So that flexibility and being able to adjust the mentality, attitude and the way you work to a new environment – the South African companies are not able to do that. There is always going to be a clash, and not only with the partners they are dealing with, but even to the customers they serve. . . .
    On the positive side, there is a lot of knowledge. They have had a lot of training, which is very positive when you apply it. So if you apply that knowledge to different environments in the way you should – and you have to encompass everything, not just the knowledge. A is A in any language, but how do you pronounce A in Cantonese? – so that is very positive, I think there is a lot of knowledge from the South African companies.

The main capability that was lacking in the above relates to local embedding. There was also a pervasive sense that the South African MNE did not belong in the host environment:

There is an attitude issue and that attitude starts from South Africa saying they are "coming to Africa," but they are not Africans. That is the biggest mistake because to us, you are coming to look down at the rest of us.

The executive was adamant that "You can't serve people with arrogance," and repeated:

You cannot come to East Africa, and tell me for these long years how you must actually cook rice. You don't.

In addition to a lack of embedding with the local customer base, the local firm pointed out that it had extensive networks in the region, networks that the South African MNE had been unable to establish:

We have the partnerships in those countries irrespective of the differences in regulatory frameworks and the others normally that go with.

In summary, the South African MNE that failed in East Africa had a strong set of capabilities, but it fell short each time it was necessary to adapt those capabilities for conditions outside of South Africa. In terms of its business acumen, its strong product portfolio did not take into account local preferences. In terms of the MNE network, it did not consider the possibility that the partner would be anything but keen to learn from (especially the parent in) the MNE network, and it also did not manage to embed locally. On the contrary, there was a strong sense that the MNE was arrogant, inflexible, and "out of sync" with local requirements and values.

5.5   Discussion

In relating the insights from the South African MNEs operating in the wider African to the other cases in this book, Table 5.5 provides a summary. It is clear that the South African MNEs studied here possess a large number of capabilities – and indeed, within their home country, all four firms are successful. This chapter however documents a number of factors that the MNEs identify as important, even though they are not always able to develop those capabilities.

The MNEs in this context resemble many of the catch-up cases that previous scholarship has documented since Dunning's (1956/1998) pioneering work. It is perhaps not surprising that most of the capabilities have long been documented by scholars (e.g. the large body of work on embeddedness), or even that capabilities such as those relating to business acumen are taken for granted by most scholars. Indeed, the evidence from South Africa gives credence to the view that emerging MNEs are essentially at an earlier stage of their evolution (Narula, 2012) rather than being fundamentally different to advanced MNEs. The question can then be asked how a study of South African MNEs in wider Africa can open up opportunities for novel theorizing. We wish to highlight three.

The first opportunity for theorizing relates to the development of basic business acumen. In countries with a large informal sector, principles that are regarded as fundamental in most management research may instead often be novel: for example, cost management and customer-centricity. The "spillovers" literature has examined the process by which those principles are introduced into the local business context at a high level of aggregation (see the review by Meyer & Sinani, 2009), but examining those processes with greater granularity is likely to yield important insights on organizational learning. In particular, it seemed to us that the MNE headquarters was the main reservoir of this capability. But in developing that capability over its entire network, it risked maintaining a headquarter-centric approach, limiting capability upgrading in subsidiaries.

Table 5.5 *Capabilities of South African firms studied*

Major Capability Category	Subcategories	South African banks in Africa*		South African agri-business in Africa*	
		Case 1	Case 2	Case 1	Case 2
Obtaining resources	Resource identification	✓	✓	✓	✓
	Ability to purchase product inputs			✓	✓
	Ability to develop resources internally	✓	✓	✓	
Product/service capabilities	Product manufacture	✓		✓	✓
	Research and development			✓	
	Local product adaptation	✓	✓	✓	
Operations and management	Production management			✓	✓
	Supply chain management			✓	✓
	Hard skills	✓	✓	✓	✓
	Soft skills	✓	✓	✓	
	Entrepreneurship	✓		✓	
	Cross-cultural management	✓			
Marketing	General sales capabilities	✓	✓	✓	✓
	Understanding the market and local customer needs	✓	✓	✓	
Managing the external environment	Political and negotiating capabilities	✓		✓	
	Relationship capabilities	✓	✓	✓	✓
	Adjusting to poor infrastructure			✓	
	Knowledge about the national context	✓	✓		

* Firms not identified by name due to nondisclosure agreement.

The second opportunity for novel theorizing relates to learning at the level of the subsidiary. The subsidiaries we interviewed were keen to learn and were quick to highlight learnings both from the parent and from sister subsidiaries. In addition, the evidence from the failed partnership suggests that an openness to learning is key to the success of the foreign venture. But although its importance was recognized by executives at the headquarters, executives rarely saw learning and enabling learning across the MNE as central headquarters tasks. Our evidence strongly suggests that intra-MNE learning is embedded in these MNEs, but the capability seems anchored in subsidiaries rather than in the parent. This raises the question of how subsidiaries acquired the strong awareness of the importance of learning, appreciation of the superior technological skill of the parent, and capability of engaging with sister subsidiaries. More generally, it raises the question of what are the triggers for capability upgrading and the sharing of learnings among subsidiaries.

The final opportunity for theorizing relates to the attitudinal dimension of local embedding, or perhaps more specifically to the lack of local embedding. Even though "not invented here" (Antons et al., 2017; Burcharth & Fosfuri, 2014) and a consequent lack of local adaptation are known to stem primarily from (unhelpful) attitudes about the local market, a construct like such as liability of foreignness (Zaheer, 1995) has not integrated an attitudinal dimension. Instead, foreign firms are argued to lack some capabilities, for example an understanding of local labor laws, as discussed in the work of Mezias (2002). We argue that negative attitudes toward the host location, for example arrogance, can also constitute a liability of foreignness. We suggest that this is a particular risk when the home country is at a higher level of development than the host country. Whether and how this functions is an area for future research.

5.6   Conclusion

South African MNEs play an important role in wider Africa, but as emerging MNEs, they lack some of the capabilities developed by advanced MNEs. This raises the questions of which capabilities they need in the wider continent, and how they can develop them.

From interviews with twenty-one executives of South African MNEs both at headquarters and at subsidiaries in host countries, three main types of capabilities emerge. The basic capability of "business acumen" is often overlooked by scholars and practitioners from advanced economies. However, our interviewees suggest that business basics such as cost control and customer-centricity are important for managing in volatile and underdeveloped contexts.

Embedding within the MNE is another important capability, and although the parent is a central source of new technology, recognized as such by subsidiaries, the headquarters of South African MNEs need to do better in recognizing lessons from subsidiaries. Although subsidiary–subsidiary embedding emerged as an important element of intra-MNE embedding, this seems to have been driven by peer subsidiaries at least as much as by the parent companies.

The third and final key capability was local embedding. This involves creating ties with the local government and regulators (and the local regulatory agenda), with suppliers where possible, and also with customers. Successful MNEs were able to articulate all these types of embedding with great detail, while the failure to embed locally was the main explanation for the failed foray of a South African MNE.

Relying on insights from headquarter-based executives in relatively better-developed South Africa and from executives at subsidiaries across the continent, this chapter provides evidence of key capabilities of South African MNEs in wider Africa. It suggests that the MNEs are effective in deploying existing capabilities across the continent, but that they struggle when they have to take seriously their (less developed) host locations and develop new capabilities to operate there. The fast-growing but under-developed turbulent African context thus provides a useful testing ground for the applicability of international business studies generally, and for emerging MNEs in particular.

6   Five Cases on Strategic Capabilities of Russian Firms

Natalia Guseva

6.1   Introduction

Competitiveness depends on the availability of specific resources, skills, and strategic capabilities that differentiate companies from competitors, allowing them to achieve success in domestic and foreign markets by maximizing customer satisfaction (see, for example, Seyhan et al., 2017; Ferkins et al., 2005; Ordanini & Rubera, 2008).

While the strategic capabilities of multinational companies (MNCs) in developed markets have been widely studied, the capabilities of MNCs in emerging markets are an insufficiently explored topic (exceptions being London & Hart, 2004; Burgess & Steenkamp, 2006; Sheth, 2011; Cuervo-Cazurra, Newburry & Park, 2016). A few scattered studies of Russian MNCs focus on assessment of different categories of strategic capabilities (e.g. Greenley, 1995; Golden et al., 1995; Farley & Deshpandé, 2006; Roersen, Kraaijenbrink & Groen, 2013; Guseva, 2016; Gurkov & Saidov, 2017; Smirnova, Rebiazina & Khomich, 2017). There are currently no comprehensive studies of the critical strategic capabilities of Russian firms, or of the evolution of these capabilities at different stages of their development, crucial for achieving competitive advantages in global markets.

Russian MNCs obtained the opportunity to enter foreign markets in the mid-1990s, following the liberalization of foreign economic activity. The resource-exporter model represented most Russian MNC activity, and this peculiarity remains predominant to this day. Russian companies have faced many obstacles in developing their strategic capabilities and upgrading them to the international level to become major players in different segments of the global market.

This chapter describes the strategic capabilities of five Russian MNCs operating in both local and foreign markets. The research team selected firms – each a leader in a different segment of the Russian economy – that differ by activity type, affiliation to broad industry sectors (high-tech and services), and degree of internationalization. The chapter explores the existence and development of their strategic capabilities and discusses the principal stages of their entry into foreign markets and the obstacles and major problems they faced. The chapter also analyzes the strategies of MNCs that have succeeded in the Russian market.

The first part of this chapter presents the country's background. This is followed by a theoretical framework of capability development in Russia and a description of the methodological approach used in the case studies. The fourth section presents the major findings of strategic capability development in Russia, based on the five firms studied. The final section compares strategic capabilities among the five firms and presents research conclusions.

6.2   Russia: Country Background

Country Profile

Russia is geographically the largest country in the world, with a territory of over 17 million square kilometers. Russia ranks ninth in the list of countries by population, with 146.8 million people living on its territory,[1] largely concentrated in urban areas (72.8 percent)[2] and predominantly in the European region of the country (77 percent).[3] Russia contains 30 percent of the world's natural resources,[4] making it the most resource-rich country in the world.

The country relies mostly on energy revenues to drive its growth and is particularly vulnerable to oil price fluctuations. This vulnerability, reinforced by Western sanctions since 2014, led to an economic decline in Russia. In 2016, Russian GDP declined by 0.2 percent. However, in 2017 observed growth was 1.6 percent. A strong dependency on prices for natural resources and energy supplies has affected commodity prices, government finances, and foreign trade. The inflation rate was 5.4 percent in 2016, with a decline to 4 percent in 2017 and a slight increase to 4.3 percent in 2018.

After the economic downturn in 2016, when the share of exports in GDP fell to 21.89 percent, the trend became positive. In 2017, exports amounted to 22.38 percent of GDP. This growth accelerated in 2018, with exports providing 26.84 percent of GDP. In 2018, GDP increased by 4.5 percent, while exports increased by 25.3 percent. In 2016, almost 50 percent of Russian exports were mineral products, such as crude and refined oil and natural gas. However, despite the measures taken by the Russian government to shift the focus from a heavily resource-based orientation to an innovation-driven economy, the share of exported natural resources keeps growing, reaching 56 percent in 2017.

The European Union is the largest of Russia's foreign trade partners, with 54.5 percent of Russia's trade in 2018, while Asian partners accounted for 36.8 percent. Per country, China occupies the leading position in the list of Russia's trading partners, with USD 56 billion and 12.5 percent of total Russian exports. China is followed by the Netherlands (USD 43.5 billion, 9.7 percent) and Germany (USD 34.1 billion, 7.6 percent). Since 2017, the USA has dropped five places in the ranking and is now tenth, with exports from Russia at USD 12.5 billion (2.8 percent); this decrease is mostly due to the complex political relationship between the two countries.

Inward Foreign Direct Investment

In recent years the Russian government has been seeking to improve and simplify conditions for doing business in Russia. The World Bank's report *Doing Business 2019: Training for Reform* (World Bank, 2019a) measures regulations in ten areas that affect the ease of doing business, among them construction permits, electricity supply, getting credit, paying taxes, and enforcing contracts. The 2019 report ranks Russia 31 out of 190 economies assessed during the study, compared to the country's rank of 40 in 2017 and 123 in 2011. The strengths of the country are described as "Registering property" and "Enforcing contracts." In Russia, commercial disputes take less than a year to settle on average, compared to a global average of almost two years. Another remarkable difference is the speed of property transfers – fifteen days in Russia compared to 1.5 months globally. Recent regulations introduced in certain regions of the country have further simplified construction permit management.

Inward foreign direct investment (FDI) volume decreased by 32 percent in 2017 compared to 2016, mostly due to new economic sanctions imposed by the USA and the EU. However, total FDI volume did not change significantly, as Russia found alternative investment targets to minimize the consequences of the sanctions. Table 6.1 displays the dynamics of inward and outward flows of foreign investment, 2013–2017.

The distribution of direct investment in Russia is heterogeneous. The Russian National Rating of the Investment Climate in the Regions (2018) noted five regions in Russia that were leaders in terms of inward FDI.[5] The Tyumen region was in first position due to significant investment in oil and gas projects by multinational companies.[6] Moscow, the business, financial, and administrative capital where the majority of MNCs have installed their subsidiaries and representative offices, ranked second. The third place went to the Republic of Tatarstan,

Table 6.1 *Inward and outward flows of FDI in Russia (billion USD)*

	2013	2014	2015	2016	2017
FDI inflows	53,397	29,152	11,858	37,176	25,284
FDI outflows	70,685	64,203	27,090	27,272	36,032
Total FDI	124,082	93,355	38,948	64,448	61,316
International ranking in outward FDI	4	6	15	20	12

Source: UNCTAD, http://unctad.org/en/Pages/DIAE/World%20Investment%20Report/Annex-Tables.aspx; http://unctad.org/en/PublicationsLibrary/wir2016_en.pdf

mostly due to large projects in the oil and gas sector; fourth was Saint Petersburg, the northern capital of Russia; and fifth, the Tula region.

Outward Foreign Direct Investment

UNCTAD ranked Russia twentieth in its Global Outward FDI ranking in 2016, and twelfth in 2017 (UNCTAD 2016, 2017b). The largest portion of Russian outward FDI traditionally lies in natural resources (oil and gas) and infrastructure. The most significant Russian multinational projects are the 2 billion USD Karachi–Lahore gas pipeline in Pakistan, led by RosTec Global Resources; the 2.5 billion USD Kalimantan railway in Indonesia, operated by Russian Railways (RZD); and the deployment of the Nord Stream 2 pipeline by the Gazprom Group, estimated at over 8 billion USD. However, Russian companies have recently increased their presence and activity in high-tech innovative industries. For example, Kaspersky Lab maintains its world leadership position in the endpoint protection platforms market. Such firms have contributed to significant projects of social value, such as the Winter Olympics in Sochi in 2014 (USD 51 billion) and the Football World Cup in 2018 (USD 20 billion).[7]

The main constraints on the expansion of Russian companies into global markets are currently related to Western sanctions and embargoes, which have limited access to financial markets for Russian firms. Previous studies have revealed the top ten Russian multinational companies in terms of foreign assets (Guseva, 2018) (Table 6.2).

The "anti-offshore" law introduced by Russia in 2014 has significantly impacted Russia's outward FDI. Among the top ten recipients of Russian FDI are Austria, Singapore, Germany, and Kazakhstan (with investments by Russian companies in the real-estate sector). However, the difficulties

Table 6.2 *Top ten Russian multinationals by foreign assets, 2017*

Company	Main industries	Foreign assets (million USD)[a]	Foreign sales (million USD)[b]	Motivation for foreign investment
Gazprom	Oil and gas	14,943	81,741	International underground gas storage expansion (objective: 5% of annual exports by 2030)
Sovcomflot	Maritime transport	6,919	954	Market expansion, ownership and use of ships, ship management
Rusal	Metallurgy	3,674	6,317	Market expansion, mining, joint ventures and projects
Russian Railways (RZD)	Rail transport	3 418	4 683	Market expansion, augmentation of passenger and freight railway turnover and operation services
Lukoil	Oil and gas	2,662[c]	70,198	Construction of oil refineries (currently 3 abroad) and sales of oil and gas products locally (over 50% of gas stations abroad)
Evraz	Metallurgy	2,385	4,633	Market expansion of iron ore and steel products; expansion of steel and vanadium production
VimpelCom	Telecoms	914	5,942	Expansion of client base worldwide through partnerships and joint ventures
TMK	Production of metal pipelines	865	917	Expansion, M&A, localization of several types of production (completion of wells, service maintenance of pipe products, etc.)
Rosneft	Oil and gas	544	37,561	Exploration and expansion of oil and gas production
Holding Metalloinvest	Metallurgy	373 (data for 2015)	2,573	Market expansion, sales growth, mining

Source: company annual reports.

[a] Average yearly RUR–USD exchange rates used for conversion; investments in foreign subsidiaries and joint ventures were considered.

[b] For this indicator, sales of foreign subsidiaries were considered.

[c] Carrying value of investments, total assets amounted to 37,398 in 2014.

Table 6.3 *Main recipients of Russian outward FDI (million USD)*

	2014	2015	2016	2017
Total investments in all countries	**57,082**	**22,188**	**22,314**	**39,049**
Cyprus	23,546	4,308	9,827	21,352
Austria	1,135	746	258	6,739
Singapore	817	383	888	6,136
Switzerland	6,927	203	1,433	2,281
Luxemburg	639	785	1,633	1,856
Virgin Islands	718	3,296	1,795	1,401
Bahamas	756	1,028	1,205	1,300
Jersey	261	1,258	112	865
Kazakhstan	657	643	476	727
Germany	1,016	738	393	724

Source: www.gks.ru/free_doc/doc_2018/fin18.pdf

of exporting capital abroad and the withdrawal of financial flows into offshore zones by Russian companies remain problematic. In the period from 2014 to 2017, the leading destinations for outward FDI from Russia (see Table 6.3) were Cyprus, Switzerland, and Luxemburg, followed by the Virgin Islands, the Bahamas, and Jersey.

The low transparency of Russian companies is a key problem for researchers. The barriers to data disclosure for subsidiaries and associated companies, and data on countries in which the company operates, also apply to the transparency of outward FDI statistics. Transparency International assessed the largest Russian companies based on the following criteria: corporate anticorruption programs, disclosure of data on subsidiaries and affiliated companies, and disclosure of data on countries in which the company is present. The Transparency International index is the average of these three criteria (Transparency International, 2018). The most transparent Russian companies were in the telecommunications sector, while the least transparent were in the infrastructure, construction, agriculture, and food industries.

The present study of the strategic capabilities of Russian companies operating in foreign markets and multinational companies present in the Russian market accounts for current trends in inward and outward FDI in Russia. Thus the pool of assessed companies includes Russia's largest exporters from the high-tech sector. Moreover, the study includes Russian companies headquartered in countries that are Russia's priority strategic partners.

6.3   The Evolution of the Capability Development Concept in Russia

Russia has undergone tremendous changes since the beginning of the 1990s because of a transition from a planned to a market economy. This period was characterized by a radical reassessment of successful performance and competition by Russian companies in domestic and foreign markets. Russian research literature for that period shows a limited understanding of the concepts of core competences and strategic capabilities. Few (Some) researches focused on organizational development in a competitive environment and the acquisition of competitive advantages (e.g. Azoev, 1996; Barinov & Sinelnikov, 2000; Yudanov, 2001). Barinov and Sinelnikov divided competitiveness criteria into two types: adaptation criteria and innovation criteria. Innovation was supposed to determine the ability of firms to adapt, and therefore turn threats into opportunities (Barinov & Sinelnikov, 2000).

Russian companies started to conduct foreign economic activities independently following the liberalization of the mid-1990s. Firms used the availability of natural resources as their main strategic capability for entering foreign markets. The Russian economic model was – and still is – based primarily on the activities of large companies and is resource-oriented. For instance, the proportion of small and medium businesses in the Russian economy is even today only 21.9 percent.[8] This resource orientation is primarily due to Russia having 30 percent of the world's natural resources, making it the most resource-rich country in the world.

The competitiveness of Russian multinational companies and their success in foreign markets was largely limited by a combination of unstable prices for natural resources and deficiencies in organizational capabilities. The series of economic crises in 1998, 2008, 2013, and 2014 had a strong influence on Russian companies and forced them to reconsider their development and growth possibilities. Thus economic instability, the pressure from shareholders for further development, and the desire to diversify risks required them to review the concept of strategic resources and capabilities, and how to gain competitive advantages in the first decade of the twenty-first century.

The classification of competitive advantages (Azoev & Chelenkov, 2000; Ageeva, 2002) and the discussion of how to acquire them became the major focus of Russian business researchers in that period (Fatkhutdinov, 2005; Vorozhbit, 2008; Sarith, 2004). Azoev and Chelenkov (2000) suggest a number of criteria for the classification of competitive advantages:

1 the nature of the source;
2 the type of dependence (market conditions, government policy, activities of competitors);
3 the validity period;
4 the nature of the dynamics (unstable, stable);
5 the level of hierarchy (product, company, industry, economy);
6 attitude to price (price-sensitive, non-price-sensitive);
7 ease of imitation (unique, easily imitated);
8 sector specifics (production, R&D, sales, services).

Ageeva notes that for Russian companies, unique assets or special competences within important areas of activity can be a basis for building competitive advantages (Ageeva, 2002). Moiseeva links firm competitiveness with a change in customer satisfaction over time and with time spent on production (Moiseeva, 2007).

Thus studies of Russian companies' competitiveness were for a long period focused on competitive advantages. However, the 2014 crisis shifted the emphasis to the importance of strategic capabilities that provide a base for competitive advantages. According to Bgashev, strategic capabilities are those that allow the company to create a strategy that is difficult to replicate and is most relevant to the company's activities (Bgashev, 2012). Patrakhina emphasizes that strategic capabilities support the unity of the company's unique features, which can be divided into "minimally acceptable opportunities" and opportunities for competitive advantage (Patrakhina, 2015).

Lischuk considers the concept of dynamic capabilities, when an organization maintains its long-term competitiveness through its ability to update and recreate its strategic capabilities to meet the needs of a changing environment (Lischuk, 2014). Alkanova and Smirnova traced the development of marketing-related capabilities in Russian firms (Alkanova & Smirnova, 2014).

Thus, after the 2014–2015 crisis, Russian enterprises, particularly multinationals, were focusing on two key tasks in developing their strategy in foreign markets: the identification and development of their strategic potential, and its transformation into a strategic competitive advantage.

In 2018, there were twenty-five Russian companies among the largest 2,000 companies in the world, according to Forbes.[9] In 2019, the top 100 companies in the world included four Russian companies.[10] These were Gazprom (ranked 40), Sberbank (47), Rosneft (52), and Lukoil (97). Such rankings confirm the successful development of strategic resources and capabilities among Russian multinational companies.

Russian companies have begun to realize (slowly enough) that if they combine a long-term perspective, strategic intent, the ability to adapt dynamically to a changing environment, and the three components of strategy – competitive advantages, distinctive capabilities, and strategic fit – they will be better able to develop the strategic capability needed to create long-term competitive advantage.

Among researchers there is a constantly increasing interest in understanding the concept of strategic capabilities among Russian firms, the achievement of competitive advantages, and the development of effective strategies in domestic and foreign markets: this has become a dynamic and promising area of research (Voronov, 2001; Fatkhutdinov, 2005; Safiullin & Safiullin, 2008; Bgashev, 2012; Lishchuk, 2014).

6.4   Methodology

This study aims to examine major strategic capabilities of domestic and multinational companies operating in Russian and foreign markets, based on interviews with leaders in selected industrial clusters. The sample is compiled of four large high-tech companies and one firm in the service industry (Table 6.4). The domestic firms are SIBUR, Gazprom M&T, and ByTerg, and the MNCs are Ecolab and Swilar. In-depth interviews were used to collect raw data. Executives from the five companies, including the founders, strategic decision makers and those responsible for strategic activities, were interviewed.

The selected sample represents substantial diversity in the set of opinions of company executives on the major strategic capabilities of domestic and global companies operating in the high-tech industry. Petroleum and gas giants Gazprom and SIBUR are included in the high-tech sector; their technologies in extraction and refinery are unique and complex. Moreover, those large exporters own subsidiaries that focus on delivering value not related to gas extraction and refinery, such as logistics, trading,

Table 6.4 *Characteristics of Russian firms studied*

| | | Firm category | |
		Exporter	Multinational
Industry	Hightech	SIBUR Gazprom M&T ByTerg	Ecolab
	Services		Swilar

and financial risk hedging. Those activities rely heavily on digital technologies and data analysis and require competencies that are also demanded in traditional high-tech industries. Thus, especially among Russian companies, SIBUR and Gazprom M&T can be included in the high-tech category.

The semi-structured interviews covered questions about each firm's profile and its strategic capabilities, which are critical both to doing business in Russia and to entering foreign markets as a Russian company. Several questions also focused on the evolution of strategic capabilities at different stages of the firm's development. The companies and interviewees are listed in Table 6.5, and some key elements of the companies' profiles are shown in Table 6.6.

6.5   Major Findings: Development of Strategic Capabilities in Russia

Case 1: SIBUR – Siberian-Ural Petrochemical and Gas Company

SIBUR is the largest integrated petrochemicals company in Russia.[11] The group manufactures and sells petrochemical products in Russian and foreign markets in two business segments, one including olefins and polyolefins and the other including plastics, elastomers, and intermediates. SIBUR's petrochemicals business relies mainly on its own feedstock produced by the midstream segment using byproducts purchased from oil and gas companies. SIBUR also sells liquefied petroleum gas (LPG) in Russian and foreign markets within this midstream segment.

The Russian government established the company in 1995 with the primary objective of relaunching the industrial integration of petrochemical enterprises from the former USSR. Between 1998 and 2002, the company rapidly increased its assets. In 1998–1999 alone, SIBUR acquired over sixty assets across multiple segments of petrochemical and related industries. At that time, the company's activities crossed Russian borders – assets were also acquired in Hungarian chemical companies. SIBUR's leadership planned to pursue foreign expansion into the Czech Republic and Serbia. As a result, SIBUR experienced a growth-related disease – a managerial and financial crisis. The situation was further complicated by a global petrochemical recession that coincided with the necessity of integrating new assets.

The period 2003 and 2006 saw a complete restructuring of the business, accompanied by changes in the management team that created a new foundation for greater growth and efficiency. To achieve long-term sustainable growth, SIBUR needed to balance production capacities

Table 6.5 *Russian company and interviewee descriptions*

Company	Industry	Major international activities	Interviewees (person, position, location)
SIBUR LLC	Gas and petrochemical	Exporter (headquarters in Russia); subsidiary SIBUR Int. in Vienna; business in 80 countries	Vsevolod Starukhin, director of sales and marketing development, Moscow
Gazprom Marketing & Trading	Natural resources Gas retail	Exporter (headquarters in Russia); subsidiary Gazprom M&T registered in London; business in 6 countries	Yuri Virobyan, general director, Paris
ByTerg	High-tech (mobile video)	Exporter (headquarters in Russia); part of production in China	Andrey Prudnikov, founder and CEO, Moscow
Ecolab– Nalco	Chemicals Water treatment process, polymers	Multinational (headquarters in USA); business in 170 countries	Larisa Shishkina, Russia & CIS HR director, Moscow
Svilar	Consulting services	Multinational (headquarters in Germany); business operates in Germany, Austria, Russia	Daria Pogodina, founder and CEO, Moscow

Table 6.6 *Russian company profiles and financial data*

Company and industry	Sales, USD	Assets, USD	No. of employees	Exports,[a] USD	Exports, USD	No. of countries business conducted with
SIBUR LLC Gas and petrochemical	7.8 bn	18.58 bn	27,000	2.76 bn	3.28 bn	~80
Gazprom Marketing & Trading Natural resources, gas retail	377.1 mn	1058.8 mn	450	258.6 mn	n/a	6
Ecolab-Nalco Industrial chemistry (USA)	13,838 mn	19,962	48,400	2,953 mn	n/a	170
Swilar Consulting service (Germany)	743,000 k	184,5 k	13	4,650	0	3
ByTerg High-tech	18.7 mn	7.7 mn	177	4,225	241,000 k	3

[a] Earnings before interest, taxes, depreciation, and amortization.

at different stages of processing, build infrastructure and new plants able to compete with leading companies in the Russian and foreign markets, and bring production and labor productivity in line with international standards.

SIBUR started to develop global partnerships around 2014. For example, in the high-priority segment of basic polymers SIBUR built projects on a global scale, and in the rubber business, alliances with leading manufacturers were pursued in the main growing markets, China and India. In 2013, a joint venture with a Chinese corporation, Sinopec, was organized around on the Krasnoyarsk synthetic rubber plant, which exports a significant part of its products to China.

The creation of a joint venture between SIBUR and Indian Reliance Industries Ltd, which involved installing a new production complex for butyl rubber in India with a capacity of 120,000 tons per year using SIBUR's own technology, is unique to SIBUR and to the entire Russian petrochemical industry.

In December 2015, the company acquired their first foreign shareholder. A deal was signed with Sinopec to join SIBUR as a strategic investor with a 10 percent share. In 2016, an agreement was signed on the sale of a 10 percent stake to the Chinese Silk Road Fund.

The SIBUR business model focuses on four main production processes: gas processing, gas fractionation, cracking, and polymerization.[12] The company is committed to improving its global competitiveness and expanding its export markets. Its employees, numbering around 27,000, contribute to the success of SIBUR's clients in industries including chemical, fast-moving consumer goods, automotive, construction, and energy in 80 countries worldwide.

In January 2018, SIBUR joined the Operation Clean Sweep initiative to prevent the release of polymer particles into the environment during their production and transportation. The initiative was supported by 60 percent of the companies that are members of the association PlasticsEurope, accountable for 80 percent of the total plastics manufacturers in Europe.[13]

To determine the main strategic capabilities of the company at different stages of its development, an interview was conducted with Vsevolod Starukhin, director of sales and marketing development, whose career has included experience in many countries, such as Holland, Brazil, Poland, Hungary, and France. He outlined the key strategic capabilities and competitive advantages of SIBUR, including feedstock base, production capacities and their effective use, sales channels, and a diversified customer base.

Starukhin notes:

If we consider strategic capabilities in the context of our company, the development of our markets and customers, we should first of all note the importance of feedstock base, modern technologies, and product development ... When launching new, advanced products we carefully evaluate the availability of the production licenses as well as our R&D capacity to meet customer needs. Your long-term competitiveness depends on how quickly you "upgrade" your product portfolio, reducing share of "commodity" products and grades.

Because SIBUR is a large or even a dominant player in some products in the Russian market, sales channels and a diversified customer base become secondary in Russia given that "it's impossible to pass us." However, the situation is different in export markets, as SIBUR becomes one of many players and enters the global competition for customers.

SIBUR conducts business in eighty countries, with its most significant presence being the CIS countries, Europe, and China. Markets are determined by the balance of production with demand and the full cost competitiveness of specific products.

A significant part of our current product range can be attributed to the "commodity +" category, so the logistics from production site is an important factor. Consequently, sustainable sales presence depends on the "logistics leg," where you can effectively supply and sell. Regarding a particular segment of our products – LPGs, like propane and butane – the most effective export is to Central and Northern Europe. If you consider the polyolefins group, e.g. polyethylene, polypropylene – it covers the CIS, Europe, Turkey, and China.

However, the success of regional sales is determined not only by supply efficiency but also by customer demand for specific product grades. In order to stay in the game, it is crucial to follow local trends, engage with customers to understand their application needs, and translate this knowledge into internal product development.

In foreign markets, SIBUR must compete not only on delivery terms and prices, but also paying a great deal of attention to customer satisfaction ... If you are a large manufacturer, then you can ensure the reliability of your supplies to export markets – this is also one of our strategic capabilities ... We try to understand and take into account our customer preferences and offer a range of services which are important to specific export market clients. For example, as we have to deal with a longer logistics leg than European manufacturers, in some cases we have to set up local warehouse facilities to deliver products to our customers on a "just in time" basis.

At different stages of the company's expansion into foreign markets, the business model of SIBUR evolved and its strategic capabilities changed accordingly. If initially the company undertook export sales from the

Moscow office and acted only through distributors, then the next step was to get closer to their clients to offer them products and services with a higher added value. Therefore, sales offices were opened in Austria, Turkey, and China. A team of salespeople was built to launch sales not only through distributors but also directly to customers. SIBUR has formed multicultural teams of professionals with a knowledge of market specifics to enable effective interaction with local partners.

Moving to direct sales, we now offer customers not only flexible payment and delivery terms, but also provide technical services, e.g. we help to solve issues related to the processing of our products, adopting production recipes. Thus, getting closer to the customer requires a better understanding of their needs, which is one of our key strategic capabilities.

SIBUR's interest in developing business in new export markets focuses on opportunities for growth.

Growth in foreign markets is quite attractive, it pushes us to leave our comfort zone, adapt and change our ways of working to unlock new opportunities as our shareholders expect the company to continue solid profitable growth ... Secondly, newly installed production capacities of petrochemical plants often exceed the demand of domestic markets. And finally, foreign expansion is a perfect opportunity to diversify our presence and hedge currency risks through foreign exchange earnings.

Case 2: Gazprom Marketing & Trading

Gazprom Marketing & Trading (GM&T), which provides marketing, trading, and supply chain services for electricity, LNG, and petroleum products, is part of the Gazprom Group (see Figure 6.1). The company was founded in 1999 in London and since then has become one of the major players on the commodities and foreign exchange markets, with over 450 employees and subsidiaries in Europe, Asia, North America and South America.

GM&T is a wholly owned subsidiary of the Gazprom group, the world's largest gas producer and one of the world's largest energy companies. GM&T describes itself as aiming to build a unique environment of excellence, providing innovative energy solutions, and building a leading integrated supply, trading, and marketing business. The key values GM&T promotes are innovation and the ability to think outside the box, a passion for excellence, growth and learning, and teamwork. Gazprom describes teamwork as being "one team with our customers, our parent company and each other, understanding each other's needs." They aim to use innovative thinking in business and relationships with their customers to provide tailored energy solutions.[14]

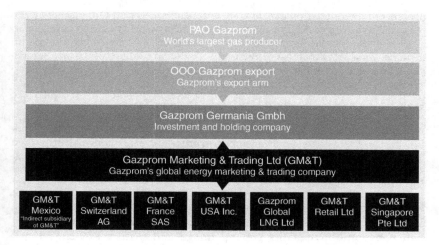

Figure 6.1 Gazprom Marketing & Trading, a subsidiary of the Gazprom group
Source: www.gazprom-mt.com/WhoWeAre/Pages/default.aspx

To understand the major strategic capabilities that allow GM&T to implement their values and be one of the world's leading gas players, the research team conducted an interview with Yuri Virobyan, general director of GM&T (based in Paris). He noted that the company was one of the first Russian resource companies to enter foreign markets, which it did in the late 1990s.

Virobyan notes that the history of Gazprom's foreign development took place in three stages. Throughout the first stage – 1970s – sales of the gas produced in Russia were carried out through contracts with leading major national gas companies, such as Gaz de France in France, Ruhrgas in Germany, Eni in Italy, and OMV in Austria.

Gas was sold across the Russian border for a fixed price and in large quantities, however Gazprom did not attribute much importance to what happened to their product after sales. Back then nobody was interested in where it was resold, transported, used, and what were the prices on the domestic markets in Europe.

At the second stage, "the realization came that perhaps we need to move further" and "in this regard we began negotiations to create joint ventures together with foreign partners as we in turn were afraid to perform direct sales." Agreements on joint ventures were signed with the same partners. However, as Virobyan notes, it appeared that a conflict of interest with the main competitors persisted [...] Our partners were interested in buying from us at a lower price, and we were interested in selling at a higher price, and the joint ventures we created at that time barely resulted in anything. Subsequently most of them closed, except for one, which was signed with a large gas consumer – the German company BASF. This is the only joint venture that still exists to this day.

At the third stage, according to Virobyan, Gazprom

understood the necessity to streamline the entire supply chain – production, and transport and sales to the final consumer, in order to create our own distribution network. At that time – the beginning of the 2000s – the European market opened up to competition, opportunities for direct sales of gas to the European market arose.

Thereafter Gazprom began "to create our own trading companies in European countries, primarily in the UK due to its large gas market, high consumption, and its general image and history of being a gas country."

Throughout these stages of Gazprom's foreign expansion, the most important strategic capabilities they developed included:

1 unique access to raw materials
2 substantial expertise and technical base
3 the financial resources of the Gazprom Group
4 knowledge of the market and customers
5 the creation of trading centers.

The first strategic advantage was the unique access to raw materials. "We are the largest gas producer in the world," said Virobyan. "As far as resources are concerned, we have more than anyone. Our share in the European market will be large in any case, with variations depending on the country – 20 percent in France, 40 percent in Germany, and 100 percent in some countries like Hungary or Romania."

Second, Virobyan pointed to Gazprom's substantial expertise and technical base. "From the production, transportation and storage standpoints, we are perceived by the market as a very serious industrial player."

Thirdly, financial power was also seen as an important competitive advantage.

There was a time when Gazprom was in the top three largest companies in the world in terms of capitalization, even though our positions have slightly declined since then. It makes a real difference when you come to your client and say: "we have no problems with financing" rather than saying: "we only have three euros in our account." The client chooses their business partner accordingly to their financial stability.

An important factor is knowledge of the market: "customer understanding" and the creation of "one team with the customers." In Europe, "there is no one-size-fits-all approach to selling gas. It is necessary to adapt to the peculiarities of the market, the specifics of our clients," Virobyan emphasizes.

We focus on the British market, firstly due to its size, large volumes of consumption and its history as a gas country, while France for example was historically centered on electricity. . . . The French and British markets are built in a completely different way: in England the market has been open for competition for a long time, and gas and electricity there are viewed as commodities. In other words, buying gas is very simple: compare two or three prices on the Internet and in two clicks, you have your gas running. In France, decisions on gas and electricity are serious. A dedicated meeting with explanations is required, the client wants to be certain about the advantages and why they should buy from us and not from others. Regardless, French customers believe that there is no better supplier than the traditional one, Engie for example (former Gaz de France). Therefore, in France we either build direct contacts with consumers, or sell gas through regional distributors. Lately we began to focus increasingly on the end user.

GM&T also pays special attention to building a highly professional team to understand the specific needs of their customers.

We have designed a high-performing commercial structure. For example, our team in France is 90 percent French, consisting of professionals with broad expertise in foreign companies like Engie and EDF. Sometimes our clients wonder how they will do business with us if we are "so far away in Siberia," and are concerned about the risks of shipping interruptions. Thus, we explain to them that GM&T is registered in the same Chamber of Commerce of Paris as Engie for example, and in case of any issue, the client can defend their interests in court, as they would do with Engie. To us, as a global Russian company, the local legislation is applied in the same way as for any other French company. Therefore, all customer requirements are respected and business with us is no different than with any other large European player.

An important strategic resource of our company is the presence of a trading desk in London, which drives operations throughout Europe. Today, trading is required to support gas supplies to end consumers and optimize the hedging of risks. Our trading desk is one of the largest in Europe. In the UK, it is in the top three, and in the top five in Europe. We have very competent traders managing risk. Thanks to the creation of a single trading center in Europe, GM&T can offer competitive prices and stable supply.

In the conclusion to his interview, the GM&T CEO noted that current political sanctions against Russian companies in the foreign markets, along with recent changes in EU legislation to restrict the activities of non-European companies, are hindering the development and expansion of the business.

At the moment, it would be fair to say that the problems we face are increasingly political. From an economic standpoint, our product is of high quality, sold at an attractive price, we have a good team, and we benefit from the support and financial assistance of the parent company. In other words, we do not feel any serious economic problems, however political constraints can unfortunately hinder us.

Case 3: ByTerg

ByTerg is the largest Russian manufacturer of video cameras for stationary objects and vehicles. The company produces a wide range of video cameras designed for outdoor surveillance under Russia's severe climate conditions: from −50°F to +50°F. The stated aim of ByTerg is to supply high-tech solutions for integrated protection of objects, to customers with enhanced requirements for security systems.

Since its 1996 launch, ByTerg has produced more than 1.5 million video cameras. According to an IMS research report, *East Europe and Russia Market for CCTV and Video Surveillance Equipment*, between 2010 and 2012, ByTerg became the largest CCTV supplier in Russia and the third largest in Eastern Europe, as well as Russia's largest CCTV camera manufacturer.[15] In 2017, the company employed 250 people, of which 20 percent work in research and development. The current production volume is 100,000 CCTV cameras per year.

In 2010, ByTerg began cooperation with selected Chinese manufacturers and transferred some of its production facilities to China. This partnership is based on principles of "no opposition," "no competition," and "no disclosure." At the same time, the company's priority products – video cameras for the transport sector and government projects – continue to be produced at its Russian plants.

During the interview, ByTerg's CEO, Andrey Prudnikov, identified five groups of key strategic capabilities that allow ByTerg to maintain leadership positions in its market segments:

1 use of the most advanced and effective technologies in the global security systems market
2 reliability of equipment and a high level of service
3 knowledge and understanding of peculiarities of the local (Russian) market
4 friendliness and individual approach to each client and partner
5 engaged team of highly professional employees

Looking first at innovative technologies. Prudnikov noted that since the beginning of the mass production of video cameras in 1996, the process itself has been repeatedly changed. If initially it was a "screwdriver" hand assembly, currently almost all of the components of video cameras are manufactured on a production line using modern technological equipment.

Today, innovation, technology, and the ambition to quickly implement all of the world's latest inventions make ByTerg a hallmark in the video surveillance market in Russia. One of the company's latest achievements is the introduction of specialized premises for "dry" assembly. To minimize the presence of moisture inside a video camera, all components are kept for a long period in specialized dry storage cases with relative air humidity not exceeding 1 percent (as compared to relative air humidity in regular premises at around 70 percent). Video cameras are assembled in a special "dry" room where the microclimate is maintained by special equipment all year round. The introduction of the "dry" room solved the problem of condensate precipitation on the glass of a sealed camera in case of sudden temperature changes.

The second of ByTerg's key strategic capabilities is the reliability of the equipment it produces and the high level of service it provides. The CEO emphasizes the importance of quality control stages in production. Each multiformat video camera (MVC) undergoes multiple levels of testing under carefully controlled conditions so as to guarantee the reliability of its operation for an extended period. ByTerg's multiple stages of quality control include checking and testing of input components; burn-in and vibration testing of the video module; and checking the cameras for impermeability – air- and water-tightness and absence of moisture inside the camera body.

Thanks to this quality control, MVCs have a five-year warranty. Prudnikov notes that it is precisely because of the quality control that MVCs are so popular. They are not only used for solving security surveillance problems: MVCs have also been used to study the process of ice forming on aircraft wings during Tu-214 aircraft testing. They have, too, been installed under water for observation of the life of the Moscow Dolphinarium inhabitants – without any additional adaptations needed. Finally, the firm helped Russian drivers to win the Paris–Dakar rally – miniature MVCs were installed on Kamaz vehicles' side panels to monitor wheel conditions.

Special emphasis is put on post-sale service. ByTerg's specialists provide comprehensive technical support to customers and partners on the entire range of equipment in the company's list – at purchase decision and consultation stages in addition to during product operation.

The third strategic capability discussed was knowledge of the local market. ByTerg reacts promptly to changes in the market. The company closely follows the latest developments in the field of complex real estate security. Monitoring of the world's largest manufacturers is carried out so that any significant development – in both the field of CCTV and other areas of security – does not go unnoticed.

Since their development, MVCs have earned recognition in the Russian security systems market. In 2008, these cameras received two ZUBR awards (for strengthening security in Russia) in the categories "Market Choice" and "Time Proven."

The fourth strategic capability mentioned by the CEO was customer orientation, focused on specific segments such as security for public transport, the automotive industry, maritime transport, and aerospace. In the CEO's opinion, it is very important to "make friends with customers," as it affects the understanding of existing "hidden" problems in the security industry. In order to offer effective solutions, it is necessary to obtain "access" to these existing problems.

The company focuses on specific segments of new product development, such as public transportation, including safety enhancement for buses, trams and electric trains, and maritime and air transport. Thus ByTerg has managed to take into account problems developing around the video equipment currently installed on public transport, such as low temperatures and vandalism, and to offer an innovative solution – a universal IP-video surveillance system using anti-vandal multifunction cameras and video recorders of its own production.

Particular efforts are dedicated to relationship management with the company's dealers. ByTerg seeks to develop individual, personalized approaches with partners. Mutual respect and open, transparent relations are keys to mutually beneficial cooperation, according to Prudnikov.

The last strategic capability discussed, but certainly not the least and probably one of the most important, is a highly engaged and professional team of like-minded people. These "awesome specialists" are imbued with team spirit. Particular attention is paid to the involvement and engagement of employees. For instance, it has already become a yearly tradition for the ByTerg team to ascend the legendary peaks of the world. The "Mountain Club" has conquered, among others, the Olympus, Mont Blanc, Elbrus, and Kilimanjaro.

ByTerg supports various social projects. Since 2008, the company has led the "Charity instead of New Year's souvenirs" initiative – on New Year's Eve, the "souvenir budget" is spent on charity and help for children.

Case 4: Ecolab

Ecolab Inc., headquartered in St. Paul, Minnesota, is a global supplier of cleaning, sanitizing, and maintenance products and services for the institutional, hospitality, healthcare, and industrial markets. The firm claims that around the world, businesses in foodservice, food processing, hospitality, healthcare, industrial, and oil and gas markets choose Ecolab products and services to keep their environment clean and safe, operate efficiently, and achieve sustainability goals.

Ecolab started its operations in Russia in 1991 and today employs more than 840 people throughout Russia. In 2013, Ecolab began implementing a large-scale localization strategy in Russia. In 2015, the company received the "Company of the Year" award from the American Chamber of Commerce in Russia, which recognized the firm's strong growth, the active development of its partnerships with local suppliers, the attractive working conditions of its employees, the commitment of the team to corporate and social responsibility, and their compliance with business ethics.

A high level of localization – covering local demand by installing local production plants – helps the company to get closer to its customers. To date, localization has reached 75 percent in the sector of chemical solutions for oil extraction. For refining industries, it is even higher – around 99 percent. Ecolab produces its brands in Russia on a contract basis with ten factories in Russia and the CIS, and all products receive a corresponding certified trademark in compliance with requirements of the Russian government.

Larisa Shishkina, the HR director for Ecolab Russia, noted during her interview that the most important strategic capabilities for the success of the company in Russia are:

1 unique technologies and business diversification
2 sustainability
3 research and development
4 localization and merger-and-acquisition projects in Russia.

Ecolab's unique technologies and business diversification mean that the firm is a trusted partner for over one million customer locations and the global leader in water, hygiene, and energy technologies and services that protect people and vital resources. With sales of USD 14 billion in 2017 and 48,000 employees, Ecolab delivers comprehensive solutions and on-site services to promote safe food, maintain clean environments, optimize water and energy use, and improve operational efficiency for customers in the food, healthcare, energy, hospitality, and industrial markets in more than 170 countries around the world.

The company has a long history of breakthrough innovation resulting in game-changing technologies. Since 1998, Ecolab has invested millions of dollars each year in research and development in Russia to introduce products and programs that not only meet government and regulatory standards, but also increase safety and reduce environmental impact. The firm's core technologies have been developed and expanded in direct response to customers' evolving needs.

The second strategic capability discussed was sustainability. Ecolab Russia is working at more than 978 customer locations, helping companies rethink operations and business strategies to reduce the use of natural resources and ensure long-term viability. Increased demand for goods and services presents significant opportunities for the business across industries.

Research and development is a third important strategic capability in Russia. Ecolab has nineteen global technology centers with 1,600 scientists, engineers, and technical specialists, among them over 500 PhDs, and possesses 7,700 patents, which is a strong strategic capability to leverage business in Russia. "Indeed," Shishkina noted, "our R&D experts share their experience and research with different countries, including Russia." Moreover, the Ecolab research and scientific center in Kazan is among the best in Russia, with modern equipment and highly qualified personnel.

As an example, Core Shell™ polymers – high molecular weight latex flocculants (chemical compounds that accelerate water cleaning) – were specifically developed for wastewater treatment applications, sludge dewatering, and processing aids in the municipal water and wastewater treatment markets including papermaking, petroleum refining, mining and mineral processing, and food and beverage production in Russia.

As another example, Nalco Water, an Ecolab subsidiary, develops solutions and ensures the optimization of industrial processes in the water treatment industry. Master Chemicals Nalco Champion, another subsidiary, offers unique differentiating chemical technologies to optimize oil production processes, as well as traditional oilfield reagents. This part of the Ecolab business is in charge of the development, local production, and incorporation of chemicals for the oil industry.

Mergers and acquisitions (M&A) and localization projects are a crucial strategic capability of Ecolab in Russia. In 2017, the company acquired its first fully owned production facility in Sterlitamak, Russia. Founded in 2006, Promkhimservis Co. specializes in the production of solutions for energy customers. Its location is a major asset, as it will enhance supply chain logistics and efficiencies, bringing the company much closer to the customers in the region. New production lines may double the plant's capacity. Ecolab also plans to further develop the plant's certified laboratory on site with R&D capabilities. In addition to expansion opportunities, localization is also a requirement of Russia's energy and oil giants, such as Gazprom and Rosneft.

Following the development of foreign operations, as Shishkina noted, the key strategic capabilities shifted. At the time of entry into the Russian market, the target was to find a niche and determine what branches of industry the company would focus on. New technologies played a crucial role at that time. At the current stage, sustainability, localization, and M&A projects are the crucial strategic capabilities for future growth and increasing operating income in Russia.

Shishkina highlighted that among the 170 countries where Ecolab does business; the most important are the emerging markets, such as Russia, China, India, and Brazil, because of their rapid growth. Ecolab is growing its presence in the Russian market and had sales of over USD 180 million worldwide in 2017.

Case 5: Swilar

Swilar is a German consulting company, offering to German and international small and medium-sized enterprises (SMEs) a full range of services to help them penetrate or expand their presence in the Russian market. The company has two offices in Germany (North Rhine–Westphalia and Bavaria) and one in Russia (Moscow).

Swilar was founded in 2011 by Georg Schneider, Tobias Schmid, and Daria Pogodina. Each founder contributed their own experience and history of working with foreign companies in Russia. In the following years the company developed actively, attracting experienced specialists from Russia, Germany and Austria.

In 2015, in response to market demands, the partners jointly set up a third company in Moscow, Swilar Admin Ltd. In this way they created the opportunity to run clients' subsidiaries as a management company – both formally and virtually, by managing operational processes and personnel. During its development, the company focused on the provision of a full range of services: legal support, accounting, financial and management reporting, controlling, and interim management.

Reducing client risk and improving administrative efficiency issues became the goal and mission of the firm.

A sales manager should have the time and ability to deal with sales, without being disturbed by administrative processes, and a managing director should get access to any required information without further effort.

SMEs were and still are the main target group of Swilar. It has become very attractive to get competent services from one source, to have direct contact with project managers, and not to spend resources on administrative issues. This is exactly what the partners and employees of Swilar are focused on.

The Swilar team has more than 20 years of experience in the Russian market. A competent team of specialists from different areas makes a reliable partner for successful business in Russia. Swilar takes an active part in Russian and German business life and is a longstanding member of the German–Russian Forum, the German–Russian Chamber of Commerce, and ICV (International Controller Verein).

According to Daria Pogodina, managing partner of Swilar Ltd, the most important strategic capabilities that have help the company succeed are:

1 intellectual (managerial), with skilled and experienced employees and the application of an optimal management system;
2 cultural – understanding the differences in German and Russian approaches to doing business, thanks to their international team of employees and managers who are citizens of Russia and Germany;
3 market-related:
   a in contrast to major competitors, the ability to work with SMEs;
   b the ability to provide a full set of business management services and simplified market access in Russia – their clients being European companies requiring project management, accounting, subsidiaries managing services, or potential investors seeking investment prospects in Russia and seeking a better understanding of risks and opportunities that await them;
   c opportunities for advertising, such as periodicals within the German business environment in Russia, sponsorship of events dedicated to Russian–German relations, word-of-mouth through partners and the network developed by the partners over the years.

The company's main strategic resources include the ability to swiftly respond to the needs and requests of potential and existing customers and adapt to the changing conditions of the market by offering new services, flexible contractual conditions, continuous self-improvement, and proximity to skilled labor markets.

According to Pogodina, the key skills and competencies of Swilar's employees that have helped it to successfully operate in the Russian market since its foundation are:

1 a creative approach to sales and business development;
2 a client-oriented approach;
3 proficiency in at least three languages (Russian, German, English);
4 problem-solving skills;

5 flexibility;

6 project management skills.

The crucial competitive advantage for Swilar when working in Russia, as Pogodina notes, is the high quality of its services, reputation, and networking:

In the environment of German SMEs, a good reputation and networking are the most critical aspects for our company as they require substantial timing and physical resources. Top SME managers (in Germany they are often family companies) tend to deal with partners who they can trust based on word-of-mouth recommendations. Furthermore, they want and need to be prepared for the peculiarities of the Russian market – by someone who knows both German and Russian business strategies with proven experience.

Human resources are less critical – the labor market in Moscow is sufficiently saturated with skilled workers.

Due to active marketing among German SMEs in Russia, and the networking efforts of partners, Swilar has became significantly more recognizable than in the first two years in the Russian market. The ability to solve – and avoid – problems for these specific company segments through an individual approach to clients has become one of our main competitive advantages.

Pogodina considers that the company's competitive advantages are sufficient for yearly long-term growth, maintaining the current rates of customer retention and customer base expansion. The main competitors of the company are large well-known global or German consulting firms. These competitors' advantage is a wider recognition in Germany. Their shortcoming is price, which is often not clearly defined for the client for an all-in-all project. Having started working, the customer soon realizes that a project is going to be much more expensive than planned and often the customer does not have direct contact with the managers and decision makers. Swilar provides good services, long experience, direct communication, and clear costs for this specific group.

6.6   Comparison of Strategic Capabilities and Conclusions

Each of the domestic and global firms selected for the study has a unique combination of strategic capabilities that allow them to maintain leadership positions in certain segments in local and foreign markets. This study identified the following strategic capabilities (Table 6.7).

This study was based on the methodological tools designed by the Centre for Emerging Market Studies (CEMS) for comparative analysis of the strategic capabilities shared by the selected firms. The research

Table 6.7 *Strategic capabilities identified in domestic and multinational Russian companies*

Company	Industry / firm category	Major strategic capabilities
SIBUR LLC	Gas and petrochemical / domestic (exporter)	Feedstock base Production capacities and effectiveness use of them Sales channels Diversified customer base
Gazprom Marketing & Trading	Gas retail / domestic (exporter)	Access to unique raw materials Substantial expertise and technical base Resources of the Gazprom Group Knowledge of the market and customer understanding Creation of trading desks
ByTerg	Mobile video / domestic (exporter)	Innovative technologies Reliability of equipment and high level of service Knowledge of local market Customer orientation for specific segments: public transport security, automotive industry, aerospace Engaged upper-level professional team
Ecolab-Nalco	Chemicals / multinational (headquarters in US)	Unique technologies and business diversification Sustainability R&D Localization and M&A projects in Russia
Swilar	Consulting services / multinational (headquarters in Germany)	Intellectual: high-competence team Cross-cultural competencies Market competencies: focus on small and medium size enterprises, full line services, different promotion channels

team enriched this analysis to identify strategic resources of companies specific to the Russian market through qualitative study. We used CEMS methodology to divide strategic capabilities into six main groups: obtaining resources, product/service capabilities, operations and management, marketing, managing the external environment, and strategy.

This research allowed us to identify the major strategic capabilities of domestic companies in local and foreign markets, as well as multinational companies that are successful in the Russian market. These companies differ from each other in their competitive resources due to their development history; their experience in conducting operations in domestic and global markets; their use of various competitive strategies; their degree of product innovation, sales, and promotion experience; and their interactions with customers and the capability to take into account their peculiarities and preferences.

The research team ranked the strategic capabilities, grouping them in three categories:

1. Very important – mentioned by at least four of the five companies
2. Important – mentioned by three of the five companies
3. Less important – mentioned by two or fewer of the five companies.

The first group – very important strategic capabilities – includes customer orientation based on an understanding of local and foreign customer needs, general sales capabilities, and product manufacturing (see Table 6.8). All five companies highlighted customer orientation, belonging to the fourth group of strategic capabilities – marketing – as a critical strategic capability regardless of the degree of internationalization, activity, or ownership. The second very important dimension was general sales capabilities, which also belongs to the marketing group and was highlighted by four out of the five companies. A third very important dimension was product manufacturing. This parameter, in the product/service capabilities group, was highlighted by all the Russian exporters and by Ecolab.

The second category – important strategic capabilities – comprised two capabilities in the category of obtaining resources: resource identification and the ability to develop resources internally. Those capabilities were highlighted by SIBUR, Gazprom M&T, and Ecolab. Gazprom M&T especially accentuated the capability to generate and use the financial resources of its parent company, the Gazprom group. Capabilities in local product/service adaptation, a subcategory of product/service Capabilities, was mentioned by ByTerg, Ecolab, and Swilar.

Other important strategic capabilities were in the categories of operations and management: hard skills (mentioned by ByTerg, Ecolab, and

Table 6.8 *Comparison of the Russian firms studied, by strategic capabilities*

Major capability category	Subcategories	SIBUR	Gazprom M&T	ByTerg	Ecolab	Swilar
Obtaining resources	Resource identification (3/5)	✓	✓		✓	
	Ability to purchase product inputs	✓	✓	✓	✓	
	Ability to develop resources internally (3/5)	✓	✓	✓		
Product/service capabilities	Product manufacturing (4/5)			✓	✓	✓
	Research and development					
	Local product / service adaptation (3/5)					
Operations and management	Production management	✓		✓	✓	✓
	Supply chain management	✓	✓	✓	✓	✓
	Hard skills (3/5)	✓		✓		✓
	Soft skills (3/5)					✓
	Entrepreneurship					✓
	Cross-cultural management (3/5)		✓		✓	✓
Marketing	General sales capabilities (4/5)	✓	✓	✓	✓	
	Understanding local and foreign customer needs (5/5)	✓	✓	✓	✓	✓
Managing the external environment	Political capabilities					
	Relationship capabilities					
	Adjusting to poor infrastructure					
Strategy	Portfolio management				✓	
	Long term perspective and sustainability				✓	

Swilar) and soft skills and cross-cultural management (Gazprom M&T, ByTerg, and Swilar). Three out of five companies noted the use of national culture as an additional strategic capability, plus the opportunity to obtain cultural synergies through the effective management of cross-cultural differences. This confirms the importance of cultural diversity as a strategic capability for achieving competitive advantages in the global economic landscape (Guseva, 2016).

It is important to note that none of the companies taking part in the study mentioned the capability of managing the external environment, including political capabilities, relationship capabilities, and adjusting to poor infrastructure. Russian exporters noted the negative impact of political factors, expressed in the form of restrictions imposed by EU legislation and sanctions on Russian companies operating in the European market. Interviewees also mentioned other strategic capabilities, including long-term perspective and portfolio management.

The results obtained in this study summarize the experience of domestic and multinational companies present in Russia and the necessity of possessing appropriate strategic capabilities for successfully doing business in Russia. Additional study is required to fully understand the key strategic capabilities of Russian companies in global markets. The subject of strategic capability differentiation, depending on the company's globalization phase, also remains open for discussion.

In conclusion, the comparative analysis conducted as part of this study and the results represent pilot data for Russian companies operating in the foreign markets, and MNCs operating in Russia. These developing strategic capabilities are based on a thorough understanding of customer orientation, the acknowledgement of general sales capabilities, and the continuous development of product manufacturing.

Notes

1. www.worldometers.info/world-population/russia-population/.
2. www.gks.ru/free_doc/new_site/perepis2010/croc/perepis_itogi1612.htm.
3. www.oceanunite.org/round-up/pre-empting-russias-year-ecology/.
4. https://raexpert.ru/releases/2017/Dec15a.
5. https://asi.ru/eng/investclimate/rating/.
6. http://naukarus.com/inostrannye-investitsii-v-ekonomike-tyumenskoy -oblasti-analiz-sovremennyh-tendentsiy.
7. www.themoscowtimes.com/2014/05/21/factbox-russian-mega-projects-12 -of-the-best-a35656.
8. www.rbc.ru/economics/05/02/2019/5c5948c59a794758389cfdf7; www .gks.ru/wps/wcm/connect/rosstat_main/rosstat/ru/statistics/accounts/.
9. www.forbes.com/global2000/list/2/#tab:overall.

10. www.gazeta.ru/business/2019/05/16/12358009.shtml?updated.
11. www.sibur.ru/en/about/overview/.
12. www.sibur.ru/en/about/products/production/.
13. www.plasticseurope.org/en/resources/publications/1804-plastics-facts -2018.
14. www.gazprom-mt.com/WhoWeAre/VisionAndValues/Pages/default.aspx.
15. www.byterg.ru.

7   Strategic Capabilities of Polish Firms

Mariola Ciszewska-Mlinarič and Krzysztof Obłój

7.1   Introduction

The long era of socialism in Poland, 1945–1989, suppressed international expansion by Polish firms during the country's internal economic and political transition. The "shock therapy" initiated in 1989 (Slay, 1994) transformed political, economic, and social systems and moved Poland from a planned to a market economy. From that point, the rapidly growing domestic economy offered local companies numerous opportunities for development within Poland, while international expansion, particularly outward foreign direct investment (OFDI), appeared more risky and less attractive. Initial internationalization activity focused on exports, as reflected in export growth from the mid-1990s. OFDI from Poland gained momentum only after Poland's accession to the European Union, nearly a decade later. Polish companies had to start from scratch: acquiring resources, gaining operational experience in the local market economy, then developing the products and capabilities needed to support their efforts to enter foreign markets.

This agenda was far from easy. First, local firms had not been able to develop appropriate competences and knowledge sets under the Communist regime, as export activities were restricted to designated international trade agencies. Kriauciunas and Kale (2006) and Shinkle and Kriauciunas (2012) show that these long-lasting impediments limited managerial motivation and abilities to renew and improve existing competences. The extent of socialist imprinting on a firm's knowledge set inhibited its adaptation to the evolving market and institutional conditions.

Second, Polish companies had very limited resources (either tangible or intangible), and generally lacked firm-specific advantages to offset the "liability of foreignness" in international markets (Bruton, Lau & Obłój, 2014). Third, at the initial stages of transformation Poland lacked institutions supporting internationalization, such as insurance coverage or a legal system that protected exporting companies. Emerging market firms often face poor home country conditions that hamper their international growth orientation and efforts (Cuervo-Cazurra, Newburry & Park, 2016).

Finally, rapid growth of the domestic economy during later stages of transformation offered extraordinary opportunities for development in the local market, for both existing and new ventures. This situation had two effects: firms did not have to internationalize to grow, and firms could also learn and develop new knowledge sets and competences in the relatively safe and well-understood local market. Therefore, in line with the "big step hypothesis" (Pedersen & Shaver, 2011), most Polish companies were slow to make their first international investments, as they first had to develop the resources, competences, and infrastructure needed to support foreign operations.

The objective of this chapter is to broaden our understanding of capabilities that enabled Polish firms to overcome such barriers and liabilities in order to expand into foreign markets. With this aim, we present and analyze six case studies of firms representing different industries and different modes of servicing foreign markets (exporting and OFDI). Our findings suggest that Polish firms enact opportunities to enter international markets by actively building capabilities primarily in three areas: product improvement, relationship development, and cultural and market sensitivity. Typically, they learn and develop basic management capabilities in the domestic market. Then they slowly enter international market, and in order to cope with their lack of resources and initial liabilities, they invest in their technological competences and products upgrade. Such moves make them more credible partners to local distributors and buyers in other countries. Over time, they learn that development and maintenance of these relationships is a competence of crucial importance.

Finally, the companies under study stressed the value of extreme local responsiveness. They have *good enough* products and services, local support and embeddedness, yet limited resources and reputation. Hence, they search for entry points and niches by studying the idiosyncrasies and demands of local markets, and adapt appropriately. In some cases adaptation takes the form of extraordinarily attentive services; in others it involves flexibility, speed of reaction, or aligning products to cultural values and norms. In essence, firms use the three capabilities noted above as a toolkit to build a viable internationalization template that helps them to neutralize (at least partially) their inherent liabilities of foreignness, origin, and outsidership, and to enhance performance in international markets.

The chapter is structured as follows. First we will present the country background, followed by a methodological note outlining the selection and profiles of the firms to be studied. The final section presents the study findings, which view the firms' development in foreign markets through the lenses of the capabilities they developed and deployed along the way.

7.2 Country Background: Poland

Economic Outlook

Poland is one of the largest countries in the European Union (EU), with a population of approximately 38 million citizens (ranked 6), and the ninth-largest economy in terms of GDP (524.7 billion USD in 2018). Since the transition process that started in 1989, systemic reforms led to Poland's successful transformation from a socialist and centrally planned economy to a market-driven economy. The country steadily earned a reputation as being business-friendly, improved its standing in international rankings – as measured by the World Economic Forum's annual *Global Competitiveness* reports (n.d.) and the World Bank's *Doing Business* (n.d.) – and attracted a wide range of foreign investors. Between 2014 and 2018 the Polish economy performed well, with an average growth of real GDP above 3 percent.

Exports of goods and services now account for more than 52 percent of GDP, as a result of declining oil prices, the improved economy in the euro area (with a key trade partner, Germany, accounting for 27.3 percent of exports and 23.4 percent of imports), and the depreciation of the polish zloty (PLN). Table 7.1 shows figures on GDP, international trade, and FDI in Poland. In 2016, NPB (the central bank of Poland) reported that both FDI stock and outflows had reached record levels, having increased in comparison to 2014 by 25.7 percent and 34.8 percent respectively (NBP, 2017). The majority of Polish OFDI is located within Europe (86.4 percent), particularly in the eurozone countries (70.6 percent). In 2014, there were 1,437 enterprises headquartered in Poland, and they held shares in 3,194 entities abroad. The government recognizes the importance of active internationalization for Polish firms (exports, outward FDI) and has systematically increased the budget for the Polish Investment & Trade Agency, which supports international activities.

Economic and Political Transition, 1989–2017

Under the conditions of a centrally planned economy (1945–1989), the state made nearly all economic decisions, and specialized state-owned

Table 7.1 *GDP, international trade, and FDI trends in Poland, 1990–2017*

	1990	1995	2000	2005	2010	2015	2016	2017
GDP at constant prices, 2010 (USD millions)	226,663.6	252,409.4	326,204.7	379,768.5	479,321.5	556,360.9	573,400.0	600,956.5
GDP growth rate	−11.5	7.0	4.6	3.5	3.6	3.8	3.1	4.8
GDP at current prices (USD millions)	65,977.7	142,138.3	171,887.0	306,126.8	479,321.5	477,577.4	472,030.0	526,211.9
GDP per capita at current prices (USD)	1,738.3	3,696.5	4,458.8	7,979.8	12,507.3	12,480.7	12,348.9	13,785.7
Inward FDI: stock at current prices (USD millions)	109.0	7,843.2	33,476.7	86,345.5	187,602.2	185,986.4	186,310.2	234,440.7
Outward FDI: stock at current prices (USD millions)	95.0	539.3	267.8	1,776.4	16,406.5	27,492.1	29,286.8	30,982.2
Imports of goods and services at current prices and current exchange rates (USD millions)	15,095.0	33,821.8	57,312.2	109,155.5	201,917.8	221,464.6	227,232.1	264,157.4
Exports of goods and services at current prices and current exchange rates (USD millions)	19 037.0	35 711.3	46 429.9	106 062.0	191 786.8	236 026.8	246 060.5	286 799.0

Source: UNCTAD (2018).

organizations monopolized international trade, depriving both state-owned and smaller private companies of internationalization knowledge and experience. The political and economic bureaucracy (*nomenklatura*) set inputs, production goals, and prices for goods and services (Hunter & Ryan, 2001). In the 1980s, limited demonopolization of foreign trade was introduced, although the quality of "Made in Poland" products was unsuited to meet the demands of Western European customers, while demand from other communist bloc countries was weak (Belka, 2013). In the late 1980s the economy suffered from severe shortages, misallocation of resources, controlled prices, sluggish or zero GDP growth, and inefficient companies.

The Polish case has been praised as a fast and holistic transformation from a planned to a market economy (Slay, 1994). The program of economic transformation was based on five pillars: rapid introduction of free trade, stabilization, privatization of state-owned enterprises, construction of a social safety net, and mobilization of foreign financial assistance. In 1990, trade was demonopolized and liberalized through radical decreases in tariffs and the elimination of most export quotas and import quotas (Ciszewska-Mlinarič, Obłój & Wąsowska, 2018). Foreign trade (first imports, then exports) did not begin to grow systematically until the late 1990s, while OFDI gained momentum in 2004, accelerating with the accession of Poland to the EU.

The period from 2001 to 2004 was characterized by constant negotiations preceding Poland's accession to the EU, accompanied by the convergence of market and legal institutions in Poland with those of the EU. Internal convergence increased as normative and cognitive institutions caught up with regulatory reforms (such as governmental legislation and new industrial agreements and standards), accelerated by increased mobility of people travelling abroad for business and tourism, and transformation of the education system. The latter started with massive management training programs, with the support of Western funds and scholars, in the early 1990s.

External convergence responded to EU demands and led to the adaptation of Poland's institutional logic to European standards. Poland, as a newly accepted EU member, was granted grace periods to implement the necessary changes after 2004. These changes were of an incremental nature and aimed at eliminating frictions and encouraging adaptation to EU regulations and institutions. Table 7.2 presents a summary of the main changes in the business environment and key institutional pressures that characterized the Polish economy in this period. From 1995, exports from Poland showed nearly continuously growth (punctuated by a decrease in 2009), but OFDI activities gained momentum only a decade later (Figures 7.1 and 7.2).

Table 7.2 *Institutional characteristics of Poland's economic and political system and their impacts on firms' strategies and performance*

	Economic and political system features	Firms' strategies and performance
Institutional transformation and frictions, 1990–2004	Democratic, multiparty system introduced Development of modern financial and banking sector Huge incentives to inward FDI (tax holidays, tax breaks, low prices of assets) Radical inflation controls through high interest rates Tax reforms Early marketization – liberation of prices, elimination of subsidies, internal convertibility of currency introduction Lifting of legal barriers to private entrepreneurship, promotion of small business development Massive privatization of state-owned enterprises through commercialization, employee ownership plans, foreign direct investment, public offerings Chaotic development of "wild capitalism" resulting from a combination of incomplete institutional reforms, lack of clear property rights and contract enforcement, unstable tax system, and constant introduction of new institutions, combined with slower adaptation of normative and cognitive structures	Functional, survival-oriented, tactical restructuring and cost cutting – getting rid of over-employment, over-capacity, redundant resources and services (e.g., shops, cinemas, schools, restaurants, holiday resorts for employees) Incremental introduction of modern management methods and techniques, especially marketing tools and financial reporting Incremental development of mostly cost leadership and occasionally differentiation strategies Profit orientation Change of organizational cultures toward more open, cooperative, and effectiveness-driven values Focus of most firms on fast-growing internal market with occasional export contracts

Institutional convergence and incremental adaptations, after 2004	Bankruptcies of big and heavily indebted enterprises caught in "credit trap" under conditions of high interest rates and state-owned agricultural sector	Strategy development and implementation, with support of modern IT and consulting services
	Modernization of infrastructure	ROE, ROA, and cash-flow orientation
	Small and medium business promotion	Competitive strategies toward MNCs operating in Polish markets
	More balanced inward FDI policy	Development of export-oriented and OFDI strategies
	Export and outward FDI promotion and support (insurance and credit)	High-tech and born-global firm creation
	Proactive employment policy	
	Consumer protection and competition regulation	
	Property rights enforcement	
	Harmonization of legal system with EU regulations	

Source: Ciszewska-Mlinarič et al. (2018).

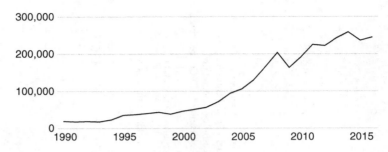

Figure 7.1 Exports of goods and services from Poland, 1990–2016 (million USD at current prices)
Source: UNCTAD (2017a)

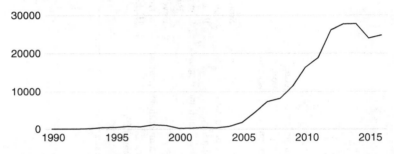

Figure 7.2 Stock of outward FDI from Poland, 1990–2016 (million USD at current prices)
Source: UNCTAD (2017a)

Poland's OFDI is low by comparison to the world, even though it is the largest within the Central and Eastern Europe (CEE) region. The trend is for Polish firms increasingly to invest abroad, with major investments in European service sectors (though Canada and the USA were among the top ten capital recipients). The high geographic concentration of Poland's OFDI reflects its limited financial resources and investor experience. Those companies that decide to invest in more distant locations are either among the largest Polish firms and able to finance large projects and bear greater risks, or those that have competitive advantages in specialized areas. There is only scant research that describes and explains the logic of this process (Wąsowska, Obłój & Ciszewska-Mlinarič, 2016; Nowiński, 2017; Wach, 2017) or the capabilities that companies develop while experimenting with exports and outward investments (Trąpczynski & Gorynia, 2017; Götz & Jankowska, 2018; Ciszewska-Mlinarič, 2016; Wrona & Trąpczynski, 2012).

Table 7.3 *Data collection matrix for the selection of Polish firms as case studies*

		Firm category	
		Exporter	Multinational
Industry	High-tech	Kooptech	Aplisens
	Low-tech	Granna	Nowy Styl Group
	Service	Prochem	Audioteka

Selection of Cases

The researchers' aim was to answer the question "What are the strategic capabilities of internationally oriented Polish firms?" To do this, they used a multiple case study method. Two criteria guided selection of the companies to be studied (Table 7.3). The first criterion, the coverage of different industry types, meant the inclusion of service industries as well as manufacturing industries of different technological intensity. Second, the stage of internationalization differentiated between exporters and firms involved in foreign direct investment, labeled here as multinationals. Table 7.4 summarizes characteristics of the chosen companies. All of them are internationally oriented and – with one exception – they were founded after 1989. Data collection was based on secondary sources – corporate reports, websites, media releases – and primary sources – at least three face-to-face interviews at each firm, with company owners and other key decision makers. The case material focuses on each firm's internationalization history and its development of capabilities enabling growth in foreign markets.

7.3   Findings

All quotations that appear in the case descriptions that follow come from interviews conducted by the authors with the managers and owners of the companies examined.

Aplisens

In 1992, six engineers left the Industrial Institute of Automation and Measurements to set up a new business. Their newly founded civil

Table 7.4 *Key characteristics of Polish firms studied*

	Multinationals				Exporters	
Case	Aplisens	Nowy Styl Group	Audioteka	Kooptech	Granna	Prochem
No. of interviews	4	6	4	3	4	3
Industry	High-tech Manufacturer of process instrumentation	Low-tech Manufacturer of office furniture	Service Publisher of audiobooks and provider of audiobook platform	High-tech Manufacturer of accessories for cinemas (washing, drying, & distribution of 3D glasses)	Low-tech Publisher and manufacturer of board games	Service Engineering and general construction (turnkey projects)
Founding year	1992	1992	2008	2010	1991	1947
No. of employees (FTE)	430	6,000	60	14	120	210
Age at internationalization	7	3	3	1	12	24
No. of markets	80	~100	23	9	24	4
Key foreign markets	Germany Belarus Russia	Germany Switzerland Ukraine Russia	Czech Republic Slovakia Sweden Spanish- & French-speaking	USA	Ukraine Czech Republic Slovakia	Belarus
Sales turnover, 2017 (million EUR)	18	300	12	2.2	5	45
FSTS (2017)	43%	85%	70%	95%	47%	10%
Entry mode	WOS JV Export	WOS JV Export	WOS JV Export	Export only	Exports of products Contract manufacturing (France, Germany)	Exports of turnkey projects and technologies

Notes: FTE = full time employment; FSTS = foreign sales to total sales ratio; WOS = wholly owned subsidiary; JV = joint venture.

partnership bought technologies, production in progress, and materials from the Institute, and started to develop industrial measurement instruments. Currently, Aplisens occupies a leading position among domestic suppliers of solutions in the field of industrial control and measurement equipment (including differential pressure transmitters, hydrostatic level probes, level transmitters, valves, and digital indicators). The company sells products – generally labeled as process instrumentation – and offers consultancy and maintenance services to industrial buyers in many industries. The company also has an accredited pressure laboratory, which provides services for its own needs and other manufacturers in the field of calibration of pressure transmitters and differential pressure. Over the years, product quality has improved, with the company successively obtaining certifications (ATEX, PED, SIL, PZH, HART, PROFIBUS, NACE), expanding the research and development department, launching technologically advanced production plants, and expanding the offer range.

The company's turnover exceeds 18 million EUR, of which about 43 percent is revenue from foreign sales. The main foreign markets where the company also has subsidiaries are Belarus, Russia, Ukraine, Germany, Romania, and the Czech Republic.

After a period of development and strengthening their position in the domestic market, the company started in the late 1990s to export, especially to CEE markets. Initially, the choice of the eastern direction (Russia, Belarus, Ukraine) was opportunistic, driven by the motive of following domestic buyers expanding in this direction. In 2001, Aplisens opened its first sales subsidiary in Russia in the form of a joint venture with a local partner. The absence of Western competitors in Eastern markets motivated their initial focus there. The managers were aware that the quality of Aplisens products was good enough for Eastern and Central Europe, but not for Western Europe. The CEO reflects that:

First there was Russia, then Belarus and Ukraine. It was also a time when it was quite easy to enter these markets because they were largely unnoticed by the West. ... At that time, the level of our products was sufficient for these markets, not for Western markets.

Internationalization to Western and non-European markets gained momentum when Poland joined the European Union. By this time, Poland had removed many tariff and nontariff barriers, but even more important was the increasing development of products that began to be comparable with offerings from Western producers. According to one top manager:

It was the first time we managed to launch new products and develop them to such a level that it was possible to function in the European Union. And then there was entry to the EU, yes, and a completely new situation – in Poland you could sell what you want, there were no barriers, so all companies went to Poland, and we went to the West then.

According to Aplisens managers, entry into Western markets was possible due to the development of product and technology capabilities in the 1990s. Competition with Western firms triggered learning and led to further technological improvement and product development. The presence in Western markets was also beneficial for Aplisens' position in Poland, where foreign companies increasingly operated. The reputation effect appears clearly: "If they did not know us from the West, they would not accept us in Poland."

Since 2009, Aplisens has been listed on the Warsaw Stock Exchange. Capital from the issue of shares allowed the company to further expand and modernize its production capacity in Poland. With regard to key foreign markets, Aplisens managers have decided on direct investments, to gain greater control and deeper understanding of the market:

In large markets, we want to have organizations that depend on us so that we have full information about the market and access to the client.

The Aplisens Group consists of wholly owned sales subsidiaries built from scratch – as in Germany (2008), France (2010), and Ukraine (2005) – or joint ventures (JVs) with a local partner – as in Russia (2001; 90 percent ownership), Belarus (2004; 60 percent), the Czech Republic (2011; 75 percent), and Romania (2015; 51 percent). Regardless of the specific investment mode, the creation of a wholly or partially owned subsidiary is always preceded by export activities. Additionally, in the case of JVs, Aplisens always has a majority share.

In markets with lower sales potential, the company uses exports, developing a network of distributors who receive adequate support in terms of product knowledge or advertising materials. The adopted model of cooperation is generally based on the principle of "One market, one distributor." Close relationships with foreign distributors allow the company to keep stock of spare parts and products, and these buffers are particularly important in more geographically distant markets.

Nowadays, Aplisens' products have high quality and are technologically advanced. Due to the specialized and technical nature of Aplisens products, the company has had to develop the skills of acquiring and maintaining industry certificates to allow its products to be traded on different markets and in different regions. Over the years, the company gained knowledge about how to adapt products to technical standards in particular markets (acquiring country-specific certificates) or in specific industries (technical adaptation). They also gained skills in adapting their products to individual customers' requirements, which gives them an advantage in comparison with large Western competitors. The trade director and CEO highlight the role of adaptation:

Our adaptation processes are more oriented on industries than countries. We are constantly upgrading and adjusting our products to the needs of new industries. There are many apparatus manufacturers, our partners, who need something specific and then we actually do for them a special sensor with special measures, special features and so on ... Our advantage is that, compared to Western companies, we are still a small company, therefore we can do what the client wants, that is, we create dedicated solutions, which makes us more attractive to some of our clients than large Western companies.

In summary, the set of capabilities that helped Aplisens to successfully grow and operate in foreign markets includes product development capabilities; knowledge and skills in acquiring and maintaining certification; high customer responsiveness and meeting individual customer demands; long-term relationships with distributors and the creation of buffer warehouses; and reputation development, with their international image enhancing the odds of successful cooperation with foreign customers in Poland.

Nowy Styl Group

The case of the furniture manufacturer Nowy Styl Group has already been examined by the authors in another publication to explore how and why learning modes change as rapidly internationalizing ventures mature and grow (Ciszewska-Mlinarič et al., 2019). For the purposes of this chapter, however, the analysis of the empirical material is focused on capabilities per se, rather than on learning modes.

Two brothers, Adam and Jerzy Krzanowski, founded Nowy Styl in 1992. In the very beginning, the company offered only three types of chairs, assembled by seven employees. Three years later, regular exports to the markets of Central and Eastern Europe began, but the Russian crisis in 1997–1998 forced the company to reorient its exports to Western Europe. Today, Nowy Styl Group is the third largest producer of office furniture in Europe, employs over 6,000 people, and has revenues of EUR 320 million, including 85 percent from more than 100 countries around the world. Nowy Styl Group has its own foreign sales organizations in seventeen countries and has established fifteen production plants in Poland, Ukraine, Russia, Germany, and Switzerland. The Krzanowski brothers are still managing the company, though the executive board has been enlarged.

The company's first years were characterized by high growth in the domestic market, broadening of product offerings, and increasing employee numbers. The initial business model of the firm assumed a low level of vertical integration – the company cooperated with numerous suppliers. However, some difficult experiences with unreliable suppliers in early 1990s led the founders to adopt the strategy of vertical integration: maintaining their own production of various components in order to enhance quality control and lower the bargaining power of suppliers. Nowadays, the firm's value chain is one of the most vertically integrated in the European furniture manufacturing industry. The CEO states:

We produce almost everything at home, from metal, chrome, wood, plastic, upholstery, foam, we have all these technologies.

The firm's early international efforts, mainly regular exports to Eastern Europe since 1995, were motivated by the search for growth and the improvement of efficiency using gradually expanded production capacities. At that time, the quality of the company's products was good enough for other post-Soviet markets, but far from meeting the expectations of Western buyers. However, the collapse of the Russian market in 1997–1998 forced the reorientation of exports to Western Europe:

When Eastern markets were rapidly drying up, it was necessary to shift our production quickly and adapt to completely different needs.

The company's first larger contracts in the West concerned contract manufacturing (components or entire products), which provided a very strong motivation for company development in terms of products, technology, and service quality. At that time, relational capabilities were particularly important, enabling the company to learn from their partners' product and production competencies, but also deepening their understanding of local markets and developing a network of distributors.

Encouraged by growing export revenues, the founders decided in 1999 to establish several joint ventures on a 50/50 basis with local partners – former distributors or export intermediaries – in order to control distribution in the larger and more affluent Western European markets such as France, England, and Germany, but also in Ukraine. Over time – after accumulating market knowledge, and then seeking greater control – Nowy Styl has increased its shares in JVs to 100 percent.

The exception is in Ukraine, where Nowy Styl's strong local JV partner occupies a unique role: the Ukrainian business unit not only performs sales and distribution functions but also runs two production plants in Ukraine and Russia. Indeed, due to a number of cultural, administrative/ institutional and economic differences, the Ukrainian business is seen nowadays as additional to the core, and its Ukrainian co-owners and managers enjoy great autonomy. They have easy access to Nowy Styl product and technological knowledge and can count on their Polish partners to support the business financially if needed (for instance, it was necessary to build a new factory in Russia due to the political conflict between Ukraine and Russia). Such solutions enable Nowy Styl to achieve benefits resulting from their presence in Eastern Europe, without being directly exposed to political and business risks (relational capabilities).

Since 1999, the company has been involved in continuous product diversification: it produces wooden parquets under the brands Baltic Wood, which offers systems of office furniture; forum seating, including auditorium seats designed for concert and lecture halls, cinema and theatre armchairs, stadium seats, and telescopic tribunes; and BN Office Solution, its own brand of high-end office furniture and equipment.

The development of the BN Office Solution brand was preceded by close cooperation (JV, 50/50) with an Austrian company, Bene, one of the European leaders in office furniture and equipment for the high-end segment. Next to sales and distribution, the cooperation also assumed codevelopment of products, which created an important learning opportunity. However, after two years, in 2005, Bene started to have serious financial problems in Austria, so Nowy Styl Group bought 50 percent of their shares.

In 2008–2009, the founders decided to reorganize. They enlarged their management board by appointing three new board members, and then designed a new international structure to optimize organizational processes within the group. Thus the management of subsidiaries was restructured, moving from a high level of autonomy to central coordination along different functions from the headquarters in Poland. These changes enhanced knowledge sharing and minimized unnecessary redundancy.

In 2011, the company started to use an acquisition strategy to increase market shares, build legitimacy in foreign markets by owning local high-end brands, and obtain new competences, particularly needed for the corporate design segment: rather than selling only products, Nowy Styl sells office space solutions to corporate clients). The first target was Sato Office, a German firm that owned two brands (Sato Office, Grammer Office) and a developed distribution network in Europe, the USA, Australia, China, Russia, and the Middle East. In 2013, Nowy Styl acquired Rohde & Grahl, a furniture manufacturer with subsidiaries in

Germany and the Netherlands. The following year, the company bought 50 percent of shares in a Turkish manufacturer, TCC, and in 2015 it acquired SITAG AG in Switzerland. Initially, post-acquisition integration was a challenge due to several cultural issues (a clash of national and organizational cultures), but, with time, Nowy Styl Group management learned how to manage the integration process. The specificity of this management mode is that Nowy Styl Group focuses on integration that respects and allows for local differences. According to one of its board members:

These acquisitions were a challenge. We bought German companies, and they operated in the market a little longer than we did. And then it turned out that the Poles "rule" them. We had to find ways how not to "rule" them but make them feel part of the group.

As Nowy Styl became one of the three largest firms in Europe in its industry, its brand and reputation started to serve as a magnet for new business opportunities, including acquisition offers. As of 2017, the company's sales, distribution and/or production subsidiaries were all located in Europe, although it also had more than 100 export markets. This concentration in Europe is a result of previous experiments with JVs in Argentina and Mexico in the first years of the twenty-first century. In both cases, after about two years, the company's management decided to exit those markets due to geographical distance, cultural differences, and challenges in maintaining close cooperation. These experiences made the managers believe that the company's knowledge, competences, and business model are better suited to geographically closer European markets.

The growing significance of the corporate design segment in Nowy Styl's strategy was reflected in the 2016 marketing slogan: "We know how to make your space." The company offers not only its product, production, and delivery capacity to business clients, but also a design capability coupled with advice on how to arrange office space that responds to contemporary challenges of changing work patterns. As noted by the company's trade director:

We can design, produce, and deliver all that is needed – the interior plan, products and customization, delivery, assembly, everything. . . . We become an attractive supplier for many international corporations that have subsidiaries in many countries. They often prefer to have their headquarters negotiate one contract for the supply of furniture and equipment in many countries.

In 2015 two new departments were created, Workspace Research and Consulting (WRC) and International Key Accounts department (IKA), to support internal knowledge development and sharing. WRC is dedicated to collecting all knowledge relevant to the design segment (e.g. how to create a great office space, what programmers need, etc.) and training the salesforce. IKA coordinates all international activities related to serving corporate clients in the design sector.

Although its products are classified as low-tech, the company employs advanced technologies. For instance, at international fairs, it uses virtual reality goggles in its showrooms. The factory opened in 2014 in Poland was one of the most modern and largest plants in the furniture business in Europe, equipped with state-of-the-art global technology to cut down delivery times, make customized production easier, and improve product quality.

Nowy Styl's managers recognize the significance of the diversity of foreign markets in terms of buyers' expectations (e.g. specific require-ments when it comes to ergonomics or the shape of chairs), different competitors, and varying distribution channels. They have developed understanding of local markets and the need for product adaptation. They clearly indicate that due to such differences it is not possible to sell the same products everywhere:

We have a different strategy in every market. We do not have one universal strategy for the whole world, because each market is different. In each market we have a different position, different competition. ... It means that you have to sell different products on every market, differently positioning them in terms of prices, presenting them in a different way, or using different distribution channels.

It took Nowy Styl twenty-five years to achieve the position of number three in Europe and to generate 85 percent of its sales in international markets. Over this period, the business model of the company evolved from selling simple individual pieces of furniture in one country to the development of complex furniture systems and the offering of design and advisory services to corporate and international clients in many markets. Is business modeling a capability, or rather the effect of other capabilities' development that was driven by the founders' entrepreneurial spirit, a desire for learning new routines and experimenting with existing ones? Leaving this question open, among the most important capabilities explaining the company's international success are the following:

- product capabilities and research and development (R&D) activity, enhancing the quality and range of their portfolio;
- strong vertical integration and production skills, with the most modern factory in Europe;
- high responsiveness to market differences;
- cross-cultural management, with the integration of acquired firms and an adaptable international structure;

- achieving legitimacy through the acquisition of high-end Western brands;
- reputation, becoming a "magnet" for acquisitions.

Audioteka

Audioteka is an internet-based digital platform that sells audiobooks in eleven languages, reaching more than six million users in twenty-three countries. Marcin Beme, an entrepreneur with degrees in mathematics, economics, and computer science, founded the company in 2008. He set up the business with two friends: a sound engineer who worked at the time in Polish national television and radio, and the CEO of K2 Internet SA, the largest digital marketing agency in Poland.

Initially, the business focused on the domestic market, offering 120 audiobooks through its website. A key challenge was to develop content and establish relationships with traditional publishers, convincing them that audiobooks would not destroy their printed-book market but should instead be seen as an additional distribution channel. Then, in 2009, Audioteka's founder initiated a cooperative agreement with Nokia. The partners agreed that Audioteka would develop its own mobile application to be preinstalled on 250,000 Nokia e52 phones, together with one of its audiobooks, and in turn, Audioteka's logo was placed in all promotional materials and marketing activities promoting the phone in Poland. The success of the project encouraged further development of applications for iPhone and Android and enabled the firm to establish relationships with large international players, both producers of mobile devices (HTC, Samsung, and Apple) and service providers (T-Mobile, Orange, and Play).

At that time, the founder redefined the company's business model, recognizing that in addition to content (which was locally bounded and depended on the relationships with local publishers), Audioteka could offer platform solutions to both audiobook and traditional publishers by developing their own, dedicated distribution channel of audiobooks via internet service, mobile, and car applications. Two engines could drive the company's growth. One was content development: permanent recordings of the latest bestsellers with exclusive rights, plus distribution of already developed audio content. The other was platform development. Audioteka's owner realized that the company's advantage could be transferred abroad:

At first sight, Audioteka is not a scalable business – we sell audiobooks in Polish. So what is scalable here? Nothing. But the notion that ... our product is not an audiobook but a platform was eye-opening. We "just" have to add content. It turned out to be possible. In the end, it's relatively easy.

The international expansion of Audioteka started in 2011, when the company established a joint venture with a Czech partner, a major book distributor. The partner was in charge of managing relationships with local publishers, acquiring copyrights, and providing local content, while Audioteka supported the new venture with an internet portal and mobile applications that were a simple "clone" of the Polish platform.

A search for financial resources that would enable further international expansion and technological development led to a contract with an Israeli venture capital fund, which in 2011 invested 2 million PLN (0.44 million EUR) in exchange for a 20 percent stake. The next year, the company signed a contract with a French car-maker. The partners agreed that Audioteka's application would be preinstalled in the manufacturer's vehicles available in France and Spain. The founder attempted to establish contacts with French and Spanish publishers. The French publishers were reluctant to cooperate with an unknown firm from Poland. This forced Audioteka to register the company in France and to recruit a manager with experience in the French publishing industry. In the case of Spain, the company employed a young translator as a country manager. By the end of 2012, the company's website and its mobile and car applications were available in both languages, and the company's catalogue included several hundred audiobooks for each market.

Since then, the company has launched versions of its service in several other languages, usually managing content issues (contact with publishers and acquisition of copyrights) from Poland, where a team of country managers, many of them native speakers, work. However, it employs approximately 25 people in its subsidiaries in the Czech Republic, France, and Turkey. Over the years, the company has developed a reputation for being technologically advanced, with its own IT team; company managers recently began analyzing the possibility of developing an application for robots designed to assist elderly people. Audioteka's brand and international reach makes content acquisition and management easier, enabling the company to develop long-term relationships with publishers. Audioteka's model complements the publishers' business, as the company offers additional distribution channels, organizing and financing the recording of books in various languages.

As of 2017, Audioteka's online platform (welcome.audioteka.com) offered services in eleven languages – Polish, Czech, Slovak, Spanish, Italian, French, German, Swedish, Lithuanian, Turkish, and English – and applications for Apple (iOS), Android, and Windows 10. Their catalogue of titles contains approximately fifty thousand items, of which about six thousand are in Polish. For the French and Spanish versions, the real traffic is not generated by citizens of these countries but by readers in French-speaking African countries and in Latin America. This explains why registered users come from twenty-three countries, despite there being "just" eleven language versions.

For many years, the company's management decided on target markets using a simple rule: "Avoid markets where Audible dominates." In 2017, however, Audioteka won a tender, in competition with Amazon/Audible, to provide an app for a German mobile operator. Marcin Beme promotes a bold vision of Audioteka's future as holding second place in the global landscape, just behind the unbeatable Audible. Only time will tell if his company can do it. At present, the international growth of Audioteka is fuelled by the founder's entrepreneurial orientation – proactive and risk-taking behavior, presence at conferences and events, search for new partners and business opportunities – in combination with the company's reputation and brand and the team's relational and business modeling capabilities.

Kooptech Cinema

Kooptech Cinema is a small high-tech company producing machines that wash and dry advanced 3D glasses for cinemas. With a growing number of 3D movies, the demand for such machines has grown, but it is still a relatively limited market: cleaning machines are very effective, and one is usually enough for a whole cinema complex. Kooptech was established in 2010 and employs 14 people. It has a turnover of 2.2 million EUR and exports all its products to almost 40 countries; the USA, with 60 percent of sales, is the largest single market.

The company did not invest in sales force and marketing. Instead, it allied with a large Japanese supplier of cinema equipment to reach its main customers in the USA and Asia. For smaller markets (e.g. in Europe) the firm serves itself, having developed an informative webpage, and attends cinema equipment fairs and shows. This has allowed its team to develop some marketing flair to complement the distribution provided by its Japanese partner.

Initially the company focused on development of the product, essentially a washing machine combined with a dryer. The technological secret lies in the perfection of components, with the assembly and application of appropriate fluids and processes to make the glasses perfectly clean and dry. The firm considers its market knowledge as a key resource and capability. The owner states:

We have a good product but it is not very important. We spent a lot of time to learn the logic of the industry, how is it organized, to figure out what is the business model of 3D glasses and such movies. Machines, technologies, and almost every-thing can be easily bought today. But we have this unique knowledge about the logic of the market that allows us to better address our clients' demands.

Another crucial capability, in the managers' opinion, is their customer service focus. The company tries to respond immediately to each request or complaint. The owners of the company or top managers often travel to customers' locations in order to place the machines and later to service them. Currently, their policy is to deliver free parts:

We want to build long-term credibility. And we want our customers to feel that we will never leave them without support. How much money we can make on parts? Almost nothing, compared with our margins. Hence, customers cover travel and lodging costs of service person, and the parts are for free. And we never ask if they still have a warranty or not.

Industry knowledge and customer focus are of crucial importance in the opinion of the managers, equally important in every export market. However, the ways they are presented and sold differ. The managers view the key distinction as being that in some markets, personal relations must support business, while in others, this factor is less important. One of them described it in the following way:

In the USA, you have to know your partner as a person and mix business and personal credibility. The firm is just an organizational form – they do business with you, personally. In Germany you are just a firm – you sit down at the table and negotiate a contract. In the Middle East you have to develop and build both personal and business relations and it takes time. And you have to allow them to negotiate and win something. Generally in Asia it is important that partner gets something in order to be satisfied – a discount, faster service, or a bribe. And in former Soviet Union you have to sit down with them and drink. And become friends. So every market is the same, but different.

Among the most important capabilities explaining the company's inter-national success are its R&D efforts to develop high-quality equipment for the cinema industry; absolute focus and personalized customer service that is a source of competitive advantage in many markets; flexibility and adaptability in the approach to each international market, and a drive to learn industry and markets specificities.

Granna

Granna is a family-owned business that publishes educational games for children, youth, and adults. Ewa and Konrad Falkowski founded the company in 1991. As parents of two daughters of preschool age, they were well aware of the poor offering of educational games. The idea of the company arose from their passionate drive to make children happy when they learn. The early years of the company are reminiscent of the history of many entrepreneurs – a small production facility in a rented garage and distribution by the owner himself.

Currently, the company's offerings include over 120 titles, it employs 120 people, and its games are available in more than thirty countries, among which the most important are Ukraine, Czech Republic, Slovakia, Italy, Lithuania, and Canada. It has a turnover of five million euro, of which 17 percent accounts for game exports, and 30 percent for exports of services (contract manufacturing).

The first, sporadic attempts to sell to the Russian market were in 1996–1997, but the economic crisis in Russia forced the founders to retreat from this market to focus on Poland's growing domestic market. As the company grew successfully in its local market, it postponed the decision to resume exports for several years. Finally, in 2003, a small entrepreneur from the Czech Republic approached the founders, expressing interest in distributing their games. It was a signal for the owners that export through local distributors might be an interesting option. Since then, the company has been regularly exhibiting at international toy and games fairs, expanding its contacts and its range of markets. Growing revenues in foreign markets encouraged the owners to further expand their production capacity and invest in new games. An important moment in the company's history was the release of "Super Farmer." The game became a blockbuster title in Poland, translated into many languages and offered in twenty-five markets. It eventually reached a record level of one million copies sold.

The company builds its presence in foreign markets only through exporting and local distributors. Some bad initial experiences with licensing and cooperation with an American partner made the owners reluctant to use this entry mode. The owners believe that good relationships with distributors are essential for the company's growth in foreign markets.

In each market, Granna cooperates with one distributor who has exclusive rights to sell its games. The owners are convinced that their local partners have the best knowledge and access to sales channels. Each local distributor takes responsibility for the organization of sales and marketing activities in the local market, while Granna's managers and employees offer assistance with the selection of games, necessary adaptations (translation of instructions and text on the packaging), organizing transport, and preparation of promotional materials in the local language, covering the cost of printing and graphic design. Additionally, the company offers its partners the option of placing their logo on the packaging, even with small orders.

Although the final selection of games is made by distributors, Granna's managers offer assistance, and they carefully select and develop new games for export markets. With time, they developed a sensitivity to cultural differences, recognizing that certain graphic symbols or narratives in a game description may be problematic, such as a red cross in Turkey, breeding pigs in Israel, or a mention of World War II in Hungary (the Kingdom of Hungary was a member of the Axis powers). At the stage of creating and preparing games for foreign markets, the company now attempts to eliminate culturally sensitive symbols that may be unacceptable in certain regions of the world. Thus, for example, in the game "Rancho," an extension of "Super Farmer," pigs are not present among the farm animals.

Over the years, the process of selecting new distributors has become more structured and less opportunistic. A dedicated export department conducts the search for new partners, with contacts initiated mainly at trade fairs. The search for partners is preceded by a selection of potentially productive foreign markets. Aspects such as the size of the product market, growth forecasts, the popularity of board games as leisure activities, and transport costs are taken into account. Entering a specific market is thus the result of the interest of managers in a particular country, after analyzing and recognizing suitable markets, and discussions with potential partners or distributors at trade fairs.

In recent years, sales of production services to foreign publishers (contract manufacturing) have become an important revenue stream. Their partners from developed Western European countries increasingly recognize the company's production skills, combined with publisher experience, as a valuable capability. For example, the German market for board games is one of the largest in the world, with a strong culture of game playing and many internationally recognized local firms. Granna's efforts to enter this market with its own games have been unsuccessful except for a few sporadic export contracts. However, the company recently entered this market as a supplier of production services to German games producers that recognized that Granna production has a better combination of quality, prices, and delivery time than other, often Asian offerings. Moreover, Granna's publisher experience is an additional differentiator and value-adder, as Granna can provide advice on how to improve the partners' game logic, spotting inconsistencies or difficulties.

Nearly half of Granna's revenues (47 percent) are now generated from exports of goods and services (contract manufacturing). The key capabilities that have enabled this family business to achieve a high degree of internationalization include games development capability, relational capabilities (long-term and good relations with distributors in many countries), sensitivity to cultural differences when developing new products, and production capability.

Prochem

Prochem is a classic engineering firm specializing in the chemical industry. It designs installations and entire factories, buys and assembles equipment, and monitors investment processes. Over its more than seventy years it has operated mostly in Poland, with occasional contracts carried out in the Middle East and CEE countries. It currently employs approximately 200 specialists and has a turnover close to 45 million euro. The turnover depends mostly upon economic conditions, and in some years (especially when the company has a large international contract), revenues have exceeded 70 million euro.

The firm has resources and capabilities typical of a professional service firm in this industry. Its core resources are reputation, competent and experienced teams of diverse specialists, and established relations with suppliers of equipment and construction companies. A capability to perform and monitor the total investment process, with the support of 3D design processes using sophisticated software, is the key technological capability, but it is not unique globally. In essence, every modern engineering company must have this capability nowadays, but it is still not standard in Poland. Engineering companies differ mostly in their industry specialization (energy sector, railroads, consumer, mechanical, or chemical) and Prochem has unique history and knowledge accumulated in the chemical industry.

Prochem used to operate internationally in the 1970s when Poland exported chemical technologies and factories to Africa and Asia, but always as a subcontractor to Polish foreign trade organizations. These projects ended in the 1980s and today, the firm bids opportunistically for international contracts of two kinds – turnkey factories and as a second-tier supplier of engineering services. In both cases, the major resources – software, teams of competent engineers, international experience, and references – are important, but none of them creates a particular competitive advantage, because every bidding party must have them. As one of our interviewees indicated:

Some of our resources and capabilities are internationally useful, and some are useless. Generally our Polish reputation is not very relevant internationally. Knowledge of our engineers is the key but we do not get any premium for our tools and software. And our relations with suppliers are not important, because in many international markets you have to work with local suppliers because only they have necessary local certifications ... Local markets are very idiosyncratic due to local regulations and it is impossible to build competitive advantage if you are not a global player.

Large international players in this sector have substantial advantage over Prochem, especially in bidding for turnkey projects. They either control patents for particular chemical technologies and installations or are allied and promoted by suppliers of particular technologies that come almost invariably from developed Western countries. Also, as they operate worldwide, they can show many more factories or installations of particular types as their references. As a top manager of Prochem stated:

For example Fluor can sell three installations of particular type per year. We, in Poland, can sell one per ten years and therefore we cannot accumulate such knowledge, experiences and use them as references in the bidding process ... We are a good shoemaker, but we do not know how to design shoes and sell them worldwide.

Occasionally Prochem exports its services and works for international players, but the firm has found it very difficult to develop unique resources and capabilities in this area. In some cases, for example working for oil platform contractors, Prochem learned that such companies carefully break down the total task into many elements and always control the final and most difficult elements of the design to prevent diffusion of knowledge. Also, other companies have made very good offers to the best engineers and designers from Prochem at the end of such contracts, and many of them have moved, thus taking their knowledge, experience, and contacts with them. Finally, as a person responsible for this type of contract stressed, exporting such services is not easy in spite of cost advantage because global players are not eager to share their work:

They often even did not want to use us as a supplier of design and engineering services in spite of the fact that we can do it equally well and cheaper. The reason is very simple – when buyers learn that they use cheaper suppliers of professional services they immediately demand lower prices.

Thus Prochem has resources and capabilities, but they are distinctive only in the company's local domestic market. It has a long history, reputation, accumulated knowledge, certifications, competent staff, and an ability to manage large projects. These capabilities are also important in international markets, especially in CEE countries, where from time to time Prochem wins a contract for large projects (e.g. in Hungary or Belarus) due to its unique experience or being part of larger alliance. However, it does not have specific capabilities that make Prochem competitive in Western European markets other than lower costs. Therefore, it occasionally provides large Western engineering companies with specialized engineering services, but these contracts have never led to long-term cooperation.

7.4   Conclusions

Table 7.5 summarizes the major capabilities identified in the Polish companies studied. A descriptive summary of the firms' key capabilities is presented in Table 7.6.

The extant literature suggests that exploration motives drive emerging market firms to undertake international expansion in more developed markets. They intend to acquire more sophisticated assets and capabilities owned by developed country multinationals, either to offset home market competition (Luo & Tung, 2007), upgrade their resource pool to compete successfully with advanced-market peers in global markets (Amsden & Chu, 2003; Guillén & García-Canal, 2009), and/or to escape poor home country conditions, such as underdeveloped institutions or economic backwardness (Cuervo-Cazurra et al., 2015; Cuervo-Cazurra & Ramamurti, 2017).

At the beginning of the political transformation of Poland, most Polish companies benefited from the combination of high market growth and relatively low buyer expectations. Entrepreneurial strategies and "good enough" products and technologies sufficed in the marketplace (Obłój, Obłój & Pratt, 2010; Gorynia et al., 2014). Over time, companies improved their offerings, but only after they started exporting or tried outward investments and discovered that their "good enough" products and technologies were not good enough for advanced international markets. Also, they discovered that they lacked managerial skills and experience in international operations, and they had to overcome the liability of a foreign country of origin.

While the sequences in which the companies studied addressed these issues varied, the pattern of development of strategic capabilities was similar. Our findings reveal that the performance of Polish firms, especially in foreign markets, is shaped by their ability to develop strategic competences in three areas: product and technology improvement, relationship management, and local responsiveness.

The drive to improve products and technologies emerged because managers had to change their mental maps and accept that their products and/or processes were not good enough to compete internationally. Research and development, technologies, and production facilities had to adapt to the demanding conditions of international markets. Processes to upgrade, adapt, and certify products were put in place over time, resulting in real capability development. Some companies used adjacent

Table 7.5 Capabilities of Polish firms studied

Major capability category	Subcategories	MNC			Exporters		
		HT	LT	S	HT	LT	S
		Aphsens	*Nowy Styl Group*	*Audioteka*	*Kooptech*	*Granna*	*Prochem*
Obtaining resources	Resource identification	✓	✓				
	Ability to purchase product inputs						
	Ability to develop resources internally	✓	✓				
Product/service capabilities	Product manufacture	✓					
	Research & development	✓	✓		✓	✓	
	Local product/service adaptation	✓	✓		✓	✓	✓
Operations and management	Production management			✓			
	Supply chain management			✓			
	Hard skills						
	Soft skills						
	Entrepreneurship		✓		✓		
	Cross-cultural management		✓				
Marketing	General sales capabilities		✓				
	Understanding local customer needs	✓	✓				
	Corporate brand and reputation	✓	✓	✓	✓	✓	✓
Managing external environment	Political capabilities	✓	✓			✓	
	Relationship capabilities	✓	✓	✓	✓	✓	✓
	Adjusting to poor infrastructure		✓				
Other	Business modeling		✓	✓			✓

Notes: HT = high-tech manufacturing; LT = low-tech manufacturing; S = services

Table 7.6 *Strategic capabilities of Polish firms studied*

	Multinationals			Exporters		
	Aplisens	Nowy Styl Group	Audioteka	Kooptech	Granna	Prochem
	Internal development of products' quality (own design offices, extensive R&D operations) to face competition from developed market firms Knowledge and skills in acquiring & maintaining certificates Flexibility & customer responsiveness – meeting individual customer demands (high flexibility and competent support as differentiators) Relationship with distributors (buffer warehouses)	Product capabilities and R&D activity → as a result of internal development, contract manufacturing (early stages) and acquisitions of Western companies High vertical integration and production skills (most modern, automated factory in Europe) High responsiveness to markets' differences Cross-cultural management → integration of acquired firms and adjusting international structure	Leveraging relationships with mobile phone manufacturers, mobile operators, and later car makers to penetrate domestic and then foreign markets Business modeling → from selling content to selling content and platform solutions (website, apps for smartphones, software for cars); leveraging waves of mobility (people, content, technology) Reputation & brand Founder's entrepreneurial spirit in-built in organizational culture	R&D capabilities (patents and technical solutions) Understanding industry challenges & issues Understanding markets & customers Customer focus (solving customers' problems) Founder's entrepreneurial spirit in-built in organizational culture	Creative games development Cross-cultural capabilities that help in development of culturally sensitive games (graphics, descriptions) Production skills, combined with publisher reputation and experience → contract manufacturing Long-term, close relationships with distributors	Specialized engineering capabilities (chemical installations), recognized in CEE markets Lack of (transferrable) ownership advantages to be leveraged in Western markets; ownership advantages regionally bounded

Reputation – international image enhances odds of successful cooperation with foreign customers in Poland

Product and production capacity

Business modeling – from simple individual pieces of furniture to developed furniture systems & design segment (corporate clients)

Reputation – "magnet" for acquisitions

Founder's entrepre-neurial spirit in-built in organizational culture markets of former communist countries as an intermediary stage in learning how to do these things, but usually it was competition in Western markets that triggered real development of the necessary capabilities for improvements in products and technologies. As explained by one of the CEOs:

We are competing with Western companies that spend millions on development, improve parameters. If we do not do it, we will fall. Therefore, we have to invest in development to have the same parameters.

Two other very specific but related capabilities that we observed in practically all studied cases are the development of relationships with partners in international markets (e.g. distributors) and of sensitivity to the local cultural and business environment. All the companies we studied stressed the importance of being able to develop lasting relations with local partners. There are two main reasons. First, practically none of the companies we studied had sufficient resources to manage their growth and internationalization on their own. Hence they needed local partners to help them access resources, gain knowledge and experience, and develop distribution. Next, liabilities stemming from being foreign made operations in international developed markets difficult. Therefore good partnerships helped the firms to attain legitimacy and good reputations. In essence, the capability to develop and manage relationships help to embed a company in the local environment.

While relationship capability is essentially a matter of "how to connect," resolving the issue of being foreign requires adaptation to new conditions and efforts to develop competitive advantage. The companies we studied became sensitive to their target cultural and business environments and keen learners of idiosyncrasies in the local contexts. These capabilities helped them to adapt their products and technologies and gain local certifications in response to local demands, but additionally they signaled that they were making an effort and were prepared to adapt to almost any demands of their new partners and customers. In such ways they differentiated themselves from both local competitors and multinationals from Western markets. Their local sensitivity and responsiveness exemplified the motto "we try harder" as a vehicle to gain reputation, build trust among local partners and customers, and overcome the liability of being from a foreign country.

The final strategic capability common to the companies studied is the ability to combine acquired capabilities into an "internationalization template." Each of the firms accumulated knowledge and transformed tacit knowledge into financial and operational procedures for managing international operations, local responsiveness and product adaptation, and long-lasting relationships, in a manner proposed by the Upsalla framework (Johanson and Vahlne, 2009). For each of these companies, the template was different, depending upon countries that they entered, their mode of entry, and the results. The template of Prochem is simple and related primarily to export of services and occasional turnkey projects in formerly communist countries. The template of Nowy Styl Group is very complex and reflects the size and maturity of this large multinational corporation. Each of these templates is in itself a strategic capability in the management of international operations that may allow these companies to repeat complex and risky strategic moves in new locations in the future.

8   Emerging Market Multinationals

The Case of Kazakhstan

Venkat Subramanian and Almira Abilova

In recent years, scholars have sought to understand the outward internationalization of emerging market multinational enterprises (see, for example, Luo & Rui, 2009; Gubbi et al., 2010). This stream of research has focused mainly on motivation for internationalization and "gives little indication of how well companies will succeed when investing and operating overseas" (Luo & Rui, 2009); it therefore seems necessary to advance the research on the successful internationalization of emerging economy enterprises (Lau & Bruton, 2008; Gammeltoft, Barnard, & Madhok, 2010).

The focus of this chapter is to explore the factors that influence success in the market-seeking activities of emerging market firms, and the capabilities they bring to these activities. We examine these dynamics within the context of Kazakhstan. The objective of this chapter is to identify key contextual conditions in a transitioning and emerging country that has unique historical and administrative heritage, and link such conditions to the evolution of companies in a variety of industries. Institutionally, Kazakhstan is evolving, and firms have had to adapt to this changing and uncertain environment. Economically, the country is dominated by a few resource-based industries. We drew the firms in this study from non-resource-based industries such as transport, banking, and retail. These firms have attempted to build country-specific competitive advantages in Kazakhstan, and such capabilities have in turn created value in particular international markets. However, the scope of such expansion is limited, given the early stages of internationalization in these companies, few of which have capabilities that are mobile across borders beyond neighboring countries.

Kazakhstan is a relatively new country, having been a nation-state for about twenty-five years, since the collapse of the Soviet Union. The country moved into the upper-middle income group in 2006. It went through a painful and somewhat chaotic transition from a planned economy, with almost complete state ownership of economic activity, to a market economy. After the Soviet Union's collapse, GDP contracted between 1993 and 1999, with a contraction of 25 percent of GDP in the

Table 8.1 *Socioeconomic indicators in Kazakhstan, 2016–2018*

	2016	2017	2018
Population size (at end of year) millions	17.9182	18.1573	18.3956
Employed population, millions	8.5536	8.5852	8.7097
Unemployed population, millions	0.4455	0.4423	0.4419
GDP, billion KZT	46,971,150.0	53,101,281.80	58,785,737.70
GDP, million USD	137,278.3	162,887.4	170,536.8
Volume of industrial output (goods, services), billion KZT	19,026,781	22,790,209	27,576,067
Mining and quarrying gross output (service) production, billion KZT	9,397,619	11,568,785	15,202,227
Agriculture gross output (service) production, billion KZT	3,684,393.2	4,070,916.8	4,388,637.2
Manufacturing industry output production, billion KZT	8,046,845	9,400,848	10,427,356
Investments in fixed capital, billion KZT	7,762,303	8,770,572	11,130,171
Investments in fixed capital, million USD	22,686.2	26,903.6	32,288.5
State budget deficit, billion KZT	−737,717.6	−1,455,319.8	−833,072.3
State budget deficit, percent of GDP	−1.6	−2.7	−1.4
Volume of retail trade, billion KZT	7,974.4	8,892.9	10,069.7
External trade turnover, million USD	62,113.6	78,102.9	93,489.7
Export trade turnover, million USD	36,736.9	48,503.3	60,956.2
Import trade turnover, million USD	25,376.7	29,599.6	32,533.5

new country's first two years. However, after a difficult adjustment, the economy grew between 2001 and 2008 (World Bank, 2018a); within the past two decades the economy transitioned from the lower-middle income level to the upper-middle. Since 2002, GDP per capita has risen six-fold and poverty incidence has fallen sharply. In the early to mid-2000s, the GDP growth rate was on average 10 percent a year, the highest growth rate among all the countries of Central Asia. Table 8.1 shows general socioeconomic indicators of Kazakhstan for 2016–2018.

Thanks to natural resources such as oil, gas, and minerals the country has expanded its reach and built strategic partnerships with Europe, the USA, and China. The country enjoys a good strategic location: neighboring China, the world's largest and fastest-growing economy; connected by rail with Russia and Europe; and with ports in the Caspian Sea. From the beginning, Kazakhstan was able to secure international contracts with neighbors: completing major oil agreements with China in 1997, building an oil pipeline from the Caspian to the Russian Black Sea port of Novosibirsk in 2001, and signing a deal with China for construction of an oil pipeline to the Chinese border in 2003 (Alvarez, 2016).

The economy, though, remains poorly diversified: beginning in the early 2000s, oil and gas have accounted for more than half of Kazakhstan's industrial output and more than two-thirds of its exports, and many of its other industries are dependent on oil (World Bank, 2018a). In the post-Soviet era, the labor-intensive agricultural sector became steadily less productive. In the manufacturing sector, however, there has been growth in the production of construction equipment, agricultural machinery, and some defense items (Library of Congress, 2006).

Thanks to revenues from energy sources and natural resources, Kazakhstan's economy stabilized somewhat beginning in 2000, enhancing its ability to invest abroad. In 2010, Kazakhstan joined Russia and Belarus to establish a customs union in an effort to boost foreign investment and improve trade. The customs union evolved into a Single Economic Space in 2012 and the Eurasian Economic Union (EAEU) in January 2015. The economic downturn of its EAEU partner, Russia, and the decline in global commodity prices from 2014 to 2015 contributed to an economic slowdown in Kazakhstan, which continues to experience its slowest economic growth since the financial crises of 2008–2009 (Mostafa & Mahmood, 2018). In 2014, Kazakhstan devalued its currency, the tenge (KZT), and announced a stimulus package to cope with its economic challenges. In the face of further decline in the ruble, oil prices, and the regional economy, Kazakhstan announced in 2015 it would replace its currency band with a floating exchange rate, leading to a sharp fall in the value of the tenge. Since reaching a low of 391 to the US dollar in January 2016, the tenge has modestly appreciated, helped by somewhat higher oil prices.

Kazakhstan's outward foreign direct investment (OFDI) grew significantly from 1998 to 2002. Between 2001 and 2002, its OFDI grew tenfold from $42.6 million to $463.9 million (UNCTAD, 2006). The rapid increase was due mainly to increased outward investment by the energy sector, the search for new resources and markets, and investments in developed countries.

As Figure 8.1 shows, from independence until about 2007, Kazakhstan's net foreign assets were relatively small. In 2007, KazMunai Gas made a purchase of the Romanian firm Rompetrol, increasing its net foreign assets. In the second decade following its independence, Kazakhstan became one of the largest outward investors among the former Soviet Union countries. The major source of Kazakhstan's OFDI are quasi-public and private companies such as Kazatomprom and national companies such as KazMunaiGas in search of new markets for oil exports, new refineries, and new processing technologies. Due to this improvement in

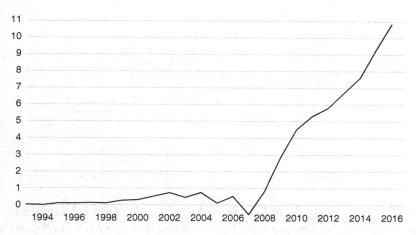

Figure 8.1 Net foreign assets in Kazakhstan, 1993–2016 (trillion USD)

OFDI, Kazakhstan's OFDI world performance index rose from a position of 128 in 2006 to 46 in 2007.

The main beneficiaries of Kazakhstan's OFDI are Georgia and countries in Central Asia. For example, Kazakhstan has around 1 billion USD in net foreign assets in Kyrgyzstan in sectors such as banking, construction, energy, and metal mining and production.

Kazakhstan's challenging external environment caused a broad-based economic slowdown in 2014 and put upward pressure on inflation. In 2017, more favorable terms of trade and increased oil production supported an economic recovery and improved economic indicators in Kazakhstan. Despite some positive institutional and legislative changes in the last several years, investors remain concerned about corruption, bureaucracy, and arbitrary law enforcement, especially at regional and municipal levels. An additional concern is the condition of the country's banking sector, which suffers from low liquidity, poor asset quality, and a lack of transparency (CIA, 2018).

In the rest of the chapter, we will discuss the strategies and activities of Kazakh and regional companies that have tended to use a capability-based approach to internationalization.

8.1   Selected Kazakh and Regional Companies

We chose to study the following companies: Air Astana, Sberbank Kazakhstan, Kamaz Kazakhstan, Sportmaster, and Tsesna. These companies were chosen based on their profiles and their internationalization

Table 8.2 *Data collection matrix for the selection of Kazakhstani firms as case studies*

		Firm Category		
		Purely domestic	Exporter	Multinational
Industry	High-tech			Kamaz
	Low-tech		Tsesna	
	Service	Air Astana		Sportmaster
				Sberbank

strategies following the collapse of the Soviet Union. Of these five firms, two originate from Soviet times – Sberbank and Kamaz – while Air Astana and Tsesna are newer domestic firms that have tried to develop specific competitive advantages. Sportmaster evolved in the immediate aftermath of the dissolution of the Soviet Union. Another basis for our choice of firms was our wish to understand differences in the industry structures in which these companies operate and the effects of the specific institutional, economic, and social context of Kazakhstan. Table 8.2 shows the distribution of the selected firms by type of industry and level of internationalization.

The firms' managers were interviewed two or three times with follow-up clarifications on the phone, involving at least two senior executives from each company. In the sections that follow, we will examine the different cases in more detail and to how the selected companies expand into overseas markets.

Air Astana

Air Astana Company is Kazakhstan's national flagship carrier, with two main hubs: Almaty, the financial, industrial, and cultural capital of the south of Kazakhstan, and Astana, the capital in the north of the country. Its mission statement is "From the Heart of Eurasia, we are building one of the finest airlines in the world" (Air Astana, 2017). Air Astana serves sixty-four domestic and international routes with a fleet of thirty-three aircraft.

The airline's international strategy has evolved to develop two major thrusts – one focused on passenger routes and the other on providing maintenance, repair, and overhaul (MRO) services to other airlines in the region. In both cases, the airline leverages its location and lower costs as advantages to gain a foothold in overseas markets.

Starting in 2015, the airline rapidly expanded its regional and international network, using its locations in Astana and Almaty as hubs. Route expansion focused on neighboring China and broader Asia, including India, and destinations in the former Soviet Union and Europe. While initially the airline focused on passenger traffic within Kazakhstan and some select international destinations, the strategy evolved by creating a transit hub in Astana and Almaty to ferry passengers from China and India to European destinations and destinations in the former Soviet Union.

The specific capabilities for this strategy were to build the brand and a network, and to make alliances with other airlines to fill in "holes" in the network. The airline was a relatively new one in a new country and as such had a small network with little brand value and few alliance connections. Initially the airline focused on service quality, winning several international quality awards. In a second stage, the airline expanded into neighboring countries and European destinations and formed alliances with regional airlines to feed into its hubs. As part of this initiative, the company formed alliances and code-sharing partnerships with airlines in China, India, Russia, Turkey, and Europe to add more destinations to its network. Finally, it worked with the government to upgrade airport infrastructure in Astana. As a key part of its capability building, the airline often used access to joint venture partners in Europe, learning from their operations and technology. The company also hired several expats experienced in the airline industry to improve operations to meet international benchmarks. Air Astana has emerged as a credible player, connecting Chinese and Indian cities to destinations in Europe and the former Soviet Union.

The key contextual conditions that enabled Air Astana to develop an international strategy are its shareholding structure and the support of the government. The airline's shareholders are Samruyk Kazyna, the national holding company, which owns 51 percent of the shares, and British Aerospace, which owns 49 percent. The senior management is composed of expats with global experience in the airline industry. These influences helped to professionalize the airline from the beginning, contrary to the operational styles of many other state-held airlines in former Soviet Union countries, where political patronage played a major role. Air Astana's management was given wide leeway to lead the airline based on economic considerations rather than political and noncommercial ones. The government also invested in airport modernization as part of Expo 2017 in Astana. The larger airport and the exhibition allowed the airline to leverage on increased passenger traffic to further build its brand and network.

The second thrust of the internationalization was in the area of MRO services. For a number of years, Air Astana outsourced its services to MRO firms in China and Turkey. However, with the growth of its fleet, the airline started considering setting up its own MRO facilities, which also allowed the company to offer maintenance services to other airlines in the region. Air Astana had been performing relatively simple inspections, at the level known in the industry as A-checks, on their own planes. After gaining enough experience, Air Astana was planning to perform relatively more complex maintenance works such as C-checks, which the airline had until then been outsourcing. The engineering team of Air Astana proposed to open an MRO center to undertake C-checks when the airline's fleet size reaches 20 aircraft, but analysis indicated that the MRO operation would not break even at that fleet strength. However, as the airline was planning to grow to 33 aircraft, and with 29 more planes planned for delivery within the next few years, the economics of upgrading MRO capabilities became more attractive.

While the main reason for the MRO was to serve its own fleet, Air Astana hoped to attract clients from neighboring countries such as Russia, Tajikistan, and Kyrgyzstan. There were about 2,000 Airbus aircraft in the region, mostly in China (which had about 1,300 aircraft), and Russia and Turkey (which together had about 500 aircraft). However, all these three major markets had their own MRO operators, and hence Air Astana's MRO venture faced strong competition. As the chief engineer at Air Astana says:

There are some MROs in Russia, but they are not enough, we certainly expect that some of the airlines will fly in and repair their planes in Kazakhstan.

The likely targets are airlines based in other neighboring countries such as Tajikistan and Kyrgyzstan, and neighboring regions in Russia and China. However, the MRO will first have to build up its reputation and credibility, given that Air Astana is a new entrant in this business. The airline would also have to secure the technical certifications that are required to deliver such MRO services.

Air Astana brought some competitive advantages to this business. Low hourly pay rates in Kazakhstan potentially lower the cost of services; however, potential obstacles are fierce competition and the long distance to transport planes for major airlines from Russia. The engineering staff at Air Astana are experienced in maintenance services. For the many years Air Astana has been in operation, its engineers travelled to China and Europe to observe the maintenance work performed there. Therefore Air Astana had a pool of local staff in engineering and is not expected to hire expats when starting its own MRO.

However, the venture was relatively less successful compared to the initiative to increase international transit passengers. One reason was because the MRO required more experienced engineers and technical staff than Air Astana initially thought. There was only one academy of civil aviation in Almaty. However, EU standards of aviation were not applied and taught there, hence the students who graduated were not really qualified to work in the MRO operation. Previous attempts to create internship programs for students with engineering degrees also failed, because the majority of those interns did not like the career prospects or the entry-level pay in the engineering departments of the airline. As the chief engineer at Air Astana says:

We had students from top engineering schools interning with us. We took them in the hope that they would want to work with us after graduating; however, they did not want to work with us, they wanted to go directly to offices, become directors, and we understand that.

Therefore, Air Astana had to consider opening an aviation maintenance school, in which students would receive European certification upon graduation and would be qualified to perform aircraft maintenance at the MRO. The length of the study period would be fourteen to twenty-four months and the students would be high-school or college graduates, which meant a lead time of around two years. The training would be given by experienced local engineers who had worked for Air Astana for many years. As a result, Air Astana understood that some capability gaps still existed in their quest to build an internationally competitive operation in MRO, and they have started the process of developing these capabilities in-house.

For Air Astana, its international strategy is at times constrained by the national context. Kazakhstan is a long distance from both Western Europe and North America; therefore, the logistics and transportation of spare parts, aggregates, equipment, and materials from those regions becomes complicated and expensive. This situation is in contrast to having an MRO in Europe, where ten or twenty other MROs are located nearby, and in case of emergency parts can be easily traded with no customs control and relatively low logistics costs. Whereas in Kazakhstan, for Air Astana's MRO, one has to fly to the nearest MRO location, usually in China or Turkey. This means crew and aircraft have to pass through customs control and pay additional fees for transportation and customs clearance. All these additional steps can eventually delay repairs. Customs legislation in Kazakhstan, which tends to be rather cumbersome, further complicates the process. Air Astana often experienced having necessary parts or materials stuck in customs for a very long time. Air Astana has more recently agreed with the government authorities on a speedy customs process in Almaty.

Sportmaster

Sportmaster is the largest multicategory multibrand sport and outdoor retail chain in the former Soviet Union, with a strong presence in Kazakhstan. The company has 475 retail stores in Russia, Kazakhstan, China, Ukraine, and Belarus. It claims to be number ten globally among sport and outdoor retail companies.

The company started operations in Kazakhstan in the 2000s. There are twenty-four stores in Kazakhstan, with the second highest inventory turnover after Russia. The retail offering is almost the same throughout its five international markets. The store format adopted in Kazakhstan is the Super format, in contrast to the ones in Russia and Ukraine, where the company uses the larger Hyper format. The key capabilities in this business in Kazakhstan are similar to those in other national markets – product assortment, logistics, scale, supply chain, human resources, and IT. The company developed many of these capabilities in-house and subsequently scaled them through its network across its five markets.

Making choices on the right product offering is a key a capability in the retail business. Sportmaster applied advanced IT infrastructure and used analytics to learn about customer preferences and needs, and constantly updated the product offerings. The company partnered with IT software and hardware companies such as Cisco, IBM, Hewlett Packard, and Oracle. Its large IT team worked to ensure smooth processes and timely system updates, and made necessary improvements whenever issues arose. While the company collaborated with global technology firms, the company's internal IT team further customized these products.

Sportmaster's IT development team was located in Russia; however, the IT team sought to tailor localization updates for each country based on that country's specific needs. A central system helped to track the inventory in real time online. The analytics of the program included hourly sales, assortment of sales, the average sales check, the average cost of goods, and various coefficients of customer service, product turnover, etc. The system allowed the generating of many types of report in case the user needed to make decisions based on real-time data.

One crucial factor for success in the retail industry was an efficient supply chain. Sportmaster created a fast merchandising model served by an agile supply network. The company developed a multilevel hub-and-spoke distribution model, in which every country has its own large distribution center. The largest distribution center in Moscow occupied an area of 106,000 square meters. Shipping goods from supplier to the main hub for redistribution to countries downstream enabled economies of scale and enhanced quality control.

Originally, the company carried only mainstream brands and did not have a private label. The drawback of relying on mainstream brands was the relatively low margin. Tapping customer experience and knowledge gained from twenty years of operations, Sportmaster began in the late 1990s to develop its own private brands (such as Demix) to address specific market niches and harvest growth in store numbers and in the customer base. However, developing brand management capabilities and knowledge of different national markets went more slowly than did building up the firm's technical capabilities.

The aim of developing the private label was to offer customers more affordable prices yet trendy and high-performing solutions. Sportmaster products under private labels were manufactured through a scalable sourcing system operating in China, Bangladesh, Vietnam, India, and Indonesia, among others. Through cooperation with OEMs, the company developed supplier management capability.

To control supplier quality, the company established quality control hubs across the sourcing base. These hubs monitored the selection and regular audit of manufacturers and suppliers; quality control of materials, components, technologies, and end products; testing of functional features of products and materials; and shipments of end products. When an item that was displayed in a given retail store was identified as having a defect, every store in the network received an alert, thanks to a unified system. Every store would then remove the item from display or sale, thereby reducing possible customer complaints and the costs associated with returned goods.

Currently Sportmaster carries more than half its goods under its private label, having learned global branding practices from the top brands they have served. The company has continued to carry mainstream brands in order to keep attracting customers who are loyal to these brands. To develop their in-house private brand, the company set up a research and development center in Singapore in collaboration with the UK's University of Loughborough, renowned for its sports technology research. This unit, tasked to pioneer breakthrough sport technology, is associated with the Institute for Sports Research at Nanyang Technological University (NTU) and had the support of Singapore's Economic Development Board.

Competency in human resources is another key investment. Sportmaster developed its own educational centers to build this capability. For example, they established a center based on a prototype retail store in Almaty, where Sportmaster sends prospective employees for training. The candidates who successfully complete the training receive certificates. The training time was about a month. Candidates who passed all the exams and received the certificate were given a position. The company also established distance-learning and certification programs using videoconferencing for continuing personnel training.

Sportmaster also developed a culture of sharing experiences among the national networks within the company. Top and middle management frequently met to exchange ideas and share experiences. When Sportmaster was setting up its new business in China, subsidiaries from Russia, Kazakhstan, and Ukraine sent their specialists to build up the infrastructure and set up the store network in Shanghai and Shenzhen. The company emphasized sharing new technology and analytics across its network. Such sharing of experiences, the intensive use of technology, and optimization of the store network all provided the company with tools for effective cost control.

Some of the key challenges in Kazakhstan relate to the underdeveloped supplier network and changing institutional conditions. In the Kazakhstani market, the task of sourcing quality products was challenging. The majority of service providers had been newly established companies seeking to focus on short-term profits at the expense of building long-term relationships. Although Sportmaster established a lengthy and thorough selection process for suppliers, in the end some of suppliers still tended to be unreliable.

The Kazakh government sought to use technology to improve tax reporting, including e-submission of tax declarations and online submission from point-of-sale terminals. While the new regulations had the potential to simplify business reporting and perhaps increase the ease of doing business, the implementation of such processes tended to lag behind due to underdeveloped infrastructure and lack of IT personnel, among others factors.

As a result, businesses incurred costs of installation of such systems and also sometimes were fined for not reporting compliance on time. Usually, this occurred not because the company was not ready but because infrastructure on the government side was not up to speed. Other legal issues tended to arise because of contradictory laws for retail business that come from customer protection regulation and the tax authorities. Sportmaster worked with state authorities and business lobbies in order to resolve discrepancies in consumer and tax laws, with the aim of establishing one unified body of laws, but the regulatory agencies have tended to be slow to respond. In order to keep the business running and the customers happy, Sportmaster has tended to seek "creative solutions" to address the contradictions in different types of regulations. The company, in essence, had to build nonmarket capabilities that were not always uniquely location-specific to Kazakhstan but also applied in other neighboring countries that were experiencing similar institutional changes and evolution.

Given the risks it faces, the company's expected margins and returns are higher than in traditional Western markets. Margins of 3–4 percent tend to be considered good in Western countries, whereas in CIS countries, the company expects higher margin rates of 7–8 percent to make the risks worth taking.

Kamaz

Kamaz is the largest manufacturer of heavy load trucks in the former Soviet Union, producing 45 percent of heavy load trucks in the region, and the company is among the top twenty heavy load truck manufacturers in the world. Even after the demise of the Soviet Union, Kamaz remained the major supplier of heavy load trucks in Kazakhstan, Russia, and the broader CIS region. In the recent economic downturn, the fall of commodity prices depressed sales in Russia and the CIS region from 44 thousand units in 2013 to a low of 28.5 thousand units in 2015, but sales recovered to 38.2 thousand units in 2017.

Competing in this emerging market and other neighboring markets requires a wide distribution and service network, a range of trucks that work under tough weather and road conditions, and a price range that is attractive in this local market. In other words, the company needs engineering, manufacturing, marketing, and distribution capabilities to be able to compete effectively in this market.

For Kamaz, some of these capabilities were legacies from dependencies created by its heritage and history as the primary heavy load truck maker in the former Soviet Union. Kamaz was part of the Soviet industrialization process, and during those days, manufacturing and distribution were planned to meet government targets. Because Kamaz was the Soviet Union's only producer of heavy-duty trucks and tasked to respond to the needs of the entire country, the plant had a large capacity, allowing it to produce 150 thousand trucks and 250 thousand engines a year.

For many years, the primary goal was to be able to manufacture sufficient trucks to fulfill the government's plans. However, this period also laid the foundation for capabilities that later became the basis for the company's international expansion. During this period the company developed strong research and engineering capabilities and also established its own supply chain to feed its manufacturing facilities.

Kamaz has been operating in Kazakhstan's vehicle market for more than four decades. The Kamaz brand name became so synonymous with the heavy load truck category in the country that people called heavy trucks Kamazes. Such recognition allowed Kamaz to develop a strong brand name in Kazakhstan and the broader CIS market.

In the immediate post-Soviet era, European brands including MAN, Volvo, and Mercedes Benz entered local markets throughout the CIS, including Kazakhstan. However, such competition made only a small dent in Kamaz's dominant market share, as their trucks were in a higher price range than Kamaz. These brands took only a small part of the market and were viewed as niche, with Kamaz's cheaper prices giving it a competitive advantage over Western European manufacturers. As the director of Kazakhstan Kamaz, Marat Serzaliyev, mentions:

> The advantage is the price, which is substantial if you look at the vehicles of a similar class; Kamaz certainly wins over European brands in terms of price and quality, and of course in terms of service and spare parts availability.

In this new environment, Kamaz leveraged established assets such as its brand and its capabilities in engineering and manufacturing (which were part of its legacy), while investing in and learning new capabilities, particularly in product development, marketing, distribution, and service. While in the past the company had only a few models to offer its customers, it introduced a greater variety in anticipation of increasing competition. The company expanded its product development team, working with some of its Western competitors in selected markets to lean product design and development. Many different types of trucks, from tip trucks and heavy lorries to fire trucks, were built on chassis from Kamaz. The company sought feedback from customers through its extensive dealer network and modified or added new features to its products in response to customer requirements.

The Kamaz engineering facility in Kazakhstan also developed trucks that were particularly suitable for Kazakhstan's roads and needs. Such capabilities were established with new product development centers. Customers were able to order their preferred specifications and request customized modifications to their trucks. This contrasts with the Soviet past, when the company offered only a standard set of trucks with little customer input to the design or manufacturing.

> Because consumers come and tell us, that they need a vehicle that has this or has that or that they need something that is not in the database, but something else.

Another capability that Kamaz actively developed was the expansion of its distribution and service network in Kazakhstan, in Russia, and elsewhere abroad. From the onset of Kamaz's history, the Soviet government had ordered the company to build distribution and service networks throughout the former country. This network is now available in Kazakhstan and the whole CIS region, with seventeen service and dealership centers in Kazakhstan itself. Over time, this service network has provided a strong barrier to entry for other competitors, particularly Western ones.

In contrast to the fragmented maintenance system of the previous era, the company has implemented an integrated maintenance system built on the principle of a one-stop shop and providing a full range of services to the consumer. The development of the service network had two aims – the construction of new centers and the reconstruction of existing service centers. As for the dealers, the company was guided by an internal document called the "Guide for dealers of PJSC KAMAZ," which defines all the conditions that dealers must meet. The guide specifies the requirements for the certification of dealer and service centers, which allows the company to provide a uniform service format and recognizable official dealers for consumers and to standardize the main business processes of the dealers. Customers know that when they face technical problems with Kamaz trucks, they will have little difficulty in obtaining spare parts or getting professional service through authorized dealers.

In recent years, as Chinese companies started penetrating the Kazakh market with cheaper prices and acceptable quality, Kamaz's market share began to drop substantially. While Kamaz still has the highest market share among all the brands, Chinese manufacturers have gained a significant share of the Kazakh market through aggressive competition. Among the six most popular brands for medium- and large-capacity trucks and trucks under the age of three years, three companies from China were represented. Shacman was in second place (1,383 units), occupying more than 10 percent of the market, and second only to Kamaz. Howo had 8.4 percent of the market, occupying the fourth place, and Foton had 4.4 percent of the market at sixth place.

In order to sustain its market share in Kazakhstan, therefore, Kamaz needs to choose a different positioning strategy using the strengths and capabilities it has obtained over time being the leader in the market.

Sberbank

Sberbank is the largest bank in the former Soviet Union, founded in 1841. By the end of 2017, Sberbank had spread across twenty-two countries with about 145.6 million clients including 14.8 million internationally, with 325 thousand employees worldwide. The main activities of the bank included providing financial services to corporate and private clients. The share of international business amounted to 14 percent of the group's assets.

Sberbank is among the top five largest banks in Kazakhstan and in the fourth place by assets. It has received many awards. After 2010, many international banks and a few local banks exited the Kazakh market because of currency volatility and high dependence on commodity prices to fuel the economy. However, Sberbank remained in the market and continued to grow. The head of Sberbank's Kazakhstan retail division, Alexey Akimov, described the overall situation as follows:

Sberbank is feeling great and is growing its positions. Therefore, in general, I assess the situation as positive. Well, I also think that the proximity of the markets Russia and Kazakhstan has its influence.

Sberbank has provided a full range of banking services to consumers in Kazakhstan and positioned itself as a universal bank competing with other large banks such as Halyq, Qazkom, and Tsesna, which have strong backing from local government. After Russia and Turkey, Kazakhstan is the largest market for Sberbank. Compared to the Russian market, Kazakhstan may seem relatively small. However, the Kazakh operation is Sberbank's second largest international subsidiary, and quite a successful one. The role of Kazakhstan increased noticeably after Sberbank had to sell off its Ukrainian subsidiary for a knock-down price as a result of sanctions that prohibited money transfers between Ukraine and Russia in 2017, due to the conflict in Eastern Ukraine.

The main reasons that Sberbank has remained successful in the market are its international outlook, its sharing of knowledge and capabilities, its ability to innovate, and its focus on service quality. Other important competencies have been technology, creating a service mentality, and developing and nurturing key relationships with institutional decision makers. When the crisis of 2015 hit the region (caused by the crash in oil and commodity prices followed by currency devaluation), Sberbank had to face the same set of challenges as other local banks. However, it weathered the crisis better than other local banks, as it had a strong asset base and profits from its international operations.

Like many emerging markets, Kazakhstan is a price-sensitive market. Sberbank, being a universal bank, tries to provide its clients with a high quality of service while maintaining relatively affordable fees and charges for its services. Its prices are competitive vis-a-vis its main competitors Halyq, Qazkom, and Tsesna, but it offers better service quality. The bank has also focused on establishing a physical presence in all the regions it works in. However, the goal of Sberbank is not to grow in terms of numbers of offices but to have a mix of physical branches in the different regions combined with digital banking options.

Many of Sberbank's key competencies, such as product development and technology, have been developed through its international network and then transferred and adapted to its different national subsidiaries. Banking service quality in the Kazakh context was originally low compared to its Russian operations. By applying practices that worked in Russia to the Kazakh market, Sberbanks performance rose above that of other local banks. For example, Sberbank's Net Promoter Score increased to 87 percent, viewed as an extremely high score.

Sberbank developed a competitive advantage in the market in terms of service quality. The new banking services and customer practices they brought to the local Kazakh market became highly successful. Customers came to view the bank as having the best mobile banking app and digital banking platform in the country, which helped attract many young customers.

This meant that the bank had to develop an understanding of customer needs to succeed on product development. The needs and behavioral model of customers in many former Soviet countries, such as Kazakhstan and Russia, tended to be similar. However, the evolution of tastes among Kazakh consumers tended to lag a year or two behind the Russian market. That played to the bank's advantage when adopting practices from Russia. However, such similarities do not apply across all functions and activities. In many cases Sberbank's analysis identified variance in the preferences of people from different regions in Kazakhstan. Hence Sberbank developed and adapted products that specifically addressed local market conditions.

Another key capability in banking is technology. Sberbank is considered one of the most technologically advanced banks in the region, constantly adopting new technology into its operations. On an ongoing basis, Sberbank has transferred its technology to the Kazakh market, while creating one large platform that allowed the transfer of technology internationally across its operations.

Similarly, Sberbank has tried to leverage its international network to develop its human capital. Sberbank wanted to rely primarily on local staff and to grow more talent locally. At the senior management levels, 20 to 30 percent of the managers are expats, while middle management staff are 95 percent local. To diffuse the innovations it had developed in its international network, the bank has regularly brought in management personnel from Russia, Kazakhstan, Ukraine and other countries. The

bank's Kazakhstan operations are closely integrated into its global network, though subsidiaries have considerable autonomy to make operational decisions.

Managing regulatory relationships is another key capability, crucial in
the banking business in the former Soviet space. While at first glance,
Kazakhstan's and Russia's regulatory environments may seem similar
because of their long-shared history, there are important differences
between the markets.

One example is how the banking laws in Kazakhstan have been influenced by Western practices rather than by laws prevalent in Russia and
other parts of the former Soviet Union. The Kazakhstani banking regulatory environment is more internationalized than that of Russia and
other parts of the former Soviet Union. Another difference is the degree
of government involvement in industry and the number of government-
owned businesses. In Kazakhstan, government corporations have played
a major role in the country's economy; in Russia, the involvement of the
state was subtler.

The bank has tried to cultivate strong long-term relationships with
regulators and has played a role in the evolution of banking regulation.
Sberbank developed key relationships with regulators, who often inter-
acted with them on the banking innovations Sberbank had brought to the
region. Sberbank has become known as an innovator in the banking
sector in Kazakhstan.

The ability to develop such relationships has proved to be a key asset in
this market. The CEO of Sberbank, Herman Gref, is Sberbank's brand
face and is a well-known person globally. He was featured in Forbes as one
of the highest-paid CEOs in the CIS countries. He was born in Kazakhstan
and has developed a very good relationship with the country's president.
He makes frequent visits to Kazakhstan and has featured in many forums
and conferences there. This good relationship has helped not only to
promote the bank's brand but also to maintain its position against competition from government-supported local banks. The head of Sberbank's
Kazakhstan retail division, Alexey Akimov, described it this way:

Gref is very respected and Sberbank is very respected, and there is a very positive
attitude toward Russia, and a good relationship toward the Russian authorities, so
we are associated with Russian experience, and, therefore, listen carefully to all
the news that we bring from Russia, so here we became sort of newsmakers, we
bring information and news from all over the world tried out in Russia or even not
tried, so people really hear us.

Large local banks such as Qazkom and Halyq, Tsesna and BCK, have
announced mergers; this creates strategic challenges and questions for

Sberbank as to how to maintain its position in Kazakh market. One way would be to grow in assets and try to compete with these merged banks, or they could stay focused on profiting from existing clients, providing excellent service and growing their client base gradually. After their merger Qazkom and Halyq would control 40 percent of the market, whereas Tsesna and BCK together would control 11 to 12 percent. Sberbank, in contrast, controls 6 percent of the market. With such gaps in market shares, the bank will have to consider how to stay viable and competitive in the market.

Tsesna-Astyk

Tsesna-Astyk is a leading company in the grain-processing industry and part of Tsesna Corporation, one of the largest firms in Kazakhstan. The corporate firm is one of the strongest national brands, familiar to every Kazakhstani. Over thirty years the parent company had evolved into a diversified firm, active in retail, construction, manufacturing, grain processing, and media.

The decision to transfer Kazakhstan's capital from Almaty to Akmola, which was carried out in 1998, played a crucial role in the development of the company. In the 2000s, Tsesna focused its resources on the development of the construction business. The company participated in building many strategic facilities for the new capital, including the Ministry of Finance. Tsesnabank and its subsidiaries, the insurance company Tsesna Garant and the investment and brokerage company Tsesna Capital, along with the Russian bank Plus Bank, became key parts of the company's development. In 2017, Tsesnabank celebrated its twenty-fifth anniversary. For the bank, these were years of dynamic development, during which it earned many awards from reputable business publications.

The largest project of the corporation was undoubtedly Tsesna-Astyk. The company dates back to 1969 with the commissioning of the grain reception center in the city of Tselinograd in the Kazakh Soviet Socialist Republic. Currently the company has more than 2,500 employees. It exports around 40 percent of its production and is one of the largest refined food product manufacturers in Kazakhstan. The main destinations of the company's exports are Russia, Tajikistan, Turkmenistan, Afghanistan, Mongolia, Kyrgyzstan, Uzbekistan, and, increasingly China.

To control delivery channels and the quality of its products, Tsesna-Astyk operates its own distribution centers in Almaty, Astana, Kokshetau, and Karaganda. Developing these distribution centers increased the company's vertical integration but allowed it to scale up quality control processes across multiple centers in the country. This move also reduced its dependence on partner networks, placing the company closer to the consumer.

Kazakhstan flour is a brand known in many export markets. In 2007, Kazakhstan became the world's largest exporter of flour, holding this position until 2010, when it fell behind Turkey. Due to active protectionist measures by neighboring countries and increased transportation costs, the country lost some market share.

The popularity of Kazakhstani flour was due to its ecological purity and desirable baking properties. Given these properties, demand for flour-based products from the country grew. Currently, 70 percent of the flour produced in Kazakhstan is exported to a wide variety of countries, including Afghanistan, Uzbekistan, Tajikistan, and Kyrgyzstan. More recently, new export destinations such as Turkmenistan, Mongolia, and Russia have opened up. The most promising direction for export is neighboring China.

The key capabilities Tsesna needed for overseas expansion were access to good-quality raw materials, processing and manufacturing capacity, marketing capabilities such as brand-building and distribution, skillful selection of which markets to enter, and good relationships with overseas buyers. In terms of access to raw materials, the company developed relationships with farms and installed quality control systems and processes to improve and sustain quality. Initially, small private farmers were hesitant, but as the company co-invested with these farmers in quality control and transport logistics, the farmers were more open and became part of the process in changing the previous arms-length model.

As observed earlier, the company is relatively vertically integrated. It has been active in crop growing, cattle breeding, grain storage, flour milling, macaroni and pasta production, bread baking, feed milling, logistics, and distribution. The resources needed for value addition – such as grain processing by Tsesna and other local firms in the Kazakhstani market – were relatively large and substantial for these players. Kazakhstani millers process 5.5 million tons of grain annually, producing about 4.2 tons of flour. Of these, 1.3 million tons are targeted for domestic needs of the country. The remaining 2.9 million tons are exported. Further, expectations are that shipments of both flour and processed grain will continue to increase, perhaps by 20 to 30 percent – primarily because of increasing demand from China, but also due to irregular harvests in Uzbekistan, Tajikistan, and Afghanistan.

In terms of selection of markets, the company targeted neighboring ex-Soviet states and other nearby countries such as Afghanistan, often through international organizations. The export story of Tsesna dates back to 1995. The first major destination was Afghanistan, where Tsesna exported not only floor but also more refined products such as pasta under the Tsesna brand. This initial foray came through contracts with international humanitarian funds such as UN, the Red Cross, and UNICEF. Such contracts with humanitarian agencies have continued since, with another contract in 2015 with the UN to provide flour produce to Tajikistan. The company developed key relationships with international organizations and a reputation for reliable supply at competitive prices.

The next big market was China. For a year, the company supplied flour to China on a trial basis, during which the volume increased threefold. In the future, the company expects a thousandfold growth, which will allow Tsesna to further increase capacity. According to the Statistics Committee of Kazakhstan, the country exported 1,918 tons of wheat and rye flour to China in 2015. By 2017, flour exports had increased to 9,504 tons.

Tsesna also invested in brand-building, positioning the brand in domestic and overseas markets as offering affordable quality and a wide product range. Such positioning required investments in marketing over time and, combined with developing relationships with key distributors such as supermarkets and smaller retailers, has enabled the company to expand its export footprint.

8.2   Discussion and Conclusions

When Kazakhstan emerged out of the collapse of the Soviet Union, its movement from a socialist to a market economy saw property rights established and encouragement for private entrepreneurship. This transition, while still ongoing, produced firms that succeeded at home and made inroads into international markets.

Much of Kazakhstan's international expansion has been within the former Soviet Union and other neighboring countries, largely due to shared language and other cultural legacies. These cases of Kazakhstan-based companies that have entered the international arena fall into two categories. One set is composed of legacy firms that were relatively successful in the new environment. Brand names such as Sberbank and Kamaz are familiar in the region and rely on legacy manufacturing and distribution systems they inherited from the socialist past. These firms adapted their domestic and foreign strategies – in terms of product portfolio, manufacturing, distribution, and services – and were able to compete quite well. They developed new competencies, particularly in product development, technology, marketing, distribution, and human resources, and integrated them with those existing competencies that were valuable in the new environment.

The second set of firms were creations of the new environment. They competed aggressively domestically and then increasingly in international markets. Both Air Astana and Tsesna built strong brands and invested in product innovation and in marketing and distribution competencies and capabilities. Both initially built their domestic market shares before venturing to enter overseas markets.

In many ways, the different companies in this study are similar in terms of their approaches to internationalization. All the firms that have succeeded took a process-based approach, building up their domestic business before expanding into neighboring markets, initially with limited product ranges, then expanding their ranges. This reflects the internationalization process that has been identified in the literature (Johanson & Vahlne, 1977, 2009). While aspects of the theories of international market entry strategies apply to transitional and emerging markets, those relating to the development of the capabilities that are needed to compete appear to be very different in some cases.

The ability to survive and succeed in institutional conditions that are still evolving and changing is another similarity. All these firms developed relationship competencies in their home market and then developed similar ones in foreign markets. As the new institutions under development gained credibility, networks and political connections remained important and the ability to manage relationships played a role in most of these markets. Each firm in this study developed relationships with key stakeholders that helped it expand into neighboring markets.

Some of these companies faced strong challenges, partly due to increasing competition as markets opened; some severe challenges to long-term strategy originated in immature institutional environments that have led to instability and uncertainty. Other challenges related to the potential for leadership changes, which may render existing relationships obsolete.

9 Internationalization Capabilities of Argentine Firms

Michel Hermans and Diego Finchelstein

9.1 Introduction

Argentina is the home economy for a diverse set of companies that have internationalized along widely divergent paths. This chapter examines the organizational capabilities of seven Argentinean firms and analyzes how these capabilities influenced their internationalization strategies. Following an overview of the dynamics of the Argentinean business context and how it conditions organizational strategies, we present brief case studies illustrating the firms' internationalization trajectories. As these firms share many of the macro-level contextual opportunities and constraints, we posit that their markedly distinct internationalization trajectories result from micro-level perceptions and interpretations of the business context and from the different organizations' ability to develop the necessary capabilities.

9.2 Argentina: Historical Economic Context

Early Context of International Business in Argentina

Argentina's integration with the international economy was very limited under the exploitative Spanish Crown. The small Buenos Aires population engaged in unauthorized trade with merchants from Europe, exchanging leather products for goods that represented a European lifestyle (Luna, 1994). Argentina's international economy remained dormant until the industrial revolution, when technological advances lowered transportation costs and lengthened storage life, making Argentinean exports of wool, wheat, and meat internationally competitive (Jones, 1996). These opportunities attracted inflows of foreign direct investment (FDI), mainly to develop agricultural production and related services.

Argentinean companies were among the first emerging market multinationals (Kosacoff & Ramos, 2010). The commodity trader Bunge and

Born (later absorbed by Bunge Ltd.) marketed agricultural crops internationally, while its subsidiary Molinos Rio de la Plata provided outward FDI to install food processing plants in Uruguay and Brazil. Other examples of Argentinean companies that invested in neighboring countries include shoemaker Grimoldi, beer maker Cervecerías Quilmes, and food processing machinery manufacturer Di Tella. As the twentieth century opened, GDP per capita in Argentina exceeded that of most European countries.

Industrialization through Import Substitution

In the 1930s, the Argentine government pursued import substitution industrialization (ISI) policies to stimulate local industrialization (Katz & Kosacoff, 1989). Initially, ISI had positive effects for less technology-intensive manufacturing sectors. While the agricultural sector continued to focus on exports, Argentinean companies developed technological capabilities for use in the internal market. Only a few engaged in outward FDI.

After World War II, the government, with IMF and UNCTAD support for its import substitution strategies, intensified ISI policies (Ingham, 1995). Although these subsidies and support programs aimed to improve existing products and processes, Argentine companies found themselves needing imported inputs to manufacture industrial goods, yet unable to import more sophisticated technology due to capital constraints (Katz & Kosacoff, 1989). The process of technological upgrading placed further stress on the country's balance of payments. In 1976, a military coup put an end to the ISI policies.

Pendular Reconnections with International Business

Swings between protectionism and market openness characterize recent economic history in Argentina. Between 1976 and 1982, Argentina's military government opened its domestic market and initiated a market liberalization phase. However, exchange rate control did not keep pace with inflation, causing overvaluation of the Argentine peso. Sharp increases of imports, mainly of consumer goods, combined with a rising interest rate and political instability, led to deep crisis in the Argentine industrial sector in 1980–1981 (Katz & Kosacoff, 1989). Outward FDI from 1977 to 1982 was negative, bottoming in 1980 when Argentinean firms repatriated USD 110 million (UNCTAD, 2018).

The return of democratic government in Argentina in 1983 led to economic instability. Growing public and private debt and ineffective exchange rate intervention anticipated hyperinflation between 1987 and 1991. At its peak, inflation reached 3,046 percent in 1989 (World Bank, 2018c). In March of 1991, the Convertibility Law pegged the Argentine peso to the US dollar. Extensive market reforms, strong FDI inflows, and privatization enabled foreign debt restructuring and provided reserves to the Central Bank, used to sustain currency convertibility. Economic stability allowed Argentinean companies to engage in outward FDI, which gradually increased (see Table 9.1).

However, economic stability was short-lived. During the second half of the 1990s, currency crises in emerging markets increased the cost of foreign debt for Argentina's public and private sectors. In 2001, rumors of Argentine peso devaluation motivated the government to freeze bank deposits to avoid a bank run. The subsequent political crisis, characterized by social unrest and five different presidents in less than three weeks, one of the world's largest ever defaults on sovereign debt. By the end of 2002, the exchange rate had tripled, and risks linked to political instability, international litigation, and unresolved macroeconomic issues caused Argentinean firms to repatriate USD 627 million (UNCTAD, 2018).

In 2003, the Kirchner administration sought to stabilize the Argentinean economy through a zero-deficit current account policy (Table 9.1). Growing commodity exports, with China becoming an increasingly important trade partner, enabled this move. The renegotiation of foreign debt provided the stability needed by Argentinean firms to invest abroad. However, this stability was – again – short-lived. Increased agricultural export taxes and forced nationalization of private pension funds in 2008, followed by nationalizations of several private firms, depressed investor confidence. The following years saw increased government control of the economy through its influence on prices of consumer goods, special permits for imports, exchange rate intervention, subsidies in the transportation and utilities sectors, and political control of the Central Bank and the National Institute of Statistics (OECD, 2017).

In December 2015, a coalition came into power with a platform focused on reconnecting Argentina to the international economy. The new government deregulated the exchange rate, liberalized cross-border capital flows, and abolished export duties (ECLAC, 2017a), renewing access to international capital markets. In addition to macroeconomic measures, the government launched regional and sectorial strategies aimed at increasing the competitiveness of Argentinean firms and attracting FDI. These included development of the Vaca Muerta oil and gas deposits in Patagonia, promoting lithium and precious metal mining projects, and enhancing Argentina's receptiveness to tourism. However, the growing current account deficit (see Table 9.1) and failure to reduce public spending increased public debt,

Table 9.1 *Argentina: key economic indicators, 1992–2017*

Year	GDP Growth (%)	Debt/ GDP (%)	Exports (million USD)	Imports (million USD)	Inward FDI flows (million USD)	Outward FDI flows (million USD)	Inflation (%)	Unemployment (%)	People in poverty (%)
1992	9.6	n/a	12,235	14,872	4,431	1,166	17.5	7.0	17.8
1997	8.1	29.6	31,030	37,537	9,160	3,653	0.3	13.7	26.0
2002	−10.9	166	29,146	13,429	2,149	−627	40.9	17.8	54.3
2007	9.0	62.1	66,346	53,400	6,473	1,504	25.7	7.5	36.6
2012	−1.1	40.4	95,168	83,213	15,324	1,055	25.6	6.9	25.7
2017	2.9	56.6	73,391	89,002	11,857	1,168	24.8	7.2	25.7

Source: Based on data collected from UNCTAD – UNCTADSTAT, 2019, Estudios DEPS. 2019, ECLAC – CEPALSTAT, 2019, INDEC, 2019, ODSA-UCA, 2019, Argentina Government webpage, 2019

raising Argentina's country risk and hence the cost of capital to Argentinean firms. At the time of writing this chapter, the government, facing a recession, sought IMF support to ease inflation and exchange rate volatility. Concerns about the course of the economy seemed likely to affect the results of the 2019 presidential elections and had the potential to trigger the next swing of the Argentine economy's pendulum.

9.3 Internationalization Trajectories of Seven Argentinean Firms

Understanding Firm-Level Dynamics

Notwithstanding early FDI activity (Bisang, Fuchs & Kosacoff, 1992), recurring swings in the political and economic arenas have acted as a brake to the internationalization of Argentinean firms. Small and medium-sized firms adapted to economic swings by restructuring local operations, but they had only limited, export-based exposure to international business (Hermans, 2003). Restructuring larger firms generally required entering new lines of business, giving rise to the emergence of *grupos*: diversified and largely family-owned conglomerates (Finchelstein, 2018).

The following sections describe the internationalization trajectories of seven Argentinean firms, with a focus on the organizational capabilities that enabled the development of these firms. Given the exploratory goal of this study and the ongoing evolution of our subjects, we relied on a qualitative case study approach. We conducted interviews with directors or executives at each of the companies and complemented our fieldwork with archival information to triangulate the data obtained. For each of the companies we developed a case study along a historical timeline, followed by an in-depth analysis of the organizational capabilities that were relevant to each company's internationalization trajectory. Table 9.2 positions each of the case companies according to their main activity and their degree of internationalization. Table 9.3 provides a general overview of the case companies.

Grupo Mirgor

Grupo Mirgor: Past to Present Grupo Mirgor assembles and markets components for the Argentine car manufacturing industry, consumer electronics such as TV sets, and cellular phones for the local market. As of 2017, Grupo Mirgor operated plants in the Argentinean South and in the greater Buenos Aires area, employing 1,500 workers, with sales of USD 1,077 million. It imports some of the parts and components it uses for its domestic production and has no meaningful direct exports.

Table 9.2 *Data collection matrix for the selection of Argentinean firms as case studies*

| | | Firm category | | |
		Purely domestic	Exporter	Multinational
Industry	High-tech	Grupo Mirgor		Grupo Bagó
	Low-tech		Bodega Lagarde	Arcor San Miguel
	Service			Grupo ASSA Globant

The company originated in the early 1980s, when Roberto Vázquez, Nicolás Caputo, José Luis Caputo, and Antonio Caputo perceived opportunity in Argentina's import substitution policies. Local manufacturing of passenger and light vehicles required the development of networks of local parts and components suppliers. Local suppliers were slow to introduce technological innovations such as air conditioning. Mirgor signed an initial agreement to supply air conditioning equipment for the Peugeot 504 model. Roberto Vázquez, President of Grupo Mirgor, observed that "the only problem was that we knew absolutely nothing about air conditioning equipment for cars." The company signed a technology transfer agreement with Air Car and obtained a license to establish a manufacturing facility in the Tierra del Fuego province, which offered tax exemptions. However, legal conflicts and restrictions imposed by the provincial secretary of industry halted the company's production, leading to temporary closure of the plant. According to Vázquez, "we faced many difficult negotiations with the secretary of industry."

Due to import substitution policies of the mid-1980s, car manufacturers such as Fiat, Chevrolet, and Renault were encouraged to incorporate Mirgor's air conditioning equipment into their vehicles. During the 1990s, regulation of the local automobile industry allowed car manufacturers and their suppliers to be integrated into global production networks. This policy change pushed Mirgor to adopt international production and quality standards.

In 1994, Mirgor floated 48 percent of its shares on the Buenos Aires, New York, and London stock exchanges. A holding company in which French car parts supplier Valeo had a stake controlled the remaining 52 percent. This allowed transfer of Valeo's proprietary technologies

Table 9.3 *Argentinean company profiles and financial information, 2017*

Company and industry	Sales (USD million)[a]	Assets (USD million)	Number of employees	EBITDA[b] (USD million)	Exports from Argentina (USD million)	Number of countries with company presence
Grupo Mirgor, manufacturing	1,077	559	1,500	106	nil	1
Bodega Lagarde, wine	6.17	n/a	50	0.61	2	1
San Miguel, agriculture	202	370	1,000	11.2	n/a	4
Grupo ASSA, IT	77.7	36	1,350	7.5	28	6
Grupo Bagó, pharmaceutical	1,300	n/a	7,200	350	n/a	7
Globant, IT	413.4	344	6,753	38.4	n/a	14
Arcor, food and sweets	2,551	1,922	21,000	252	n/a	123

[a] Based on exchange rate of 31 December 2017: USD 1 = ARS 19.12.
[b] Earnings before interest, taxes, depreciation, and amortization.

and made Mirgor a supplier to Volkswagen and General Motors in Argentina, Fiat in Brazil, and Citroën in Uruguay.

Toward the end of the 1990s, management closed the Tierra del Fuego plant due to its obsolete technology and to continued recession in the Argentine economy. During 2001, demand in Argentina fell to historical lows. The company sold non-core assets and entered an agreement with Volkswagen to assemble dashboards for its Polo Classic model.

As Argentina's economy started to recover in the early 2000s, Mirgor was the local market leader for automotive air conditioning equipment. Mirgor then developed a partnership with Carrier, a global leader in air conditioning, to produce units for residential customers. Additionally, Mirgor repurchased Valeo's participation in its company, securing a license to use its technologies until 2013. Full ownership allowed Mirgor to broaden the range of licenses it held. In 2005, the company obtained a license from Denso to produce air conditioning components for Volkswagen's new Suran model, and a license from Behr for Peugeot's new 307 model. Further diversification included the development of an on-site facility in General Motors' plant in Rosario to assemble wheels and later steering components.

Law 25.539, promoting the manufacturing of technological products in Tierra del Fuego province, came into effect in 2009. The law encouraged substitution of imports with globally branded but locally manufactured products. Carrier decided to develop its own production facility to meet exponential growth in the residential air conditioning segment. Alejandro Carrera, a former independent board member, observed: "Mirgor's management had prepared for this scenario. It quickly replaced Carrier with a license from LG and was able to obtain severance payment." Mirgor acquired consumer electronics assembler Latec S.A., which began to assemble mobile phones for Nokia in 2010.

The company further diversified its production: microwaves and ovens under Whirlpool and LG licenses; DVD and Blu-ray disc players and LED screen TV sets under LG license; and desktop and laptop computers licensed by Dell. Mirgor was quick to act upon Nokia's global demise, obtaining a license from Samsung to produce mobile phones from 2014, and later television sets. In 2017, the company signed an agreement with Samsung Argentina to develop a retail channel called Samsung Stores.

Grupo Mirgor: Capability Development   Grupo Mirgor's history is characterized by the development of increasingly sophisticated production capabilities against a backdrop of constant negotiation for technological licenses, maintenance of customer relationships, and government regulation. Javier Soriano, who started his career at Mirgor in product development, observed that "during Mirgor's first decade, we grew locally with some licenses we had obtained abroad. We did what was possible for a local market that was less demanding. As from 1993, the company became more professional in response to foreign competition." The company increasingly obtained recognition as a preferred supplier from global car manufacturers, and certified its production processes according to global standards in their automotive, consumer electronics, and household appliances business units.

Management's relationship development and negotiation skills positioned the company at the interface between global technology suppliers and global clients –especially in the automotive sector. According to Carrera, "Mirgor has an exceptional capability to develop relationships with global leaders in product technology. It has been able to obtain licenses from companies such as Valeo, Nokia, LG, Whirlpool, Dell, and now Samsung." Nearly every car manufacturer in Argentina incorporates Mirgor's air conditioning equipment in at least one of their models.

Managing relationships with governments at the national, provincial, and municipal levels has been vital to both the company's origin and its competitiveness over time. In the 1980s, provincial and national industrial promotion laws not only offered tax benefits but also required car manufacturers to comply with national component quotas, thus securing demand for companies such as Mirgor. Carrera said that renegotiation of the industrial promotion laws had been "very important to Mirgor's competitiveness. Initially, the tax exemptions would expire in 2002, then 2012, and currently, they are expected to expire in 2023. Management acts at different levels to avoid expiration, mainly at the provincial level where government has an interest in protecting jobs."

Looking to the future, as the founding generation steps down to be replaced by younger managers, Carrera anticipates that "Mirgor is likely to maintain its positioning as a manufacturer of licensed technological products for the automotive industry, consumer electronics, and household appliances for the Argentinean market."

Bodega Lagarde

Bodega Lagarde: Past to Present Bodega Lagarde is a boutique winery in the Argentinean province of Mendoza and has wine storage capacity of 2.2 million liters. With sales of USD 6.17 million and exports close to USD 2 million (annual balance, FY 2017), it employs 50 workers, plus another 100 temporary workers during the harvesting season.

216 M. Hermans and D. Finchelstein

Wine production in Argentina traces back to early Spanish missionaries who brought with them high-yield but low-quality Criolla grapes. In the 1850s, Argentina's national authorities sought to improve wine quality by introducing higher-quality grapevines – including Malbec (Mateu & Stein, 2008) – and later developed the railroad system to connect producers with local consumers in Buenos Aires. In this context, Don Jose Angel Pereira founded Bodega Lagarde in 1897. Subsequent generations developed the winery until 1969, when the founder's great-grandchild found himself without heirs. He decided to sell the company to Luis Menotti Pescarmona, owner of the industrial firm IMPSA (Dengis & Dengis, 2006). The Pescarmona family maintained an emphasis on the production of high-quality wines. Over time, they acquired more vineyards and introduced varietals new to the Mendoza region.

Vertical integration and a focus on high-quality wines shielded Bodega Lagarde from shifts in the Argentine economy. For example, during the 1980s, the growth of urban areas and the development of country clubs led to closure of wine estates in Mendoza and San Juan provinces (Richard-Jorba, 2006). This trend did not affect Bodega Lagarde's supply because the firm sourced grapes from its own vineyards. Likewise, from the mid-1980s, many Argentine winemakers suffered financial stress resulting from a shift in demand toward fine and sparkling wines. As Bodega Lagarde produced only high-end wines, this shift had little impact.

In 2001, Sofia Pescarmona became CEO of Bodega Lagarde. Building on the legacy of quality wines and benefiting from the strong devaluation of the Argentine peso in 2002, the company increased its presence in export markets through select distribution agreements and international buyers, while launching new product lines. Together with her sister Lucila, Pescarmona promoted concepts that were new to the Argentinean wine industry, including a restaurant at the estate and a line of organic wines.

Bodega Lagarde emphasizes sustainability in winemaking and has implemented water conservation initiatives, ecologically responsible packaging, and waste management initiatives. In 2019, it became the first Argentine winemaker to earn B Corporation certification. This differentiated approach to winemaking warrants Bodega Lagarde's current exports to more than fifty countries, including premium markets such as the United States, Japan, France, and the United Arab Emirates.

Bodega Lagarde: Capability Development   Historically, Argentine wines were produced for an unsophisticated local market in which inexpensive jug wines dominated. While agencies such as the Instituto Nacional de Vitivinicultura or the Instituto Nacional de Tecnologia

Agricola fulfilled phytosanitary control and technical support roles, until the end of the 1990s, only a few firms achieved significant quality improvements, often as a necessary condition for exports (Richard-Jorba, 2006). Bodega Lagarde has maintained its historic profile as a high-quality winemaker consistently investing in production and quality enhancements. Currently, quality continues to be a priority. According to Pescarmona, "As we are a small winery, we can't compete with larger players based on cost. We focus on quality, especially the quality of our grapes. We grow 80 percent of the harvest ourselves and constantly monitor the vineyards from which we source grapes externally."

Building on quality in production capabilities, Bodega Lagarde developed several marketing-driven capabilities. The company's branding emphasizes tradition, with its proprietary vineyards that date back to 1906 and preservation of the historical winery that was built in 1897, but innovations allow for maintaining a connection with customers. Bodega Lagarde was the first Latin American producer to plant nontraditional varieties such as Viognier and Moscato Bianco. Mirroring developments in France and in California's Napa Valley, Bodega Lagarde diversified into estate tourism and opened a restaurant where local cuisine is accompanied by the firm's own wines. More recently, the company has responded to growing demand for sparkling wines in Latin American markets and has launched its line of organic wines. Pescarmona observes: "We have our core products, such as our Malbec wines, which drive our business. However, to keep wine critics, influencers on social media and distributors interested, we need to develop new product lines and present novelties. We present the stories behind each of our wines and need to tell different stories to audiences in different markets."

Distribution in international end markets represents a significant challenge. In the second half of the 1990s, the Argentine government attempted to bring producers into state-sponsored export consortia but did not succeed. Following the example of larger winemakers, Bodega Lagarde developed partnerships with distributors. According to Pescarmona: "We have tried to develop partnerships with large distributors but lack volume for them to adequately represent us. Currently, we have multiple distributors in large markets, such as the US, but that implies more complexity."

As a smaller company in Argentina, Bodega Lagarde has found access to resources to be a challenge. While the firm has been able to assemble a group of capable and committed staff in Argentina, it lacks the scale needed to absorb the cost of proprietary commercial representations abroad. Ownership by the Pescarmona family guaranteed sufficient funding until 2001, when Pescarmona became CEO. Today, Bodega

Lagarde relies on organically generated capital, due in part to Pescarmona's preference for low debt but also to the high cost of capital in Argentina.

Looking forward, Bodega Lagarde is branching out into new wine-making-related business. According to Pescarmona: "We would like to scale up our production, but this is not easy. We would be able to source grapes but first we need to secure our distribution channels, in particular abroad." At the same time, diversification into estate tourism and online wine clubs allows for business growth. "I often tell my staff that in the future winemaking may no longer be Bodega Lagarde's main activity."

Citrícola San Miguel

San Miguel: Past to Present   San Miguel is a multinational company that produces, distributes, and markets fresh citrus fruits and food products derived from citrus fruits. Founded in 1954 by the Mata family, the company developed an industrial facility in the city of San Miguel de Tucumán in the early 1960s to market fresh fruit domestically and abroad and to produce juice concentrates, citrates, and essential oils. In 1968, San Miguel exported its first shipment of lemon peel, and in 1973, the company sent its first shipment of fresh lemon to Poland.

The following years saw sustained investment in production capacity. San Miguel acquired several estates in Tucumán province and further developed its processing facilities in Argentina. In 1993, the Mata family sold the company to a group of investors that listed the company on the Buenos Aires stock exchange in 1997. The decision of the US Department of Agriculture (USDA) to reinstate permits to export citrus fruit from Argentina to the USA in 1999 benefited San Miguel significantly. However, the bonanza was short-lived as a class action by over 5,000 citrus growers in California and Arizona led to a court ruling in September 2001 barring access to the US market.[1] This restriction pushed the firm to internationalize its production. To escape the risks associated with sourcing its fresh fruit predominantly in one province, in 2003, San Miguel acquired the Uruguayan firm Milagro S.A.

The opportunities associated with harvesting fresh fruit in the Southern hemisphere when growers from the North are unable to respond to local demand sparked an international diversification strategy. In 2007, San Miguel's sales reached USD 200 million for the first time. To expand its countercyclical supply in terms of volume and time frame, the company developed commercial representation in South Africa in 2010 and acquired the River Bend estate near Port Elizabeth in 2011. In 2013, the United States government granted export rights to Uruguayan citrus fruit producers, which gave San Miguel renewed access to one of the largest markets for fresh citrus fruit. The company's access to the US market further improved when in 2017, the USDA lifted restrictions for exporting Argentine lemons. In 2018, San Miguel was growing, sourcing, and processing citrus fruit in three countries and selling in more than fifty markets worldwide.

San Miguel: Capability Development Initially, San Miguel emphasized development of its production capabilities, focusing on volume and efficiency in growing and sourcing produce while pursuing quality standards that allowed them to enter premium export markets. While this business model allowed for exports, San Miguel's internationalization did not take off until the company decided to focus its business on citrus fruit and professionalized its management. Maximiliano D'Alessandro, San Miguel's chief marketing officer, states: "Our products cost about USD 20 cents per kilo in their place of origin and are worth more than USD 5 per kilo in their destination market. This applies to citrus fruit, but can be extended to other products as well. Our challenge is to understand in what parts of the value chain we can be successful and in what parts we should not operate." The company's capability development follows its value chain, with ongoing assessment of ways to capture rents by widening the product range and integrating vertically.

Sustained investments in quality control and tracking software to monitor product shipments allowed San Miguel to internationalize without deploying large numbers of Argentine staff. Moreover, technology could be leveraged not only in San Miguel's current operations but also in new markets, such as when the company entered Peru in 2018, or as a service to associated growers.

In addition to widening its value chain in the growing and distribution phases, San Miguel developed capabilities to capture rents closer to end markets as well. D'Alessandro observes: "When we look at our markets and consumption of our products, about 90 percent of the added value is located in the Northern hemisphere." Presence in end markets requires the development of new capabilities, including brand development and customer service. To enable this, San Miguel has started to hire Argentinean staff from fast-moving consumer goods companies and plans to develop commercial offices in China and the EU.

Looking to the future, San Miguel's management focuses on expanding its presence in consumer markets. This could facilitate further growth of its countercyclical supply of fresh and processed fruit, incorporating new types of goods such as avocados or cherries. At the same time, presence in consumer markets allows the company to source fruit from nontraditional markets and to become a year-round supplier of branded fresh fruit. In both scenarios, San Miguel's management perceives the development of marketing capabilities to be a key driver of its business. According to D'Alessandro: "Installing a marketing mindset throughout the organization – in end markets but also in Tucumán or South Africa – is one of the main challenges we face. We have secured sufficient capital for our international expansion and have learnt how to integrate the organization. We will need our organizational culture to evolve with the business model, from a local grower to a vertically integrated and market-oriented multinational."

Grupo ASSA

Grupo ASSA: Past to Present Grupo ASSA is a technology services consulting company founded in 1992. Grupo ASSA first offered its services to small and medium-sized firms that perceived technology implementation as a challenge. The company expanded rapidly and by the early 2000s had made its first international acquisition in Brazil. Its expansion continued – currently the company has offices in Argentina, Brazil, Chile, Colombia, Spain, Mexico, and the United States. More than 90 percent of Grupo ASSA's sales originates from operations outside Argentina, and the company exports to more than forty countries.

Grupo ASSA's initial service offering was implementing JD Edwards enterprise management software at local firms. Soon, the company realized that to continue growth, they needed to create more added value. Thus Grupo ASSA shifted its focus from simply implementing technology to process transformation. The company enjoyed substantial growth in its early years; then a breakthrough came in 1996 when they landed a large contract with Telecom Argentina. Other large domestic companies followed, and later the company signed contracts with global clients such as PepsiCo, Kraft, Pfizer, and Bayer.

The company received its first external investment in 1998, when the US fund Latin American Capital Partners acquired a minor stake. Grupo ASSA used this capital to develop new software, purchase offices in Buenos Aires, and initiate its expansion abroad. In 1999, Grupo ASSA purchased Brazilian IBS Consultoria, a boutique consulting firm with sales of approximately 5 percent of Grupo ASSA's. The acquisition supplied Grupo ASSA with the knowledge, reputation, and expertise needed to successfully operate in Brazil. That same year Grupo ASSA landed its first contracts in Mexico, but it was unable to achieve consistent growth until 2002.

Grupo ASSA attempted an initial public offering on the New York Stock Exchange (NYSE), which faltered due to the end of the "internet bubble." However, the firm continued its steady growth, and in 2005 it recovered shares held by Latin American Capital Partners through a buyout. In 2008, the World Bank's International Finance Corporation (IFC) displayed its confidence by investing in Grupo ASSA, followed the next year by HSBC. Together these shareholders own roughly a third of Grupo ASSA, requiring that it complies with rigorous corporate governance rules.

More recently Grupo ASSA has continued its internationalization. In 2008 the company opened an office in Mexico, consolidating itself as a strong regional player with presence in Latin America's most important markets. In the 2010s, international contracts have allowed the company to move beyond the region and open offices in North America and Europe. As Paul Dougall, Grupo ASSA's vice president of corporate development assessed: "the client has been our best channel of internationalization." Currently, Argentina represents less than ten percent of Grupo ASSA's sales.

Grupo ASSA: Capability Development One of the distinctive features of Grupo ASSA is its continual effort to offer services that complement the application of new technology to a company's business. Grupo ASSA emphasizes proximity to clients and makes an effort to understand the clients' businesses and how technology can be strategically used to increase competitiveness. As Martin Waigmaster, member of the founding family and responsible for Grupo Assa's incubator, says: "our effort has been on making our teams have business conversations with the clients ... the key is not the technology but how it can create value by transforming the client's company." Grupo ASSA creates differential value in business solutions beyond technology implementation. This additional value has been crucial to its survival and growth in a very competitive environment, where other consulting firms from developed countries – including some of the Big Four – may have originally had a stronger reputation. A professional customized service, which has been a key feature of Grupo ASSA, is also a distinctive factor in comparison to large international consulting firms. Grupo ASSA's size and flexibility allow it to offer a relatively more customized service to its clients.

Grupo ASSA actively seeks out well-known international partners. These partnerships have been instrumental to show legitimacy and may be seen as a response to the companies' reputational challenges. For example, in 1992, the company became a J.D. Edwards partner for Latin America; in 2004, it signed an agreement with ITAUTEC, a subsidiary of one of the largest private Latin American banks (Banco ITAU), to offer technological solutions together. The investments Grupo

ASSA received from the World Bank's IFC and from HSBC bank were proof of support from two widely recognized global actors.

Grupo ASSA has been successful in organically growing its reputation. It started by obtaining contracts with smaller firms and then moved to compete for larger projects. Having obtained projects from larger corporations, its team tried to build long-term relations with these firms – most of Grupo ASSA's client relationships last more than five years – and to leverage such relations to obtain further contracts with new firms. The company is aware that a client is taking a different step when they choose them rather than a global firm. Therefore, they make a deliberate effort to show the added value they can create by offering business solutions that complement their technology and by supporting clients after the technology is implemented.

The Latin American origins of Grupo ASSA have also been instrumental. First, the flexibility and capacity to adapt to unstable environments are assets the firm was born with. Waigmaister claims that "resilience is part of our company ... we are always trying to find a solution when a crisis occurs." In this sense, the large Argentine crisis of 2001 became an inflection point for Grupo ASSA as it forced the firm to change its focus and concentrate on external markets, especially Brazil and Mexico. Early internationalization also shaped Grupo ASSA, creating cross-cultural management capabilities that have been crucial. As Dougall says: "we selected a delta force that brought our genes to the new offices ... but it is not about imposing our culture, but rather finding a blend between local and international." The firm has also tried to export its adaptability, cross-cultural flexibility and professionalism into their international branches. In most cases, Grupo ASSA placed young professionals that were from almost the beginnings of the company in top positions abroad. The goal was to combine these people's management style, which reflected Grupo ASSA's culture, with input from local experts. This has been particularly crucial for international success in places such as Brazil, where local knowledge is essential.

Entrepreneurship has also been a positive capability driving the growth of Grupo ASSA, pushing the firm to seek new markets abroad from its early stages and more recently to expand beyond Latin America. Entrepreneurship capabilities have also been successfully combined with the constant search for innovation. The most salient example is Parabolt, a fully owned business incubator with the goal of developing new business opportunities while taking advantage of Grupo ASSA technology and experience. Parabolt has been active and has already initiated projects with several partners. For instance, it works with DHL to apply technology to improve logistics, and is helping YPF, Argentina's largest oil company, to redesign and rethink gas stations for the future.

In its race to remain in the technological vanguard, Grupo ASSA recently signed an agreement with Argentina's largest public research agency, CONICET, to explore how ASSA can use the basic and applied knowledge developed by CONICET researchers to offer innovative business solutions. It is too early to see results from this new agreement, but if successful, the pact could serve as an example to other Argentine firms focused on offering added value through knowledge-intensive activities.

Grupo Bagó

Grupo Bagó: Past to Present   Grupo Bagó is a pharmaceutical company that has diversified into related activities, such as animal health, manufacturing of specialty chemicals, and distribution of pharmaceutical products, and into unrelated activities, such as insurance and early childhood foods. Sebastián and Ana Bagó founded the company in 1934. In 1945, Grupo Bagó became the first Argentinean company to locally produce penicillin-based pharmaceuticals, and over the following decades it developed multiple proprietary drugs. It became the leader in the Argentine pharmaceuticals market in 1972.

In a sector characterized by the presence of large international players, Grupo Bagó currently holds a leading position in sales in its home market. While the Bagó family continues as the primary owner, the company engages in joint ventures and has developed strategic partnerships with companies such as Astra-Zeneca, Novartis, and Pfizer. Through exports to and operation of companies in Latin America, Africa, the Middle East, Eastern Europe, and Asia, Grupo Bagó's sales amounted to USD 1.3 billion in the 2017 fiscal year.

During the 1970s, Grupo Bagó started to explore FDI opportunities. Building on an existing portfolio of product licenses for export, Grupo Bagó initiated the internationalization of its production. In 1972, it opened a facility in Mexico to manufacture active ingredients, followed by pharmaceutical plants in Bolivia in 1978 and in several Central American countries in 1982. Economic turmoil in Latin America during the 1980s stalled the company's internationalization process until the 1990s, when economic stability in the Argentinean home market allowed for a new wave of FDI aimed at completing Grupo Bagó's coverage of the principal Latin American markets.

The internationalization of Grupo Bagó in other Latin American countries required a flexible approach. According to Rallys Pliauzer, Grupo Bagó's general director for Asia, Europe, and Africa, the company would "take advantage of the opportunities in each market. At times, we would acquire an existing company, such as in Colombia, where we bought a packaging company to develop the business. In other countries, such as Peru, Ecuador, or Brazil, we started from scratch, registering and filing for licenses to market our products."

In 2001, building on the company's sound financial situation, Grupo Bagó decided to explore the potential to bring its products to Asia. This strategy allowed the company to avoid competing with large multinational pharmaceutical companies in their home markets and to leverage capabilities required for doing business in emerging markets. The company developed a commercial office in India in collaboration with local partners. From India, Grupo Bagó expanded into Vietnam, Singapore, and Pakistan, where it developed a manufacturing facility with local partners. A second step included Malaysia, Thailand, and the Philippines. A third step was entry into Russia in partnership with the pharmaceutical company Chemo. Pliauzer observed that the company "started this new wave of internationalization in 2001, and in 2008, we were present in twenty-five markets, in an industry where registration of products requires 2 to 3 years."

Only five years after Laboratorios Bagó initiated exports to China, demand for some of its products there exceeded demand in all Latin American markets combined. Likewise, in 2017, Biogénisis Bagó, the animal health business unit, developed a joint venture in China to manufacture 400 million doses of vaccine against foot-and-mouth disease per year, while the combined annual demand in Latin America was 600 million doses.

Grupo Bagó: Capability Development Manufacturing and research and development activities have been central pillars of the business strategy of Grupo Bagó since its early years. A first phase that may be identified in the company's industrial history was characterized by the development of sophisticated manufacturing facilities in Argentina and the creation of the Instituto Bagó de Investigaciones, which focused on developing extensions of, and finding new applications for, drugs that the company had obtained licenses for (Campins, 2015). The renewed Argentinean import substitution policies of the early 1970s marked a brief second phase, where Grupo Bagó developed a facility to produce active pharmaceutical ingredients in Argentina, a new division focused on animal health, and a division focused on turnkey projects for the pharmaceutical industry. These changes allowed for the internationalization of production within the Latin American region. The third phase started in 1974, when Grupo Bagó anticipated the end of Argentinean import substitution policies and focused on strengthening its research and development capabilities. Concentrating on enhancing the anti-inflammatory properties of medications for which strong demand existed, the company built a proprietary knowledge base for which it holds numerous patents. During the following decades, Grupo Bagó widened the scope of its research and development activities to include medication for oncological, endocrinological, and cardiological purposes, among others.

The most recent phase is linked to its international expansion. As Grupo Bagó internationalized, compliance with pharmacotechnical production standards and obtaining licenses from regulatory agencies became an increasingly important capability. Whereas the quality of products was controlled by the company itself and had been a driver for investments in manufacturing facilities outside Argentina, obtaining licenses for marketing products locally required learning. Pliauzer observed that "the Argentinean market was more demanding than other Latin American countries. When we disembarked in Asia, we found ourselves with very different licensing and registration requirements."

Managerial capabilities, such as risk management, organizational learning, and cross-cultural management, were essential to Grupo Bagó's internationalization strategy, especially to its entry into markets in Asia, Eastern Europe, and Africa. Pliauzer suggested that the company was able to "manage crises. We consider this to be one of our strengths. We identify and assess risks well because we are used to this kind of situation." Likewise, as the organization gained experience in new markets, it frequently needed to adapt its original strategic plans and to anticipate or postpone market entries, taking advantage of potential partnerships or withdrawing from markets where Grupo Bagó's approach did not function according to senior management's criteria.

Regarding the future, Pliauzer expects the company to continue its emphasis on emerging markets. With local and international partners, Grupo Bagó is evaluating investment projects, some of which are in Africa. "We contribute technological know-how to our partners, and allow for production at optimal efficiency levels, as we are able to market excess production in international markets."

Globant

Globant: Past to Present   Globant is a technology services company that provides services related to application development, testing, infrastructure management, and application maintenance. Listed on the NYSE, the company generated revenue of USD 413 million and a net income of USD 30.5 million in 2017. At that point it operated thirty-seven service delivery centers distributed across twelve countries and employed more than 7,200 "Globers."

Globant was founded in 2003, shortly after the global 2001 dot-com crash and Argentina's default on its public debt. The low cost of qualified Argentine IT talent sparked the creation of numerous IT outsourcing companies that emulated the service model of Indian companies. Globant's founders perceived a similar opportunity – as reflected in the company's original name, IT Outsourcing S.R.L. Unlike many of its local competitors, Globant was able to leverage the founders' network to work with highly visible international clients such as EMC, Santander, and Citibank. The principal market for Globant was the United States, given small time-zone differences, cultural fit, and regulations that favored data protection and intellectual property measures to reduce risks associated with outsourcing IT projects.

The company soon entered an exponential growth trajectory. Google chose the young company for one of its first outsourced software development projects, boosting its international reputation. The increased business volume required the company to expand its capacity. In 2005 Globant closed a first round of financing, followed by a second round in 2007 and a third in 2008. The company used this capital to open delivery centers in Latin America and to acquire companies to expand its service offering and client base. These include acquisition of Accendra, an Argentinean software company with a strong client base in Chile, Colombia, and Mexico, and Openware, a company focused on IT solutions. On the flipside, an Indian company came close to acquiring Globant in 2009. Although the acquisition did not occur, Globant's leaders understood that its future autonomy would require the company to become larger and truly global.

Over time, Globant shifted its strategy from outsourced IT services to a product-oriented offering focused on digital journeys. On one hand, this shift responded to the appreciation of exchange rates in many Latin American countries that eroded Globant's cost advantages. On the other, the company now had a knowledge base that allowed it to position itself in more specific product market segments. Early experiences with the integration of wearable technology, web and mobile content, and payment solutions for Disney's theme parks and cruise lines anticipated the emergence of their new digital journey offerings.

New acquisitions aimed at broadening the company's knowledge base included the San-Francisco-based mobile technology oriented company Nextive, Brazil's Terra Forum, and the British Huddle Group, which specialized in training and media. Adding to the company's international profile, the cofounder of LinkedIn, Reid Hoffman, joined Globant's Board of Advisors in 2012. Two years later, the company filed an initial public offering on the NYSE and raised USD 58.5 million (Crunchbase, 2018) to fuel its future growth.

While maintaining operational headquarters in Buenos Aires, Globant moved its administrative presence to Luxemburg and continued its international expansion through acquisitions. Between 2015 and 2018 it acquired Clarice Technologies in India, the service design firm WAE in the UK, and, in the USA, the design, development, and quality assurance firm L4 Digital, the multiscreen firm Ratio, and the mobile design and development firm PointSource (Crunchbase, 2018). The expanded knowledge and client bases resulting from these acquisitions enabled Globant to accelerate its internationalization trajectory, servicing more than 300 customers including Google, LinkedIn, BBVA, Electronic Arts, and Coca-Cola. The geographic breakdown of second-quarter 2018 revenue was 78.4 percent from North America, 8.5 percent from Europe, and 13.1 percent from Latin America and other regions.[2]

Globant: Capability Development   Globant developed a broad set of capabilities to sustain its international expansion. In its early years, cost management was an important driver of business success. In an industry where labor represents between 70 percent and 80 percent of the total cost structure, the post-2002 economic collapse was an opportunity to leverage the comparatively low salaries of programmers in its Argentinean delivery centers. Labor cost arbitration continues to be relevant to Globant, which operates service delivery centers throughout Latin America and in India.

However, cost management alone does not suffice to explain Globant's international growth, as comparatively lower labor costs were equally available to competitors. Our interview with Guillermo Willi, the company's vice-president of human resource management, revealed technological expertise as a second important capability. "At Globant, we found a balance between the efficiencies associated with the scale of large system integrators and outsourcers, such as those in India, and the highly specialized boutique firms that are at the forefront of emerging technologies." The company's knowledge base reflects IT trends, such as gaming, social networking, virtualization, cloud computing, and online marketing. "Access to new technologies is not an issue for us. For example, we have more than 1,000 employees in the US, where VPs of particular technologies and commercial staff that interact with demanding clients inform the organization regarding new technologies."

To leverage its technological capabilities, Globant uses agile work methodologies. It has adopted an organizational structure based on "studios," units that focus on specific practices and technologies such as gaming, cloud computing, social media, and big data. Globant also uses artificial intelligence to enhance its knowledge management. It uses tools such as *Glow*, a software algorithm that allows for assembling hyperteams based on talent information, personality profiles, 360-degree feedback, career aspirations, project history, and industry and technology expertise. It also holds a stake in Collokia, a software plug-in that detects users' interests and expertise as they do their jobs and allows for connecting with and collaboration among subject matter experts. According to Guillermo Willi, "We are currently facing the challenge of managing an increasingly complex organization. Globant operates in different regions, uses different technologies, and works for different clients. We need an organizational model and management style that allows for flexibility and speed, while maintaining an integrated organizational culture."

As of 2018, global spending on software continued to be strong with positive projections for the near future (Gartner, 2018). To seize global growth opportunities, Globant needed to recruit IT talent and professionals able to contribute to the creation and operation of digital experiences. According to Guillermo Willi, Globant is "facing the challenges of a growing organization. Over the past years, revenue has grown at a twenty-plus yearly rate, and most of our businesses revenue is directly linked to headcount."

Looking forward, Globant views its main challenges as sustaining its organizational growth based on access to talent. The company succeeded in securing funding for its expansion and development of a globally competitive knowledge base. According to Globant's CEO, Martin Migoya, "Globant will need to continue performing as it has done until now, thinking about how to position itself in the market of the next 20 years ... We cannot let short-term concerns overtake our focus on decisions for the long term."[3]

Arcor

Arcor: Past to Present   Arcor is one of the largest food producers in Argentina and one of the country's main multinationals. It has forty-seven manufacturing facilities in five Latin American countries and sells its products in more than 120 countries. With approximately 21,000 employees and global sales over 3.1 billion dollars in 2017, Arcor is currently the largest producer of hard candy in the world and the largest confectionery exporter in Argentina, Brazil, Chile, and Peru.

Created in 1951, the company followed a pattern of continual growth, which included rapid product diversification since the 1960s, followed by international expansion since the 1980s. Arcor distinguishes itself from most Latin American business groups by implementing a clear vertical diversification strategy, as opposed to a horizontal model. As Luis Pagani, president of Arcor, affirms: "since our beginnings we thought about vertical integration ... before we created Arcor my family already had a cardboard production company."[4] Its three main business units are links along the chain of production. The Arcor agribusiness and packaging units supply its mass consumer food division with crucial inputs. In both cases, Arcor built production capacity beyond its needs and exploits its surplus capacity. For instance, the packaging division is the largest producer of corrugated cardboard in Argentina.

Only a decade after its creation, Arcor began taking a strategic view of external markets. Its first exports were in 1964, and in 1976, Arcor started local operations in Paraguay. During the decade of debt crises in Latin America, Arcor continued to invest abroad, opening commercial offices in Uruguay (1979), Brazil (1981), and Chile (1989). During the 1990s, the group continued focusing on finding new markets and opening factories abroad. It opened commercial offices in the United States, Peru, Colombia, and Ecuador, and later in the decade opened factories in Peru, Brazil, and Chile.

From the 2000s, Arcor pursued a globalization strategy. It developed joint ventures with important international players, becoming the largest cookie and snack producer in Latin America in partnership with the French firm Danone, and opening a factory in Mexico with local Grupo Bimbo. Simultaneously, Arcor ventured beyond the Americas, opening commercial offices in Europe, the Middle East, Southeast Asia, Africa, India, and China.

Although the global penetration of Arcor products is high, the company occupies a middle step in terms of its internationalization process. Argentina still represents roughly 72 percent of its total sales and 64 percent of its total employees. All its foreign production units are located in Latin America, where cultural, economic, and institutional distances are not large. This will soon change: in 2018, Arcor announced its plan to develop a joint venture with an Angolan firm to open their first factory beyond Latin America.

Arcor: Capability Development Arcor's early experience allowed the company to develop production and operational capabilities that sustain its key competitive advantages. Thanks to this early experience, brand management and foreign trade are among Arcor's core capability areas. The opening of a network of commercial offices has been key to marketing its products in distant areas such as the Middle East or Africa, and Arcor used its flexibility to customize its products to enter demanding new markets such as Japan. As Marcelol Siano, manager of mass consumption, maintains: "Arcor is a company that is used to transformation."[5] The company frequently adapts ingredients to fulfill specific market requirements.

In developed countries, where brands in Arcor's industry sector are quite consolidated, Arcor deployed an aggressive strategy to obtain contracts with large retailers such as Walmart and Carrefour to sell its products under the retailers' brands (Kosacoff et al., 2002). In emerging markets, Arcor has consolidated its own brands. Arcor successfully replicated its marketing experience from Argentina in other Latin American markets and exported some of its most successful brands into other Latin American countries, in some cases (i.e. Chile) acquiring already consolidated brands. Its joint ventures with Danone and Bimbo also optimized Arcor's brand and distribution expertise.

One of Arcor's most important achievements is that the public as well as the business community have perceived its brand very positively. Arcor was elected eight consecutive times as the firm with the highest reputation in Argentina,[6] surpassing well-known global companies such as Unilever and Google. Its recognition within the business community has allowed Arcor to form different types of alliances with well-established multinationals such as a cobranding agreement with the Coca-Cola company in 2010.

Another salient feature of Arcor is that it continues to be privately owned. The same founding group of families – led by the Pagani family – continues to retain full control of the firm. Pagani highlights that "our growth in each country that we are in has been achieved with our own resources."[7] Although the firm complies with all financial regulations and corporate governance standards that are required for a firm to be publicly traded, the company's good reputation, combined with its consistent financial indicators, allow it to find other sources of capital for its continual international expansion while retaining the autonomy and flexibility need to take decisions.

Vertical integration has also been crucial to Arcor. This corporate structure has helped reduce its costs and increase its profits. Additionally, it provides Arcor with tight control and guarantees the quality of its products. It also offers the possibility for developing a great variety of products, which is essential in the confectionery industry, where a great number of new products emerge every year. Vertical integration has also supported entry into distant countries by making it easier for Arcor to adjust its ingredients and packaging to the particular needs of the country to which they are exporting.

9.4 Comparison

In most Latin American countries the main actors in international business are diversified *grupos*, with many of them deploying their core competences to become multilatinas (Peres, 1998). As the preceding case studies illustrate, Argentinean firms do not uniformly fit this model. Some *grupos* have focused on core competences: for example, Arcor concentrated on the development of capabilities that enabled it to become a leader in consumer foods, in particular confectionery. However, other *grupos* continued their internationalization trajectories as diversified organizations, building on potential synergies across units. An example of this approach is Grupo Bagó, which combined pharmaceutical products for human use, products for animal health, and turnkey development of manufacturing facilities to establish its presence in international markets. Some Argentinean multinationals do not fit the *grupos* template. For example, in the IT sector, Globant developed technological capabilities to service specific clients.

Several of the companies discussed in this chapter depend on location-specific comparative advantages, such as Bodega Lagarde's vineyards or San Miguel's estates in Tucumán province. However, these advantages are insufficient in themselves to secure success in international markets. As can be observed in Table 9.4, production-related capabilities are necessary, but these require a complement of client-oriented marketing capabilities. San Miguel offers clients a wider supply window but increasingly aims to add value through online merchandise tracking, which it can deploy in other lines of fresh produce exports. Likewise, Globant initially leveraged the low cost of creating software in Argentina but then evolved to offer client-specific services with higher added value, and Grupo ASSA delivers higher added value through client-specific services. Their internationalization trajectories suggest that these firms initially focused on structuring production by securing access to necessary resources and inputs. Over time, capabilities in understanding client needs and sales processes, whether managed in-house or by partners, become more important.

The managerial challenges faced by leaders of the companies we analyzed differ according to their degree of internationalization. Firms that mainly operate locally or are exporters face difficulties in constructing viable longer-term strategies and obtaining required financing because of their exposure to volatility in the home market. Access to capital was far less of an obstacle to firms that are further along on the internationalization path. Most larger firms continued to rely heavily on local talent for financial management and operations, which often require close

Table 9.4 *Capabilities of Argentinean firms studied*

Major capability	Subcategories	Arcor	ASSA	Grupo Bagó	San Miguel	Globant	Bodega Lagarde	Grupo Mirgor
Obtaining resources	Resource identification	✓	✓	✓		✓		✓
	Ability to purchase product inputs	✓		✓	✓		✓	
	Ability to develop resources internally	✓	✓	✓	✓	✓	✓	
Product service capabilities	Product manufacturing	✓		✓			✓	✓
	Research and development	✓		✓✓				
	Local product adaptation	✓	✓	✓✓		✓		
Operations and management	Production management	✓		✓✓	✓✓		✓✓	✓✓
	Supply chain management	✓			✓	✓✓		
	Hard skills	✓	✓✓					
	Soft skills	✓	✓					
	Entrepreneurship		✓✓			✓✓	✓✓	
	Cross-cultural management						✓	
Marketing	General sales capabilities	✓	✓	✓	✓✓	✓	✓✓	✓
	Understanding local customer needs	✓			✓		✓	
Managing external environment	Political capabilities		✓	✓	✓		✓	✓✓
	Relationship capabilities		✓	✓			✓	
	Adjusting to poor infrastructure	✓		✓	✓			

coordination with headquarters. However, as more firms internationalize, Argentine talent with good soft skills, cross-cultural skills, and the ability to understand the needs of foreign clients becomes scarcer. Foreign nationals more frequently occupied positions that required interaction with clients and other stakeholders, as in the cases of Grupo ASSA, Globant, and Arcor, or are managed by partners, as with Bodega Lagarde and Grupo Bagó.

Finally, to the extent that firms internationalize, their ability to manage their external environment decreases. At one extreme, Grupo Mirgor is an ongoing balancing act in which managers take advantage of political agendas and shape stakeholder interests to allow for continued operations. The actors in the political environment that the company needs to manage are clearly identifiable. At the other end of the spectrum, companies such as Arcor and Globant rely less on one specific political context and hence focus on complying with regulation, occasionally acting to shape it. For example, San Miguel actively lobbied for requests by the Argentine government to the USDA to obtain permission to export lemons to the USA.

9.5   Conclusion

While Argentina was home to some of the world's first emerging market multinational companies, their globalization continues to be a work in progress, even in comparison to other countries in the region (Finchelstein, 2017). While the adversity inherent in the national context may justify flight-driven internationalization strategies (Cuervo-Cazurra & Ramamurti, 2017), most Argentine firms pursued strategies more focused on risk diversification within the local context rather than developing the capabilities needed to compete in the global arena. This may be partly due to the pendular swings that have characterized Argentina's domestic economy and that condition its integration with the global economy.

However, a shift in the Argentine internationalization paradigm may be in the works. Building up production and local market capabilities to support gradual internationalization takes time for those engaged in traditional activities, such as Arcor in food processing and Grupo Bagó in pharmaceuticals. Family ownership and restricted access to capital markets frequently delays professionalization of management and internationalization. In contrast, firms in newer sectors of the economy, such as Globant and Grupo ASSA, are less capital-intensive and can target international clients from their inception.

The capabilities that have sustained internationalization in these cases are remarkably similar. Analysis of the internationalization trajectories of the seven firms included in this chapter suggests that once firms have secured production capabilities that comply with international market standards, they venture abroad. Relying on an entrepreneurial approach, they develop beachheads in foreign markets that allow for organizational learning, in particular regarding the needs of international clients. Another constant is the shift in criticality of resources along the internationalization trajectory. While domestic and exporting firms are highly sensitive to exchange rate shifts and restricted access to capital, the more international firms appear to have overcome these limitations but need more talent geared to a global mindset.

Taken together, our analysis of the internationalization trajectories of these Argentinean firms reveals the requirement to consider how the economic context and managerial perceptions influence capability development. While limitations (such as licensing agreements) may entirely bar certain companies from internationalization, other Argentinean firms are learning how to internationalize faster, access alternative sources of capital, leverage new technology, and develop human capital.

Notes

1. United States District Court for the Eastern District of California, CV-F-00–6106 REC/LJO.
2. http://investors.globant.com/news-releases?item=115#assets_43_115–3
3. www.lanacion.com.ar/1711303-la-argentina-globant-debuto-ayer-en-la-bolsa-de-nueva-york.
4. Celano Gómez, 2018.
5. Manzoni, 2018.
6. Kantor, 2017.
7. Celano Goméz, 2018.

10 Building Strategic Capabilities in Brazilian Firms

Maria Tereza Leme Fleury, Cyntia Vilasboas Calixto,
Cláudia Sofia Frias Pinto, and Afonso Fleury

10.1 Introduction

As emerging market firms expand globally, they can become more influential and, in some cases, lead their industries. Such firms possess a set of strategic capabilities that enables them to overcome the liabilities of foreignness (Zaheer, 1995) and the institutional inefficiencies of their home countries. These strategic capabilities include the skills and knowledge firms need to succeed.

This chapter analyzes six cases of Brazilian firms, in different industries and at different stages of internationalization, and highlights the specific capabilities that have enabled them to succeed both locally and internationally. The presentation and analysis of the six cases will follows a brief review of the concept of strategic capability and the country background in Brazil.

Firms must possess a number of basic capabilities in order to operate as businesses. While the concept of capabilities is not new, a rather thick terminological haze hovers over its conceptualization and application. In this chapter, we will consider capabilities to be the socially complex procedures that determine the efficiency with which organizations are able to transform inputs into outputs (Collins, 1994).

Scholars argue that a firm's sustainable competitive advantage results from the construction of strategic capabilities (Stalk, Evans & Shulman, 1992) with three distinctive characteristics: they create customer value; they are better than the capabilities of most competitors; and they are difficult to imitate, substitute, or replicate (Hubbard et al., 1996).

Strategic capabilities are associated with firms' processes of strategy development and execution. They are unobservable and difficult to quantify, and, as they are embedded in organizational routines and practices, they cannot be easily imitated or traded (Day, 1994).

To create economic value and sustain competitive advantage, firms need a wide range of strategic capabilities. Every firm develops its own set of capabilities, rooted in the reality of its competitive market and past experience and dependent on its anticipated requirements (Day, 1994). Nonetheless, certain categories of capabilities appear in many firms and are identified in the literature. Technological capabilities – such as product and process development and operations management – allow the firm to keep costs down and differentiate its offerings. Market-related capabilities – such as market sensing, channel and customer linking, or technology monitoring – allow the firm to respond to changing customer needs and to exploit its technological strengths (Day, 1994). Marketing capabilities – such as skills in segmentation, targeting, pricing, and advertising – enable the firm to take advantage of its market sensing and technological capabilities and formulate and implement effective marketing programs (Song & Parry, 1997).

Other strategic capabilities include information technology, enabling the firm to spread market information effectively across the functional areas and exploit new product development processes. Management-related capabilities support all the other capabilities, encompassing human resources and financial management. While not all firms need to develop all these capabilities to attain competitive advantage (Day, 1994), every firm develops its own set of strategic capabilities over time, according to its experiences, the specificities of its country of origin, and the demands of its markets.

10.2   The Emergence of Brazilian Multinational Enterprises

Brazil pioneered OFDI – outward foreign direct investment – among emerging countries, leading the wave of so-called third world multinationals in the 1970s (see Figure 10.1). In 1980, Brazil had the largest stock of OFDI from emerging countries. However, during the 1980s, which many refer to as Latin America's "lost decade," Brazil suffered from a debt crisis and macroeconomic instability, and Brazilian OFDI lost momentum. The rise of Brazilian firms resumed in the mid-1990s when Brazil experienced a series of economic and political changes (so-called promarket reforms) that led to more open markets and increased competitiveness. Brazil's OFDI flows showed an upward trend that lasted through the accelerated growth years of the mid-2000s. In this era, Brazil became the largest investor in Latin America. In 2006, Brazil's OFDI decelerated. This trend resulted partly from the evolution of intracompany loans between Brazilian firms and their overseas subsidiaries. From 2008 onwards, Brazilian firms have had to deal with a particularly

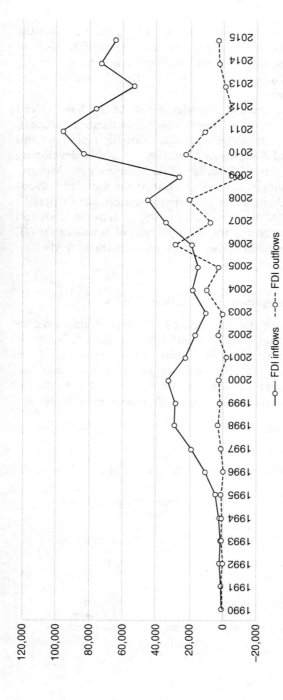

Figure 10.1 Evolution of Brazil's outward and inward FDI (USD million)
Source: UNCTAD, FDI STAT On-line database, Available at: http://unctad.org/en/Pages/DIAE/World%20Investm
ent%20Report/Annex-Tables.aspx

turbulent political and economic environment, which may explain the loss of Brazil's lead position among emerging countries in OFDI stock. In the context of the overall economic and political crises facing Brazil, divestment appeared as a strategic topic on the agenda of many Brazilian firms in recent years.

The geographical distribution of Brazilian firms' OFDI has evolved substantially since 2000. Early in their internationalization process, Brazilian firms targeted developing economies, primarily neighbors and other Latin American and Caribbean countries. In 2001, developing countries attracted 81 percent of Brazilian OFDI (Casanova & Miroux, 2016), with Caribbean financial centers accounting for about two-thirds of the total. Since then, there has been a significant change in Brazil's OFDI destinations: in 2001, developed economies such as the USA and eurozone countries accounted for about 19 percent of Brazilian OFDI, whereas by 2014 that figure had risen to 54 percent (Casanova & Miroux, 2016).

10.3   Capability Development in Brazilian Firms

In this section, we examine the strategic capabilities of six Brazilian firms (see Table 10.1) that have helped them to achieve success. The firms are in different stages of internationalization and from different industries. We identify which capabilities have enabled these firms to advance, the actions and processes that have facilitated their development, and the strategies they have used to reduce their liabilities.

Table 10.1 *Data collection matrix for the selection of Brazilian firms as case studies*

		Firm category		
		Purely domestic	Exporter	Multinational
Industry	High-tech			WEG
				Fanem
	Low-tech		Grendene	
	Service	Dr.Consulta		Stefanini
				Integration

Case 1: WEG

Headquartered in Jaraguá do Sul, Brazil, WEG operates worldwide in the electric engineering, power, and automation technology sectors. WEG began in 1961 as a small producer of electric motors and has become a leading global supplier of electrical and electronic products and coatings. The company produces electric motors, generators, transformers, components, and industrial paints and other coatings. WEG has operations in around 100 countries in five continents (with subsidiaries in twenty-two countries), with approximately 31,000 employees. WEG is the largest electric motor manufacturer in Latin America and the second largest in the world. The firm appeared in the Forbes *Global 2000* list of the world's largest public companies (Forbes, n.d.). In 2015, the Brazilian business magazine *Exame* ranked WEG as the ninth most competitive company on the South American continent (Rossi, 2015).

WEG's internationalization process occurred over three stages. The first, from the 1970s to the 1990s, was its expansion to Latin America, South Africa, and Canada, based on building up channels by commissioning local representatives and distributors. WEG's first internationalization, to Uruguay, also involved technology exports to Colombia. WEG selected this expansion mode to reduce investments and risks while building its expertise in foreign markets. WEG intensified its foreign expansion, mainly to Latin American countries, searching for foreign distributors and increasing its participation in international fairs. According to WEG's CEO, "our goal was to increase the participation in post-sale foreign markets. To accomplish that, WEG invested in the formation of technical assistants" (Melo, 2010). In this stage, WEG created a quality policy and produced its first motor to attain ABNT and IEC standards. In addition, WEG opened a Technological Center (in 1980) to develop new technologies and innovate their products, earned ISO 9001 certification (in 1992), and received the National Quality Award (in 1997). In the 1970s, WEG also created a statement of principles and a manual of corporate governance that remain in use today (Rossi, 2015). WEG standardized its work system, which defined the actions and competencies encouraged and accepted in the firm. Their aim was to simplify understanding for all, increase production quality, reduce costs, and improve safety in the work environment (Moraes, 2004). According to WEG's CEO, "the firm works with simplicity. We like to do everything simple, as quickly as possible, at the lowest possible cost, and always searching for sustainability."

In the company's second stage of internationalization, WEG opened several sales subsidiaries. During this period, the firm rethought the investments made in previous decades and decided to focus only on the segments related to electric motors and equipment. Facing difficulties in resolving conflicts of interest among their foreign distributors, WEG decided to implement its own sales units. In some cases, WEG acquired operations from their distributors, who already had stock, staff, and market knowledge (Melo, 2010). WEG expanded its investments and reinforced its partnership with a German firm. Also, they opened sales subsidiaries in Fort Lauderdale (USA), Brussels (Belgium), and Victoria (Australia) to develop regional markets. The European subsidiary was a failure and closed. The best results came from the Australian subsidiary. WEG also opened commercial offices in Japan, Germany, England, Spain, France, and Sweden. Since the beginning of its foreign expansion, WEG has balanced its concerns regarding results with cultural awareness. According to WEG's CEO, "at this time we created an annual meeting, to present not only the results, but also what we learned by operating in different countries and interacting with cultures different from the Brazilian culture."

During this second stage of internationalization, the joint venture between WEG and an Argentinian firm failed and was dissolved. The Argentinian firm had financial problems. These ended up affecting WEG, which had to deal with debts to workers that were their partner's responsibility (Melo, 2010). The manager of the Argentinian unit recalls that "the union filed a lawsuit against WEG ... the Argentinian was the most important firm in the city." WEG had to learn how to deal with international legal systems and manage their businesses beyond national borders (Moraes, 2004). This event was a milestone in WEG's internationalization: from this event onward, the firm used only entry modes that gave them full control of their international operations.

WEG's third stage of internationalization was marked by several international acquisitions. WEG identified these as investment opportunities but did not have the knowledge to operate in foreign markets. According to WEG's CEO, "we acquired firms because we did not understand the foreign market, but we were interested in the business model of the firms." WEG started by acquiring a plant from Asea Brown Boveri in Mexico. Then WEG made acquisitions in Portugal, Argentina, China (acquiring a state-owned firm), India (a new plant), and then again in Mexico (two plants acquired from the same owner in 2005 and 2008) to supply the US market. WEG sought to move up the value chain and compete globally by becoming an integration firm that supplied technological solutions.

In acquiring the Chinese firm (2005), WEG obtained full control of state-owned Nantong Electric Motors Manufacturing from the Weifu Group. Their machinery and productive process were outdated, and although WEG carefully led the firm through a restructuring process, its management had to accept the continuing presence of the Chinese government in the acquired firm. WEG's CEO in the Chinese unit stated:

There are some people who are part of the government party and are untouchable, 3–4 people that are from the Communist Party, we cannot dismiss them. As we are a foreign firm, we need the relationship. These people end up being good, have great influence in the government and help us a lot.

WEG hoped to conquer the Chinese market with their traditional products (premium line). This failed and WEG had to adapt to the local market by creating specific products, working with local suppliers, and transforming the Chinese subsidiary into an export platform. According to WEG's CEO in the Chinese unit:

WEG was not competitive, because several suppliers were from outside China (bearings from Europe, copper wire . . . all the raw material and insulation materials were brought in from outside), because WEG did not have the knowledge about the Chinese market and did not develop the supply chain in China. The electric engine that came from Brazil was too sophisticated and had too many options . . . the Chinese market was not used to [this] and did not buy.

WEG now adapts their products and practices to the local reality (Moraes, 2004). WEG works in partnership with acquired firms, gradually establishing management practices and performance criteria. Usually WEG retains local employees. According to the WEG CEO:

WEG always seek to respect local culture . . . in Argentina, Mexico, China . . . it did not go there and transform everything . . . WEG sent one or two Brazilian employees, usually a director or general manager, to talk with the local general manager and someone from the financial department, to understand the local firm.

WEG has standardized procedures to maintain product quality. The firm conducts training in its acquired firms to maintain conformity. According to WEG's CEO: "All managers complete training and become familiar with the quality and training manuals, which are then applied to the employees." Moreover, WEG promotes the exchange of employees between their units to increase knowledge of the firms of the group and instigate improvements in production processes. WEG's CEO says,

Employees of different levels are encouraged to make trips abroad to experience the logic of other markets and the state of practice of international competitors, including their production processes.

WEG diversifies in order to increase their portfolio and acquire technology. The WEG CEO says, "The best way to do this quickly is to incorporate who already has it ready."

Each manager who works abroad evaluates global opportunities for WEG. They have the ability to identify deals within their coverage area more easily than the team at the parent firm in Brazil. The managers have the autonomy to seek new opportunities and present them to the group. According to WEG's CEO:

We have a corporate orientation for all the directors of subsidiaries overseas to stay tuned for opportunities. It is not only a block in Brazil that is concerned with expansion ... no, all directors, superintendents, managers, directors of subsidiaries abroad are.

Post-sale service is a source of differentiation for WEG. The firm develops capabilities to train technicians in Brazil and abroad, thus making their service more agile, which their clients value. They develop products on a common platform for standardization, but follow customers' specifications for flexibility. According to WEG's CEO:

the parts are interchangeable ... they fit together because it's the same platform. It does not matter where the engine was bought and where it goes. The guarantee is global and the service part, the exchange part, is done in a very fast way, since there is no product differentiation. That is a way to stand out, since the main competitors have different platforms.

Case 2: Fanem

Fanem – Fábrica de Aparelhos Nacionais de Eletro Medicina – is a pioneer in the manufacturing of medical and laboratory equipment. It is a medium-size family business, with about 300 employees in Brazil and 30 abroad. Arthur Schmidt founded the firm in 1924, and it grew significantly in the 1930s. Researchers brought new ideas to Fanem, the firm moved to new facilities, its business expanded, and Fanem boosted production and consolidated its distribution network. In 1940, interruption of imports due to World War II caused shortages of raw materials. The firm searched for alternatives and began a series of innovations in the production of medical equipment. Fanem was the first South American company to use glass similar to Pyrex and neon tips to build test tubes for use in the firm's centrifuges. In addition, Fanem used tinplate to replace scarce standardized iron plates in the firm's ovens. These innovations allowed Fanem to compete with imports of similar products to theirs. In the 1940s Fanem was the market leader in Brazil, and it remains the pioneer in medical equipment in Brazil (Fanem, 2015).

In 1970, Fanem started to expand to international markets: Colombia and then Mozambique. In 1974, Fanem formed a joint venture – signing a technology transfer agreement in exchange for 24 percent of capital –

with the American firm Air-Shields Inc., the world leader in the incubator industry. The technology was rapidly transferred, leading to the upgrade of Fanem's product line. This association led to the creation, in 1975, of the first incubator with air circulation, which became an international reference in neonatology. In subsequent decades, Fanem increased exports. Between 1990 and 2000, its main market was Latin America. In 2000, Fanem started selling in Arab countries, such as Egypt, Morocco, Algeria, United Arab Emirates, Saudi Arabia, and Libya. In 2006, Fanem held 85 percent of the Brazilian market and 20 percent of neonatology's international market, exporting to eighty-nine countries, twenty-nine more than in the previous year. In 2011, it was selling to eleven sub-Saharan countries, a number that grew to twenty-seven in subsequent years. In 2013, Latin America accounted for 40 percent of the company's total sales; the Middle East, Africa, and Asia, 30 percent; and Europe, 20 percent. About 35 percent of Fanem's annual revenue, estimated at USD 50 million, came from foreign markets.

Fanem continued to expand their operations to new international markets by opening a commercial office in New Delhi and establishing an industrial unit in Bangalore. According to Fanem's CEO, the company wanted to move into a country where a baby is born every second. Both India's strategic location and especially the country's similarity to Brazil in terms of healthcare were taken into account. The participation of an Indian distributor and the experience of the subsidiary's native CEO were critical for successful implementation of the company's operations in India. Products assembled by Fanem India supply the domestic market and other Asian countries. Complementing the expansion strategy, in 2011 Fanem opened an office in Amman, Jordan, to be the main channel for the Middle East and North Africa. In 2016, Fanem continued its internationalization strategy and invested USD 800,000 in a new industrial unit in Guadalajara, Mexico. The firm's goal is to reach the impressive local market which, due to a high birth rate, consumes about USD 40 million per year in neonatal equipment. According to the CEO of the Mexican subsidiary, the Mexican government undertakes 75 percent of the purchases of neonatal equipment. Mexican regulations limit participation in contract bidding processes to local firms, or firms from regions with free trade agreements with Mexico. To overcome these restrictions and expand its business in Mexico, Fanem needed a physical presence. Another reason to set up an industrial unit in Mexico was to serve Central American, Caribbean, and Asian markets, taking advantage of logistic facilities and free trade agreements.

To participate in international contracts sponsored by the United Nations to supply medical equipment to African countries, Fanem joined integrated projects with other companies, such as Philips.

One of Fanem's priorities is training its representatives to boost sales and provide technical support to their customers. In the 1980s Fanem began to bring its international representatives to Brazil, to let them get to know their facilities and to train them in using the company's products and equipment. In 2003, Fanem created a study center to promote research and maintain the high technology level of its products. The Fanem Study Center is responsible for the exchange of knowledge between the health industry and the academic centers of major Brazilian universities, bringing innovation and new technology to the development and improvement of its products. The Study Center also offers educational activities such as courses and workshops. By 2008, Fanem was training professionals from Colombia, Ecuador, Peru, Bolivia, El Salvador, and Chile. Currently, the Fanem training program offers courses and annual training to more than 6,000 professionals and distributors from Brazil and abroad.

The quality and range of Fanem's products placed the firm at the level of its world competitors. In search of innovations and quality since the 1980s, Fanem signed technological agreements with several universities and research centers. Between 1990 and 2000, Fanem launched and had certified twenty-eight products. In 2000, Fanem received Mercosur certification for its products, and two years later European certification. In the following decade, Fanem continued to have a significant number of electromedical equipment certifications in the Brazilian healthcare sector and internationally, including from Inmetro and Anvisa (Fanem, 2017). In 2014, Fanem invested in the startup, SensorWeb, to improve its equipment based in the concept of eHealth and telemedicine. Currently, the firm invests 8 percent of its annual revenue in research and development and holds eight patents.

Innovation has been the Fanem hallmark since its foundation. Fanem operates in a high-tech market niche, unusual among Brazilian firms. Expansion, a pioneering spirit, and a strong sense of nationality have marked the firm's trajectory. Fanem sees the recipe for success as: always invest in innovative technology and in skilled labor; and develop the ability to identify the right distribution channels. These are Fanem's main strategic capabilities.

Case 3: Stefanini

A geologist aiming to teach mainframe skills to local business people founded Stefanini in 1987. It is now Brazil's largest IT firm and one of the main players in Latin America, operating in forty-one countries through twenty-five subsidiaries, with more than 25,000 employees worldwide. In 2016, Stefanini reached US\$ 821 million in revenues; more than 53 percent came from international operations (Stefanini, 2017).

By 1990, Stefanini was focusing on outsourcing and technical support for Brazilian companies. Anchored in partnership with financial institutions, it developed expertise to meet local needs and built a software factory. Stefanini's main clients were from the financial sector. However, as Brazil opened its markets, Stefanini was hit by competition from international players such as IBM. These multinationals had strong methodology and structured processes. Competing with them required Stefanini to put in investment and time. Stefanini improved its services, created better methodology, and strengthened its management processes. In 1996, it achieved ISO 9001 certification and decided to internationalize its activities to increase its competitive advantages (Godinho, 2011).

The first step was toward Argentina in 1996, through a partial acquisition. Stefanini then opened small offices in Chile, Peru, Colombia, Mexico, and the US. The company foresaw the need for quality enhancement once multinational companies became certified. In 2002, it obtained its first Capability Maturity Model (CMM) certification, which was important not only in the USA but also for the European market. Three years later, Stefanini was the first company in Brazil to reach CMM's highest level. It acquired the Tech Team company in the USA (2009) and increased its international coverage considerably (from seventeen to twenty-eight countries). Tech Team not only enlarged the size of the company but also expanded its business portfolio. This acquisition created the opportunity to apply cross-selling services among different operations (Stefanini, 2017).

The company's experience in acquisitions generated a checklist of information needed for the acquisition process (essentially an acquisition template). Among its Brazilian acquisitions, Stefanini acquired Orbitall in 2012. The firm provides card processing, online payment systems, and contact center services. It also gave Stefanini the opportunity to create different solutions and become a pioneering Brazilian fintech.

Stefanini needed to differentiate itself from competitors. The largest competitors focused on global services and standardized solutions. On the other hand, small companies were supplying customized solutions for local business, especially in Europe. The company increased its market share by doing both: offering standard services, but being flexible enough to accommodate customer needs and local specificities.

In 2015, Stefanini acquired a Brazilian Engineering firm – IHM Engenharia – that focused on industry 4.0 managing industrial processes for mining, pulp and paper, oil and gas, automotive, and other industries. This acquisition reinforced Stefanini's interest in optimizing industrial processes. The company believed its future would be in big data and analytics. It therefore invested in a new research center in Singapore to be close to universities and best practices in this segment. Stefanini also has research centers in Brazil, the USA, and Romania to solve clients' issues with operational efficiency and to develop tailor-made solutions. The goal is to reduce customer costs without changing operational processes, but also to create new offers for them. In the same year, Stefanini invested in cyber security in partnership with an Israeli company.

Recently, Stefanini has developed showrooms as a way to demonstrate its innovation capabilities to gather more clients, and innovation centers in Argentina, Peru, and Mexico as open workspaces that serves customers, business partners, startups, and students. It is also investing in robotics and acquiring some hardware companies, such as Saque e Pague, which developed products similar to ATM machines.

Branding was the main challenge for several of its acquisitions. Stefanini had different companies in the group and did not feel the need to integrate them as the same brand. The solution was to create a global brand for the company's main services, adding "Powered by Stefanini" to the local brand for related services, and for unrelated services to retain the original name.

Case 4: Integration

Founded in 1995 by four consultants, Integration currently has more than 300 employees allocated to different international operations. Operations outside Brazil generate between 30 and 40 percent of total revenue. Today, Integration has a physical presence in five countries, and it has developed and delivered consultancy projects in more than fifty countries (Integration, 2017).

The founding members of Integration worked in large consulting firms. They were young, with few years of work experience, and frustrated by the way their firms ran projects (Integration, 2017). In addition, they agreed on the need to get closer to the customer to provide better service. They decided to create a new company drawing on the expertise and interests of each member, focusing on strategy and process management, but adding a service that was uncommon at the time: implementation. "Seventeen years ago, it was not common for companies to act in implementation . . . companies sold knowledge . . . big consulting companies sold knowledge, a methodology" (Integration partner). These principles persist in a company "very strong in implementation, focus on results, to ensure the link with reality, to work side by side with the client" (subsidiary manager).

In 1998, the partners committed to an unusual decision for a consulting firm, which they believed would assist in understanding the implementation of projects. Integration bought a cosmetics company to understand how it worked. One partner left the day-to-day consultant position to manage the new company, while the others stayed in their functions at Integration, and the knowledge learned from running the cosmetics company helped them generate new services (Integration, 2017).

By the following year, Integration had added ten more consultants to its team. Integration was able to differentiate itself by establishing an unusual way of working.

And the idea was a bit different from other consultancies. Most of the consultancies are organized by sector or by industry and we organized ourselves by knowledge areas, just to open a collaboration path with stronger clients. (Integration subsidiary manager)

Precisely because it focuses on implementation, Integration also focused on knowing the local reality. However, customers in Brazil who were active or interested in other markets began to request that the firm deliver new projects outside the home country.

In 2002, one of Integration's clients who liked the methodology used by Integration in Brazil went to Argentina. Another went to Mexico and they commissioned projects in these countries, because they were interested in the work style: "Focus a lot on the field, to know reality, less theoretical" (Integration manager).

In 2003, they launched two international projects in parallel: one in Mexico and another in Argentina. In that moment, they began to evaluate the possibilities of internationalization: mainly by evaluating the attractiveness of a project for the team, diversifying the risk of operating in a single market and expanding their profile of completed projects. In terms of customer strategy, global projects have a larger budget and a higher level of complexity, all of which attract consultants to the company.

They chose to start international activities in Mexico, officially opening an office in 2005. According to the local Mexican manager and partner, it was a learning process for the company to develop the organizational structure in another country and create internal policies. In addition to the classic bureaucratic issues of starting a business, they needed to define important details such as cash flow, transfer pricing, and reporting issues before starting the operation.

To address the personal characteristics of Mexican culture, Integration sought a local partner to expand its operations. Consulting firms need a network to facilitate leads about potential projects through the network itself. "Consulting is a process of trust. It is very difficult to win customers with cold call" (Integration partner).

Later, Integration began to question its next steps along the international trajectory. In addition to opportunities related to the market demand in target countries, the firm also considered the interests of consultants in establishing themselves in these countries (Zanni, 2013). In 2007, activities began in Argentina, with a local director who had great knowledge of mergers and acquisitions operations (Integration, 2017). The following year, they invested in Chile, when one of their consultants showed interest in moving there and a client from the Integration portfolio agreed to sponsor their first project in the country (Zanni, 2013). Two years later, a Chilean partner took control of on-site operations.

International expansion highlighted the need for standards and brought to the forefront the need to strengthen the firm's corporate culture so that the customer, regardless of the service delivery location, would receive the same project quality.

The recruiting process is the foundation of Integration's culture, and therefore highly dependent on selection of its consultants. The company seeks people whose profiles align to company values. In addition, they invest in a training period, which shapes the way the company develops projects. The company's process included weekly follow-ups to spread its culture and create a sense of group belonging. The company's target is flexibility in serving the client according to their needs, while maintaining a high standard in the quality of services provided, regardless of which consultant is involved in the process.

The rapid expansion of the company required little investment in its early stages. Leaner units generate slow on-site growth, but positive profitability, due to lower fixed costs. This model drove their internationalization process. However, in the European continent the company decided to opt for rapid growth, requiring an up-front investment with a return in somewhere between two and four years.

In 2010, Integration decided to enter into a more mature and sophisticated market than Latin America. "Here in Europe in general, and specifically England and Germany, are the two most developed markets for consulting in Europe" (company representative). As the company understood the importance of local roots, it sought a British partner. Being a member of the Council of the Management Consultants Association, this partner raised the level of the projects carried out by the company. In 2015, Integration took another step on the European continent by opening an office in Germany with a local director and around ten consultants.

Case 5: Grendene

Grendene's case is representative of the difficulties faced by Brazilian firms in traditional industries seeking to grow internationally. In the 1980s, many Brazilian footwear producers became part of global value chains as OEMs (original equipment manufacturers). Foreign brand owners supplied the Brazilian makers with designs and production instructions, and the makers delivered the finished products to take to the markets. Among the few Brazilian firms that tried to upgrade in their value chains, Grendene is one that succeeded: it became the largest Brazilian producer to establish international operations especially for offshoring low-value-added operations.

While Alexander Grendene Bartelle and his twin brother Pedro founded Grendene in the southern region of Brazil (Farroupilha main), they located its main factory in the city of Sobral in the northeast region (Grendene, 2017) to take advantage of fiscal incentives provided by the Brazilian government. Grendene started producing plastic materials for the footwear industry in 1975 and developed its first plastic sandal, called Nuar, in 1979. In the next year they created new models, inspired by the strip-sandals of fisherman from the French Riviera.

Grendene created the market for injected plastic footwear in Brazil. Its Melissa brand sandal has been a fashion symbol since the eighties. This success followed the initiative to build partnerships with major world designers such as Jean-Paul Gautier, Alexandre Herchcovich, Sommer, Cavalera, Vivienne Westwood, and Karl Lagerfeld (Grendene, 2017).

Product development is anchored in creativity and realized by a multidisciplinary team that includes architects, economists, fashion designers, and businesspeople that analyze not only the footwear market but also trends in different areas to foment creativity inside the organization. Furthermore, Grendene invests constantly in technology to allow creativity to join innovation. The firm focuses on premium production processes aligning comfort, texture, and fashion. Grandene's mission is to make democratic fashion, that is, translate fashion trends with affordable prices, and Melissa is the firm's brand for Pop Luxury (Calixto, 2013).

In 1984 Grendene opened a kids' brand, transferring some capabilities from women's products to kids'. Grendene Kids is licensed by Disney, Barbie, Marvel, Mattel, and Cartoon Network to produce sandals decorated with the main characters of cartoons. In order to produce for those companies, the firm is certified to guarantee high quality control and human resources practices. In 1986, Grendene invested in the male segment and created the brand Rider, combining design with comfort. Later, it opened two different brands – Grendha (1994) and Ipanema (2001) – targeting a different female customer than Melissa did. Grendha focuses on comfortable sandals for women about 30–40 years old and Ipanema emphasizes affordable beach sandals for every age (Grendene, 2017).

According to the export director, exporting since its early stages (1979 with Melissa) helped prepare the firm for external auditing and quality control. Also, Grendene invested in a more developed production and managerial methodology in order to promote high quality and efficient processes. Recognition in this area came in 2005 and 2006, when Grendene was awarded Walmart Supplier of the Year in footwear. In 2012, the firm was awarded Best Licensee Worldwide by Mattel and the Best Overall Licensee by Cartoon Network.

As for any fashion company, the footwear challenge is to discover niches and work on brand management. Grendene covers multiple niches with its different brands without disrupting the company's mission. Nowadays, Grendene exports to more than 100 countries, and since 2003 it has been the leading footwear exporter in Brazil by number of pairs. Its largest markets are the United States, Latin America (Paraguay, Bolivia, Colombia, and Mexico), China, and Australia. Grendene's initial public offering occurred in 2004 with shares trading in the São Paulo Stock Exchange, but it is still under the founder family control.

Grendene has a completely vertical production process, controlling all stages starting with polyvinyl chloride and ethylene vinyl acetate manufacturing, which are the main inputs for plastic injection in shoe manufacturing. The firm also creates its own shoe molds, giving it more flexibility for manufacturing. Moreover, internal financial resources drive the innovation process, providing agility to develop better products and processes. It launches about 1,000 new products every year.

Grendene has the capability to produce 250 million pairs of shoes per year, entirely in Brazil, and it is considered the largest firm in the world for injected plastic footwear (about 1 percent of the total world production). The firm commercializes its products through direct exports and distributors around the globe, reaching approximated 20,000 points of sale worldwide. Most of its sales involve Grendene's brands. One of the exemptions is Walmart, which required its own trademark. In addition, Grendene invested in three Melissa concept stores in São Paulo, New York, and London to create a connection with its potential customers through brand experience combining art, culture, and fashion. In 2014, Grendene opened a showroom with a local distributor in Milan.

Grendene's source of competitiveness is production scale: it produces customized products only if the target market is interesting for positioning its brand. To guarantee an efficient production process and scale, the firm developed an online order entry system, where distributors worldwide register their interest in products available in the system for a specific period. Then Grendene places an order with its fabrication unit to meet the requests. To facilitate communication with distributors, Grendene generated a downloading center with product information and promotional material.

The marketing department positions each brand according to its DNA. Marketing campaigns use Brazilian celebrities such as Gisele Bündchen and Ivete Sangalo to emphasize Brazilian tropicality. The firm believes in associating its brands with quality and design, and patents all its industrial drawings and brands worldwide to protect its reputation. Today, they are the world's largest maker of sandals.

Regarding environmental issues, the company reuses all leftovers and unused or damaged PVC remnants. In addition, all inks are removed from the water and both are recycled. In 2015, Grendene was awarded a prize in the Environmental Management Category because of its water reuse in operations (Grendene, 2017).

Case 6: Dr.Consulta

Dr.Consulta is a health management firm providing outpatient services through a network of its own medical centers in São Paulo. Its goal is to provide high-quality and low-cost outpatient medical care to people who have inadequate access to health care, largely the low-income segment of the population. Thomaz Srougi and two business partners, Guilherme Azevedo and Renato Cardoso, founded the firm in 2011. The project began with one medical center in Heliopolis, the largest slum in São Paulo. In 2014 the project began its expansion phase, attracting foreign capital – six international funds have already invested USD 95 million (more than BRL 300 million) in the project, money that is being fully invested in new medical centers and equipment. In 2017, Dr.Consulta was providing medical consultation in fifty-six specialties, more than 1,000 types of medical examination, and more than 100 types of low-complexity surgery in forty-five medical centers located in São Paulo.

In Brazil, there are more than 150 million uninsured people and around 100 million people without medical access. The Brazilian public health-care system, the SUS, should be responsible for providing healthcare to that population but, with an annual demand of more than 1.3 billion consultations, SUS is no longer capable of providing that service.

Moreover, the SUS is intrinsically inefficient. Currently, when a patient tries to schedule a consultation, it will take him about 100 days to see a doctor and 135 days to get an exam. In practice, it will take almost a year to get a diagnosis. That creates a huge market opportunity for firms capable of satisfying the needs of that population. Dr.Consulta claims to complete the diagnostic process in no more than fifteen days.

Although Dr.Consulta was founded recently, the concept and value proposition required a lot of thought. In the first two years, the partners invested their time and resources in validating the value proposition. It took them two-and-a-half years to develop a value proposition that would drive Dr.Consulta to profitability. After that they began scaling up, raising capital, structuring the management team, and investing in IT. To Thomaz Srougi, "IT is fundamental to healthcare service firms. There will be no healthcare service firm in the future that will survive without IT. So, we are heavily investing in IT. Half of our overhead is spent in developers, programmers, and so on."

Additionally, they created a concept and replicated it. According to Thomaz Srougi,

there is a reason for everything in Dr.Consulta medical center . . . the layout, the colors, and size of the letters . . . we studied and learned a lot in these past years. There is a lot of engineering, lean services, and concepts behind all we do and offer. We have to be very effective. Patients expect quality and agility. So it is all 100 percent aligned: the more productive we are, more social value and more profits.

Dr.Consulta's mission is to offer consultations and examinations at low and competitive prices, guaranteeing fast service and high quality. According to Thomaz Srougi, "high quality for us is process, equipment, and trained doctors." To ensure the high quality, the firm relies on IT. Scheduling can be done by phone, internet, and smartphone. Arriving at the medical center, the patient undergoes procedures managed by software similar to an airline firm, able to identify bottlenecks in care and correct delays in the process. All patient health information is stored in integrated digital medical records throughout the network, and accessible to all health workers who are in contact with the patient through an online platform. The same information also enables monitoring the health status of the patients receiving medium- and long-term care, enabling prophylactic follow-up for prevention and diseases, maintenance of quality of life, and reductions in health costs for episodic, prechronic, and chronic patients. At the end of the consultation or examination, the patient can evaluate the medical care by responding to a survey via SMS. According to Thomaz

Srougi, by optimizing these processes, they are able to offer prices 60 to 90 percent lower than the average of the private healthcare services market.

Considered to be a social impact firm, Dr.Consulta received two LATAM Founders Awards (in 2016 and 2017) in the category "Most Impacting Firm" and received Interbrand Breakthrough Brand 2017 recognition as the only Brazilian brand among those with great leadership potential in their industry.

Dr.Consulta's major strategic capability is IT, in which they continuously invest. Its integrated information system provides patients with access to their medical history in a single platform, not found in the Brazilian public system or other private service firms, or even health insurance providers. Applying artificial intelligence concepts, the system analyzes not only the patient's medical history but also the probability and risk of that patient developing certain medical conditions or diseases over a long period. The growth strategy is based on offering business-to-business healthcare services to small firms and families without health insurance, and healthcare management (customized services) to medium-sized firms.

10.4   Conclusions

In sum, the main strategic capabilities (see Table 10.2) identified in the selected cases are resource identification, ability to develop resources internally, general sales capabilities, and understanding the market and local customer needs. It is clear that these firms are extending their cross-cultural management and research and development capabilities thorough their international expansions. Table 10.3 sets out the firms' capabilities as they apply to future challenges in internationalization.

The sample of Brazilian companies analyzed in this chapter can serve as models for different segments of economic activity. They are not the "usual suspects," iconic Brazilian multinationals like Petrobras or Embraer, but all of them outperform others in their respective markets.

In manufacturing, both WEG's and Fanem's cases reveal that internationalization trajectories present different stages. Initially, the company adopts one specific strategy associated with a defined set of strategic capabilities and as the company moves along its internationalization trajectory, a recursive process takes place, and the set of strategic capabilities and internationalization strategies evolves. At the core are technological capabilities associated with world-class manufacturing and product innovation. As the company increases its degree of internationalization, the need to develop capabilities such as cross-cultural management becomes crucial. Both WEG and Fanem rely on their own

Table 10.2 *Strategic capabilities of Brazilian firms studied*

Major capability	Subcategories	WEG	Fanem	Stefanini	Integration	Grendene	Dr.Consulta
Obtaining resources	Resource identification	✓	✓	✓	✓	✓	✓
	Ability to purchase product inputs	✓	✓	✓	✓	✓	✓
	Ability to develop resources internally	✓	✓	✓	✓	✓	
Product/service capabilities	Product manufacture	✓	✓	✓	✓	✓	✓
	Research and development	✓	✓	✓	✓	✓	✓
	Local product adaptation	✓	✓	✓	✓	✓	✓
Operations and management	Production management	✓	✓	✓	✓	✓	
	Supply chain management	✓	✓		✓	✓	
	Hard skills	✓	✓	✓	✓	✓	✓
	Soft skills	✓	✓	✓	✓	✓	✓
	Entrepreneurship	✓	✓	✓	✓	✓	✓
	Cross-cultural management	✓	✓				
Marketing	General sales capabilities	✓	✓	✓	✓	✓	✓
	Understanding the market and local customer needs	✓		✓	✓	✓	✓
Managing external environment	Political and negotiating capabilities	✓	✓	✓	✓	✓	✓
	Relationship capabilities	✓	✓	✓	✓	✓	✓
	Adjusting to poor infrastructure	✓	✓				
	Knowledge about the national context	✓	✓	✓	✓	✓	

Table 10.3 *Major international activities and major strategic capabilities and challenges among Brazilian firms studied*

Company and industry	International activities	Strategic capabilities and challenges
WEG Electromechanical/ energy	Global consolidator for electric engines; operations in 100 countries; subsidiaries in 22 countries	Strong technological capabilities; management of global manufacturing and services network Challenges: developing new products; upgrading in global value chains
Fanem Medical equipment	Global innovator; exports globally to more than 100 countries; built plants in India and Mexico to supply regional markets; office in Jordan	Product innovation; flexibility to serve different markets directly and through global value chains Challenge: penetrating developed markets
Stefanini IT services	Follow-source supplying large MNEs across the world; operates in developed and emerging countries; three R&D labs, subsidiaries in 37 countries (acquisitions, JV, and greenfield)	Customer orientation combining standard services and flexibility; using big data and analytics Challenge: brand development
Integration Consulting	Created niche market in the consulting business; offices in 6 countries, both developed and emerging	Working with clients in both strategy and implementation Challenge: scaling up
Grendene Footwear	Largest producer in Brazil; exporter; partnership with fashion designers	Management of local supply chain Challenge: creating international brand
Dr. Consulta Health services	No international activities	Standard procedures and metrics development for cost efficiency in business-to-consumer transactions at bottom of pyramid Challenge: business-to-business ventures

international manufacturing networks, with a low level of offshoring or subcontracting; this reduces the capabilities required for supply chain management. In terms of the capabilities needed for international operations management, the degree of integration among WEG's plants is greater than Fanem's, whose plants still operate on a stand-alone basis.

WEG's and Fanem's activities tend to be more business-to-business (B2B) than business-to-consumer, aside from certain Fanem businesses. Although a strong brand name is useful, understanding the final markets (the so-called "Intel inside" effect) is less important; the crucial demand is to establish sound B2B relationships within the value chain, which requires a specific type of marketing capability that is closely aligned to the interests of the participants.

Finally, both WEG and Fanem are firms that adopt a posture of compliance with institutions, both national and international, and seek to negotiate within their realm. This requires the capabilities to create knowledge about national contexts and to use this knowledge to manage relationships.

The genesis of service firms Stefanini and Integration reinforces the argument that the initial set of capabilities developed to succeed in the local market provides a driver for internationalization. Consolidation of a set of differentiated capabilities needed to provide services in one emerging market – Brazil in these cases – became a source of competitive advantage for internationalization in their respective fields of operation. The capabilities they consolidated at home were only a factor of survival and growth in the local market, but they became resources they could exploit to succeed in foreign markets. To build worldwide operating scale, these service companies coped with market demands by following the basic principles of their management models (or their managerial technologies). Stefanini's expansion in the IT industry reveals rapid growth through mergers and acquisitions, and dependence on strong capabilities in both pre- and post-acquisition activities. In contrast, Integration's international growth path is essentially organic, requiring capabilities associated with country and location choices, then scaling up their operations.

Grendene's case illustrates the limits of capability building for internationalization even when the firm has strong comparative advantages. Having mastered the capabilities needed for product development and production, the company was unable to develop the branding and aggressive marketing capabilities required to compete in the global footwear industry with its own brands. Its strategy relies on its role as supplier to global marketers on an OEM basis. Grendene's case shows production and operations as key capabilities for international operations through exports, while innovative design and production processes support its strategy in the local markets.

Finally, Dr.Consulta exemplifies the rise of new business models in emerging countries. Having identified the deficiencies of the public health services and the unaffordability of private services for those at the bottom of the pyramid, Dr.Consulta developed a platform that connects available medical resources, both equipment and expertise, with public demand. This case represents the clever integration of a set of capabilities including entrepreneurship, innovation, and technological mastery.

To summarize, these cases highlight the following points regarding capabilities.

> **Country-of-origin effects**: the features of the local environment deeply influenced capability development in the initial stages of the companies' trajectories. Two dimensions require attention: resources and institutions. Although Brazil is considered a rich country in terms of natural resources, it lacks wealth in terms of qualified human resources and financing, a lack that led these firms to invest in capability building to overcome those barriers. If one adds the turbulence of the political and economic environment, then that building process becomes challenging, resulting in firms that display sound financial capability and high organizational flexibility in association with their previously shown core capabilities.
>
> **Production capabilities**, for both goods and services, are driven by innovation that emerges more from immediate market needs than from the search for scientific breakthrough type of innovation (Fleury et al., 2013).
>
> **International marketing capabilities** were not developed by those Brazilian firms that became accustomed to their operations as suppliers in global value chains.

It should be noted that the degree of direct exposure to international competition substantially enhanced the development of all the above capabilities.

11 Building Strategic Capabilities in Chilean Companies

Developing a Global Competitive Advantage

Santiago Mingo and Francisca Sinn

11.1 Introduction

Outward foreign direct investment (FDI) by firms from emerging markets is an increasingly important issue in international business (Hernandez & Guillén, 2018). In this context, many Chilean companies have expanded and deepened their foreign presence over the last three decades; some are now industry leaders in Latin America. According to Boston Consulting Group (BCG, 2018), Chile is home to eighteen of the 100 most important Latin American multinational companies, even though the country represents only 5 percent of Latin America's GDP. Chilean companies have developed strategic capabilities of varying types to enable their internationalization. Such companies have faced many challenges in this process, and most still lack (or are underdeveloped in) important capabilities that would enable them to compete in developed country markets.

Strategic capabilities in Chilean firms are particularly interesting due to the country's characteristics and its economic development path over the last four decades. Two factors have significantly influenced the internationalization of Chilean firms: first, Chile is relatively small, which limits domestic growth compared to larger Latin American countries, and second, Chile initiated its liberalization process a decade before most other Latin American nations.

This chapter examines the internationalization processes of seven Chilean firms. Through interviews and company information, we explored the role of strategic capabilities developed and used by these firms as they ventured abroad or considered international expansion. Some interesting findings have emerged from our analysis of these companies. First, the companies generally focused their internationalization on Latin American countries. Transferring their strategic capabilities and resources to countries that are geographically near and share similar characteristics is a natural path to internationalization. However, these (and other) Chilean companies typically adopt a very conservative and cautious approach to establishing subsidiaries outside Latin America.

Second, these companies sought to go abroad to enter new markets that promised opportunities for continuous expansion and growth. Going overseas to acquire new strategic capabilities or other resources was not a main driver for internationalization. Most Chilean multinational companies conform to these two patterns.

Such patterns may shift: in the next decade, we expect that internationalization of successful Chilean multinationals will require them to venture beyond Latin American markets. We also anticipate that Chilean companies will go abroad not only to increase revenues but also to develop new capabilities and acquire the knowledge and resources needed to increase their competitiveness.

11.2   Chile: Country Background

Table 11.1 gives an overview of Chile's economic profile. Chile is located in the southwestern part of South America. In 2018, it had a population of

Table 11.1 *Chile: country fact sheet – annual data, 2018*

Population (m)	18.2
GDP (USD bn; market exchange rate)	298.2
GDP (USD bn; purchasing power parity)	476.7
GDP per capita (USD; market exchange rate)	16,388
GDP per capita (USD; purchasing power parity)	26,195
Historical averages (%)	**2014–18**
Population growth	0.8
Real GDP growth	2.2
Inflation	3.5
Current-account balance (% of GDP)	−2.2
FDI inflows (% of GDP)	5.3
Major exports 2018	**% of total**
Copper	37.0
Fresh fruit	7.5
Salmon & trout	6.3
Cellulose	5.6
Leading markets 2018	**% of total**
China	33.5
USA	13.8
Japan	9.3
Brazil	5.7

Source: Economist Intelligence Unit

more than 18 million and a GDP of 298 billion dollars. Given its GDP per capita of more than USD 26,000 (purchasing power parity), the World Bank classifies Chile as a high-income country. The population is mostly located in urban centers, with only 10 percent in rural areas. Santiago, the capital city, contains around 40 percent of the population. Chile is one of the most developed and stable countries in Latin America, with a category of "very high" in the Human Development Index. The country has a strong institutional environment – compared to other emerging markets worldwide – and has enjoyed a high level of economic freedom for nearly three decades.

Chilean exports are very concentrated: 37 percent of exports derive from copper mining. Fresh fruit, fish, wine, and cellulose are among its other important export products. China receives more than 33 percent of Chilean exports and the United States almost 14 percent. Chile is involved in multiple free trade agreements with countries all over the world, including the United States, China, the European Union, Japan, and many countries in Latin America and Asia. The country is a founding member of the Pacific Alliance, a trade bloc it established in 2012 with Colombia, Mexico, and Peru, and has been a member of the OECD since 2010.

Outward FDI in Chile started to become relevant after the country's economic liberalization in the mid-1970s. Structural reforms – including trade liberalization and privatization – were implemented more than a decade earlier than in most Latin American nations (Del Sol & Kogan, 2007; Edwards, 1995). This early exposure to liberalization and promarket reforms enabled some Chilean companies to acquire know-how about transitioning to and operating in a more competitive business environment. This knowledge proved useful when they launched their internationalization processes throughout Latin America in the late 1980s and early 1990s. The expansion of Chilean companies within the region coincided with the implementation of promarket reforms and transitions into more market-friendly economies in other Latin American countries.

Chile never developed specific policies to promote outward FDI or to create national champions (Razo & Calderón, 2010). Economic stability and a market-friendly economy led to development of more sophisticated and competitive firms, which began international expansion to sustain their growth only after they consolidated in the relatively small Chilean domestic market.

Outward FDI increased steadily throughout the 1990s until the onset of Argentina's economic crisis in 2001. This crisis had a significant impact in Chile because at that time, Argentina was the main recipient of Chilean outward FDI. After this recession, outward FDI resumed growth. FDI growth continues, both in terms of flows and stock (Figures 11.1 and 11.2). Peru and Colombia are very important destinations for Chilean

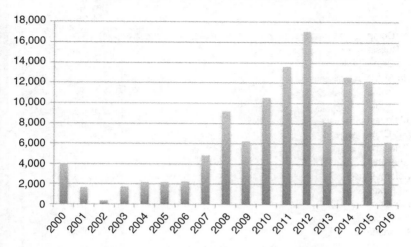

Figure 11.1 Chile's outward FDI flows, 2000–2016 (USD million)
Source: UNCTAD

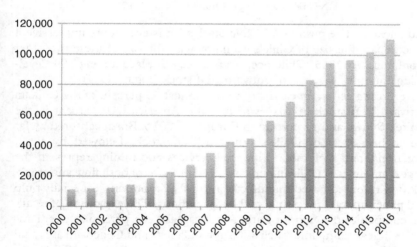

Figure 11.2 Chile's outward FDI stock, 2000–2016 (USD million)
Source: UNCTAD

outward FDI, and Brazil acquired more attention from Chilean investors during the 2010s. Today, many of the larger companies listed on the Chilean stock market generate more than 40 percent of their revenues abroad. Over the last decade, Chilean outward FDI was consistently among that of the top three Latin American countries, joining Brazil

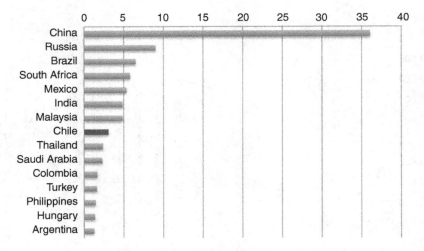

Figure 11.3 Chile's outward FDI stock as a percentage of total outward
FDI stock from top fifteen developing countries, 2015
Source: UNCTAD and World Bank Group (2017)

and Mexico. The position of Chile on this list is even more impressive if
we compare the size of Chile's economy with the size of these two other
economies. In 2015, Chile occupied the eighth place among 109 developing countries in terms of outward FDI stock (Figure 11.3).

Regarding geographical distribution, almost 45 percent of the Chilean
outward FDI stock in 2016 was in Latin America,[1] 10 percent in the
United States, and 12 percent in Europe. In 2016, Brazil captured by far
the highest level of Chile's outward FDI stock, followed by Peru,
Argentina, and Colombia. Financial services and mining represent the
largest amounts of Chilean outward FDI, in terms of both flow and stock.
Natural resource-based manufacturing is also important, especially pulp
and paper, metal processing, and hydrocarbons. The expansion of retailing companies throughout Latin America has been particularly remarkable: Chilean companies such as Grupo Falabella and Cencosud are retail
giants throughout the region. In the transportation sector, LATAM airlines and the shipping company CSAV stand out.

11.3   Methodology and Company Selection

The investigators used a qualitative approach to study the role of strategic
capabilities in the internationalization process of Chilean firms. Our analysis

Table 11.2 *Data collection matrix for the selection of Chilean firms as case studies*

		Firm category		
		Purely domestic	Exporter	Multinational
Industry	High-tech			ALTO
	Low-tech	BeitGroup	Kunstmann Casas del Toqui	Forus*
	Service			Forus* Derco eClass

* Forus is involved in services (retail) and some low-tech manufacturing.

is based on case studies of actual companies that have already internationalized, or that have the potential to do so. We chose seven companies from different economic sectors, of different sizes, and at different stages in their internationalization processes (see Tables 11.2 and 11.3). Methodologically, our study and analysis followed four stages. First, we reviewed a list of potential strategic capabilities typically associated with firm success and discussed how these might apply to the specifics of the selected companies and their internationalization processes. Second, we reviewed publicly available company information to familiarize ourselves with each firm. Next, we performed company interviews. Each of these face-to-face interviews – which are the heart of this study – was attended by both authors of this chapter and by at least one of the top executives or board members that were familiar with the history of the company, its strategic capabilities, and its international activities. Although we prepared a list of questions and topics to guide our discussions, the interviews were relatively unstructured and exploratory. Interviews lasted between 80 and 90 minutes. The fourth stage was a follow-up to gather missing information about the company or clarify issues that emerged during the interviews. Finally, after writing up the company cases, we carried out cross-case analysis to compare and contrast the companies and the roles played by their capabilities in the internationalization process. The data collection process and interviews took place between September 2017 and March 2018.

11.4   Company Cases

Based on our interviews with executives and archival information, we analyzed each company's strategic capabilities to identify those playing

Table 11.3 *Selected data for Chilean firms studied*

Company name	Year of foundation	Assets*	Sales*	Percentage of sales overseas	Number of employees	Foreign countries with subsidiaries	Interviewees
eClass	2004	Confidential	Confidential	Confidential	300	Peru, Colombia, Paraguay, and Panama	Luz María González (CEO), Largio Romero (VP Strategy and Technology)
ALTO	2003	Confidential	Confidential	50%	470	Colombia, Mexico, Spain, and the United States	Jorge Encina (CEO), Juan Cristóbal Palacios (Country Manager, Chile)
Kunstmann	1991	47	32	5%	125	No foreign subsidiaries; exports to multiple countries	Armin Kunstmann (Founder & CEO), Alejandro Kunstmann (Marketing Director)
Forus	1980	336	372	20%	4,120	Peru, Colombia, and Uruguay	Hugo Ovando (CEO), Marisol Céspedes (CFO)
Derco	1959	1,350	2,278	40%	4,700	Bolivia, Peru, and Colombia	Ramiro Urenda (Board Member and former CEO)
Casas del Toqui S.A.	1994	10	4	90–95%	45	No foreign subsidiaries; exports to multiple countries	Ricardo Court (President and CEO), Diego Callejas (CCO), Fernando Vargas (Export Director)
BeitGroup	1955	32	30	<1%	507	No foreign subsidiaries	Jorge Jadue (Founder & CEO)

* Assets and sales figures are approximate and in USD millions, 2017 or latest year available.

a crucial role in each firm's domestic and international success. In our analysis of each company, we sought to

- identify strategic capabilities seen by the firm as critical in its domestic market;
- analyze how the firm transferred these capabilities abroad and adapted them to a different country context; and
- identify capabilities that the firm lacks, but that its leaders view as important for success in foreign locations.

eClass

Founded in 2004, eClass is a Chilean e-learning company with head-quarters in Santiago. Currently, it has operations in Chile, Peru, Colombia, Panama, and Paraguay. The company offers online and blended-learning programs to both individual and corporate clients,[2] providing more than 220 courses in business, English as a second language, education, health, and other customized areas. Students may enroll in courses on a standalone basis or within certification programs consisting of four to six courses. Throughout its history, eClass courses and programs have benefited more than 500,000 students, and around 600 companies use eClass programs to train their employees. The company initiated its internationalization process in 2009 with operations in Peru. Subsequently, eClass entered Colombia (2011), Paraguay (2015), and Panama (2016).

According to company executives, a firm must possess certain critical resources and capabilities to succeed in the online learning industry. The first is the technology platform used to deliver the learning experience, which eClass developed internally. The e-learning industry is relatively underdeveloped throughout Latin America, especially in the countries entered by eClass. In Chile, the industry started developing earlier than elsewhere in the region. Thus the eClass technology platform translated into an important source of competitive advantage within Latin America. Yet in markets where e-learning is more developed, such as the USA and Spain, a good technology platform is a necessary but not sufficient condition for success. The company's preferred internationalization strategy is to enter foreign countries with nascent or incipient e-learning industries.

Another resource needed to succeed in this industry is a strong reputation as a well-established educational institution in the target market. When it began operating in Chile, eClass lacked these credentials. To solve this problem, the firm established long-term alliances with leading educational institutions in the country, especially universities. These partners typically provide content and course instructors while eClass benefits from their reputation and credibility. A key resource for establishing these alliances has been eClass executives and board members with strong networks of professional relationships within the country. The company developed the capability needed to successfully maintain and manage these alliances. For internationalization, the capacity to establish these alliances is even more important. However, it is significantly more difficult to establish networks of professional relationships that are as strong as in their home countries. This explains the "seize-the-opportunity" approach followed by eClass in their internationalization process. For example, a contact in Universidad de los Andes triggered entry into the Colombian market; this contact facilitated establishment of an alliance with the university.

Finally, another interesting route to the internationalization of eClass was to follow some of their Chilean multinational clients overseas to offer e-learning services in their subsidiaries. Corporate programs are a crucial component of eClass offerings. Finding corporate clients requires a network of contacts in the country, a capability to sell custom-made programs, and a strong reputation in the market. Naturally, the network of contacts is much easier to develop in the home country than abroad, especially when the mode of entry into another country is a solo greenfield investment. The networks of eClass's founders and executives were crucial assets when the company was young. Later, as eClass developed a network of corporate clients and the company's reputation became stronger, capability to sell custom-made programs acquired more importance. Most countries entered by eClass had weak e-learning industries. Individual programs were easier to sell in foreign settings due to their more standardized nature. However, even for a strong e-learning company that offers corporate services, and even when it has alliances to long-standing educational institutions, a lack of both local networks and reputation in the foreign destination is a barrier.

A flexible and dynamic organizational culture has played a crucial role in the eClass internationalization process. The company has won multiple awards for its high-performing workplace culture. Its corporate culture is consistent with the organic test-and-learn approach they follow when venturing abroad. Starting small with an organic entry mode, they have been able to exploit this organizational culture effectively. Other entry modes such as acquisition would prevent them from taking full advantage of their organizational culture.

Certification also played a role in their internationalization process. Relevant international certifications – such as ISO 9000 or B Corp – can be a strategic resource when entering a new country. Such certifications can substitute for lack of reputation in the host country and help attract individuals, companies, and potential allies in educational institutions.

ALTO

Founded in 2003, ALTO is a Chilean loss prevention company head-quartered in Santiago. ALTO Alliance[sm], the most traditional solution provided by ALTO, focuses on reducing retail theft.[3] The company protects more than 7,000 stores in over 100 cities and operates in Chile, Colombia, Mexico, Spain, and the United States. ALTO's business model combines advanced surveillance technology to monitor assets, extensive data analysis to prevent theft, marketing techniques to deter criminals, and intelligent criminal prosecution. Collaboration is crucial in ALTO's businesses: ALTO not only collaborates with clients but also collaborates with communities to fight theft. ALTO developed its pro-prietary technology platform to provide real-time reporting to clients about theft attempts and occurrences. One innovative ALTO feature is the use of marketing tools to prevent retail loss – particularly interesting is the use of messages sent directly to offenders and criminal networks to dissuade them from coming to their clients' stores and shipping facilities.

ALTO initiated its internationalization process in 2006 when it opened in Colombia. Subsequently, they entered Mexico (2011), Spain (2016), and the United States (2016). The decision to enter Colombia was unplanned; ALTO simply followed their Chilean clients that were start-ing operations in Colombia. In some ways, the start of their internatio-nalization process was relatively "safe." Although the decision to enter Mexico was more deliberate, a prior relationship with Walmart in Chile allowed them to secure a key pilot program with Walmart Mexico on their entry to Mexico. In the case of Spain, the decision to enter linked to an opportunity that presented itself. The ownership structure of this sub-sidiary is also different due to the involvement of a Spanish counterpart. According to our interviewees, the entrepreneurial and "colonizing spirit" of the founder was the main driver for ALTO's internationalization into the United States.

According to ALTO executives, establishing a close and cooperative relationship with clients is an important capability. Success in this busi-ness requires trust and collaboration between the company and its clients. For instance, to be able to take full advantage of its sophisticated technol-ogy platform, clients need to provide ALTO with all the data it needs. The collaboration between ALTO and its clients also plays an important role in the criminal prosecution process. Developing such close relationships with clients takes time and involves a significant level of commitment from all sides. This is even more challenging in foreign countries because ALTO's "liability of foreignness" enters the equation. In part, this explains why ALTO entered Colombia following Chilean retail companies that were already their clients in Chile and had operations in other Latin American countries. In the case of Mexico, something similar occurred. Through Walmart Chile, which was a client of ALTO, they were able to secure Walmart Mexico as the first client in Mexico. Taking advantage of the fact that Walmart Mexico oversees the Walmart operation in other Central American countries, ALTO is using Mexico as a platform to enter those countries too.

The ability to develop a strong network of contacts is another of ALTO's important strategic capabilities. The contacts and connections of executives, founders, and board members can be especially important for a company offering a nontraditional service and product, such as ALTO. For firms offering novel products and services to large clients, the reputation of executives, founders, and board members is a critical asset. Contacts and connections with the business world can help build this reputation and open doors. This strategic asset is particularly important in emerging markets. In contrast, ALTO's executives found that in the USA the business culture is more meritocratic, and clients are willing to try new service ideas such as the one ALTO provides. In Latin America, a robust commercial strategy and an innovative product is not sufficient. For instance, the absence of a network of contacts in Colombia and Mexico has always been a challenge for ALTO.

Another resource critical to ALTO's business is the contextual knowledge and capacity to understand the local circumstances related to the product and services on offer. To prevent losses, ALTO's business model requires deep knowledge about the national culture and value system, the political situation, and the country context, especially aspects related to theft practices, insurance, and prosecution. Any loss-prevention firm expanding overseas will face this challenge. However, these factors could be particularly problematic for ALTO due to the unorthodox nature of their solution. ALTO has developed its capability to absorb contextual knowledge through its experience entering and operating in other countries.

Research and development (R&D) capabilities are fundamental to ALTO's business. The company's product and service offerings depend on a proprietary technology platform to manage the intelligence and other information needed to prevent loss. Also, their solution requires constant upgrading. Machine learning allows continuous improvement of the platform as the system acquires more information. Although every country requires some degree of technology platform adaptation, ALTO has been able to successfully deploy its software internationally.

According to the executives interviewed, ALTO's technology has increasing strategic importance. For instance, even though the initial objective of entering the USA was to find new markets to expand the size of the business, the company has found new technologies and start-ups there that will help improve the technological sophistication of their proprietary software. Interestingly, as the technology platform becomes a more prominent strategic resource, it becomes easier to introduce into other markets.

Finally, the executives interviewed highlighted ALTO's flexible and entrepreneurial organizational culture. This resource has played a fundamental role during the firm's internationalization process. ALTO's international expansion has been organic, building foreign sub-sidiaries from scratch. Thus entering a new country is essentially found-ing a new venture – many of the challenges encountered are similar to the ones any new business venture faces. The newness and innovativeness of their product and service offerings require a lively and entrepreneurial organizational culture to which potential and current clients will respond. Identifying and attracting new talent that fits into this emerging corporate culture is also a crucial, yet somewhat undeveloped capability.

Kunstmann

Cervecería Kunstmann is a Chilean premium beer producer founded in 1991 by Armin Kunstmann and his wife, Patricia Ramos, in their home kitchen in the city of Valdivia (southern region of Chile). In 1997, they built a production facility and expanded the original business by adding a restaurant next to the brewery. This unique concept offered beer and food and included a souvenir store and a beer museum. The continuing presence and involvement of the Kunstmann family is critical to the process of building a unique experience around their beer. Kunstmann recently installed a beer pub in Santiago to bring the Kunstmann experi-ence closer to their customers in a major urban center. The manufactur-ing and restaurant businesses complement each other and generate important synergies that strengthen the premium position of the Kunstmann beer in the Chilean market.

Kunstmann's first internationalization attempt occurred in 1999 when they started exporting to Japan and the USA. Their entrance into these markets was in response to opportunities that presented themselves, rather than a deliberate internationalization strategy. Later, they stopped exporting to these two countries.

In 2002, the company entered into a joint venture with Compañía Cervercerías Unidas (CCU), a leading Latin American beverage company based in Chile. CCU purchased 50 percent of Kunstmann's beer production business. CCU is the largest Chilean brewer, the second-largest Chilean carbonated soft drinks producer, and one of the largest Chilean wine producers. It is also the second-largest Chilean wine exporter. In addition to Chile, CCU has operations in Argentina, Bolivia, Colombia, Paraguay, and Uruguay – in Argentina, it is the second-largest brewer.

A more systematic internationalization plan began in 2009 when Kunstmann started exporting to Argentina, taking advantage of CCU's already established distribution network. In the next few years, they started selling their products in Brazil and Colombia through independent distributors. Subsequently, they entered Paraguay and Uruguay with the help of CCU. Kunstmann also exports sporadically to other countries outside Latin America, such as Spain, New Zealand, and Taiwan. They currently plan to internationalize into the Peruvian and Bolivian markets.

In general, distribution capabilities are crucial to the beverage industry. The case of Kunstmann is no exception. Distributing is more challenging than distributing domestically. Having access to and developing strong relationships with local distributors in foreign locations requires negotiating skills plus knowledge of the distribution process in the destination country. The partnership with CCU has been critical in this respect. CCU has a strong distribution network in the Latin American countries where they operate. Kunstmann has been able to "borrow" CCU's distribution capabilities, both domestically and abroad. Even though Kunstmann benefits from CCU's distribution network in some Latin American countries, they still participate in other markets where CCU is not present. Thus they have also been developing their own distribution capabilities abroad, especially negotiating skills and relationship capabilities that have helped them to establish agreements with local distributors. It is certain that the capabilities provided by CCU played a crucial role in the development of Kunstmann's distribution capabilities.

CEO and founder Armin Kunstmann is also a strategic resource, as the architect of the Kunstmann experience. Having the founder as the CEO helps nurture the magic glow that surrounds the creation and history of the company. In addition, Armin's prior experience working in his parents' family business exposed him to exporting realities. His expertise was vital to the successful international expansion of the company.

Other important capabilities held by Cervecería Kunstmann relate to manufacturing the product and obtaining high-quality inputs and ingredients. Their capacity to manufacture premium beer is also strong, both in terms of the quantity they can produce and the quality they can achieve. Because they are exporters, all Kunstmann's foreign operations benefit from these capabilities and there is no immediate need to transfer these production capabilities to foreign markets. However, if Kunstmann were to start beer production outside the home country, transferring these capabilities could be difficult and the magic surrounding the brewing location would be lost.

The Kunstmann product itself represents another important strategic resource and capability. The quality and tradition of Kunstmann beer, combined with its unique position in the market, are among the most important factors that enable the company's success. This is what the CEO and founder calls "the Kunstmann experience." This strategic resource is difficult to imitate. However, taking advantage of this resource abroad required adaptation. For example, in an international context, the manufacturing location – the city of Valdivia – is typically unknown. To resolve this issue, the company linked the beer to the region where Valdivia is located – foreign consumers are more familiar with this region (Patagonia, at the southern end of South America). The pub/restaurant business also plays a role in transmitting the Kunstmann experience and the magic surrounding the product. In 2014, they opened a beer pub in Bariloche, Argentina. This was their first beer pub in a foreign country. They plan to open twenty Kunstmann beer pubs throughout Latin America over the next few years.

Forus

Founded in 1980, Forus is a Chilean publicly traded company that produces, imports, designs, distributes, wholesales, and retails fashion products from top international and domestic brands. Forus sells multiple specialized brands of footwear, apparel, and accessories online and through its network of 494 stores. The competitive advantage of the company revolves around the strength of their portfolio of brands, the operation of a large network of stores, the outstanding retail experience provided to consumers, and the excellent quality of their products. Each of their stores is typically dedicated to selling a specific apparel or footwear trademark. Currently, Forus manages a portfolio of more than thirty brands. Most of these brands are internationally recognized for their designs and high quality, such as Columbia, Cat Footwear, Merrell, Patagonia, Hush Puppies, and Nine West. At its founding, Wolverine World Wide (WWW) owned 30 percent of Forus. The Chilean businessman Alfonso Swett owned the remaining 70 percent of the company.

WWW is a company that spans multiple countries and owns a wide portfolio of prestigious brands – many of these brands are the ones that Forus has been promoting since its inception. In 1991, the ICL group led by Alfonso Swett acquired WWW's stake in the company. However, Forus and WWW still maintain a close strategic partnership.

Forus initiated its internationalization process in 1993, entering Uruguay. This decision was not part of a comprehensive internationalization strategy but rather an opportunity that presented itself. The company started operating in Uruguay with the Hush Puppies brand. More than a decade later, Forus entered Peru (2006) and Colombia (2006). This occurred during the year that Forus became a publicly traded company. The company's entry in to the Peruvian and Colombian markets was part of a deliberate internationalization strategy.

Essential to Forus's business model is a strong portfolio of brands they sell through a large network of stores. In Chilean markets, apparel and footwear are typically sold through department stores or stores focused on selling specific brands. In the latter case, these are either stores owned directly by the manufacturer or franchisees that have the right to sell a brand in a specific country or region. What is unique about Forus is their management of a large portfolio of brands. According to their executives, this model is advantageous because it helps to achieve scale and, at the same time, a portfolio of multiple brands allows the company to manage more risks associated with the promotion of individual brands.

The development of strong capabilities to manage a portfolio of brands and operate a network of stores to promote these brands has been crucial for Forus. Naturally, if Forus seeks long-term success in other countries, they must develop the portfolio of brands and the store network in the foreign destination. Although it may be easy for Forus to transfer the capability to manage a portfolio of brands and operate a network of stores, to exploit their strategic capabilities they will need the portfolio of brands and the network of store locations. This is not easy to accomplish and takes time and heavy investment.

To internationalize, Forus needs to secure the rights to introduce and promote each brand in the destination country. If the brand is already present in the market, they will need to acquire these rights from the current operator. Naturally, Forus prefers to retail brands that they already sell in Chile. The partnership with WWW helped build Forus's brand portfolio in other countries due to Forus's preferential access to WWW's brands. Without this partnership, the internationalization process and the possibility of exploiting Forus's business model abroad would be much more difficult to achieve. The Colombia example illustrates this point. Forus entered this country focusing on the Hush Puppies trademark. Later on, they established a formal joint venture with WWW to develop a stronger portfolio of brands. In this particular case, WWW acquired a significant portion of the Colombian operation, although Forus does not have a formal joint venture with WWW. In Peru, the company has developed a strong and interesting brand portfolio.

As noted, the strategic capability of managing a network of stores to promote a brand portfolio is one of the pillars of Forus's business model. Forus followed different paths in Colombia and Peru. In the former country, Forus initially prioritized the wholesale business over the retail business. This strategy was problematic because it delayed the development of the retail business. In other words, they neglected a key strategic capability that is closely linked to their business model. This explains, in part, some of the problems and relatively disappointing results in this country. In contrast to the Colombian case, the Peruvian operation emphasized the retail business and the mixture of retail and wholesale is similar to that in Chile.

Dealing with external environments that vary from that in the home country has been a challenge for Forus. For example, in Colombia, some of the brands promoted by Forus appear in informal markets. In addition, the level of vertical integration in the Colombian apparel and footwear industry is high, which makes it more difficult to implement a business model focused on promotion rather than production. Retail business in Colombia has a strong real estate component with which Forus is less familiar. However, a transition to malls, especially in Bogota, transformed the retail model into one much closer to that of Chile and other developed markets. The failed Forus foray into Argentina reveals the importance of the external environment. Changes in apparel and footwear import tariffs made the Argentinian operation – based on importing shoes from Chile – unsustainable.

Derco

Founded in 1959, Derco is one of the leading Latin American vehicle, automotive parts, and machinery importers and distributors. The company is also a leading automotive aftermarket provider. Currently, Derco has exclusive rights to promote more than 100 internationally recognized brands in the countries where they operate. Derco's main business unit – DercoCenter – focuses on importing, distributing, and promoting multiple brands of passenger vehicles such as Suzuki, Mazda, Chevrolet, Citroën, and Renault. More recently, they have added various Chinese brands. DercoCenter sells eight automobile brands in Chile, twelve in Peru, ten in Bolivia, and four in Colombia. DercoMaq is another business unit that sells agricultural machinery, construction machinery, and commercial transportation machinery. Focusing on the vehicle brands sold by DercoCenter and DercoMaq, DercoParts is the business unit in the automotive aftermarket, importing, distributing, and marketing vehicle parts, tires, lubricants, and vehicle accessories. Derco's AutoPlanet retail chain sells auto parts and accessories to consumers.

The Derco business model is unique: they sell many well-established brands under the same roof. This model applies to both passenger vehicles and machinery. You can see vehicles from different manufacturers next to each other in the same showroom – for example, Mazda, Suzuki, and Renault. Derco stores highlight and give more prominence to the Derco brand than to specific vehicle brands. Consumers view Derco as a trusted dealer that provides a great after-sales customer experience. While vehicle manufacturers may resist the offering of multiple brands in the same store, Derco is very successful in terms of sales and been able to achieve low distribution costs and selling expenses that vehicle manufacturers are unable to match. Derco has been able to maintain its cost advantage and improve its position in the market. In addition, the company has remained in a good position to negotiate with vehicle manufacturers and is not at the mercy of their unilateral decisions. More recently, Derco has strengthened its customer relationship management capabilities, using state-of-the-art technology to take advantage of the vast amounts of information they have about their customers.

Derco ventured abroad for the first time in 1990, selling the Suzuki brand in Bolivia. They entered the Bolivian market at Suzuki's request. In 1997, they started operating in Peru under similar circumstances. Later on, they evolved these operations into their traditional multibrand model. Interestingly, the internationalization into these two markets was "pushed" by Suzuki – it was not the result of a planned strategy of foreign expansion. The slow start in Peru and Bolivia soon evolved into a deliberate international expansion plan and deployment of their unique business model in the Latin American region. More than a decade after entering the Peruvian market, Derco entered Colombia (2009). In addition to their machinery and truck business, Derco Colombia focused on selling passenger vehicles manufactured by Chinese companies. In terms of plans, the company expects to continue its internationalization throughout Latin America except in countries that are members of the Mercosur trade bloc.[4] Although Derco's unique business model – based on the strength of the Derco brand and the sale of multiple vehicle brands from different manufacturers – is successful, its dependence on contracts with vehicle manufacturers is an inherent risk. The internationalization of Derco may ameliorate the risks associated with this situation.

One relevant factor that can affect success in the marketing of vehicles is political capabilities. In some countries – such as Brazil and Argentina – the government protects the domestic automobile industry, and companies manufacturing vehicles domestically carry a lot of clout. On the other hand, in countries such as Chile, vehicle sales rely on imports and domestic vehicle manufacturing is virtually nonexistent. Thus, the role of political capabilities – and the capacity to handle situations that depend on government issues – can vary significantly between countries. Derco has avoided internationalizing into Argentina and Brazil for this reason. The company's competitive advantage is partly linked to its capability to handle the process of importing vehicles. Naturally, this capability is significantly less relevant in countries with strong domestic production and high import tariffs to protect local vehicle manufacturers.

Unlike other companies included in this study, Derco has not experienced major problems finding and integrating foreign talent into their subsidiaries abroad. The company avoids sending talent from Chile to overseas subsidiaries. According to the executive interviewed, local talent is readily available in the countries where they operate. A centralized approach is used to transfer and operate Derco's business model abroad. The focus is on developing an effective corporate organizational structure. The capability to successfully operate the company at the corporate level has priority.

Derco has replicated its business model with little adaptation in the foreign countries where it operates. In an international context, this allows it to transfer its capabilities in operations and logistics, management, and marketing more effectively. To use this tactic, it is crucial to choose foreign locations similar to Chile in terms of relationships with vehicle manufacturers and the importation, distribution, and retailing rules and process. Derco has developed strong relationships with its suppliers throughout its history. Vehicle manufacturers know that Derco's model works in the Chilean context. Therefore, it is likely that some automobile producers will agree to replicate a similar collaboration with Derco in other Latin American markets. Despite the success of Derco to date, its executives worry about the future of the company due to the vast changes looming over the industry, such as wider adoption of electric cars, self-driving vehicles, and ride-hailing services. Will Derco's business model and its strategic capabilities survive disruptive changes in the industry?

Casas del Toqui

Casas del Toqui is a boutique Chilean wine company currently owned by the Court family. A French wine producer – Château Larose Trintaudon from the Bordeaux region – founded the winery in 1994 in partnership with Chilean wine producers. In 2010, the Court family acquired the winery. Most of its vineyards are 100 km south of Santiago, in the Alto Cachapoal area. Casas del Toqui's winery produces high-quality wines for export to almost 30 countries around the world. Currently the winery has a capacity of 2 million liters, and the average selling price of the wines is 36 dollars per nine-liter box.[5] Casas del Toqui has been involved in exports since its inception. The Chilean domestic market was never its focus – the company exports 90 to 95 percent of its production.

The worldwide reputation and leadership of the Chilean wine industry have facilitated access to world markets, and internationalization can take place rapidly in the Chilean wine industry. Chile's wine sector is an industry cluster, defined as a "geographic concentration of interconnected companies and institutions in a particular field" (Porter, 1998: 78). The relatively advanced economic and physical infrastructure of clusters can help streamline the internationalization process of young and small companies. It would be a lot more difficult for young companies to internationalize if they were not located in a cluster. However, being part of an industry with a certain international reputation may have drawbacks for smaller producers because the country of origin of the product is determinant. Even though Chilean wines have a good reputation worldwide, the average price of 28 dollars per box is relatively low compared to average prices of wines from leading regions such as France and California. Therefore, despite the benefits of being located in the Chilean wine cluster, small and medium-sized high-end wineries such as Casas del Toqui can experience difficulty competing with high-end wineries from Europe and the United States.

The capability to vinify (produce wine from grapes) is fundamental for Casas del Toqui. They also vinify grapes from other vineyards. The company's vineyards are in locations with exceptional soil and weather conditions that are ideal for growing grapes destined to become high-quality wine. This has required the development of capabilities related to the identification and purchase of high-quality inputs. Regarding actual making of the wine, in 2011, the company performed a significant renovation of the winery to incorporate state-of-the-art technology.

Having the resources and capabilities needed to produce a premium product is not enough to compete in international wine markets. Casas del Toqui carries out many downstream activities, such as actively participating in international wine fairs around the world. Relationship capabilities are essential to the establishment of flexible and close long-term relationships with buyers and distributors. The top management team, including the president and owner of the company, are careful to show potential buyers not only the premium quality of the wine but also the "mystique" surrounding it. Casas del Toqui uses different strategies to develop the "story" behind each product. The family behind this boutique winemaker plays an important and highly visible role. The company also implements eco-friendly practices that contribute to the aura surrounding the brand.

Understanding distribution and how the market operates are particularly relevant in the wine business. The product needs to travel from wine-producing regions to wine-consuming areas. Unlike the larger wine producers, smaller producers depend completely on third-party distributors to reach the final destination. Casas del Toqui has acquired experience and knowledge about distribution. The professionalism and experience of the top management team also played a significant role in generating trusting relationships with distributors. Casas del Toqui needs to differentiate itself from the many poorly managed small and medium-sized wineries that sell their products in international markets. One interesting tactic is to approach smaller distributors instead of large ones that focus their energies on wine giants. Casas del Toqui has developed the capability of finding reliable distributors and establishing strong relationships with both distributors and buyers.

In the wine business, it is also critical to develop the capability to navigate the different regulations in destination countries. Some of these regulations relate to alcoholic drinks in general and others are specific to the wine industry. Beverage laws regulate multiple aspects of wine production and marketing, such as wine classification, protected designations of origin, labeling, and vinification and viticulture practices. Compliance with these laws and regulations is crucial, especially for companies competing in global wine markets. In the case of Chile, lax enforcement has been problematic for premium wine producers, as some small wineries try to game the system by selling products that do not comply with the specific regulations of the destination countries. This inappropriate behavior can damage the country's reputation. Casas del Toqui carefully follows destination country regulations, viewing this as key to building long-term trusting relationships with their buyers.

BeitGroup

BeitGroup – formerly known as Pillín[6] – is a family-owned children's clothing company founded by the brothers Jorge and Alvaro Jadue in 1985. The Jadue family entered the clothing business in the 1950s when Jorge and Alvaro's father manufactured and sold clothing from a property located in Santiago. Unfortunately, the business went bankrupt during the early 1980s recession. In 1985, the brothers

Jorge and Álvaro Jadue brought the business back to life by founding a new firm known today as BeitGroup. In the 1990s in Chile, clothing production grew and department stores became important buyers – nearly 70 percent of sales came from department stores. In the year 2000, BeitGroup began outsourcing production to China while local manufacturing started to decrease. Four years later, they closed their clothing factory and stopped domestic production. Since then, the company has focused on designing, distributing, and retailing clothing. BeitGroup started developing its store network in the late 2000s. In October 2007, they opened their first store in a shopping mall. The sale of clothes through department store channels became significantly less relevant as they continued opening their own retail stores.

Today, their sixty stores across the country generate drastically changed revenue patterns: 78 percent of revenues flow from company-managed stores, 21 percent from department stores, and 1 percent from online sales. The opening of a new state-of-the-art distribution center in 2016 was an important milestone for the company, and BeitGroup expects a significantly increased efficiency and reduced costs during the next few years.

The capabilities and resources required for the company to be successful evolved over time. Between 1985 and 2000, the focus was on design, production, and marketing of children's clothing through department stores and one company-managed store located next to the factory. At that time, the capabilities and resources needed for success were related to clothing design, purchase of product inputs, product manufacturing, negotiation with department stores, and sales and marketing. Particularly important was the capability to handle relationships with department stores.

Some of BeitGroup's original capabilities changed their level of importance in the 2000s. After the company phased out its manufacturing in the mid-2000s, many of the capabilities associated with this function became less relevant. However, their manufacturing know-how continues to be crucial for managing outsourcing of their production. This knowledge allows BeitGroup to be fully aware of the actions of third-party producers and to evaluate suppliers and product quality. BeitGroup's clothing design capabilities – which continue to play a key role in the company's business model – also benefit from this prior experience. For instance, it allows them to develop designs that Chinese manufacturers will be able to successfully produce.

BeitGroup's first major international business transactions took place in 2000 with the outsourcing of production to China, as proposed by the Chilean multinational Capricorn. BeitGroup had been purchasing Capricorn's textiles for use in its own local manufacturing facility.

Capricorn offered to act as an intermediary so BeitGroup could outsource some production to China. The outsourcing turned out to be a success story and local production became less important. After four years, BeitGroup closed its manufacturing facility, transferring all production abroad. The collaboration with Capricorn during the early 2000s allowed BeitGroup to start developing capabilities to handle the third-party manufacturing process in China. It is important to note that the company continued to design their clothing in-house. Even though their design capabilities were strong, they had to adapt them to the new context and develop designs that could be produced by Chinese manufacturers. As BeitGroup developed the capabilities to manage the outsourcing of their production, the company decreased its dependence on Capricorn and developed the ability to select Chinese manufacturers and build their own relationships with them. Currently, they work with almost fifty Chinese producers per season without any intermediaries.

As they moved their production abroad, they started an vigorous round of store openings during the second half of the 2000s. Naturally, needs for new strategic capabilities and resources emerged. Opening and operating a network of stores represented new challenges for BeitGroup. First, the new stores required a more complete range of products than the company had hitherto produced. The outsourcing of production to China was crucial to increasing the number of product lines, including a wide variety of shoes and accessories. Doing this through in-house production would have been extremely difficult. Second, the capability to coordinate the design of their stores also became critical. One member of the board of directors is the owner and CEO of a prestigious Chilean architecture company specialized in retail store design. Third, they had to develop capabilities to manage the operation of stores inside shopping malls and handle relationships with mall operators. Fourth, capabilities to handle the steadily increasing number of employees working at their retail stores became important. Finally, as they expanded their store network, distribution capabilities started to become crucial. To address this issue, they built and opened a state-of-the-art distribution center in 2016, requiring an investment of 7 million dollars.

BeitGroup still does not have retail operations abroad, even though its main competitor – also a Chilean company – started opening stores in Peru a decade ago. First, outstanding domestic growth has kept the focus of the company on developing and operating a strong network of stores across Chile and improving their distribution capabilities to serve this increasing number of stores. Both capital expenditures and the attention of the top management team have focused on capitalizing on the success of domestic operations. Second, they adopted a more cautious approach to international expansion, preferring a "second mover" role. Last but certainly not least, the brothers that founded BeitGroup and still lead the management team represent a critical resource that is difficult to replicate or transfer overseas.

Currently, BeitGroup is actively evaluating the possibility of opening stores in Peru and some progress has been made toward this goal. They have identified a potential partner that can support entrance into the Peruvian market, and BeitGroup plans to establish a formal joint venture with them. This potential partner has a network of seventy shoe stores in Peru plus experience in warehousing, logistics, distribution, and the operation of retail stores in that country. They also have established relationships with multiple mall operators in Peru.

11.5   Discussion and Conclusion

Table 11.4 summarizes the most important capabilities required to succeed in each of the companies and their respective businesses. We inferred the relevance of these capabilities based on the company interviews. There are a few interesting patterns that can be observed. First, eClass and ALTO – the companies that depend most on the development and use of technology – have a similar profile. In these two companies, R&D and local product adaptation are capabilities that play critical roles. An entrepreneurial and dynamic culture is also crucial. In the case of Kunstmann and Casas del Toqui, the focus on selling exclusive products requires strong capabilities to obtain high-quality resources and manufacture premium products. Marketing skills, sales capabilities, and the capacity to understand customer needs are common across the seven companies. Finally, developing skills to manage the external environment is a critical capability in every company with international activities – especially the largest, Forus and Derco. In the case of BeitGroup – the only purely domestic company – managing the external environment is relatively less important. However, when the company starts exploring international opportunities, this capability will certainly become increasingly relevant.

In this chapter, we first described Chile's situation in terms of outward FDI. Next, we examined the strategic capabilities of seven Chilean companies involved in internationalization processes and one purely domestic company that is seriously considering going abroad in the next few years. The Chilean case is distinctive among Latin American countries and emerging markets. First, major Chilean companies started their internationalizing earlier than those in other Latin American markets. This relates to an earlier liberalization of the Chilean economy compared to

Table 11.4 *Capabilities of Chilean firms studied*

Major capability category	Subcategories	eClass	ALTO	Kunstmann	Forus	Derco	Casas del Toqui	Beit Group
Obtaining resources	Resource identification							✓
	Ability to purchase product inputs	✓	✓				✓	✓
	Ability to develop resources internally						✓	
Product/service capabilities	Product manufacture							
	Research & development	✓	✓	✓			✓	✓
	Local product adaptation	✓	✓	✓				
Operations and management	Production management			✓				✓
	Supply chain management			✓				✓
	Hard skills	✓	✓			✓		✓
	Soft skills	✓	✓		✓	✓		
	Entrepreneurship		✓		✓			
	Cross-cultural management							
Marketing	General sales capabilities	✓	✓	✓	✓	✓	✓	✓
	Understanding the market and local customer needs	✓	✓	✓	✓	✓	✓	✓
Managing external environment	Political and negotiating capabilities	✓			✓	✓		
	Relationship capabilities		✓		✓	✓	✓	
	Adjusting to poor infrastructure				✓	✓		
	Knowledge about the national context	✓	✓		✓	✓	✓	

what happened in other Latin American nations – in many cases, it was more than ten years earlier. Second, economic stability and a market-friendly economy, combined with a relatively small domestic market, ignited the internationalization process of Chilean companies. Macroeconomic stability and promarket reforms improved the level of sophistication of the business environment, leading to an increase in the competitiveness of Chilean firms. Unlike other emerging economies (e.g. South Korea), Chile did not implement specific policies to stimulate outward FDI or support the emergence of national champions (Razo & Calderón, 2010). Today, Chile is a country that stands out among developing countries in terms of its outward FDI stock.

In Chile, internationalization processes that involve the establishment of subsidiaries abroad have generally focused on Latin America and particularly South America. Companies venturing beyond Latin America are significantly less common. This is also the case of the companies analyzed in this chapter. In Chile, the typical objective of going abroad is to grow the business and search for new markets while taking advantage of a business model or value proposition that has succeeded at home. Therefore, during the internationalization process of our companies, it has been crucial to successfully transfer their strategic capabilities developed at home to another country, and also to successfully adapt these capabilities to the foreign country context as needed. None of our companies decided to internationalize into another country with the objective of acquiring or upgrading strategic capabilities that they lacked or that were underdeveloped at home. The only case that is slightly different is ALTO. This company initially internationalized into the USA looking for new markets. However, the company has changed its approach and is now using the USA as a place to source new technologies and ventures to improve ALTO's technological capabilities.

One interesting common pattern across several of our companies is that their first internationalization experience was linked to an opportunity that presented itself rather than being a deliberately planned strategy. However, subsequent international expansions were generally planned, more systematic, and part of a more formal internationalization strategy. "Upstream pressure" to internationalize can also push the foreign expansion of emerging markets firms. This was observed in the case of Derco, which Suzuki pushed to enter the Bolivian and Peruvian markets, and Forus, which WWW pushed to market their brands in other Latin American markets. Another interesting phenomenon observed is what we call the "following clients" internationalization approach – ALTO chose to enter Colombia because they could follow Chilean clients that were operating in that country.

R&D capabilities were especially important in the cases of eClass and ALTO. This relates to the fact that these two companies are highly entrepreneurial, operate in dynamic industries, and offer innovative products and services. In these situations, the novelty and innovativeness of the product or service are crucial. It is important to note that eClass's and ALTO's R&D activities were concentrated in the home market. ALTO has only recently begun using the USA as a location for developing its technological capabilities. In the other companies studied, R&D capabilities were less relevant.

The capability of understanding the market and local customer needs was found to be important for all the companies, although some of them possessed this capability while others did not. Relationship capabilities were also essential for most of the companies. During international expansion, this capability is crucial in multiple situations because companies need to deal with actors in organizational cultures that may be significantly different from those in their home markets. Surprisingly, cross-cultural management capabilities were not a particularly important issue. This is probably linked to the fact that the expansion of our companies was to other Latin American countries where cultural issues and values are relatively similar, starting with the language. Cross-cultural management capabilities should become more relevant as these companies venture outside Latin America.

Perhaps unsurprisingly, large companies with unique business models – such as Derco and Forus – that succeeded in Chile typically expect to be successful in other Latin American countries. However, different strategic capabilities might be more important in other country contexts. Therefore, trying to replicate the domestic business model abroad with as little adaptation as possible can be risky. Still, reproducing a business model abroad might work for companies that enter countries that have similar industry configurations and structures, and a similar national context, to those in the home country. Derco faced this kind of situation in Colombia and Peru. Conversely, Forus found in Colombia a very different industry structure where implementing their successful Chilean business model turned out to be far more difficult than expected. In other words, some of the strategic capabilities that supported the success of Forus's business model at home were not able to provide a similar level of competitive advantage when the company entered the Colombian market.

Casas del Toqui's case illustrates the role of clusters in providing access to resources that can help companies without a comprehensive set of strategic capabilities to become competitive in international markets. In the case of the Chilean wine cluster, different types of complementors and institutions are available to support international transactions. As a result, young wine producers can internationalize more quickly and even jump into global markets right after their inception. It is also important to note that in the case of wines, the country of origin exerted a strong influence. Chilean wines have a certain reputation worldwide that helps small and less-known wine producers when they participate in international markets.

The case of BeitGroup – our only purely domestic company – also offers interesting lessons. First, domestic companies might choose to stay within borders due to strong domestic growth opportunities that require significant capital investments and managerial attention. In this type of situation, avoiding or postponing internationalization does not necessarily mean that the company lacks or could not develop the capabilities to do so. Second, a more cautious approach can also delay international expansion. Some companies wait to find out what will happen with the internationalization of local competitors before taking any action. Finally, the case of BeitGroup shows that even purely domestic companies can be involved in activities of an international nature. For instance, even though all revenues might come from the home country, companies that outsource their manufacturing to other nations require capabilities to handle these cross-border activities.

Finally, we want to highlight the case of Kunstmann and its strategic relationship and collaboration with CCU. For a relatively small company like Kunstmann, it might be difficult to develop from scratch strategic capabilities that are essential to succeed internationally. Collaborating with a giant to "borrow" strategic capabilities that are underdeveloped is an interesting solution for accelerating international expansion, facilitating access to foreign markets, and increasing the probability of success. Moreover, this borrowing can potentially facilitate the development of these capabilities in the company and can lead to a situation where the "capability lender" is not needed anymore. A similar situation happened in the case of BeitGroup. The company started outsourcing its production to China with the assistance of Capricorn. However, as they developed their own capabilities to handle third-party producers, collaboration with Capricorn was no longer necessary. Finally, Forus's joint venture with WWW during the initial stages of its operation in Colombia is another example of a strategic collaboration to support international expansion.

Certainly, more research is needed to deepen our understanding of the role played – both at home and abroad – by different types of strategic capabilities in Chilean companies. However, this study has allowed us to shed light on some patterns observed in seven Chilean firms. We hope the patterns that we have identified – or that readers have inferred – will inspire future research on the topic.

Notes

1. Outward FDI stock in Panama is not counted here because that country is generally considered a tax haven. The total Chilean outward FDI stock in Latin America increases to 58 percent if Panama is added.
2. Blended programs combine online media with traditional classroom lectures.
3. While the focus of our discussion is on ALTO's traditional retail loss-prevention solutions, the company also offers other programs. More information can be found at www.grupoalto.com/.
4. The members of Mercosur are Argentina, Brazil, Paraguay, Uruguay, and Venezuela.
5. One box is equivalent to twelve standard 750 ml bottles.
6. The name of the company changed from Pillín to BeitGroup in 2016, but the clothing brand continues to be Pillín.

12 Strategic Capabilities of Colombian Firms

Maria Alejandra Gonzalez-Perez, Ana Maria Gomez-Trujillo, Eva Cristina Manotas, Camilo Pérez-Restrepo, Maria Teresa Uribe-Jaramillo, Juan Velez-Ocampo, and Verónica Duque-Ruiz

12.1 Introduction

This chapter provides a detailed description of seven cases of a diverse set of Colombian firms in different sectors and stages of internationalization. We analyze the development of the critical capabilities and other specific resources that have contributed to the success of each company in local and foreign markets, and we then compare this phenomenon among the cases. Our findings suggest that the most relevant capabilities for these companies to succeed are their ability to obtain resources, their adaptation of products to the new context, and their understanding of local consumers' needs.

There are few published research studies (e.g. De Villa, Rajwani & Lawton, 2015; Velez-Ocampo & Gonzalez-Perez, 2015) of Colombian firms with foreign operations and of their process of internationalization. During the last two decades, such companies have demonstrated remarkable progress in their international presence and in developing the capabilities needed to remain competitive both at home and abroad.

To succeed, these companies had to learn and adapt to new situations. As Cuervo-Cazurra, Newburry, and Park (2016) observe, many emerging market multinationals face severe challenges in their countries of origin, which create difficulties for them as they attempt to become competitive at the international level.

This chapter describes and compares seven successful Columbian companies operating in different industries to identify specific attributes and capabilities enabling these firms to overcome their liabilities and become market leaders domestically or internationally. The next section summarizes the economic background in Colombia; Section 12.3 describes capability development processes of firms from emerging markets, and what we know about Colombian firms in this regard. Section 12.4 describes our methodological approach and provides profiles of the seven firms in the study. In Section 12.5 we presents our findings and compare capability development in the studied cases, while the last section offers conclusions drawn from our analysis.

12.2   Colombia: Country Background

Table 12.1 presents an overview of Colombia's recent economic trends. Colombia is the fourth largest economy in Latin America and for decades has been one of the fastest-growing economies in the region. The country has a population of 50 million, largely concentrated in urban areas (77.2 percent). Its service-oriented economy generates 59.1 percent of employment, while agriculture accounts for 15.7 percent and manufacturing 11.8 percent (Euromonitor, 2019). Colombia is a founding member of the Pacific Alliance, constituted in 2012 along with Chile, Mexico, and Peru, and became a member of the Organization for Economic Cooperation and Development (OECD) in 2018.

Household consumption is responsible for most of the recent economic growth in Colombia. The country experienced a sharp reduction in the value of its exports in 2015 and 2016. This decline followed external shocks, including a substantial drop in world commodity prices (crude oil and its derivatives account for 40 percent of Colombian exports). In 2018, the United States was Colombia's major trade partner, accounting for 25.4 percent of its exports. Other important export destinations

Table 12.1 *Colombia: macroeconomic data, 2012–2018*

	2012	2013	2014	2015	2016	2017	2018
Population (mn inhabitants)	46.9	47.3	47.8	48.2	48.7	49.1	49.5
GDP (USD mn)	370,574	381,421	381,339	293,428	282,825	311,831	330,776
GDP (% real growth)	3.9	4.6	4.7	3.0	2.1	1.4	2.8
Total exports (USD mn)	60,125	58,824	54,857	35,933	31,757	37,819	41,832
Total imports (USD mn)	59,111	59,381	64,029	54,058	44,889	46,076	51,233
Inflation (% change)	3.2	2.0	2.9	5.0	7.5	4.3	3.2
Exchange rate (CLP per USD)	1,797	1,871	2,001	2,742	3,054	2,951	2,956
Urban population (%)	75.6	75.9	76.2	76.4	76.7	77.0	77.2

Source: Euromonitor (2019)

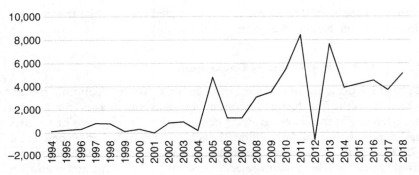

Figure 12.1 Colombia's outward FDI, 1994 –2018 (USD million)
Source: Banco de la República de Colombia (2019)

included the European Union at 10.4 percent, other Pacific Alliance markets at 9.6 percent, and China at 9 percent. Colombia is one of the top inward FDI destinations in Latin America and an important source of outward FDI to the region.

As shown in Figure 12.1, 2005 Colombian outward FDI (OFDI) began to grow in 2005, led mainly by the manufacturing sector. The growth in OFDI began its consolidation in 2008 (Aguilera et al., 2017; Gonzalez-Perez & Velez-Ocampo, 2014). At that time, favorable exchange rates and commodity prices had a major impact in increasing OFDI flow. 2011 was the peak of Colombian outward FDI. This was a response to two main factors:

1   the Colombian peso rose nearly 30 percent against the dollar since 2007, making the acquisition of foreign firms attractive and possible;
2   the financial rating (Moody) of Colombian firms improved, which reduced the borrowing costs of financing overseas acquisitions and signaled that Colombia was overcoming the stigma of being trapped in a war against drug dealers and guerrillas (Portafolio, 2011).

In 2012, the perceived political stability and potential economic growth of the country led to foreign firms acquiring many Colombian companies (Portafolio, 2012).

The year 2013 saw another peak for Colombian outward FDI, with nearly seventy Colombian firms (with previous exporting experience) deciding to expand their operations to foreign countries, largely concentrated in Latin American countries (Portafolio, 2014). The motivation of these Colombian firms to invest abroad was a response to the trade liberalization trend in Latin America, deregulation of markets, and better access to international capital markets. Although there have been a few instances of greenfield investment, foreign acquisition has been the preferred entry mode (Gonzalez-Perez & Velez-Ocampo, 2014). Note that depreciation of Colombian currency may explain the decrease of Colombian outward FDI after 2016.

12.3   Capability Development for Emerging Market Companies

Emerging market multinationals or multilatinas (multinationals from Latin America) are now global players in various industries around the world. The 2010s witnessed the rise in the number of multinationals from emerging countries such as Mexico and Brazil. These companies, once FDI recipients, are now major investors across the globe (Santiso, 2008).

As Cuervo-Cazurra, Newburry, and Park (2016) observe, many emerging market multinationals face severe challenges, including lack of support of the home country, low innovation, and awkward firm ownership characteristics such as family or state ownership. Cuervo-Cazurra et al. (2016) suggest that emerging market multinationals must develop innovation and learning capabilities to be successful in international scenarios.

To sustain enterprise performance, it is important to shape capabilities to innovate and collaborate with other companies, states, and institutions (Teece, 2007). Velez-Ocampo and Gonzalez-Perez (2015) found that successful multilatinas developed abilities to strengthen their organizational capabilities to evaluate potential allies and acquisition targets.

Sol and Kogan (2007) identify network creation and alliances as the key capabilities needed by Chilean multinationals to succeed internationally. This is consistent with Ramsey, de Magalhães, Forteza, and Junior (2010), who suggest that the success of multilatinas in international countries is associated with interfirm partnerships or strategic alliances with host companies. On the other hand, Oliver (1997) argues that for sustainability, a company must develop an ability to manage the institutional context of its resource decisions (internal culture, influence from the state, and interfirm relations). In this way, resource capital and institutional capital become determining factors for economic sustainability.

Finally, Keijzers (2002) indicates that truly sustainable enterprises deal with quality and volume aspects of natural capital related to environmental preservation and the sustainable social, technological, and infrastructural conditions of production, concluding that the world needs to pay special attention to strategic management of the sustainable enterprise.

12.4   Methodology

This paper uses a comparative qualitative case study methodology to answer the question: Which strategic capabilities did companies develop to overcome the liability of foreignness and become high flyers in domestic and global markets? This study, adopting the recommendations of Yin (2009), has three major phases. First, the researchers defined the research question, approach, unit of analysis, and companies to be studied and crafted the data collection instrument. In the second phase, data collection and analysis phase, researchers collected secondary data for each case company and then interviewed C-level executives from the case companies. After writing up a case report for each selected company, researchers carried out cross-case analysis to trace links and identify similarities among companies.

The cases were selected to include distinctively successful firms from different sectors and in different stages of internationalization. The study relies both on secondary data (corporate reports, specialized business and economics media, and official databases) and on primary data collected during interviews with CEOs or C-level executives of the case firms.

Table 12.2 classifies the companies selected for the study according to their market orientation, internationalization stage, and technological intensity. The table was designed by the Centre for Emerging Market Studies (CEMS) for use in comparing strategic capabilities in emerging markets firms.

The primary and secondary data for this study were collected between August and September 2017. Table 12.3 provides comparative financial data for the companies studied.

Table 12.2 *Data collection matrix for the selection of Colombian firms as case studies*

		Firm category		
		Purely domestic	Exporter	Multinational
Industry	High-tech	Grupo Bios	Haceb	
	Low-tech	Mattelsa	Sempertex New Stetic	Colcafé
	Service		Brainz	

Table 12.3 *Colombian company profiles and financial data, 2016 or latest available figures*

Company and industry	Sales[a]	Assets[a]	No. of employees	EBIDTA[b,a]	Exports[a]	No. of markets	Interviewees
Grupo Bios Agribusiness	889,116	337,812	7,318	n/a	No exports or foreign operations	No exports or foreign operations	Santiago Piedrahita Montoya, company president
Brainz Video games	2,096	489 (2014)	24	244	8,764	160	Alejandro González, president & founder
New Stetic Dental supplies	26,735	31,989	700	4,501	13,559	67	Juan Esteban Gómez, chief of marketing dept.
Sempertex Rubber and latex products	33,214	24,773	1,020	6,126	13,194	45	Oswald Loewy, company president (byemail)
Colcafé (Coffee production)	233,417	450,041	912	35,801	84,867	54	Francisco Eladio Gómez, inter-national business manager; Carlos Saldarriaga, international business coordinator
Mattelsa Clothing	18,952	19,718	1,170	2,184	56	No exports or foreign operations	Mateo Jaramillo, founder and general director
Haceb White goods manufacturing	253,667	271,869	2,426 (2012)	25,314	23,680	13	Andres Valencia, chief of strategic development of suppliers and materials

[a] Data in USD thousands; exchange rate as of December 2016, 1 USD = 3,000.77 COP.
[b] Earnings before interest, tax, depreciation, and amortization.

12.5   Findings: The Cases Studied

Grupo Bios

Agribusiness giant Contegral's shareholders established Grupo Bios in 2016 as a holding company to bring together a group of agribusiness companies in Colombia (Portafolio, 2017). This strategy responded to trends observed in studies such as those of the International Fund for Agricultural Development (IFAD, 2003), which identified that food production in developing countries is expected to double by 2050, mainly due to an increase in the total world population.

Grupo Bios's holdings include interests in companies from a wide range of activities such as chicken protein, production and trade of eggs, and genetic porcine improvements (Portafolio, 2017). In 2017, Grupo Bios ranked 43 among the 500 largest Colombian firms by sales (Dinero, 2017a). This holding company aims to respond to rising local and international demand for agricultural products (Portafolio, 2017).

The most important business held by the company is balanced foods, which brings together Contegral and Finca, both market leaders in Colombia (Dinero, 2017a; Portafolio, 2017). The second business of the group is production of chicken protein with Operadora Avícola SAS, with an 8 percent market share in the poultry industry in Colombia. In third place is Avicola Triple A, positioned as the fourth largest egg producer in Colombia (Hernández Bonilla, 2017). Their remaining major line of business is genetic porcine improvement through PIC Colombia SA (Grupo Bios, 2016).

According to Santiago Piedrahíta Montoya, president of Grupo Bios, the group developed various critical capabilities to help it to become successful. The main capabilities of the holding company relate to its ability to understand consumer needs: "In-depth understanding of customers' business from the productive point of view." This includes technical experts working hand in hand with farmers to improve productivity, aiming to generate impact. As the president explains:

we want to be a relevant actor in the animal protein chain, and the animal protein chain is the whole chain, from the raw material –independently if it is imported or locally produced – to the final consumer. We have to be excellent in reaching the final consumer.

These capabilities link to intangible resources including knowledge, sales orientation, customer involvement, reputational capital, and leadership skills (Guesalaga et al., 2018).

Regarding the prominent performance of the company in logistic management and efficiency, the president explains that the business group brings almost two million tons of commodities every year into its production facilities, or 200 trucks daily, and is comparable in terms of volume with the cement and coal industries. They have become very efficient in the logistic management of these commodities, investing in transport companies such as Coordinadora and Compas to add value and to reduce costs and delay in the supply chain. Piedrahita explains, "It is a very complicated logistics chain. When I arrived here, I thought that the numbers were wrong. This also implies in the organizational capabilities, the necessity to control day-to-day routines in an exhaustive manner." These capabilities can have a positive effect on firm performance, as seen in measurement of the logistics service capabilities of Taiwanese container shipping firms by Yang, Marlow, and Lu (2009).

Moreover, excellent commodity management enhances the outstanding capabilities of the company in its supply chain management, as the firm deploys its strengths in buying the huge volumes of commodities required as raw materials for operations in the companies held by the group. Grupo Bios has a specialized team that is expert in hedging currency to minimize the risks of price volatility and fluctuation. This capability involves a profound understanding of financial and commodity derivative exchanges, effective networking, and the efficient purchase of commodities in different countries.

Another characteristic that gives the company an advantageous position versus competitors, according to its president, is "the company's capability to generate a competitive paranoia that keeps them aware of market challenges and to anticipate to changes". This capability is key to maintaining high profit margins in their balanced foods business, which generates over 65 percent of total earnings.

Grupo Bios does not have foreign operations. The group is currently conducting research on potential foreign markets and has identified its main competitor in the balanced foods business. However, the internationalization process is not a priority for the company. The company has identified a strong potential to increase its market share in the domestic animal protein market. According to Piedrahíta Montoya (2017), this initiative would require more consolidation of the animal protein industry and major investments to increase productivity, improve efficiency, and reduce costs in order to reach the target of increased protein consumption within the country.

Grupo Bios developed strategic capabilities related mainly to obtaining resources. Specifically, the business group developed abilities to purchase product inputs from other countries and to develop resources internally through efforts such as planting in different regions of the country. Regarding its marketing capabilities, the understanding of local customer needs is a key factor in its strategic planning of the group, as it has a special focus on the final consumer.

Mattelsa

The Colombian fashion visionary Mateo Jaramillo Cadavid (Mateo Jaca) founded Mattelsa in 2006. For this company, the human talent of its work group is its most important success factor. As it is crucial that the company thinks and acts without borders, their working group is international, and they live and act with the mindset that they are international. "Mattelsa is a community of 1,170 people where everyone possesses the mentality of an athlete, and people are focused on finding their best version of themselves" said Mateo Jaca in an interview. Mattelsa, as a lifestyle inspirer, clothing designer, and manufacturer with direct sales operations, is highly successful in its domestic market with over fifty stores in Colombia and a presence in a number of Central American markets.

The high growth in foreign markets relative to the local market, and a desire to follow the company's clients abroad, motivated their decision to internationalize. Mattelsa decided to open their own store in Guatemala, a Central American country in constant economic turmoil. Mattelsa hopes to establish itself in Mexico in the future. However, they decided to test their business model in Guatemala through exposure to hostile market conditions, to allow the company to identify those factors that need improvement or adaptation to achieve a competitive advantage abroad. Unlike the traditional export model, this internationalization process allowed Mattelsa to undergo a process of accelerated learning and adaptation (Barkema & Vermeulen, 1998; Lu & Beamish, 2001). Mattelsa actively invested in improvement capabilities and used external and internal networks to learn and improve operational efficiency across countries, acquiring knowledge that contributes to rapid growth (Prashantham & Young, 2011; Sapienza et al., 2006, Zahra et al., 2000). The main capabilities developed in Mattelsa are associated with its abilities to develop resources internally, capacities in developing products and services, and marketing skills.

Regarding its ability to develop resources internally, knowledge is the most important company pillar. To build knowledge development capability, Mattelsa created a careful strategy of personnel selection and preserved this through the development of five pillars of corporate culture associated with food, sports, leisure, socialization, and knowledge.

Internal resources created and identified by Mattelsa dynamize their procedures and create knowledge and new skills (Kogut and Zander, 1992). Their objective of promoting integration among internal resources translates into organizational improvement and growth capability, with little or no restriction to the source that endows internal resources. This capability enabled Mattelsa to develop contingency plans for problems arising following entry into an international market.

Mattelsa's capacities associated with products and services are linked to product manufacturing and research and development (R&D) capabilities. Mattelsa develops forty different garments each week, and these processes are totally endogenous. The experience accumulated by Mattelsa through its continuous learning process is key to acquiring the skills necessary to compete in international markets (Barkema et al., 1996; Chang, 1995; Denis & Depelteau, 1985; Li, 1995). These capabilities have been very important for the stage of the internationalization process associated with international consolidation and Mattelsa's increasing commitment to its clients and markets abroad. Mattelsa has differentiated itself in the allocation of its resources for reasons such as its particular history, its experience, the application of different strategies, and the use and combination of different resources and capabilities over time. Mattelsa has sought to obtain a unique resource endowment, and that has allowed its products to be perceived as having unique characteristics.

Its marketing skills are based on its market knowledge and its innovation capacities. For Mattelsa, the most important knowledge resource when it comes to choosing a target market is its customers. Additionally, knowledge of the market allows them to increase the capacity to discover and exploit opportunities because knowledge of client problems can have great generalizability and therefore constitutes opportunities in the market (Shane, 2000; Von Hippel, 1998). Mattelsa's familiarity with its customers and knowledge of ways to serve the market enables it to recognize solutions to customer needs and to formulate an effective marketing strategy to introduce and sell their products. The marketing capacities of Mattelsa are very important across the four stages of its internationalization process: knowledge of its clients and of their needs determines the company's motivation and its strategic planning, market research, market selection, and entry mode choices.

Mattelsa's customers are the most valuable information resource for developing its marketing capabilities, enabling the firm to actively meet the needs of its customers, and to sustain a competitive advantage in its domestic and international markets.

Colcafé

Colcafé is a subsidiary of multinational food holding company Grupo Nutresa, specializing in the business of coffee processing. Founded in 1950 under the name Industria Colombiana de Café, the company has since become one of the most successful companies in Colombia. Colcafé has four brands: Colcafé, Sello Rojo, La Bastilla, and Matiz; it also produces coffee for other brands such as Starbucks (Roldán, 2015).

During 2016, Colcafé reported net sales of USD 233 million (EMIS, 2017a) and its total exports for the same year were USD 85 million, representing 36 percent of the company's net sales revenue (Legiscomex, 2017a). The company currently exports to more than sixty countries around the world. The United States is its largest export market with a value of USD 51.6 million in 2016. Other major markets are the United Kingdom, Ecuador, Peru, Mexico, Japan, and South Korea.

This firm applies a very interesting internationalization model, to which it has gradually committed resources to enter and operate in foreign markets. Colcafé began as an exporter, and over the years it has turned toward establishing strategic partnerships for its growth and expansion. This strategy involves alliances with local partners and the acquisition of dominant companies. This model is consistent with Grupo Nutresa's conservative DNA, which prefers gradual internationalization and integration to global value chains.

According to Francisco Gomez, Colcafé's international business manager, "Colcafé was born as an export-oriented company." The firm launched into international markets back in 1961, when its president, Fabio Rico, traveled to Japan and negotiated the company's first export of instant coffee, a product they had previously developed for the national market. Since then, Colcafé has maintained its presence in the Japanese market. The long-term trade relation with Japan as its main market allowed the company to develop a relationship with Japanese multinational Mitsubishi for operation in the Asia-Pacific. One of the most important moments in the relationship with this Japanese conglomerate took place in 2012, when Colcafé established a strategic alliance with Mitsubishi and Takasago International to acquire Dan Kaffe Malaysia (DKM). The firm's shares are distributed: Colcafé (44 percent), Mitsubishi (30 percent), and Takasago International (26 percent).

According to Gomez, Colcafé's successful internationalization into the Asia-Pacific markets builds upon a number of strategic capabilities such as entrepreneurship, local product adaptation, understanding local customer needs, relational capabilities, and cross-cultural management.

Entrepreneurship emerged in gaining access to the Japanese market in the 1960s, a bold move bringing Colcafé products to an unknown destination. Achieving this mission required sales capabilities along with a strong physical presence to develop and maintain relationships with their new clients. Colcafé has continued to promote intra-entrepreneurship and innovation. This is evidenced in product adaptations for new markets and in the establishment of a new innovation branch within the company in recent years.

The capabilities associated with local product adaptation emerged when Colcafé realized that to increase sales in the Japanese market, it was necessary to understand local customer needs, including their requirements and expectations in terms of quality and volume. The company specially crafted a number of products for the Asian market including special blends (with other natural ingredients such as ginger) and packages designed for smaller households in countries such as Japan.

In terms of relational capabilities, Colcafé has been very successful in building strong relationships with its Asia-Pacific partners. This is evidenced in the long-term relationship with Mitsubishi that allowed the companies to acquire DKM in 2012 and form a joint venture in 2014. The Asian firm offered market knowledge and culture, solid relationships with governments, and a consolidated supply chain across the entire region, while Colcafé contributed its product knowledge and production capabilities, both essential to consolidation as local producer in the region.

Cross-cultural management, viewed as the capacity to work with multicultural teams, is a key feature of Colcafé's human capital, especially since beginning operations in Malaysia. According to Carlos Saldarriaga, the company's international business coordinator, "The company had a long experience doing business with people from different cultures; however, their acquisition and joint venture in the Asia-Pacific region represented a new step toward consolidation of a multicultural team as this initiative required engaging local collaborators, such as managers and salesforce."

Looking toward the future, Colcafé aims to develop its networks, brand, and human capital to further strengthens its position in Asia-Pacific markets. With this perspective in mind, Colcafé plans to build upon three strategic capabilities: to nurture human capital (talented, innovative, committed to sustainable development), and brands (leaders, well known among consumers), supported by reliable products and a solid distribution network (diverse channels and segments) (De Villa, 2016).

Sempertex

Sempertex, which grew out of a firm established in 1938, is one of the world's largest producers of balloons. Its products are used for celebrations in more than seventy countries, including markets as diverse as the United States, China, Saudi Arabia, Russia, and Brazil. This family business is one of the top manufacturing companies of value-added products in Colombia, one of its largest exporters, and one of the most experienced in negotiating in Asia-Pacific markets.

Based on reported figures for 2016, Sempertex had assets valued at USD 24.7 million and generated net sales revenues of USD 32.2 million (EMIS, 2017b). For many years, Sempertex was one of the only Latin American producers of balloons to ISO 9000–2001 certification specifications.

Sempertex received the National Export Award in 2001, the Technical Achievement Award for Product Improvements in the United States in 2005, and the TÜVRheinland Proof Seal in 2008. Ernst and Young recognized the company's president as the Colombian Entrepreneur of the Year in 2015, among a number of other national and international recognitions (Ernst and Young, 2016).

During the 1990s, Sempertex decided to invest in larger production facilities, to upgrade its production technologies, and to establish an export strategy. Before economic liberalization in Colombia, Sempertex focused on the domestic market and made only occasional exports to Peru and Ecuador. Thirty years later, Sempertex is an international market-oriented company with exports valued at USD 13.2 million in 2016, and 50 percent of its production goes to international markets (Legiscomex, 2017b).

Sempertex exports to more than 50 countries directly, serving the rest through their distributors. For many years, Russia was its main export destination. Last year, the United States took over as its largest export market. Other important destinations include Estonia, Finland, China, Chile, and Japan.

Sempertex's successful consolidation as one of the most important manufacturing companies in Colombia and one of its larger exporters is due to its development of a range of strategic capabilities. In the view of its president, the firm's most important capabilities are in R&D, relationship management, supply chain management, adjusting to poor infrastructure, and understanding the needs of local customers.

Its R&D capabilities support its full-time commitment to innovation, identifying new materials and textures, and creating new designs that are attractive to their consumers. This has allowed them to create products that respond to consumer needs in their international markets, while adapting to new trends, for example LED balloons. (Sempertex has an alliance with Wakadabaloons in Denmark.) The company often invests its profits in the acquisition of new production technologies and upgrading of their production facilities.

Sempertex's relationship capabilities are evident in its participation in international fairs in the 1990s along with Proexport (now Procolombia), which helped the company expand to other Latin American markets, including Costa Rica and Mexico. Participation in international fairs in Europe, Asia, and North America was also key for Sempertex's internationalization. According to Oswald Loewy, Sempertex's president, the company uses fairs to identify local partners and distributors and build relationships. This was, for example, the way they entered Japan and China, with companies that eventually became their distributors in these distant markets. These relationships also provided the credibility Sempertex needed to sign a license agreement with Disney to produce balloons for their brands.

Their success in supply chain management required establishment of a new distribution center, allowing them same-day dispatch of product orders received before noon (Endeavour, 2016). Supply chain management is also critical to their access to latex, the main raw material for their products. Sempertex acquires over 3,000 tons of latex every year from suppliers in Guatemala and Colombia.

Despite successful internationalization of their products, Sempertex maintains its production in Colombia, demonstrating its capability to adjust to poor infrastructure. Around the start of the twenty-first century, Sempertex needed to relocate the production plant due to operational constraints. The company considered moving production to countries including Guatemala, the United States, China, and even Thailand, but opted instead to move to a different zone in Barranquilla (Periodico El Heraldo, 2016). The city offered a good balance of talented labor, a reasonable operational cost that offset the risks of not moving their production abroad, and direct access to one of Colombia's top maritime ports, a key element to minimize the costs of importing raw materials and exporting their products. This is important: high logistical cost is one of the top challenges to export competitiveness in Colombia.

Finally, their deep understanding of local customer needs, combined with a constant commitment to innovation, enabled Sempertex to become one of the world's most competitive producers of balloons. They are able to perform well in price-based markets (e.g. developing countries in Asia or Latin America) as well as quality-oriented markets (the United States, Europe, or Japan). The company has been very successful in building strategic partnerships with distributors around the world. These capabilities are fundamental to identifying consumer needs and providing a quick response time to customer issues (usually less than twenty-four hours).

New Stetic

New Stetic is a dental supplies company that has, since its inception in the 1950s, followed nontraditional patterns not only in regard to its products but also in R&D, marketing strategies, market selection, and international orientation. New Stetic is a pioneer in its industry in Colombia, with a remarkable international presence, an uncommon trait for any Colombian company not related to coffee exports.

In the 1950s, the Colombian economy followed an import substitution strategy, and most local manufacturing companies operated only in their own region. Relatively unsophisticated transportation and infrastructure, meager governmental support and promotion of exports, and a lack of international exposure among entrepreneurs and business practitioners were among the most relevant factors causing Colombian companies to remain local (Steiner & Vallejo, 2010). In 1954, Francisco Vélez acquired a small dental laboratory with six employees in Medellin. Very soon, Vélez realized that in order for the company to grow at a quicker pace, he needed to find international clients, so he filled a briefcase with acrylic teeth and traveled to dental congresses in the United States and Europe in search of clients (Gallo Machado, 2008). Fortunately, Vélez succeeded. New Stetic's exports grew rapidly in terms of volume and country of destination; furthermore, the company introduced new products that contributed to its position as the second largest Latin American company in the artificial teeth sector by 1980 (New Stetic, 2017).

After the coffee boom in the mid-1970s, the Colombian economy remained relatively stable due to its conservative fiscal and foreign exchange rate policies. However, in the 1980s, the so-called lost decade for Latin American economies, the national government promoted major promarket reforms that prompted major changes in the international orientation of the economy. New Stetic benefited from export promotion plans and activities implemented by the government. Nevertheless, Vélez's strategy to reach international markets remained the same. He attended international dental supply fairs and used a particular marketing tactic that he called the "hotel suite" to establish contact with international clients. Before visiting any country, Vélez searched for potential clients. Then he booked a nice room in a fancy hotel and invited his potential clients for lunch, so they had the opportunity to establish a personal connection without interruptions (*Dinero*, 1997).

In the early 1990s, New Stetic exported nearly 70 percent of its production to more than countries. In 1992, they exported USD 2.9 million. They were among the top 100 Colombian exporters, especially impressive for a nontraditional company in an incipient industry in Latin America. This led New Stetic to receive the "National Export Award" from the National Association of Exporters, ANALDEX, and the "Expoinnovadores" award from America Economía, DHL, and the Colombian-American Chamber of Commerce. In the late 1990s, Luis Emilio Posada acquired the company. By 2016, sales had reached nearly USD 27 million with exports of USD 13.5 million, which positioned New Stetic as the fourth largest company in its industry worldwide.

Product diversification was key to New Stetic's success. Acrylic teeth were their first products. However, the company introduced new acrylic resins, alloys, anesthetics, and other dental supplies to its portfolio. Attending key dental congresses around the world is still a preferred pathway to meet new and existing customers. Nowadays, New Stetic has its own sales subsidiaries in Mexico and the United States and sales representatives in sixty-five countries, including Madagascar, Iraq, Saudi Arabia, Thailand, Vietnam, and South Africa. Juan Esteban Gómez, chief of the marketing department, explains:

The strategy we follow to get to unconventional countries from the perspective of a Colombian company is to identify countries that meet three main criteria: economic prosperity regardless of country size, lack of competitors, and likelihood to avoid political risk by finding local distributors.

In new countries, New Stetic needs first to adapt to the regulatory system and then to the market needs. Gomez says, "the first contact we have whenever we visit a country is the national agency that regulates medicines and pharmaceutical products. For us, that contact is key to start a business in any region, then it comes to the dental fairs and the contacts with potential distributors." As this company operates in a highly regulated environment with rules that vary from one country to another, its growth is dependent on its ability to comply with local regulations and certifications and to adapt its products to the needs and rules of the markets. "Product adaptation is absolutely central to our success; we have developed a different tooth for every country or region based on dental habits, anatomical characteristics, dentists' preferences, and legal regulations," explains Gómez.

Brainz

Brainz is a story-driven global video game company specializing in adventure and strategy games for mobile devices, headquartered in Bogota.

Brainz emerged in 2011 from its parent company Zerofractal, created in 2000. In 2013, the firm shifted its focus entirely to the design and development of story-driven games for mobile and social media platforms. By 2017, the firm was exporting games translated into fifteen different languages to 166 countries (Chiquiza Nonsoque, 2017).

Zerofractal, the parent company, was created by a group of undergraduate students of architecture in the middle of an economic and real estate crisis in Colombia. Some of the founding members of the entrepreneurial team had had previous experience producing TV advertisements, designing websites, and developing multimedia. At its start, Zerofractal's primary focus was 3D animation of architectural and real estate projects, largely concentrating on clients in the United States and Canada. Around 2007, a new business partner, Mauricio Bejarano (an experienced entrepreneur and venture capital raiser), joined the company. It changed its name to ZIO studios and evolved as an animation and digital media studio. ZIO produced advertising for companies such as Guinness. Their animations earned high visibility on YouTube, leading to the realization that by leveraging social media, they could develop apps, games, and experiences and provide them to users worldwide.

The company restructured itself to carry out this new mission. According to an interview with Alejandro González, cofounder and CEO of the company, in 2010, a venture capital fund called Promotora de Proyectos in Medellin helped them raise capital. This gave the firm a boost, allowing them to employ a diverse group, with 80 employees at one point. Between 2011 and 2013, ZIO sold or merged most of its business units and reduced its labor force to 30 collaborators. In 2012, a new business partner, Jairo Nieto, joined the company and contributed to enhancing the narrative and story-driven content of the games. Since 2013, Brainz has concentrated only on video games. Between 2015 and 2016, they developed their proprietary technical platform with operations under the umbrella of Ruta N in Medellin. In 2017, the company employed twenty-four engineers and artists.

Video-game development activity in Colombia grew from eight companies in 2008 to fifty-four in 2014. By 2017, only forty-six registered studios, educational institutions, and individuals in the country were developing video games (IGDA Colombia, 2017).

According to an interview with González, who holds extensive technical and creative experience serving clients in developing TV post-production and multimedia projects for major brands, "the main differentiator of Brainz is their focus and vision to be recognized for their high-quality storytelling, artistic skills, and technical innovation".

Brainz produced games such as Vampire Season and Social Street Soccer and coproduced games including Mark of the Dragon with the Korean firm Gamevil and Hero Haven ZQ Game (Saa, 2013). They launched World War Doh in February 2020.

Brainz's success relies on a number of specific strategies and capabilities:

- focus on a single line of products, story-driven games;
- capacity to recognize their own strengths and competitive advantages;
- deep understanding of the global video games industry and an ability to identify a specific niche market in which to compete;
- hard skills, recruiting and developing human resources with high technical competencies in software and apps, graphic design, and artistic expertise;
- hiring international consultants, advisors and mentors with specific technical expertise (usability, game design, and interfaces) to support the development of Brainz employees;
- soft skills, nurturing creativity to ensure that games entertain and engage existing and new users;
- localizing products to specific markets, ensuring each game includes appropriate cultural content for consumers in target markets;
- networking, for fundraising, investors, and access, and to be more visible to distribution platforms (Apple and Google);
- overcoming the liabilities of foreignness – building a reputation as a technically strong company was not easy when coming from Colombia; Brainz has managed to position itself to overcome these liabilities.

Haceb

Jose Maria Acevedo founded Haceb in 1941 in a small workshop in Medellin. The crisis of World War II, accompanied by scarcity, became the company's opportunity to move from assembling grills to producing stoves. Washing machines, more complex stoves, and refrigerators soon followed, with the company guaranteeing impeccable after-sales technical service. In 1993, the company expanded and set up domestic branches in Bogota, Cali, and Eje Cafetero (the coffee region) to strengthen its presence in the country. Later, it obtained the Portfolio Award for the best after-sales service in the country and recognition for its leadership and commercial activity.

In 2000, Haceb adopted a new model: concentric organizational structure, versatility among company activities, and strengthened corporate culture, all of which its leaders considered key to organizational growth.

In the same year, the company implemented a call center, a centralized service that channeled customer needs to the correct company resource.

The company decided to strengthen its position in international markets in 2006. Haceb signed contracts with important multinational companies in their sector, which encouraged the company to adapt to world standards. The company also established branches in Venezuela and Mexico.

The big leap for the company occurred in 2015 through alliance with appliance giant Whirlpool, launched as Haceb Whirlpool Industrial with a new production plant in Copacabana. An investment of USD 50 million established the capacity for automated production of washing machines and created 250 new direct jobs.

By 2017, Haceb was an industrial complex covering more than 221 thousand square meters to house its internationally certified refrigeration and heating plants, employing 4,000 workers and exporting between 10 and 15 percent of its production to fifteen countries. With yearly sales of around COP 815,000 million, the company earned brand awareness of 25 percent among consumers of durable goods brands (*Dinero*, 2016).

According to Andres Valencia, the company's chief of strategic development of suppliers and materials, the most important strategic capabilities that have led the company to success relate to its understanding of internal markets, a very challenging task. Developing this capability required understanding the cultural differences in each country's regions and adapting their portfolio to provide what consumers want and need according to their stage of life.

To its founder, Jose Maria Acevedo, people have been the pillar on which Haceb was built. The strategy, vision, and mission of the company are based on the talent and capabilities of its employees. Their main focus is on employees being happy, which is then reflected in their commercial strategy, a strategy that focuses on connecting with their customers to make them fall in love with the company's products and services.

Brand reputation connects to the importance of the company to people. Because Haceb wants its customers and other stakeholders to connect with the company, they must continue building loyalty and increasing customer confidence in their brand and products. Their strong presence in social media helps the company to continue connecting with people and build the reputation of the Haceb brand.

As for Haceb's international strategy, exports have been a complex challenge as entry barriers to other countries are very high. Haceb's main export destination was Venezuela, but political instability in that country caused the company to back off. Meanwhile, Ecuador imposed technical and commercial barriers that clearly restricted Haceb's operations. In view of these issues in mind, the company's export strategy shifted and is currently concentrated in Central America and the Caribbean, with some operations in Bolivia.

According to Valencia, "Haceb believes that maintaining the same capabilities during all internationalization strategies is restrictive. The company hasn't given its export strategy the necessary attention, and it is clear that due to conditions in each country, Haceb must build its capacities to succeed." Such capabilities have not yet been fully established, which has decreased the value of the company's position abroad in recent years. Haceb set up some branches abroad that it then dismantled, such as in Peru and Mexico. Branches in Venezuela and Ecuador remain, but they have clearly lost strength. In addition, alliances have been made with marketers to manufacture some of their own brands, but this short-term effort has little impact on the long-term internationalization needs of Haceb.

These capacities, clearly, have less strength in markets outside Colombia. In other countries where Haceb wants to compete, their competitors expend huge efforts and have more resources, making it difficult for Haceb to succeed in these markets.

12.6 Comparisons and Conclusion

Table 12.4 summarizes the major capabilities identified in the companies studied.

This study identified resources and capabilities of the selected companies that were essential before, during, and after their first international activity. These companies differentiated themselves in the endowment of their resources for reasons such as their particular history, their experience, the application of different strategies, and the use and combination of different resources and capacities over time. Two of the most relevant capabilities present in the observed companies are their abilities to understand customers' needs and adapt their products to different markets, which is consistent with their not having leading positions in international markets. It is also clear that marketing capabilities, especially regarding general sales capabilities, do not strongly influence the national and international success of Colombian firms. However, other marketing-related strategic capabilities are present in most of the cases: for instance, relationship capabilities and understanding of the needs of local consumers.

These companies have developed unique competitive resources, which have positioned them as local and in some cases international leaders in their respective industries, especially because their clients perceive unique

Table 12.4 *Capabilities of Colombian firms studied*

Capability	Subcategories	Grupo Bios	Brainz	Sempertex	Colcafé	Mattelsa	New Stetic	Haceb
Obtaining resources	Resource identification	✓					✓	✓
	Ability to purchase product inputs	✓					✓	
	Ability to develop resources internally		✓				✓	✓
Product/service capabilities	Product manufacture		✓			✓		
	Research & development		✓	✓	✓	✓		
	Local product adaptation				✓	✓		
Operations and management	Production management	✓	✓	✓	✓	✓		
	Supply chain management	✓	✓		✓			
	Hard skills		✓		✓	✓		✓
	Soft skills				✓	✓		
	Entrepreneurship							
	Cross-cultural management						✓	
Marketing	General sales capabilities		✓		✓			✓
	Understanding local customer needs	✓						
Managing external environment	Political capabilities	✓	✓		✓			
	Relationship capabilities	✓	✓				✓	
	Adjusting to poor infrastructure	✓						
Others	Competitive paranoia				✓			
	Speed of adaptation and response							

characteristics of their products and/or services. Development of unique competitive resources was present in purely local firms, such as the recently founded Grupo Bios and Mattelsa, which entered highly competitive industries and developed unique internal resources based on sophisticated production practices, proximity to clients, and efficient use of supply chains. For these companies, one important element in choosing a target market is the analysis of potential customers, and such market knowledge can increase a company's ability to discover and exploit opportunities that eventually support the companies' growth. Capabilities in external relationship management, exhibited by firms such as Brainz, Colcafé, Sempertex, and New Stetic, have enabled them to develop unique resources and to better understand local customer needs.

In addition, export performance and market diversification of these companies are highly dependent on their ability to develop proactive and innovative product positioning and brand consolidation, both for their customers and distributors. Another relevant aspect for these companies is their decision-making rationality and adaptability in each stage of the internationalization process, which leads them to the development of those cooperation, negotiation, and innovation skills that positively influence their performance. Findings of this study indicate that one of the most critical capabilities contributing to the success of Colombian firms locally and internationally is their ability to obtain resources and, more specifically, the capability firms have to develop resources internally, as shown by four companies in the analysis. These companies have managed to develop not only competitive products but also a solid and close connection with both suppliers and distributors; these features assist the firms in become more competitive.

Other specific capabilities considered, such as production management, soft skills, cross-cultural management, general sales capabilities, competitive paranoia, and political capabilities, were not found to be particularly relevant for the local and international success of Colombian firms: these capabilities were not significantly identified in most of the studied cases. Additional research is needed to assess the development of such capabilities in either selected industries or a larger sample of cases.

More research is needed to deepen our knowledge of the capabilities needed for Colombian firms to be sustainable over time and to identify patterns separated by industry and ownership. As strategic capabilities evolve, the discussion is also open for the differentiation of capabilities needed in each stage of the internationalization process. In conclusion, this study offers business managers and scholars a comparative analysis of the critical capabilities needed for Colombian firms to become successful locally and internationally, contributing in this way to the growth of literature regarding the sustained growth and internationalization patterns of Colombian companies, as existing literature on this topic is scarce.

13 Capabilities of Mexican Exporters and Multinational Corporations

Miguel A. Montoya and Gerardo Velasco

13.1 Introduction

In recent years, attention among managers and scholars has shifted toward the emerging markets, which have become more influential as their firms grow and expand to other markets. There are a considerable number of studies that analyze the relation between resources and capabilities of the firm and its growth (Churchill & Mullins, 2001; Correa Rodriguez et al., 2003; Davidsson et al., 2006; Gibb & Davies, 1990; Keogh & Evans, 1998; O'Gorman, 2001; Smallbone et al., 1995). Additionally, the global economy's landscape has changed as the appearance of new multinationals and the expansion of existing ones have affected ways of doing business. In these multinationals appear different capabilities that help them grow and consolidate, both locally and internationally. Because of this, there have been various initiatives, including this one, to study the extent to which the capabilities determine the success of different types of company. Managers and scholars have recognized differences in the capabilities needed in different contexts; in this book we study the capabilities of exporters and multinational corporations from emerging markets. We also wanted to analyze the capabilities needed locally and explore whether they become limitations when trying to enter other markets.

This chapter will focus specifically on Mexican firms at three technological levels: low-tech, high-tech, and services. We selected seven firms for this study, analyzing their capabilities individually and comparatively. The study provides insight on how firms in emerging economies can become multinationals and exploit their capabilities, noting the differences in capability use between economic sectors, between local and global markets, and between emerging and developed markets.

This chapter starts with a general background of Mexico, focusing especially on the sectors that the firms analyzed are part of. This is followed by profiles of the selected firms. The capabilities found are then presented, along with a comparison of the firms' use of their capabilities. Finally, conclusions about the analysis are presented. A general trend discovered is the importance of consolidating internal processes before expanding abroad. Once commencing activities outside of Mexico, the capabilities most mentioned by those interviewed were relationship capabilities, corporative brand and reputation, and understanding local customer needs, all of which are skills related to interaction outside the firm. In order to go international, it is important to get allies abroad that can help the firm start in a new market and consolidate its position there, which will be heavily influenced by the public perception and the fulfillment of customers' needs.

13.2   Mexico: Country Background

Institutions have evolved differently throughout the world, depending on the geographic and cultural context of each country or region. In Latin American countries, in contrast to the United States, partially due to numerous political revolutions, economic processes and institutions tend to be controlled centrally (North, 1991). In view of this, Latin American firms, especially small and medium-sized enterprises, face multiple challenges to growth. Previous studies have showed that external factors such as macroeconomic conditions and public policies may affect a firm's growth (Capelleras & Rabentino, 2008).

Mexico has a population of 126.2 million, with literacy of 99.1 percent among people over fifteen years old (INEGI, 2018) Table 13.1

Table 13.1 *Mexico: country profile*

	1990	2000	2010	2018
Population (millions)	83.94	98.9	114.09	126.19
GDP per capita (current USD)	3,112	7,158	9,271	9,698
GDP growth (annual %)	5.2	4.9	5.1	2.0
Inflation, GDP deflator (annual %)	28.2	11.2	4.5	5.3
Exports of goods and services (% of GDP)	19	25	30	39
Imports of goods and services (% of GDP)	20	27	31	41
Foreign direct investment, net inflows (million current USD)	2,549	18,382	21,002	34,616
Patent applications, residents*	661	431	951	1,334**

Source: World Development Indicators database
* World Intellectual Property Organization (WIPO).
** 2017, last data available.

presents an economic profile of Mexico. It is a growing country in terms of energy reserves and has a growing middle class. Its business climate shows an emphasis on competition and performance, but hesitance toward innovation. Its workforce is young, but there are social problems in terms of corruption, a highly hierarchical and bureaucratic society, and a war against drug dealers (Hofstede Insights, 2016). One of Mexico's advantages, yet also one of its disadvantages, is its geographical location, sharing a border with the United States. According to previous studies, innovation and growth in Mexican firms have depended on internal resources and also on environmental and institutional factors (Lemus et al., 2015). There are some environmental factors in Mexico, such as the intellectual property regime (Candelin-Palmqvist et al., 2012) and access to credit (Carpenter & Petersen, 2002), that are not accessible to all firms and in which Mexico lags behind other economies. To compensate for this limitation and to obtain needed resources, many Mexican firms prefer to establish solid, trust-based alliances with other firms (Franco & Haase, 2010), rather than signing extensive and complex contracts. Because of this, multinational firms have grown by allocating their investments abroad, avoiding the limitations of their home country (Montoya & Alcaraz, 2018).

Despite these limitations, Mexico has continued developing in various aspects, such as growth of its home market, which helps the internal development of its firms and builds advantages to help them grow abroad. There are a small number of Mexican firms that are generally known to be multinationals, but this is due in part to the lack of information and records on firms operating abroad. Nonetheless, it can be calculated how much is invested in different countries. Based on UNCTAD's Bilateral Foreign Direct Investment Statistics (2014), 63.4 percent of Mexican investment is directed to developed countries, 31 percent to Latin America and the Caribbean, and the rest to other countries. Among developed countries, 39 percent goes to Europe and 61 percent to North America, with 60.5 percent of this solely to the USA (Montoya & Alcaraz, 2018).

Table 13.2 shows the evolution of Mexican foreign direct investment (FDI), arranged by destination. FDI toward the USA holds great importance. In 2011, there was a decrease of approximately 10,000 million USD in Mexico's global FDI compared with the previous year, which is consistent with a decrease of close to 13,000 million USD in the USA. In 2012, Mexico's FDI to the USA increased by 12,000 million USD and its global FDI increased by 31,000 million USD. Another relevant aspect is how the US receives more Mexican FDI than all the developing

Table 13.2 *Mexican FDI stock abroad by geographical destination (million USD)*

Region	2009	2010	2011	2012
World	**84,479**	**110,014**	**100,188**	**131,106**
Developed economies	**55,933**	**73,729**	**60,741**	**79,555**
Europe	**12,690**	**28,939**	**29,002**	**35,667**
Austria	35	11	11	870
Czech Republic	308		36	
France		9	9	−1,174
Germany	1,070	246	304	681
Hungary	1,142	1,993	1,929	1,759
Ireland	1,157			
Netherlands	2,143	8,430	5,852	13,665
Poland	39		39	
Slovakia			42	
Spain	3,123	17,591	18,417	17,457
Switzerland	2,762	333	2,144	4,909
United Kingdom	913	327	217	−2,498
North America	**43,242**	**44,790**	**31,740**	**43,888**
Canada	63	132	116	115
United States	43,179	44,658	31,624	43,773
Developing economies		**34058**	**32,694**	**40,474**
Asia		**−4**	**67**	**125**
China		−4	48	95
India			19	31
Latin America and the Caribbean	**24,360**	**34,062**	**32,627**	**40,349**
South America	**18,941**	**24,370**	**26,090**	**34,154**
Argentina	792	235	388	699
Brazil	13,194	16,186	17,827	22,377
Chile	1,179	1,773	3008	4,815
Colombia	2,848	4,105	3747	3,156
Ecuador	441	913	963	1,387
Paraguay				76
Peru	742	802	−172	1,248
Uruguay				38
Venezuela	−256	356	329	358
Central America	**2,936**	**3,243**	**3,391**	**5,220**
Costa Rica	357	177	554	1,046
El Salvador	672	897	675	945
Guatemala	864	930	1,023	1,040
Honduras	397	416	651	1,310
Nicaragua	352	384	344	357
Panama	293	439	145	522
Caribbean	**2,483**	**6,449**	**3,146**	**974**
Dominican Republic	2,321	2,577	2,310	1,035

Table 13.2 (*cont.*)

Region	2009	2010	2011	2012
Jamaica	162			−61
Netherlands Antilles		3,351		
Puerto Rico		512	536	
Unspecified	4,187	2,228	6,752	11,076

Source: UNCTAD FDI/TNC database, based on data from Banco de México

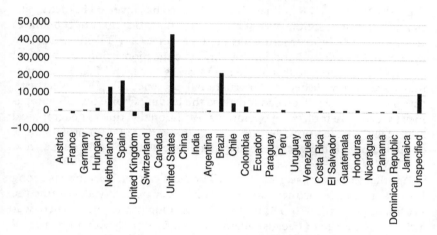

Figure 13.1 Mexico's FDI stock abroad, by country, 2012 (USD million)
Source: based on data from UNCTAD FDI/TNC database

economies combined (except in 2011, which had a difference of only 1,000 million USD).

Figure 13.1 presents Mexican outward FDI by country in 2012, showing differences between countries. The US is the greatest recipient of FDI, which may be due to its geographic location. Brazil is an important destination as well, being the second biggest recipient of FDI, receiving over half of Mexican FDI to developing countries (as shown in Table 13.2). After Brazil, the next two countries are Spain and the Netherlands, following the trend mentioned above of having a greater investment in developed countries.

There are many different sectors in the Mexican economy, but some of them are more meaningful and have a bigger impact overall. We will focus on the sectors to which the firms we selected for the study belong.

One of them is the electronics, technology, information, and communications sector (ETICS) (Capelleras et al., 2013). From 2006 to 2016 ETICS was one of the fastest-growing sectors, receiving more than 4.56 billion USD of direct investment and generating 47.59 billion USD in that time. Currently, it employs over 50,000 people and accounts for more than 2,095 firms. These firms tend to be based in urban areas because they need access to certain resources, including financial, technological, human, and knowledge-related ones (Capelleras et al., 2013).

Mexico ranked 79 of 144 countries analyzed by the World Economic Forum's Networked Readiness Index. Mexico has invested in the expansion and modernization of its IT infrastructure, but mature economies can grow such infrastructure faster; high prices for IT infrastructure access in Mexico and the low quality of education bring the national average down. Despite this, there are IT areas in which Mexican companies have accomplished an international presence. In A.T. Kearney's (2014) study, Mexico placed fourth as the leading choice for US companies to locate their offshore operations. Additionally, due to geographical advantage, Mexico provides the USA with nearly 500,000 professionals annually, increasing each year, with language skills (Cervantes-Zepeda, 2017).

Another important sector is retail. The Mexican retail sector has a long history, its first department stores opening over a century ago during the Porfiriato period (1876–1911). In the beginning of the 1990s, there was a change in the sector because alliances started forming with international retailers, such as Costco and Walmart; the latter is currently the leading company in the sector due to its economies of scale and low prices. In 2018 the Mexican retail market stood at 229.801 billion USD and the retail sector accounted for 14 percent of the country's GDP and 35 percent of employment (Montoya et al., 2018).

The entertainment industry in Mexico, including internet entertainment, music, movie theaters, and amusement parks, generated 22.8 billion USD in 2016 (NTMX Agencia, 2017). This sector increased in value by 44 percent between 2006 and 2012, having an estimated worth value of 30 billion Mexican pesos in 2012. This growth took place due to increases in urbanization by 2 percent and in disposable income per capita by 37 percent during that time. There is a substantial gap between firms in this sector: there are over 6,894 micro firms with 89 percent of market share, while the two leading companies accounted for 9 percent of volume in 2010. In 2017 the sector was predicted to grow by 43 percent within the following year, affected by several factors: predicted growth of 35 percent in per capita disposable income, 5 percent in population, and 7 percent in urbanization (Montalvo & Daspro, 2017).

13.3   Developing Capabilities in Mexican Firms

To succeed in a global market, multinational corporations need certain capabilities, which may or may not be consistent with those needed to grow in their home country. In international expansion, there are capabilities with transferable elements (competitive advantages), but there are others that are grounded in the country (comparative advantages). It is important to take both into consideration, since their presence or absence will determine the success or failure of the firm abroad (Cuervo-Cazurra et al., 2016). To deepen our understanding of this topic, we interviewed executives and managers in each of the firms we studied, so that they could explain the capabilities they have found relevant to them.

For the study, we used two methods to obtain information to deepen our knowledge: analyzing public data on each firm, and interviewing executives from the firms about their capabilities, doing a comparison between the projected information in their public outlets and the responses they provided in person. The secondary source data helped guide the interviews and also helped in our analysis of the interviewees' responses. After compiling the data, we performed a comparative analysis between firms based on the capabilities mentioned by each firm. In the light of these comparisons, we drew conclusions regarding which capabilities are most relevant for Mexican multinationals and how they are connected to the success of the firms studied.

To select the companies included in this chapter, we made a preliminary list of firms that are among the top in their respective sectors. The initial list had thirty-five possible candidates. To narrow it down, we chose companies that would provide added value to the research in that their practices are relevant both locally and internationally. We sent invitations to said firms and drafted interview questions with the information they had available for the public. Out of all the invitations, we received responses from seven companies, and we met with their representatives. Table 13.3 includes the final list of firms, arranged according to their levels of internationalization and the types of products or services they provide. A profile of each firm is presented in Table 13.4.

13.4   Findings: The Cases Studied

Seven Mexican companies of different industries and sizes were chosen:

• one of the main chains of retail in the country, Elektra;

Table 13.3 *Data collection matrix for the selection of Mexican firms as case studies*

		Firm category	
		Exporter	Multinational
Industry	High-tech	Interlub	Neoris
	Low-tech	Belticos	
	Service	Vidanta	Farmacias Similares
			KidZania
			Elektra

- the largest chain of pharmacies of Mexico, Farmacias Similares;
- one of the largest promoters of tourist time-shares, Vidanta;
- an IT consultancy, Neoris, that is an offshoot of a large building materials company;
- a children's entertainment developer, Kidzania;
- a family-run beverage company that has taken an international leap, Belticos;
- a small business of great technology and innovation, Interlub.

In all cases, we conducted interviews with CEOs, vice-presidents, owners, and/or founders. The aim of the interviews was always first to create a climate of trust between the participants and the authors and then to discuss the capacities of their companies.

Interlub

Interlub, founded in 1984 in Guadalajara, develops and produces highly specialized lubricants. From the start, the aim of the firm has been to provide high-tech solutions to companies, creating new, customized products for each customer. According to the CEO, "It is a firm that since its birth has sought to offer differentiated products, not competing in the market by volume." They began producing in Mexico for local customers. Despite not having a completely consolidated position, they started to export their products to Japan in the late 1990s and have expanded since, currently having an export and distribution network that covers over 37 countries. The CEO mentioned that this expansion was necessary because "firms need to find their path and in some cases it is important to go against the normal logic and even consultants, being honest to the vision of the firm and earning trust from the clients." They have created

Table 13.4 *Financial summary of Mexican firms studied*

Company	Industry	Sales, million USD[a]	Assets, million USD[a]	Employees, thousands	EBIDTA,[b] million USD[a]	Exports, million USD[a]	No. of markets
Belticos	Bottling and manufacture	n/a	n/a	0.7	n/a	20% of sales	10
Interlub	Oil producer	n/a	n/a	0.14	n/a	50% of Interglass sales	37
Neoris	IT	n/a	n/a	3.5	n/a	n/a	30
Elektra	Retail and financial services	3,967	10,707	70	683.379	1,099	9
KidZania	Entertainment	500	n/a	13	n/a	450	21
Farmacias Similares	Drugstore and medical practices	2,615	n/a	n/a	n/a	n/a	n/a
Vidanta	Hospitality	800	n/a	16	n/a	640	n/a

[a] Exchange rate of 1 USD = 20.4745 MXN for December 31, 2016.
[b] Earnings before interest, taxes, depreciation, and amortization.

more than 2,000 products and have more than 1,700 clients. They have also acquired numerous national and international certifications, including FSSC 22000 (Food Safety System Certification), NSF, FDA, ISO 14001, and ISO 9001 (Contreras, 2013; Interlub Group, 2016a). In 2014, they had over 140 employees and were planning to expand in South American (Interlub Group, 2016a); they now have operations in Colombia and have made efforts to open up in Brazil, a particularly difficult market (Contreras, 2013).

In dedicating their efforts in the creation of unique products for each client rather than having a generic solution, Interlub has aimed to create added value in their products but also to provide long-term solutions for their customers and help with the correct lubrication of their machinery: 6 percent of Mexico's GDP is used unnecessarily on maintenance due to unnecessary friction (Interlub Group, 2016). Interlub's team see research and development as an investment. For them, each newly developed product generates not only a solution for a client but also knowledge for the future development of new solutions, constantly updating the firm's processes and formulas. The CEO mentioned that one of the key resources for the firm is "the technology, the type of product we are capable of doing, which is a niche product that, I would say, very few companies are structured in a way that they can provide this type of solutions." Their main distinction from their competitors is this capacity to innovate and create tailored products, which most firms cannot or do not do as standard practice.

In order to best exploit technology and give optimal service to their clients, Interlub has prioritized investments in equipment and in their staff. Their laboratories provide all the machinery needed for their processes, but people are primordial for the company. As mentioned by the CEO, it is necessary to "build a structure, an organization where multiple experts can work collaboratively, which is both our greatest success and, sometimes, the biggest challenge." In that sense, they have designed the firm in a way that attracts the needed talent for the solutions they provide, but also keeping in mind the treatment these people will receive once they join the firm.

From the beginning of the firm, the aim was to produce and export to different destinations, daring to break away from the standard mindset and looking for new opportunities abroad, even prior to full consolidation among local customers. As the CEO said: "We, without knowing the concept, were born global, because we knew that if we could sell in Japan, we would be able to sell in Mexico, and now, we do not imagine our business without investing in innovation." To do this, a presence at international expositions was key, generating trust in people from all around the world and providing them with value-added products that are both attractive and functional to them, while being confident in the success they would have both globally and locally.

Credibility was the first big obstacle when expanding to the international market, since there were other firms with previous prestige with which they had to compete. Currently, trust remains a vital element in their operations, but new challenges have arisen. There is a problem with closeness to clients, since Interlub is a small firm that provides constant attention to numerous clients. To deal with this, it is necessary to hire more people and to instruct them in the Interlub mentality, being good consultants that follow the technical, cultural, and relational culture of the firm. This corporate culture is what helps trust to be maintained with customers and is worked upon from the very structure of the firm, having an organic system that revolves around principles and fulfills a purpose that makes the workforce proud. Credibility is relevant not only for the firm but also around the beliefs people have in different parts of the world about Mexican products. As mentioned by the CEO, "Sometimes we have a product in Italy or Korea and they trust us, because it has to be high-quality in order to get over there, but the same product is not accepted here in Mexico and they prefer to get a foreign or a cheaper alternative." The culture of the market is, therefore, an element that cannot be overlooked, since it can create or break apart the firm and its position. One strategy to gain credibility and trust in these cases is through history, having known and respected clients, since this affirms the quality of the product and the service provided.

Interlub's product development process also differentiates it from other firms. It is divided into two processes with different rhythms. The one that generates the most revenue is oriented toward updating and optimizing their current products and technology, which is a short-term process. According to the CEO, this is an important aspect because "the competition does not follow this path, they tend to use the same product while we get a tailored suit and optimize it continuously." The second rhythm is only possible with a firm with niche products in a long-term development process. It consists of research that may change the paradigms followed at the time, but this may not generate revenue immediately. What most firms do not consider is that "there is a way to make profit out of this, even if it is on the long run. We have to find a way to utilize it in two factors: inspiration for scientists and new talent and improvement of your current products." Research is paramount for them since it allows them to discover new things, creating knowledge that can help them directly and indirectly in the parallel processes they are running.

Among the capabilities we mentioned to the representatives of Interlub, they identified thirteen as being significant for them; they also added four capabilities. To create its specialized and customized products, Interlub has invested in the development of the methodology "SmartTouch," which includes the acquisition of resources and the research and development of products by adapting solutions and materials to both local and global clients' needs. It is important to note that production capabilities were very relevant to Interlub, but also understanding the needs of global clients, which is consistent with the ideas expressed by the founder. Since Interlub administers its own production, it requires outstanding human resources that cooperate under correct managerial guidance that allows correct sales practices to bloom. At the same time, employing relationship capabilities, Interlub workers visit customers' firms and work with their personnel to reach the best solutions. Additionally, Interlub has agreements with external research facilities, including the Massachusetts Institute of Technology (MIT), to conduct investigations that promote the expansion and refinement of the products, both in the short and the long run, breaking paradigms in the industry and establishing a positive corporate image with both current and potential clients. During the interview, he specified that the "important networking we do is with universities, with external institutes," MIT being the prime example. Along with the agreements Interlub has, it has the most advanced and flexible research center in Latin America, which allows it to develop its internal resources (Interlub Group, 2016). They use their relationship capabilities not only outwards but also inwards, creating an environment of collaboration and commitment where all the employees feel invested in their jobs and valued, while provided with all the equipment they might need.

Neoris

Neoris started as a subsidiary for one of the world's largest building materials companies, CEMEX. Its initial purpose was to reduce the adaptation time after acquisitions. Now it has become one of the top global firms in the Mexican IT sector (Cervantes-Zepeda, 2017). In the beginning, they were dedicated solely to attending to CEMEX's needs, but in 2002, they started providing consultancy services. They have operations in multiple countries, with Argentina and Europe being their main markets, and they continue expanding to other locations, such as India and the Czech Republic. They have a strong presence in Mexico and in other countries: they are the top consultancy firm in Mexico, the second in Argentina, and the third in Columbia; they are the leaders in the implementation of IT systems and solutions in hospitals in Chile; they are one of the biggest consultancies in the Middle East and provide services to the two top banks in Spain. They are the first Latin American firm to be recognized as a SAP Global Services Partner, having the most Spanish-speaking SAP consultants in the world. They have presence in more than thirty countries and have more than 3,500 employees, as well as talent development programs with twenty universities and social responsibility programs to give access to students (Neoris, 2014; Neoris, 2016).

The solutions Neoris provides may start in Mexico and may be either completed in or provided from other locations, depending on the needs of the industry and the firm in question. The attention to each client is specialized and adapts with time to further accommodate the clients, creating a relationship of trust and support and generating added value to the services due to the resulting efficiency.

Neoris provides solutions throughout the globe, so they have offices in strategic locations, such as India and the Czech Republic, to provide services to firms in other countries. In these locations, they look for comparative advantages. In India, they searched for technology at a competitive price and for software development, hiring both locals and people from Spain to run the operations in the new location. On the other hand, they went to Prague to look for a digital transformation strategy. Because of new trends, they are starting to diversify and develop phone apps to control what is happening in the firm.

Neoris also develops new solutions that are tropicalized and work for Latin America. An example is the adaptation of direct-from-store delivery to their services. They seek to find solutions that help them deal with the circumstances that may arise when they arrive in a country, not relying on standardized solutions.

Neoris identified eleven of the capabilities suggested by our research instrument as being important for their success, and they added four other capabilities. Neoris bases its activities on trends around the world, developing an understanding of both local and global customers' needs and adapting accordingly. This understanding allows Neoris to identify resources it needs and has that it will later develop with the help of cross-cultural management, soft skills, and outstanding human resources. This cross-cultural management is key to its operations, especially in cases such as opening new sites and having people from different nationalities working there (as in their Indian headquarters). Neoris has an established business model where most operations start in Mexico but are carried out in offices abroad, depending on the service and customer, and adaptation depending on the local infrastructure, which may hinder processes, especially in Mexico. This model exploits global thinking to transfer operations to the best location and ensure customers' satisfaction. Neoris holds in high regard the innovation and entrepreneurship that the company incorporates into the solutions it provides, taking advantage of hard skills and relationship capabilities to research and develop these solutions in a form that is optimal for each customer. This helps build a corporate reputation that creates long-lasting agreements and business relationships, with 70 percent of their customer relationships lasting longer than five years (Neoris, 2015; Neoris, 2016).

Belticos

Belticos is a beverage producer that makes its own products and also works as an assembly plant for other companies, bottling their products. They started out with a brand of orange juice, FrutiQueko, in 1991, having only fifty employees and two assembly lines. Now they have more than 700 employees and multiple assembly lines for hot, cold, hot & cold fill, and other beverages, as well as a water treatment system, specialized warehouses according to product type, and a waste disposal system that separates trash. In 2012 they first got the FSSC 22000 certification, which they have renewed each year. They also have kosher and organic certifications, allowing them to fulfill the needs of varying markets, as well as more specific certifications granted by certain customers. They export their own products to the United States and various countries in Latin America, but the clients of their bottling services are sold in other markets as well; among them are PepsiCo, Campbell's, Hershey's, Danone, Coca-Cola Company Mexico, and Walmart Mexico. They are planning to continue expanding to other places such as Saudi Arabia (Global Standards, 2012; Belticos, 2013; Belticos, 2016; Belticos, n.d.).

When the firm started there were no quality standards in place, but as time went by, it became necessary to get certifications to continue operating and growing, following customers' demand for more quality control and regulations. One of the founders mentioned that in the beginning they "didn't have any experience in quality systems, in controllers, in everything needed," but, as regulations became more necessary, they "became the tip of the spear and obtained the first certificate of FSSC 22000 nationally." For them, in the everyday activities it is necessary to keep improving and taking care of their quality. The cofounder also mentioned that there is a global trend in acquiring certifications, because people "want that everything is produced with quality, with people with human and technical quality and with human and technical directors." It is of vital importance to them to have not only the qualifications but also an internal environment that allows their employees to thrive, being given fair treatment and the technology needed to fulfill their jobs.

Even such regulations were mandatory, the company's first major investment was in technology, needing efficient machinery that could keep up with the evolving market. To operate said technology, there was the need to train personnel; Belticos personnel now provide assessments to clients in new product development. In addition, to ensure the quality and continuity of energy supply, they have invested strategically to produce their own energy, even getting extra income through the sale of the energy surplus from their clean electric energy production system. To be successful, they have created a team dedicated to reading market trends to create new products, developing both their own and their customers'. Becoming a leader of trends arises not from inspiration but from experience and time, knowing the industry and the markets and attending conferences and expositions. According to the CEO, "It is a combination between one's capacity and learning and trying to see what others are doing, and, from there, anticipate your move."

There has been a difference in strategy locally and abroad. The CEO said: "When we exhausted our business model, we found that the only way to survive was adapting to the specific local demands of our clients . . . we went from being a survival company to a company that grows above average, our key: Adapting to the specific needs of our customers." The population in the local market used to not be willing to pay more for better quality, but the trend has been shifting with time as a healthy diet has become more important and people have achieved greater acquisitive power. Also, managers need different capabilities operating locally or globally. International managers need to be multicultural, to master a second language, and to have technological knowledge. They also need to have leadership and to have lived abroad, as well as being resilient and knowing how to be autonomous and free while fulfilling their responsibilities.

Some limitations that Belticos has encountered include their geographic location, because it is complicated to get clean energy, but they are currently investing in this aspect by acquiring machinery. They are expanding to the USA to have a more consolidated position with added-value products, and they are making more alliances with more experienced firms in different markets that help them have a hybrid growth, either by sharing brands or by creating new ones together. With previous expansions they have searched for distributors that provide needed services and infrastructure, because, as the CEO mentioned, "it is better for both of us to take advantage of the structure our distributors and clients already have in place and their knowledge in terms of politics and market regulations, avoiding investing unnecessarily."

Belticos mentioned eleven different capabilities from our main research instrument and two additional capabilities. Given that Belticos is a low-tech firm, it is understandable that location is considered a key capability, since resources and labor are rooted in the country. In the beginning, Belticos started after a failed business attempt and the founder decided to try and use the remnants to create something, adapting the previous experience to a new business. Belticos worked first with its own orange juice brand only, FrutiQueko, but it later expanded to other products that became known on their own, eventually leading the company to also start bottling for other companies. To do this, they needed good relationship capabilities, but they also understood that different firms need different standards and certifications, for which the firm also needed political capabilities that allowed them to meet all the requirements and properly carry out these processes. This aspect became particularly relevant when they tried expanding abroad. The CEO pointed out that their executives and managers needed to be "people that are fluent in at least an additional language, that have knowledge about IT, are multicultural and with leadership skills, and that have lived abroad, but, above all, with a lot of resilience." The firm is always adapting itself to this profile, so these managers can help them grow, but they also need the infrastructure to do so. Because of this, Belticos has to invest in an outstanding staff to exploit the hard skills in engineering and production that they administer. This has allowed the processing of new products and the adaptation of previous ones, as well as increasing the number of assembly lines they had. With this new technology, Belticos has been able to file for new certifications, including the FSSC 22000, and it has dedicated efforts to polishing its general sales capabilities to assure its continued presence in the market.

Vidanta

Vidanta is a hotel, golf course, and urban development chain that has facilities in the main touristic sites in Mexico. They build hotels and golf courses in key locations that attract tourists from around the world, as well as creating housing complexes where their clients can stay. Vidanta is a service exporter, providing hospitality services to people all across the world in an integrative way, including golf courses and housing as complementary services. They do not have hotels in different countries, but they have alliances with foreign firms; of their more than 700 million USD annual income, 80 percent of their sales come from clients abroad. Each year their facilities receive more than 700 thousand visitors, of which more than half a million are foreigners. They built and run the international airport in Mar de Cortés and they currently employ over 16,000 people. They are the number one firm in the hospitality business in Latin America and they are considered the sixth best place to work in Mexico, having a personnel rotation of less than 20 percent. They have received multiple certifications, including the Five Diamond Certification from AAA and Earthcheck's Gold Certification for the ecological sustainability culture in the houses they build (Grupo Vidanta, 2015; Expansión, 2016; Instituto Nacional del Emprendedor, 2016).

Vidanta relies on teamwork to provide customers with the best attention possible. They complement their teamwork with their care for each other's well-being and with a clear corporate structure that gives each sector of the firm operative autonomy. In order to grow, they invest in new locations and new attractions that allow them to continue growing, creating alliances with key partners such as Cirque du Soleil. They also follow their customers' opinions and base their decisions on them and global trends, allowing them to exploit the best ideas.

Vidanta named eight capabilities from the main segment of our study instrument and one additional capability. The origin of the firm was to exploit an opportunity the founder saw, the beauty of Mexico as a global touristic attraction, an optimal geographical location. This drive is what made the firm grow, adapting to the bad infrastructure in the country through their soft skills (Instituto Nacional del Emprendedor, 2016). To be able to provide the best service, Vidanta identifies resources and alliance opportunities to pursue with the relationships and political capabilities it has. The people in Vidanta have defined roles and an established command line to support their soft skills. An important discovery regarding Vidanta is how most of the capabilities identified have an interpersonal element, where relationships serve a key role in their operations. Similarly, Vidanta is committed to its customers, its employees, and its expansion, so it always reinvests 90 percent of its revenues. This investment is not only for expansion, but also for improving the work conditions of the employees, providing an employee dining facility where even corporate-level guests eat and enjoy. Vidanta also invests in social programs and has set up Fundación Vidanta, which educates children from communities near the facilities of the firm (Instituto Nacional del Emprendedor, 2016).

Farmacias Similares

Farmacias Similares is a chain of drugstores with adjacent doctor's offices. The idea behind their business was, and still is, to give affordable access to medicine to people with low incomes. Mexico is one of the countries that invests the least in healthcare, dedicating only 6.1 percent of GDP to it in 2008. Farmacias Similares doctors provide consultations at a reasonable price (approximately 2 USD) and the firm supplies inexpensive medicines that it produces itself, which are bioequivalent to more expensive versions. They are the biggest chain in Latin America, having more than 6,000 sales points, and they attracted 39 percent of the participation in the sector in Mexico during 2016, accumulating sales of 2.6159 billion USD. Their first expansion was to Chile and Guatemala in 2003, both of which, at first, represented challenges due to political and social differences from Mexican culture. Currently, these two and Peru are the most important locations where they do business. They continue to expand and plan to open more drugstores, adapting their model to the needs of each specific country (Anderson & López, 2008; Farmacias Similares, 2011; Celis, 2016; Mercadotecnia FE Economía, 2016).

To improve their corporate culture, they have implemented a cultural model reinforcement program, which has been approved by the Mexican government. Along with this, the training of their doctors includes a yearly Doctors' National Congress in Mexico City, teaching the participants about the company's history and values, as well as working on service-oriented commitment to the customer. The main guidelines the doctors have to follow are respecting the consultation's price, respecting the assigned shift, and not becoming another salesperson for the drugstore, instead sticking to the appropriate treatment of patients. In the medical line, the firm is currently trying to get new sales points to continue expanding. They are also looking for alliances with laboratories so that they can become suppliers as well, always taking price into account and controlling it through mass production.

Some of the complications Farmacias Similares has encountered abroad include laws that prohibit having a doctor's office next to a drugstore, as in Chile and Argentina. Here, they placed the doctors' offices as close as possible to the drugstores, usually prescribing generics. Also, in Guatemala many indigenous people did not know any doctors and only used traditional medicine, so they had to start going down the hills to be treated and the doctors had to learn native languages to communicate. In Argentina, people tend to prefer local products, so it was difficult to establish there. In Chile and Peru there was an upside in a regulation that demands drugstores' employees to be pharmacists that can provide assessments, so that doctors' offices are not as needed there. To provide better service, in each country the drugstores are run by locals.

Farmacias Similares mentioned thirteen main capabilities from our research instrument and two additional capabilities. The start of the company was marked by low prices, looking for an alternative for people at the base of the pyramid that cannot afford medicine in other places. The idea arose from an understanding of local clients' needs, which were addressed through the adaptation of local products to the bad infrastructure in the country. This practice has been carried along to other countries. Doctors who work in the Farmacias Similares outlets see the jobs as a useful way to get experience after graduation. The incentives were significant, as explained by the medical services director at Farmacias Similares in interview: "there are thousands of doctors who are now working with Farmacias Similares. Universities tell us that we have become a source of employment for their graduates or even a second job for doctors working with public medical institutions." Farmacias Similares provides opportunities for young physicians and extra income to complement meager salaries for those more experienced practitioners who worked at public health institutions.

The firm wants to provide good quality for a low price with good general sales capabilities, using soft skills and networking and political capabilities to administer their production and supply chain. By doing this, it can manufacture products by buying inputs at low costs and developing the internal resources needed to carry out this production. In its publicity, Farmacias Similares uses a character called Dr. Simi, whose persona is intended to show the caring nature of the firm and transmit an aura of peace and safety. With this image, it also promotes social commitment, giving yearly awards to the best social programs. To grow while keeping prices low, Farmacias Similares has expanded organically, to optimal geographic locations with similar cultures to the Mexican one, and hybrid-wise, through alliances with others. Their political capabilities have helped with this expansion, given that regulations differ among countries. The firm's focus has been on developing corporate reputation through its products and outstanding human resources, training doctors on the values the company promotes and the importance of people (Mercadotecnia FE Economía, 2016; Villaseñor, 2017).

KidZania

KidZania is a firm that combines education and entertainment (edutainment), dedicated to providing children a space to explore adult life and play different roles in society, from having a profession to paying taxes.

Their first facility opened on September 1, 1999, in Mexico City under the name of La Ciudad de los Niños (The City of Children), having an initial investment of 10 million USD and twenty-five partners and sponsors, a number that increased to forty-two in just two years. They adopted the new name in 2007 after they started expanding abroad, opening their first facility in Japan in September 2006, which received 950,000 visitors in the same year. They started expanding to Indonesia, Portugal, United Arab Emirates, and South Korea in less than five years, first with their own and their sponsors' investment, but then they started franchising their parks. There is only one franchise holder per country, and they must make the investment and get local sponsors for the new parks. They currently employ more than 6,500 people around the world and each park receives between 500,000 and 800,000 visitors per year. In 2014, they had 10 million visitors worldwide, and as of 2015, 50 percent of their revenue came from abroad. Currently, they have plans to expand to the United States, opening three facilities that have an investment of between 30 and 53 million USD (Güemes-Castorena & Díaz Prado, 2014; Forbes, 2017; Montalvo & Daspro, 2017; Notimex, 2017).

Each of KidZania's franchises around the world is different from the others, having local sponsors that are representative of the daily life there. For example, in Japan children work preparing sushi; in Indonesia, in a noodle factory; and in Mexico, preparing tortillas. What KidZania looks for in its partners are allies that fulfill the motto "Know How, Know Who": those who know how to succeed locally and who can help them succeed and grow in the new host country as well.

KidZania has explored multiple countries in Asia and the Middle East. Despite the different cultures, the concept has been generally welcomed and there have been some surprises. An example is that women in certain countries are not allowed to do certain activities, such as drive, yet the girls at the KidZania centers have no problem driving and their parents permit it. Another case is in South Korea, where the rules were adapted so the adults could accompany their children at all times, bringing in a cultural element of closeness with the children.

Future plans for KidZania involve exploring the possibility of a smaller-sized KidZania in Doha, which could open new opportunities to target middle-sized cities. They also have the project of opening a car-themed facility in Johannesburg. They have to adapt their technology to their activities, since they need to keep updating the service while respecting the key idea of human interaction.

KidZania named ten main capabilities and three additional capabilities. The fundamental element for KidZania is relationship capabilities, especially with their sponsors. KidZania's initial twenty-five partners and sponsors helped pay for the construction and running of the firm. Without them, it would have been impossible to start operations, and even more to continue expanding abroad. KidZania started as a local facility, so it needed to understand local clients' needs. Once it was established, it could analyze the factors that allowed success locally along with needs from a global perspective, adapting their plans accordingly. According to André Fabre, KidZania's Director of Operations in Mexico, the firm's unique focus on formative "edutainment" that is both value-driven and educational captured an important national and global tendency in the industry (Montalvo & Daspro, 2018). In itself, then, the model helped the firm attract clients, but they needed to adapt the facilities to each location. With their local knowledge, it was possible to identify the elements that could help the expansion abroad, complementing this with the political capabilities the team had developed over time. KidZania learned how to set up beneficial contracts and franchises, using communication and teamwork with the franchisers, but also creating extensive contracts that establish the rules for the use of KidZania's intellectual property; the first contract in Japan was twenty-five pages long, while the most recent ones are more than 200 pages. Protecting this intellectual property is key for them, since they are prone to being copied, with more than fifty imitations existing in China alone; but the company prevails due to its corporate reputation (Forbes, 2017). Soft skills have helped KidZania to adapt local products through the research and development undergone in the planning for each center. These efforts are possible due to the firm's cross-cultural management and entrepreneurship from within the firm, promoting intra-partnerships that help the firm's overall performance.

Elektra

Elektra is one of the top domestic retailers in Mexico, having an income of 81.2 billion Mexican pesos in 2016 (Grupo Elektra, 2017). It was founded in 1950 as a radio manufacturer, but in 1959 they opened their first store, providing the option of weekly payments so that low-income customers could purchase their products. They opened Banco Azteca to carry out their banking services, which started only with the weekly payments but added other services, such as loans, savings accounts, and transfers, to match customers' demands. Their first franchise opened in 2005 and they have a presence in El Salvador, Guatemala, Peru, Honduras, Panama, and the United States. Their banking services represent 62 percent of their income, doing between 8 and 10 million transactions every day and having an investment of more than 220 million USD in technology to operate the banks. In the last few years they shown steady growth, with an increase of 9.0 percent in their consolidated income and of 9.1 percent in their consolidated EBITDA between 2011 and 2016 (Grupo Elektra, 2017; Montoya et al., 2018).

There are cultural differences to be taken into account in the Latin American countries where the company operates. They had to do deep analysis, because even though the host country cultures are similar to Mexican culture in some respects, there are others in which they are completely different, and the model needs to be adapted. For example, the voice of Ingrid Coronado was used in Mexican commercials but a different singer was needed for commercials in Peru, because the locals couldn't understand what Ingrid was saying.

There have been setbacks in their expansion abroad. The first problem was moving two businesses, retail stores Elektra and Banco Azteca. Elektra required less regulation in order to open in different countries, but the bank needed a new license for each country and needed to prove it was a working model, which was very difficult at first since it had had little time operating in Mexico. Brazil and Argentina proved to be particularly complicated cases, with the result that the company had to withdraw its operations in those countries. In El Salvador, the Elektra stores were closed due to low revenue, but Banco Azteca continues to operate there to date. In the future, Elektra aims to expand to Colombia, so they are undertaking an environment analysis and gathering information in order to take the best decision. Despite this plan, the main focus right now is consolidating their current position and improving their internal structure.

Elektra said it had eleven main capabilities from our research instrument and three additional capabilities. Elektra started with a demographic definition, understanding the needs of the local low-income population and the need to adapt to the Mexican infrastructure. General sales capabilities and hard skills helped Elektra buy needed inputs, manufacture the ones it could, and develop internal resources, always attending to low-waged workers while building their corporate brand (Grupo Elektra, n.d.). According to Pedro Padilla, current Director of Grupo Salinas (a business group to which Elektra belongs), Ricardo Salinas "wanted to improve the quality of life in people's homes giving them the items that would make their lives easier and more pleasant," inspiration that lives on in Elektra's sales practices. To carry out the financial aspects of their operations and deal with credits, Elektra created the banking service Banco Azteca, but it was meant to deal solely with credits in the beginning. By analyzing the situation and studying customers' demands, Elektra noticed that people wanted additional services, such as savings and money transfer, so the business model changed and adopted new activities that fulfilled these needs. For their international expansion, Elektra analyzed the situations of different markets and opted to move the established business model to countries with similar characteristics and culture. Once in the countries, some differences were perceived and some adaptations were made, using political capabilities and understanding and adapting to the global clients' needs, leaving only Banco Azteca in some countries and withdrawing completely when necessary. Elektra promoted entrepreneurship in the different branches, having an intercultural administration that was able to share different perspectives (Grupo Elektra, 2017; Montoya et al., 2018).

13.5   Comparison and Conclusions

Table 13.5 shows a comparison of the capabilities found and the companies that stated those capabilities were necessary for their success both locally and globally. Along with strategic capabilities that were predicted to be important at the start of the study, we have included the category of "additional capabilities," which were identified during the study as being relevant.

This study has shed light on the capabilities that a variety of Mexican firms deem necessary to succeed locally and globally. It is important to note that most capabilities were mentioned three or more times, except for supply chain administration (only Farmacias Similares) and intra-partnership (Interlub and KidZania). Farmacias Similares needs strong control over the supply chain and production to keep prices low. Interlub and KidZania are firms that need a lot of teamwork, so intra-partnership is an important capability for them. In the case of Interlub, it was also mentioned that it is particularly necessary to have a good relationship within the firm and with customers in order to provide the best products for clients.

Another relevant discovery was that there were three capabilities mentioned by six out of the seven firms: understanding local customer needs (mentioned by all but Vidanta), corporate brand and reputation (all but Vidanta), and relationship capabilities (all but Elektra). The first two capabilities are connected to the consolidation of the local position, which is normally the first step toward internationalization. In the case of Vidanta, the idea was not to target only one group but to attract customers from abroad. Relationship capabilities become important when firms try to expand and rely on alliances. In the case of Elektra, since it has grown by its own means, it does not have the need of developing relationship capabilities in the same manner the rest of the firms do.

Table 13.5 *Resources and capabilities of Mexican firms studied*

Capability	Subcategories	Belticos	Interlub	Vidanta	Neoris	Farmacias Similares	KidZania	Elektra
Obtaining resources	Resource identification		✓	✓	✓	✓	✓	✓
	Ability to purchase product	✓	✓	✓	✓	✓	✓	✓
	Ability to develop resources internally	✓	✓					
Product/service capabilities	Product manufacture	✓	✓			✓	✓	✓
	Research & development	✓	✓		✓			
	Local product adaptation	✓	✓	✓	✓	✓	✓	
Operations and management	Production management	✓	✓	✓	✓	✓	✓	
	Supply chain management			✓		✓	✓	
	Soft skills	✓	✓		✓			
	Hard skills	✓			✓			
	Entrepreneurship	✓	✓		✓	✓	✓	✓
	Cross-cultural management	✓	✓		✓	✓	✓	✓
Marketing	General sales capabilities	✓	✓			✓	✓	✓
	Understanding local customer needs	✓	✓		✓	✓	✓	✓
Managing external environment	Political capabilities	✓	✓	✓	✓	✓		✓
	Relationship capabilities	✓	✓	✓	✓	✓	✓	✓
	Adjusting to poor infrastructure	✓	✓	✓	✓		✓	
Others	Brand and reputation	✓			✓	✓	✓	✓
Additional capabilities	Adaptability to global needs		✓	✓	✓	✓	✓	
	Intra-partnership				✓		✓	
	Understanding of global clients' needs				✓			
	Optimal geographical location	✓				✓		✓
	Outstanding human resources	✓						

When analyzing the different types of firms, it can be seen that all three exporters share two capabilities: production management and relationship capabilities. The fact that they are exporters means that they need alliances that allow them to distribute or develop their products and services or to expand their activities. At the same time, they all need to administer the production of their products and services to ensure quality and correct procedures following required parameters and certifications.

Two capabilities were repeated throughout all the multinational corporations and indeed shared by all the firms studied except Vidanta: understanding local customer needs, and corporate brand and reputation. As mentioned earlier, multinational corporations need a consolidated presence in their home country. In order to succeed abroad, it is necessary to understand their home culture and needs and to create a reputation that supports their image abroad and works as a distinguisher. This discovery is particularly relevant because Vidanta has most of its revenue coming from abroad, which gives it more flexibility regarding this capability. On the other hand, Interlub's CEO mentioned that they were born global, yet they consider this capability relevant, since it is important to know the customers and their needs in order to tailor their products. It is important to analyze the mindsets both firms have to understand the origin of this difference; a relevant distinction might be the idea of tailoring vs. standardizing. Vidanta as a hotel chain needs to have all processes the same so that they cover, not the specific needs of each customer, but all the general needs any given customer might have. Interlub's approach is creating specific products while cooperating with the client, so they work closely to fulfill the individual requirements the firm has.

The capability of obtaining resources was the most significant for two out of three exporters (Interlub and Vidanta), mentioning all three subcategories as key for their business, while Belticos listed none. The main resource for this may be that Belticos is a firm dedicated to bottling and product development for itself and others, but the main resources needed are already identified, such as access to water. Interlub and Vidanta, being in high-tech and services, need a constant update at a higher rate than Belticos; therefore, their ability to identify, purchase, and develop resources and products quickly becomes a prime need. Among the multinational corporations, KidZania did not mention any of these capabilities and the others three firms identified two each, repeating ability to develop resources internally across firms. The way KidZania is structured, it does not need concrete resources, but key partners that can provide said resources, so their ability to acquire them becomes secondary. Neoris is an IT firm, so it is particularly important for them to identify resources and develop them internally, not purchase them, because high-tech firms need constant updating and internally generated breakthroughs, as in Interlub's case. Farmacias Similares and Elektra are service firms that sell both third-party and their own products, so they need to develop resources but also to be able to buy those products they do not create themselves.

For product/service capabilities, two exporters (Belticos and Interlub) listed all three subcategories, while Vidanta did not mention any of them. Vidanta is a service company oriented toward standardization of processes and meeting any customers' needs; therefore, research and development and adapting locally are not relevant by comparison for them. Belticos and Interlub, being product providers, require the skills to manufacture and adapt them for their customers and to do the research needed in order to fulfill their specific needs and requirements, particularly in terms of sanitary qualifications for Belticos and technological tailoring for Interlub. Among the multinational corporations, KidZania mentioned all the capabilities, Farmacias Similares identified two, and Neoris and Elektra listed one each. KidZania needs to research their markets and analyze how their centers will fit within said markets, even if the plan itself will be carried out by the franchise holders and their partners. Farmacias Similares controls the manufacture of the products, in order to regulate the prices, and adapts them to the target demographic as well as their healthcare services, for example in countries that do not allow a physician's office adjacent to a drugstore. Neoris and Elektra do not need the local product adaptation capability in the same way as other firms, since their services are already designed around their clients. Neoris is based on IT solutions, so they do not adapt products for their customers, but rather develop new ones for them and then give the support needed. Elektra, on the other hand, focuses on product manufacture in terms of getting the correct approach for the customers and their needs, as in their banking services that meet a specific necessity, but they create their own systems rather than adapting existing ones in the target market.

In the category of operations and management, all the exporters and Farmacias Similares mentioned production management as a significant capability. This is consistent with Vidanta's need for standardization and for product control on behalf of Belticos, Interlub, and Farmacias Similares. This is important for Belticos for certifications and for both Belticos and Interlub in order to fulfill customers' requests, but for Farmacias Similares it is particularly important in terms of costs. Belticos also mentioned hard skills, which is related to the firm being operations-related, while both Interlub and Vidanta mentioned soft skills. These two firms need this capability in order to coordinate the efforts within the firm, with the CEOs of Interlub and of Vidanta both mentioning the importance of collaboration between people and having a good work environment. Interlub also listed entrepreneurship and cross-cultural management, which is consistent with the CEO's statement about looking for managers that have lived abroad, are fluent in other languages, and have the talent and the drive to grow. From the multinational corporations, all but Farmacias Similares mentioned entrepreneurship and cross-cultural management, and all but Elektra listed soft skills. Farmacias Similares hires locals for the branches abroad, so being cross-cultural is not as necessary as if they sent people from Mexico abroad, and their approach to entrepreneurship is closely related to the manufacture of their products, not to the sales department, which is the strongest section of the firm locally and abroad. For the other firms, entrepreneurship helps them look for new alternatives and cross-cultural management allows them to understand the local customers while focusing on internal affairs. The working environment and communication are particularly relevant for these firms, but for Elektra it is more significant to have hard skills that ensure the correct running of the operation. Neoris also listed hard skills, which is consistent with their line of work in IT solutions.

Among the additional capabilities mentioned, there are different patterns to be observed. Both high-tech firms mentioned the same three capabilities: adaptability to global needs, understanding of global clients' needs, and outstanding human resources, sharing the first two with KidZania as well. The first two capabilities are related to global trends and adapting to them, so it is logical for Neoris and Interlub, two firms oriented toward tailored solutions and products for their customers around the world with constant innovation, to focus heavily on them. KidZania reads the trends in order to open new centers and to analyze the plans for each one of them, taking into consideration lessons from other centers as well as knowledge of the local situation. Outstanding human resources capabilities were also identified by Belticos and Farmacias Similares, mentioning that it was important for them to have well-trained personnel, but also satisfied employees. Intra-partnership was only mentioned by Interlub and KidZania, being the two firms that most heavily emphasized the importance of collaboration within the firm. Optimal geographical location was mentioned by all firms, except for Interlub and KidZania. The reason behind this may be that those companies take their decisions and do their research in specific places, but their products and services are taken to different parts of the world that are not directly dependent on their behalf, since lubricants are shipped and the locations for KidZania centers are found by the franchise holders. For the other firms, the location is important because of the access to certain resources or locations, for touristic attraction, or for closeness to the end user, where Neoris offers on-shore services and Elektra and Farmacias Similares run their physical stores on site.

Of the seven major categories, the three most repeated among the firms were (among the "others") corporate brand and reputation, managing external environment, and marketing. This is important in that it shows that the firms place more importance on elements that are directed outward – people's perceptions and dealing with third parties – than on internal elements. This shows how the firms start to look outwards when they begin the internationalization process, rather than focusing on internal affairs that have to be consolidated prior to this expansion.

This chapter provides new input to the study of emerging markets, and Mexico in particular, and the capabilities that multinational corporations consider important. There are further important elements to be considered. The study was done by analyzing public data, which tends to be incomplete, and the interviewees' perspectives, which could be biased. A possible study to deepen the new understanding of these capabilities could be to measure the degree to which the firms actually have and exercise said capabilities, beyond the perspectives of their representatives, in order to have a more objective comparative ground. It may also be important to compare the results of multiple firms from within one industry to analyze trends, or the lack of them, in each sector of the economy.

14 Building Strategic Capabilities in Emerging Market Firms

The Case of Peru

Armando Borda Reyes and Carlos Cordova Chea

14.1 Introduction

Emerging markets have large institutional voids that affect the nature of competition and the capacity of firms to develop ownership advantages, and emerging market firms are often at a disadvantage when competing against developed country firms. For example, when the Spain-headquartered multinational Banco Bilbao Vizcaya Argentaria (BBVA) entered Peru in 1995, it announced a "one-thousand-day plan" through which BBVA would become the market leader in the Peruvian banking system (Schwalb & Casafranca, 2000). The domestic Banco de Credito responded to this threat and maintains its market leadership even today. The Banco de Credito acted on different fronts. The company heavily invested in state-of-the-art IT equipment and systems, adapted its upstream processes to respond rapidly to customers' requests, and changed the traditional "wait and see" behavior of credit officials by encouraging them to go out of the building and follow potential customers in their relevant markets. The case of Banco de Credito demonstrates that emerging market firms are not passive victims of new entrants, at the mercy of a highly capable foreign firm. On the contrary, it shows that domestic firms can defend their market positions, upgrade, and develop new capabilities that allow them to successfully compete, even against strong foreign firms. This chapter shares our understanding of why some domestic firms can withstand the entrance of international competitors, develop or strengthen their strategic capabilities, establish market leader positions, and, in some cases, venture abroad to compete internationally.

We selected a group of leading Peruvian firms to identify the core capabilities developed by these firms and to examine the process of building them over time. The analysis of each firm uncovers interesting commonalities among the companies.

This chapter first provides the country background. Next, we briefly describe the companies selected for this study and the methods used to

337

gather data about them. We then share overviews of our in-depth case analysis of the companies included, and we uncover their specific sources of competitive advantage and the processes followed to develop their capabilities. Finally, we present the patterns of capabilities and paths of capability development observed among the companies included in the study.

14.2   Country Background

Located in the west of South America and with a population of more than 30 million (see Table 14.1), Peru has experienced dramatic institutional, social, and economic turbulence during the past thirty years. In the late 1980s and early 1990s the country was on the verge of economic bankruptcy and a civil war. The country landscape started to change with the adoption of promarket reforms (Export.gov, 2017a).

From 1990, when Alberto Fujimori became president, Peru has followed a consistent path of market liberalization and economic integration (Borda et al., 2017). The country has signed seventeen free trade agreements and is a member of the Transpacific Partnership and one of the founding members of the Pacific Alliance (IADB, 2014). Achieving average growth of 5.7 percent between 2005 and 2016, Peru is currently one of the region's fastest-growing economies (CIA, 2017). In parallel, poverty levels have steadily decreased, from 56 percent in 2005 to 20.7 percent in 2016 (Export.gov, 2017a).

Although the country has gradually improved its legal framework, several challenges remain. For example, decisions by the judicial system are often slow and unpredictable, and once legal decisions have been ruled on, the capacity to enforce the rulings is weak. Perceptions of widespread corruption play a major role in generating uncertainty (Export.gov, 2017b).

Table 14.1 *Peru: country profile*

	1992	1997	2002	2007	2012	2017
Population (thousands)	22,737	24,827	26,601	28,293	30,159	32,165
GDP (USD million)	35,884	58,144	54,796	102,202	192,650	211,403
GDP growth rate (%)	−0.5	6.5	5.5	8.5	6.1	2.5
GDP per capita (USD)	1,578	2,342	2,060	3,612	6,388	6,572
FDI Inflows (USD million)	−79	2,139	2,156	5,491	11,788	6,769
FDI outflows (USD million)	0	85		66	78	262
Inflation rate (%)	73.5	8.6	0.2	1.8	3.7	2.8

Source: UNCTAD (2019)

At the industry level, Peru is a service economy. The service sector makes up almost 60 percent of Peru's GDP. The other 40 percent includes extractive industries (18 percent), manufacturing (14 percent), and agriculture (7 percent) (Global Edge, 2017). The country's economic growth is reliant on commodity-related sectors, especially mining activities.

At the firm level, the predominant organizational form is a family business group that relies on the domestic market for growth. In comparison with companies from other countries in the region, relatively few Peruvian firms venture overseas. While a few Peruvian firms started to internationalize during the mid-1990s, most firms that have ventured abroad began their foreign operations only in the mid-2000s. Exporting is the preferred mode used by Peruvian firms to enter international markets.

14.3   Companies Selected

While the six Peruvian firms selected for study (listed in Table 14.2) vary in scale, sector, and level of internationalization, they share at least one common trait: all have responded effectively to the challenges flowing from Peru's market liberalization and to the resulting increases in the inflows of foreign direct investment (FDI). All the selected firms belong to family business groups. Alicorp, the largest in the sample, is part of the Romero Group, of one of Peru's largest family business groups.

All companies in the sample are successful in their industries. Deltron, a distributor of computers, peripherals, and accessories, competes in the domestic market by focusing on streamlining its value chain. Cantol, a manufacturer of door locks and padlocks, is the only company in the sample that is primarily an exporter, and has been able to leverage its innovation capacity and exploit control of its distribution system to

Table14.2 *Data collection matrix for the selection of Peruvian firms as case studies*

		Firm category		
		Purely domestic	Exporter	Multinational
Industry	High-tech			Resemin Group
	Low-tech	Deltron	Cantol	AlicorpYobel
	Service			Lolimsa

compete successfully. Finally, each the four multinationals competes successfully in international markets. While Alicorp (food production and distribution), Yobel (supply chain management), and Lolimsa (software supplier to the health industry) are regional multinationals, Resemin (underground drilling machinery for the mining industry) has operations in Latin America, Africa, and Asia. Alicorp's and Yobel's success is dependent on operational scale and replication of their home business models, while both Resemin and Lolimsa focus on niche markets in their global industries.

Cantol/Canepa Business Group

Created in 1972 by Raul Canepa Sr., this company was a response to the insecurity faced by Peruvian homeowners. In some urban areas, burglars broke into houses with impunity (a situation that has not changed much). Local producers failed to respond to the demand for effective solution to this threat, and their products merely reproduced readily available but ineffective imported products. In this scenario, Canepa founded the company and created a modern door lock suitable to the Peruvian market.

Imported door locks and locksets did not fully respond to local market needs. While imports from developed countries offered features not found in products then available in Peru (such as the knob-lock set category), they failed to fully address the unique requirements of emerging economies. In developed countries, thieves do not generally force their way into houses as aggressively as in Latin American countries such as Bolivia, Colombia, Ecuador, Mexico, Peru, and Venezuela.

Immediately after market liberalization, Cantol was unprepared to compete with international players. Fortunately for the firm, imported products would have required extensive product adaptation to adequately serve the local market. According to Raul Canepa Jr., current CEO of the firm, this entry barrier insulated the domestic market for several years, giving Cantol the opportunity to increase the quality of its products, to streamline its operations, to invest in technology, and to innovate its product offerings. To start with, Cantol specialized in an improved product category, the rim lockset, capable of enduring high levels of force.

Raul Canepa Jr. stated that to improve its competitive capability, Cantol invested in modernizing its manufacturing plant and operational management systems. First, Cantol identified activities in its value chain that could compromise the quality of its products and focused its investment decisions on these. Later, the firm detected bottlenecks in its manufacturing processes that were inhibiting growth. The company's investment decisions have favored bringing new equipment to minimize these bottlenecks. At later stages, Cantol invested in machinery that provided economies of scale, following analysis of expected costs and long-term benefits. To identify useful new machinery, Cantol's managerial team travels to advanced international trade fairs such as those in Chicago, Milan, and Hanover. According to Canepa, regional conferences tend to present offerings of a relatively lower technological standard.

In parallel, the firm demonstrates product management capabilities and a constant commitment to quality. Cantol is the most important promoter of the Peruvian technical standard for locks. The objective is to identify the conditions and characteristics with which a product must comply to be sold in the marketplace. The company works closely with the Peruvian Agency of National Quality (INACAL) to develop norms that will reinforce its position as a high-quality producer. The firm's ratio of returned products to total manufactured products is less than 0.01 percent.

Over time, the firm has also developed product-related and marketing capabilities to innovate its products and product portfolio. According to Canepa, the firm constantly monitors the needs and requirements of the marketplace through its strong distribution network, which currently reaches more than 10,000 points of sale throughout the country. Most of them are traditional small retailers, and working with them has required the cultivation of long-term relations. The founder (Mr. Canepa Sr.) and his team visit every province of the country twice a year, gathering a deep understanding of customer needs. Traditional retailers are the firm's most important source of information about new needs from customers and new offerings from competitors.

Strong control of its distribution system enables the firm to identify economies of scope, through distributing products not only from Cantol but also from well-known international vendors seeking to enter the Peruvian marketplace. Canepa believes this distribution system, developed over decades, provides Cantol with a difficult-to-imitate capability that will act as a source of long-term competitive advantage.

To deepen its understanding of potential responses to emerging local needs, the firm has developed strong research and development (R&D) capabilities. Cantol is among the Peruvian companies with the most patents registered in all industry segments by the national authority. While most of its patents are regionally oriented, Cantol registered those with a global reach in Geneva.

These capabilities have allowed Cantol to export its final products to other emerging economies in the region. Nevertheless, while Cantol has received requests from several Latin American countries, the firm has been cautious about increasing its exporting commitment. Canepa stated that as part of its market assessment process, Cantol explores three conditions. First, to reduce retaliation, Cantol identifies markets where local manufacturers of locks do not exist. Second, the firm explores whether customer requirements are relatively similar to the Peruvian market, so as to minimize product adaptations and maximize plant utilization. Finally, considering their own experience in the local market and the importance of controlling the distribution channel, Canepa noted that the firm makes an estimate of its potential to gain access to the correct distribution network in a particular host country. Where these three conditions are not all present, the firm attends to the market without scaling up its commitment to exporting there.

The firm's second family generation, led by Raul Canepa Jr., realized that its metal mechanical locks and its distribution activities must respond to evolving industry dynamics. They decided to reorganize the company to respond to existing challenges and enable diversified growth in the future. Cantol is now the holding company for the Canepa Group, responsible for creating new business units and providing administrative services (legal services, accounting, human resources, etc.) shared by all business units. Currently there are two main business units under its wing: Tecnopress, the metal mechanical lock arm of the group responsible for manufacturing Cantol locks, and Distrimax, responsible for the distribution of Cantol products and for obtaining exclusive rights to distribute international brands.

Cantol has seven lines of products with a portfolio of more than twenty product categories, earning annual revenues of more than USD 70 million. The company has more than 450 employees and international presence in Bolivia, Costa Rica, Chile, and Ecuador (through exports). Its yearly growth rate was more than 10 percent during the period 2010–2017, and its international revenues represent more than 7 percent of its total sales.

Lolimsa

Rolando Liendo (CEO), together with Abraham López and Ezequiel Munárriz, founded Lolimsa in 1987. According to Liendo, two decisions with long-term consequences differentiated the firm from other players in the domestic market in its early stages: the decisions to follow a niche strategy and to sell standardized software packages (as opposed to custom-made software).

The dominant business model in the industry at the time was to offer a one-stop solution for all technological requirements. Liendo created Lolimsa as a specialized company, and its first client determined its sector of specialization. A US company that had gained a long-term contract with the Peruvian government hired Lolimsa to develop specialized software in epidemiology.

This project lasted almost six years, and the firm developed a unique understanding of the health care industry. Liendo suggests that this particular experience shaped the niche strategy of the firm. Lolimsa is now a software company that exclusively targets the health sector (hospitals, labs, pharmacies, doctors' offices, biostatistics, etc.). Its R&D efforts, one of the cornerstones of its strategy, are concentrated on this industry. Lolimsa is one of the leading Peruvian companies in technological patents filed with the domestic patent authority. Further, the firm protects its intellectual property internationally through World Intellectual Property Organization agreements.

Liendo never envisioned Lolimsa as a tailor-made software development company. He was intrigued by the worldwide sales of Microsoft's standard packages (i.e. Office) and their ease of installation by users. Liendo believed the most efficient way to support the standardized services (Carmel, 2012) provided by the health sector would be through a standardized software package incorporating the best practices in health-related service management.

Initially, Lolimsa aimed to serve only the health care market in Peru. However, Liendo soon realized that not only was the domestic market small and fragmented, but also that it favored custom-made solutions. Consequently, revenue from domestic sales of their packages were insufficient to cover the total costs of maintaining its operations. To survive, it was necessary to expand the firm internationally.

Consequently, the firm started to explore neighboring countries such as Ecuador, Colombia, Bolivia, and Venezuela. For country selection, Lolimsa relied on a network of partner institutions previously developed in its home market. Liendo realized that both pharma labs (i.e. Roche) and tech firms (i.e. Microsoft and Oracle) were global players in the health industry and that Lolimsa needed to work with when they ventured abroad. These partners could provide unique context-specific knowledge and specific leads to help Lolimsa develop its business internationally. Therefore, Lolimsa's international expansion built on the key contacts provided by its global partners. Following this relational strategy, the firm expanded to Ecuador (in 1994) and thereafter to Colombia, Venezuela, Bolivia, and beyond.

Lolimsa's internationalization strategy evolved over time. Initially, the firm used contractual agreements with credible technological and distribution partners. When the interests of stakeholders failed to align (as when channel partners did not prioritize selling Lolimsa products), the firm began to explore greenfield investments. While such investments provide full control of operations, the downside is the level of investment needed and the increase in fixed costs. Consequently, according to Liendo, Lolimsa again shifted its strategy to move to a product and trademark franchise system, in which Lolimsa sells the product to the local franchisee, which manages local operations with minimal supervision. Lolimsa established its current business model in 2010: the firm holds a minority equity stake in the franchisee, thus retaining a limited degree of control over the partner's decisions. Under this scheme, Lolimsa receives 40 percent of total revenues.

Beyond building the R&D and relational capabilities required to internationalize, Lolimsa needed to remain resilient in the face of dramatic changes in local and regional market conditions and capable of managing its external environments. These issues are of major importance in Latin America in both the institutional and industry arenas. At the institutional level, several countries – including Argentina, Venezuela, and Bolivia – within the region remain ambivalent regarding adoption of the Washington consensus on trade liberalization and privatization, while others, including Peru, appear to be on the verge of retracting their commitments. At the industry level, the shift from stand-alone pharmacies to pharmacy chains has altered the rules of the game. The resulting scale efficiencies mean the entrance into an area by one store from a chain has the power to close more than thirty nearby stand-alone pharmacies. Lolimsa has a unique advantage over foreign competitors due to its resilience and flexibility to rapidly adapt its operations to compete in changing and often unpredictable environments.

While firms from outside the region tend to perceive Latin American countries as similar, Lolimsa has developed cross-cultural managerial capabilities which it can leverage in its negotiations. Liendo realized that in the Latin American IT industry, being a foreign company often provides an edge over domestic firms. According to Liendo, demonstration of a deep understanding of local situations and culture in the host country provides key advantages over other nondomiciled firms by signaling the capacity to adapt payment conditions, support in selling activities, and public relations to the specific context of the host country.

Finally, the firm has demonstrated that they produce innovative and high-quality products in the industry. To reinforce this position in international markets, Lolimsa relies on obtaining demanding global certifications to demonstrate its qualifications. For example, Lolimsa has CMMI (Capability Maturity Model Integration) level 3 and CCHIT (Certification Commission for Health Care Information Technology) certifications.

Lolimsa has achieved continuous growth throughout its lifespan. Its annual growth rate averages between 5 percent and 6 percent. Liendo believes the firm will continue to grow at this pace in the near future. However, its international strategy will favor penetrating deeper into existing markets, rather than entering new ones. Lolimsa currently has operations in eleven countries (all in Latin America) and its foreign operations account for more than 70 percent of its revenues.

Resemin Group

James Valenzuela founded Resemin in 1989 as a provider of spare parts for maintaining mining drilling equipment from established brands such as Caterpillar, Atlas Copco, and Sandvik, among others. Valenzuela has a deep knowledge of the Peruvian mining landscape. During his childhood he lived with his parents in Toquepala (a mining camp). He studied mining engineering in one of the most prestigious Peruvian universities, and his initial working experience was in rock drilling. Using his industry-specific knowledge and the window of opportunity provided by widespread scarcity of potential competitors in the country at that time, Valenzuela decided to enter the market with the aim of gaining an important role among mining companies, mining contractors, and suppliers of international mining equipment brands.

The company's beginnings were difficult. According to Valenzuela, as a Peruvian company, Resemin was at a disadvantage in Peru. In some cases, its products were viewed as counterfeit versions of ones from established brands. This experience gave the firm resilience, one of its most important capabilities. Resemin has relied on this capability several times during its history.

In the face of this discrimination, the firm continuously invested in R&D activities and in improving its manufacturing facilities. Initially the company reverse-engineered parts from its competitors, but it then evolved by developing improved components compatible with those provided by international brands. This evolution helped Resemin consolidate its position in the Peruvian mining industry as a supplier of parts and pieces and to strengthen its confidence in designing and producing its own equipment for underground mining, a niche in the mining industry served by the firm for several years.

In 1996, Resemin designed a complete underground drilling equipment system and outsourced the manufacturing process to a US company. Unfortunately, as Valenzuela revealed, the result was not as expected. There were huge differences between its internally designed product and corresponding products from competitors such as Atlas Copco and Sandvik. While the firm lost much of this investment, the learning experience gained helped Resemin identify technological gaps and improve its local manufacturing capabilities by investing in its plant and in specialized software.

Resemin's second attempt to develop drilling mining equipment was in 2002. The firm not only designed but also manufactured the main components of their equipment for underground mining. Because of the firm's control of the operation and the relative simplicity of the product's design and operation, the product was very successful in the Peruvian market.

While the firm initially focused on serving the domestic market, Glencore, one of the largest mining companies in the world and with operations in Peru, bought Resemin equipment for their facilities in Zambia in 2002 and requested that Resemin operate the machinery there. In response, the firm created an independent service unit that works as a mining contractor. Resemin followed a similar strategy in the Republic of Congo in 2009 and in India in 2012. The manufacturing process is concentrated in Peru, and each mining service unit contracts to operate the equipment in the host countries. Further, Valenzuela revealed that as these are independent units, they can acquire products from Resemin or from its global competitors (i.e. Atlas Copco) to comply with customer requirements. By working on widely dispersed and varied emerging markets, the firm has developed operational and managerial capabilities, especially those related to supply chain and cross-cultural management.

The firm continuously invests in fine-tuning its product/service capabilities by investing in product adaptation and innovation. According to Valenzuela, underground mining is "one of the worst environments to work" because of the lack of oxygen, high corrosion, excessive humidity, and extreme smoke during operations. Thus the equipment must be highly functional and fairly simple to use so that workers can stay in tunnels for the shortest time possible without sacrificing productivity. This firm's mission is to develop new equipment capable of competing with hardware from the large multinationals serving this specific niche. While the latest technology may offer "nice to have" characteristics, functionality, flexibility, and simplicity are "must have" features in this product category.

Valenzuela revealed that the company developed several product innovations that go from mining jumbos, alternators, and more recently, micro jumbos, which were the smallest front-facing drilling vehicles able to work in underground mining. Their latest product, the Muki, has the characteristics of a game changer: only 1.05 meters wide, it can work in extremely narrow veins. This product received a US patent (Molina, Olivari & Pietrobelli, 2016).

Flexibility is a characteristic not only of its product lines but also of the company itself. As Resemin is close to the market and relatively small, the firm can easily adapt its products to customer requirements. This provides them with a competitive edge in the market. Currently preparing its next generation of products, Resemin bought the engineering division of a German manufacturer of scoop loaders to fine-tune its R&D capabilities and complete its product portfolio for the underground mining industry.

While contracting provides an attractive international growth path in Africa and Asia, it is not as attractive in South America. In fact, according to Valenzuela, Resemin's customers are not only mining companies but also mining contractors, which make up an important part of its business. Following the same path in Latin America as in Zambia would seriously impact these revenues. As a consequence, Resemin created independent commercial companies to manage its portfolio in the region. The firm created Resemin Argentina in 2006 and Resemin Mexico in 2012. For other regional markets, Resemin uses a network of distributors to serve host markets. Their unique understanding of the industry and the interests of its customers allow the firm to compete globally against established multinationals such as Sandvick and Atlas Copco.

Resemin Group has evolved from a solo firm that supplied parts for underground drilling machines to a business group with independent but complementary lines of businesses. One is dedicated to manufacturing a product portfolio with six product lines, the second acts as a mining contractor, especially in Africa and Asia, and the third oversees commercial units located in Latin America. Currently, Resemin Group has annual revenues of more than 100 million USD and has experienced an annual growth rate of 40 percent in the period 2014–2017 (Escalante, 2017). The group has more than 7,500 employees globally and physical presences in Argentina, India, Mexico, Peru, Republic of Congo, and Zambia.

Alicorp

Founded in 1956 as Anderson Clayton & Company, the company was acquired by the Romero Group in 1971 and renamed Compañía Industrial Peru Pacífico (CIPPSA). CIPPSA mainly produced and sold edible oils. After a series of mergers and acquisitions beginning in 1993, the company added products to its original portfolio such as noodles, biscuits, flour, dairy products, sauces, and animal food. The company was renamed Alicorp in 1997.

After Peru liberalized its market in the early 1990s, the company's top management team saw a high risk of entrance by regional competitors with competitive advantages in its main line of business (edible oils). As a response, Alicorp needed to pursue different lines of action.

First, the firm needed to improve its operations to reach international standards in a relatively short period. The company invested in state-of-the-art machinery and redefined both its main processes and its organizational structures (Alicorp, 2000). Since its inception, the firm has leveraged strong capability in sourcing and purchasing commodities (Osores, 2015). This knowledge is crucial, especially for its success in the farinaceous and oil business. The company nurtured this capability over time, and Alicorp is now the biggest importer of wheat in Peru and among the top three in Latin America. It also imports other commodities such as soybeans. Its ownership of warehouses and plants along the entire Peruvian coast allows the firm to store and process commodities faster and at lower costs than their competitors.

Alicorp needed to establish high entry barriers to international competitors. The company originally concentrated its efforts on strengthening traditional distribution channels, as opposed to modern retail. Once modern retail dominates the distribution system, any international company with sufficient resources can enter the market to compete head-to-head. Alicorp decided to strengthen its traditional distribution system by assigning geographic areas to local independent partners controlled by the firm. Over time, the company established a strong distribution network that currently reaches around 100,000 points of sale in Peru.

Alicorp's profound understanding of the traditional distribution channel is one of the core capabilities in its business model (Osores, 2015). The firm coined the term "Go to market" to capture its capacity to cover vertical and horizontal markets faster and more efficiently than its competitors, especially when launching new products or distributing existing ones. Its distribution network allowed Alicorp to gain scope efficiencies that their competitors cannot easily match.

The firm has also developed brand management capabilities over time. Being in a closed economy with little competition in the early 1990s, the company initially lacked employees with branding skills. To resolve this gap, Alicorp attracted talent from competitors that were well-orientated to the market. With the strong commitment of the management, Alicorp hired people from international firms to develop a marketing culture and a customer focus, now embedded in its business model. The firm developed knowledge and expertise in defining the correct value proposition, strategy, and market segmentation, and in identifying growth potential for each of its brands. Currently, the company manages nearly 200 brands in the Latin American region. The brands that Alicorp possesses compete in premium segments.

In parallel, the firm needed to generate products with value added. To compete internationally, the firm needed an attractive portfolio of products. With only one basic commodity (edible oil), it would be impossible to internationalize. The company therefore expanded its portfolio of products. In 1995, CIPPSA acquired La Fabril (oils, noodles, biscuits, flour, and laundry care), and in 1996, it acquired Nicolini (noodles, flour, and animal food) and Molinera del Peru (noodles). With these acquisitions, the firm obtained a broader portfolio of products capable of generating added value.

After its consolidation in the local market, Alicorp decided to grow internationally by acquiring well-established firms. Alicorp acquired Eskimo (ice cream) in Ecuador, 2007; Value Brand Company in Argentina (personal and home care) and Propersa in Colombia (personal care), 2008; Sanford in Argentina (cookies and candy), 2010; Italo Manera in Argentina (cakes and pasta), 2011; Pastificio Santa Amália in Brazil (consumer goods), 2013; and Industrias de Aceite in Bolivia (cooking oils), 2018. This history of mergers and acquisitions enabled the development of strong organizational capabilities to generate synergies and efficiencies among its operations (Osores, 2015).

More recently, Alicorp has updated its organizational structure to deal with its increasingly diversified portfolio of industries, products, and countries, and to gain efficiencies within and across different business units and geographic areas. Its three business units are mass consumption, industrial services (business-to-business), and animal nutrition. In its mass consumption business unit (the most important in term of revenues), Alicorp's management believes that the firm has developed expertise in six core platforms of products: farinaceous, oils, homecare, personal care, sauces, and impulse (confectionery) products (*Gestion*, 2013). Consequently, when deciding to acquire a company or expand its current portfolio, Alicorp analyzes the fit of the target company with its six core platforms.

Further, considering its exponential growth and its mode of expansion through domestic and international mergers and acquisitions, Alicorp's management team believed it was necessary to improve the control, coordination, communication, standardization, and knowledge transfer among subsidiaries and from headquarters to its subsidiaries. The firm implemented the "One Alicorp" program to shape and promote one corporate culture across the entire organization (Alicorp, 2019). This involved a corporate reconfiguration in which all supporting areas of every country (finance, human resources, supply chain, and raw materials) stopped reporting to the country manager. Now they report to functional corporate vice-presidents of each of these areas, who are based in company headquarters. This reconfiguration allows better knowledge transfer of best practice within the organization. Under this scheme, workers with expertise in different areas travel to all the countries in which Alicorp operates to train people or look for efficiencies, innovations, and best practices.

Alicorp's sales revenues rose from USD 80 million in the early 1990s to nearly USD 2 billion in 2016. The company has approximately 7,500 workers and operations in seven countries within Latin America: Peru, Argentina, Bolivia, Brazil, Chile, Colombia, and Ecuador. Alicorp exports its products to twenty-three countries around the globe.

Deltron

Oscar Zevallos and Nestor Quispe founded Deltron Group in 1989. At that time, companies such as IBM, Compaq, and Acer (among other multinationals) dominated sales of personal computers and peripherals. This market was rapidly evolving toward a new model, assembling generic and less expensive yet compatible personal computers.

While established brands failed to pay attention to this trend in the beginning, they soon realized that market preferences might be about to change dramatically. The business model of assembling generic computers offered better prices, more flexibility and (at least perceived) similar performance to branded computers. Hence, the model benefited from a boom period that started in the late 1980s and that would last for more than a decade.

In this scenario, according to Zevallos, Deltron's top management team perceived a window of opportunity for the company to exploit. Given that small and medium-sized domestic enterprises assembled the generic computers, Deltron saw these firms as requiring a reliable, efficient, and economical source of supply of parts and components of good quality. Further, assembling companies would require sufficient variety at any given point to respond to the preferences of their customer base. Zevallos and Quispe founded Deltron to be an importer and wholesaler of internal computer hardware such as read-only memory, motherboards, and hard drives, among other components.

As stated by Zevallos, from its inception, Deltron built its business model around its strong procurement capabilities. The firm needed to identify and build an international network of suppliers in the United States, China, and other places around the globe to buy computer hardware. This entailed the capacity to identify and anticipate in the international market the resources needed to meet local demand, and also the ability to understand and negotiate with different suppliers from multiple countries, in search of the best balance between quality and price. The company developed cross-cultural managerial capabilities to efficiently deal with foreign suppliers.

The development of this international network and its understanding of the domestic market allowed Deltron to provide a good product mix, to maintain an adequate stock of products, and to sell products of good quality at lower cost than their domestic and foreign competitors. Further, as reported by Zevallos, while the company is fully devoted to serving the domestic market, it has established two overseas offices to further streamline its procurement process. The first one was established in 1992 in Miami, Florida. At that time, the USA was Peru's most important trading partner for computer parts and accessories. Deltron established its second office in 2014 in China after Asian countries became the most important commercial partners for Peru in the category (OEC, 2014).

According to Zevallos, the capability to be fast in procurement has been crucial to its success in the market. The knowledge of the procedures and operations of foreign and Peruvian customs, the development of an international network of suppliers, and the ability to select the appropriate maritime or aerial transport carrier allowed Deltron to offer a wider variety of imported products, shorter delivery periods, and lower costs than their competitors in the market. Despite the entrance of international competitors, Deltron has been successful in sustaining its leadership in Peru.

As the Peruvian market evolved, Deltron's core competence in procurement remained unchanged but its business model evolved from being a wholesaler of internal hardware parts to providing finished goods (computers, printers, and other accessories). Moreover, Zevallos noted that given its predominance in the domestic marketplace, Deltron has developed profound capability for understanding local consumer needs. As a consequence, the company obtained representation agreements for global brands and is now an official wholesaler distributor and strategic partner of several major global manufacturers such as HP, Intel, Samsung, and Creative, among others.

Based on its local understanding of market conditions, Zevallos recounts that Deltron decided to segment the marketplace to serve each segment more efficiently. The firm identified small assemblers, retailers, government, and corporate clients as the relevant segments for its business. While business-to-business models serve most segments, the governmental sector requires a different model. Each segments has its own particularities and preferences, and Deltron relies on its procurement capabilities to develop and provide suitable and unique value propositions.

For small assemblers, the most important factors are range of components, cost, and quality. As mentioned in different focus groups, assemblers consistently consider Deltron as their first option "because they can find all the variety of products they need." Further, given that this segment is fragmented and assemblers often do not have access to formal financial services, Deltron developed capabilities to minimize financial risks to these small companies. The management of credit and receivables policy during its early years provided a source of competitive advantage that the firm has fine-tuned over time. While the firm was initially financially exposed, its "know your customer" policy plus the use of collateral and guarantee letters keep its credit risk under control.

For retailers, it is essential to have appropriate volume, flexibility, and rapid delivery. According to Zevallos, retailers value Deltron's capacity of "offering the volume of products they need and being flexible in terms of negotiating the prices." To serve both the government and corporate segments, Deltron created the Advance brand. Initially, the firm obtained ISO 9001 certification to manufacture its own computers. Currently, as stated by Zevallos, the firm leverages its commercial office in China to import to the domestic market computers, tablets, TV sets, and other equipment carrying its Advance brand.

Deltron is now by far the biggest domestic wholesaler of computers, computer hardware, and accessories in the Peruvian computer market, employing around 500 people and earning about USD 220 million in annual sales revenue. The firm has operations in the Peruvian cities of Lima, Trujillo, Chiclayo, Huancayo, Cuzco, Iquitos, and Arequipa. The company aims to reproduce its business model internationally in the near future by expanding to other Latin American countries they view as institutionally and culturally similar to Peru such as Bolivia, Ecuador, and Colombia.

Yobel

Yobel was created in 1967 by the brothers Fernando, Eduardo, and Jorge Belmont as part of the Belmont business group. The group has operations in the cosmetics, personal care, and manufacturing/logistics industries.

During its early years, the Belmont business group had continuous growth due to, among other things, the adoption of the direct sales model created by Avon. By 1977 the group had internationalized to Ecuador by replicating its direct sales model and later opened similar operations in Colombia and Argentina. The manufacture of its products remained concentrated in Peru.

After this early success, in 1988 the Belmont brothers decided to split the group into three stand-alone units, with Fernando Belmont in control of Yanbal-Unique (cosmetics and personal care), Eduardo Belmont of Belcorp (cosmetics and personal care), and Jorge Belmont of Yobel (manufacturing and logistics). Yanbal-Unique and Belcorp not only remained independent but also aggressively competed with each other to consolidate their market positions. Yobel continued to manage the manufacture and supply chains of the other two companies until 1990. Due to the intense competition, Yanbal-Unique decided to vertically integrate its operations to both manufacture its own products and manage its supply chain directly. Belcorp maintained its business model by out-sourcing its manufacturing and supply chain to Yobel.

According to Francisco D'Angelo, CEO of the firm with almost thirty years of experience in the company, Yobel has developed a unique experience in the cosmetics industry by efficiently managing the complexity of the entire supply chain of its counterparts. This included dealing with multiple providers, manufacturing processes, clients, and stock-keeping units. This understanding is path-dependent and has developed and accumulated over time.

As stated by D'Angelo, Yobel's value proposition is as the "one-stop shop" for customer operations, achieved by providing services across the full spectrum of supply chain management: demand and supply planning, sourcing, manufacturing, and logistics. Thus Yobel's value proposition embraces two key roles: as manufacturer and as logistics operator. Each of these roles has completely different business dynamics in terms of margins, operations, and potential for replication in other countries.

D'Angelo noted that for its international expansion, Yobel uses a "follow the client" strategy. In particular, the firm established logistic operations in each country entered by Belcorp. This strategic arrangement provides Yobel with a smooth internationalization process by providing an exclusive and regular anchor client abroad (Belcorp). While establishing a production plant was not always possible, access to logistic operations in host markets permitted the firm to obtain scale economies in the Peruvian plant and to cover its fixed costs in the host country, while gaining host-country-specific knowledge. Yobel has logistic operations in Chile, Colombia, Costa Rica, Ecuador, El Salvador, Guatemala, Mexico,

Puerto Rico, Dominican Republic, and the USA. Further, it has plants and logistic operations in Peru and Mexico.

From its operations in Peru and Mexico, Yobel serves other markets and fulfills its value proposition of being the "one-stop shop" for its customers. As noted by D'Angelo, Yobel's domestic revenues currently represent 60 percent of its total sales.

D'Angelo observed that in 2003, Yobel's top management team decided to expand their client universe above and beyond Belcorp in Peru and in the rest of the Americas as well. D'Angelo noted that the firm relied on several capabilities to do this. First, Yobel used its capacity to manage the entire supply chain. Further, it leveraged its presence in international markets to be attractive to large multinationals. Yobel can now be the one-stop shop for Peru and ten other Latin American countries. Second, given that its manufacturing process favors flexibility over full automation, Yobel can manufacture different types of products in the same production line. This provides economies of scope that are not easy to duplicate. Finally, considering Yobel's experience with a direct sales model and its knowledge of traditional retail, the firm can reach more than 700,000 points of sales in the region, providing good coverage of markets in which the firm has a presence. With these assets in mind, the firm moved to diversify its customer base.

Yobel considered industries that faced similar issues to those met by the cosmetic industry: many vendors, many clients, many stock-keeping units, and horizontal distribution. Hence it targeted industries such as personal care, food, homecare products, jewelry, and in general, other mass consumption goods. Among its multinational customers are 3M, Unilever, L'Oréal, Procter & Gamble, Johnson & Johnson, Beiersdorf, Kimberly Clark, Colgate, and Alicorp. The results of its customer diversification strategy vary between home and host countries. In Peru, 35 percent of its revenues flow from Belcorp. The rest comes from operations of large domestic companies (e.g. Alicorp) or multinationals (e.g. Proctor & Gamble). In contrast, for its international operations, Belcorp represents 70 percent of Yobel's revenues.

D'Angelo explained that the objective of the firm over the upcoming years is to continue diversifying its portfolio of customers in countries where the firm has already established operations. In manufacturing (representing 50 percent of company revenues), Yobel achieves good margins but competes with existing plants of its customers (e.g. Unilever in Colombia). Therefore, growth plans are contingent not only on efficiency gains but also on new investments in infrastructure that customers might prefer to avoid. However, in the supply chain business, Yobel competes with other logistic operators. Here, the margins are fairly small and require attractive volumes to gain operations. Given the economies of scope provided by its main customer, Yobel may be able to increase this line of business internationally and become fairly competitive.

Yobel currently employs nearly 5,000 people and earns annual sales revenues of about USD 150 million, with 40 percent of its revenues from international operations.

14.4   Conclusions

This chapter has aimed to identify the strategic capabilities used by Peruvian firms and to evaluate the processes of developing them to enable the firms studied to compete with foreign competitors in domestic and international markets. Table 14.3 summarizes the main capabilities identified in the study. We observe many commonalities in their strategies, despite their having originated in different sectors and having various company-specific strategic capabilities.

First, it seems that Peruvian firms leveraged existing institutional conditions to either identify and exploit windows of opportunity or to deter the entrance of foreign competitors. For example, Resemin entered the market because of restrictions imposed on the importing of spare parts for drilling machinery at the time. Similarly, institutional conditions insulated the country from foreign competition, giving Cantol the time to upgrade its core competences. Further, Alicorp, cognizant of its weaknesses, decided to strengthen its traditional distribution channel to deter the entrance of foreign competitors. One of the most important capabilities developed by Peruvian firms is adjusting to the poor infrastructure that is a legacy of the institutional conditions faced by the country during the 1980s and 1990s.

Second, most firms seemed to favor the upgrading of manufacturing, production management, local product adaptation and supply chain management capabilities. Yobel developed strong production and supply chain management capabilities due to its relations with Belcorp. Its ability to manage flexible manufacturing processes helped the firm diversify its customer base in domestic and international markets. Alicorp invested in state-of-the-art machinery and leveraged its ability to purchase commodities to overcome cost disadvantages. Deltron based its business model on exceptional procurement processes. Cantol adapted its door locks and locksets to align with national and Latin American realities; the firm also invested heavily in modernizing its plant and machinery. Resemin's manufacturing capabilities allowed them to produce highly specialized drilling mining machinery. Lolimsa demonstrated a deep understanding of host-country

Table 14.3 *Resources and capabilities of Peruvian firms studied*

Capability	Subcategories	Cantol / Canepa	Lolimsa	Resemin	Alicorp	Deltron	Yobel
Obtaining resources	Resource identification				✓	✓	
	Ability to purchase product inputs				✓	✓	✓
	Ability to develop resources internally	✓		✓			
Product/service capabilities	Product manufacture	✓	✓	✓	✓	✓	✓
	Research & development	✓	✓	✓			
	Local product adaptation	✓		✓			✓
Operations and management	Production management	✓	✓	✓	✓	✓	✓
	Supply chain management	✓	✓	✓	✓	✓	✓
	Hard skills		✓				✓
	Soft skills						
	Cross-cultural management						
Marketing	General sales capabilities	✓	✓	✓	✓	✓	✓
	Understanding the market and local customer needs	✓	✓	✓	✓	✓	✓
	Corporate brand and reputation				✓		✓
Managing external environment	Political and negotiating capabilities				✓	✓	✓
	Relationship capabilities	✓		✓			✓
	Adjusting to poor infrastructure	✓	✓		✓	✓	✓

situations and cultures and a strong capacity to adapt its offerings to the singularities of host markets.

Third, Peruvian firms with international presence in different regions (using Rugman and Verbeke's typology; 2004, 2008) are characterized by playing niche roles in global industries. Both Resemin and Lolimsa based their business models on a constant effort to innovate in their corresponding areas of expertise. Given their presence in different geographic markets, these firms have needed to complement their product and service capabilities with cross-cultural managerial capabilities. In interviews, the representatives of these firms emphasized the resilience and flexibility that have allowed their companies to overcome difficult environmental conditions.

Fourth, marketing, sales, and control of a traditional distribution channel became crucial strategic capabilities for many of the firms analyzed in this chapter. For example, Alicorp developed the capacity to create valued brands and has rapid vertical and horizontal market coverage of their products. Yobel uses its access to 700,000 points of sale within Latin America to attract foreign multinationals. Cantol deploys its distribution capacity to attract international vendors interested in operating in Peru through traditional channels such as hardware stores. Deltron has become the preferred distributor of internal computer parts and peripherals in Peru. The strategic byproduct of access to traditional distribution channels is the potential to gain a profound understanding of local customer needs, which drives innovation across product categories.

Fifth, R&D capabilities are also salient to the success of Peruvian firms Cantol, Lolimsa, and Resemin. Cantol holds many registered patents, which have allowed the firm to compete in the local market and to start exporting its products to other emerging markets within the Latin American region. Lolimsa's R&D efforts are one of its main sources of competitive advantage, enabling the production of innovative and high-quality software oriented to the healthcare industry for eleven emerging markets. Its technological patents are registered internationally by the World Intellectual Property Organization. Resemin's investments in R&D have permitted the company to identify technological gaps in the design and production of world-class equipment for specialized underground mining in six countries on three different continents.

In this chapter, we have shown how some Peruvian firms withstood the entrance of international competitors in their home countries, established dominant positions in domestic markets, and in some cases ventured to compete abroad. In doing so, we have provided not only in-depth case studies based on primary data from interviews with company founders, CEOs, or top executives, but also a comparative analysis of the strategies used by Peruvian firms to upgrade their capabilities. While more research is certainly needed to fully understand this process, this chapter represents a step toward this goal.

15 Examining Strategic Capabilities Across Emerging Markets and Their Firms

Alvaro Cuervo-Cazurra, William Newburry, and Seung Ho Park

Emerging markets and their firms are often referred to as a collective group but in fact display a significant amount of variety in their individual characteristics. Given the diverse challenges presented by their home-country operating environments (Khanna and Palepu, 2010) which result in large variations in operations (Grosse & Meyer, 2019) and internationalization (Cuervo-Cazurra & Ramamurti, 2014; Ramamurti & Singh, 2009), it would not be surprising to find that emerging market firms have needed to develop particular capabilities to achieve success (Williamson, Ramamurty, Fleury, & Fleury, 2013). However, leaving aside theoretical arguments, we know little about the actual capabilities that these firms perceive as strategic to their success, and the degree to which these capabilities vary across different operating conditions. Instead, most of the research in global strategy has studied how emerging market multinationals build their capabilities as they expand abroad (Cuervo-Cazurra, 2012; Cuervo-Cazurra & Genc, 2008; Guillén & García-Canal, 2012a; Luo and Tung, 2007; Peng, 2012; Ramamurti, Williamson, Fleury & Fleury, 2013).

Hence, in this chapter, we use interview data and insights from the preceding country-based chapters to examine the capabilities that managers of emerging market firms have identified as being strategically important for their firms' competitiveness. In addition to examining overall patterns in the data, we analyze differences and similarities in strategic capabilities based upon the firms' level of internationalization (purely domestic, exporter, or multinational), type of industry in which they operate (low-tech, high-tech, and service), and country-level characteristics.

We have studied emerging market companies headquartered in Emerging Europe (Russia and Poland), Asia (China, India, and Kazakhstan), Latin America (Argentina, Brazil, Chile, Colombia, Mexico, and Peru) and Africa (South Africa). As such, our sample comprised firms from five continents, including all of the BRICS countries plus seven additional significant emerging markets. A total of thirty-four authors representing twenty-one universities participated in our data collection efforts. Information was collected

359

from seventy-two companies in our twelve study countries. This amount of diversity should allow us to detect patterns across many of the major emerging markets.

Although focus of this chapter is to determine patterns in the capabilities the leaders of emerging market firms identified as being strategic for their success, we also reconcile the degree to which these capabilities are consistent with existing theoretical models of capability development, such as the four broad capability development methods or stages discussed in Chapter 2 – imitation, integration, incorporation, and internal development, or four-I within the broader discussion of resources and capabilities (Barney, 1991; Eisenhardt & Martin, 2000; Teece, Pisano and Shuen, 1997; Wernerfelt, 1984), their development (Helfat & Peteraf, 2003; Capron & Mitchell, 2012) and their use in internationalization (Lessard, Lucea & Vives, 2013; Luo, 2000; Tallman and Yip, 2009).

15.1   Overall Strategic Capability Usage

Before proceeding to analyze how strategic capabilities might vary depending on how our sample is subdivided, we first examine overall patterns across the companies in the study sample to provide a broad overview of the capabilities that emerging market multinationals identify as being strategic. Looking at Figure 15.1, we can see that the capability most frequently mentioned is understanding local customer needs, which was mentioned by 56 out of 72 companies. The ability to relate to local customers is a well-established tenet of much international business theory (e.g. Prahalad & Doz, 1987; Bartlett & Ghoshal, 1989), so this result is not surprising. It appears highly consistent with the imitation and integration methods of capability development presented within Chapter 2's theoretical framework. Imitation requires understanding what products customers are currently using while integration with local players is a key method of accessing and developing an understanding of these needs. Emerging market firms from countries with lower and middle levels of development would use these capability methods more intensively. While some of the countries represented in our study are approaching advanced development levels (e.g. Chile), most are still at the level where these methods of capability development would still be most viable. Understanding local needs will also be important for firms from more advanced emerging markets consistent with this being the highest overall capability identified in our sample. As countries and their firms progress to utilizing higher-level capability development methods such as internal development, their relative reliance on this capability may diminish.

Looking more specifically at our interviews, it became apparent that understanding local customer needs requires a certain degree of locally

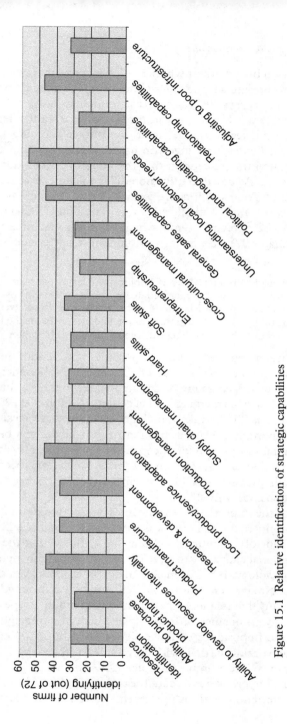

Figure 15.1 Relative identification of strategic capabilities

embeddedness in host markets where foreign investment occurs and that having an appropriate attitude was important for this to occur. For example, our interviews in South Africa (see Chapter 5) revealed that a common problem is South African firms holding an attitude that they are apart from the rest of Africa, with the phrase "coming to Africa" having been used when they invest in other countries within the continent. This created the perception that the investor looked down on the host environment. As one executive noted, "You can't serve people with arrogance" and "You cannot come to East Africa, and tell me for these long years how you must actually cook rice. You don't" (Chapter 5).

For Poland's Kooptech Cinema, which produces machines that clean 3D glasses (Chapter 7), addressing customer needs goes well beyond the product, as the company's owner stated:

We have a good product but it is not very important. We spent a lot of time to learn the logic of the industry, how is it organized, to figure out what is the business model of 3D glasses and such movies. Machines, technologies and almost everything can be easily bought today. But we have this unique knowledge about the logic of the market that allows us to better address our clients' demands (Chapter 7).

The second most mentioned strategic capabilities were relationship capabilities, which were noted by 47 out of 72 companies. Relationships are commonly acknowledged as important across many markets, but seem to be particularly valued in emerging market contexts (Smith et al., 2012; Chen et al., 2017; Peng, 2003). Like the ability to understand local customer needs, while important to all firms, relationship capabilities may be relatively more important for firms with lower capability development levels based on early-stage imitation and integration processes. After firms become more sophisticated, they learn to develop capabilities internally rather than relying solely on relationships with others.

Examples of the importance of companies' abilities to develop relationships were prominent throughout the interviews. For example, Mr. Carrera of Grupo Mirgor of Argentina (see Chapter 9) noted that the company "has an exceptional capability to develop relationships with global leaders in product technology. It has been able to obtain licenses from companies such as Valeo, Nokia, LG, Whirlpool, Dell, and now Samsung."

It is noteworthy that relationships occurred with multiple types of parties across our study companies. For example, Mexican company Interlub's CEO noted the importance of university relationships, stating that the "important networking we do is with universities, with external institutes," where MIT is the prime example (Chapter 13). Although corporate political connections are important across countries (Cui, Hu, Li & Meyer, 2018), in China, government relationships seem to be particularly crucial

(Chapter 10). Thus, an executive of Brazil's WEG stated: "There are some people who are part of the government party and are untouchable, 3–4 people that are from the Communist Party, we cannot dismiss them. As we are a foreign firm, we need a relationship. These people end up being good, have great influence in the government and help us a lot" (Chapter 10). For Indian pharmaceutical firm Biocon, collaboration with other pharmaceutical firms reduced investment risk and expanded capabilities (Chapter 4). For example, in 2009, Biocon and Mylan signed one of the earliest partnerships in the global pharma industry to codevelop biosimilars. This resulted in Trastuzumab, the first jointly developed biosimilar product authorized to treat cancer, receiving US FDA approval in 2017.

While relationship capabilities were seen as being highly important, the company leaders interviewed in our project also recognized that the nature of this capability varied depending on the country of investment. Thus, according to an executive at Kooptech Cinema of Poland:

In the USA, you have to know your partner as a person and mix business and personal credibility. A firm is just an organizational form – they do business with you, personally. In Germany, you are just a firm – you sit down at the table and negotiate a contract. In the Middle East, you have to develop and build both personal and business relations and it takes time. And you have to allow them to negotiate and win something. Generally, in Asia, it is important that the partner gets something in order to be satisfied – a discount, faster service, [...]. And in the former Soviet Union, you have to sit down with them and drink. And become friends. So every market is the same, but different (Chapter 7).

Three additional capabilities were in close running for third among our study firms: general sales capabilities with 46 mentions, local product/service adaptation with 46 comments, and ability to develop resources internally with 45 mentions. The importance of local product/service adaptation builds on the first two capabilities, suggesting the importance of the abilities to develop relationships, and to become embedded within local environments (Meyer, Mudambi & Narula, 2011), in order to adapt products and services to customers' particular needs. This differs from the strategy, commonly employed by many developed country multinationals, of attempting to develop products that can be used globally with limited adaption. This is despite the commonly noted tensions between global standardization and local adaptation (e.g. Prahalad & Doz, 1997; Newburry & Yakova, 2006).

The trade director and CEO of Aplisens in Poland highlighted the role of adaptation:

Our adaptation processes are more oriented on industries than countries. We are constantly upgrading and adjusting our products to the needs of new industries. There are many apparatus manufacturers, our partners, who need something specific and then we actually do for them a special sensor with special measures, special features and so on ... Our advantage is that, compared to Western companies, we are still a small company, therefore we can do what the client wants, that is, we create dedicated solutions, which makes us more attractive to some of our clients than large Western companies (Chapter 7).

The CEO of Belticos in Mexico says: "When we exhausted our business model, we found that the only way to survive was adapting to the specific local demands of our clients ... we went from being a surviving company to a company that grows above average, our key: Adapting to the specific needs of our customers" (Chapter 13).

General sales capabilities will be discussed in both the industry and multinationality sections later in this chapter, and so we will forgo a detailed discussion of general sales capabilities here. We only make the summary point that general sales capabilities may be particularly important when competing in commodity and other price-sensitive industries. Similarly, the ability to develop resources internally will be discussed in the industry section of this chapter. However, given the desire of many emerging market multinationals to advance beyond competing in commodity or other low-cost industries (Cuervo-Cazurra et al., 2019), the ability for a company to develop its resources internally would again seem to be a desirable capability across emerging markets and their firms.

While Figure 15.1 examines the number of times that individual capabilities were identified in our study, Figure 15.2 groups these capabilities

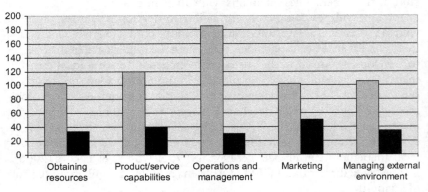

Figure 15.2 Strategic capabilities by value chain segment

across five value chain areas (Porter, 1985): obtaining resources, product/ service capabilities, operations and management, marketing, and managing the external environment. As can be seen from the figure, while the value chain area of operations and management had the largest total number of strategic capability item mentions, on average the items in the category were identified by fewer companies than the others in the study. The marketing category items, which comprised marketing, sales, and understanding local customer needs, scored the highest number of company mentions on average. Product/service capabilities, which included product manufacture, research & development, and local product/service adaptation, scored the next highest. Both these higher-scoring areas involve some degree of interaction with customer needs – either in upfront product manufacture or in later marketing and sales functions. Given that a company's domestic capabilities may not always apply in foreign locations in terms of understanding customer needs, it is not surprising that these two areas received relatively higher emphasis among the value chain areas.

15.2   Identifying Systematic Differences

Of course, even among developed country firms, the importance of particular strategic capabilities varies depending upon multiple factors such as industry, degree of multinationality, and home country. After examining similarities and differences across these three variables, we will conclude by integrating the findings to examine how differences occur at multiple levels of analysis.

Industry Differences

Industry type has a significant impact on the operations of firms in emerging markets (e.g. Newburry, 2010; Contractor, Lahiri, Elango & Kundu, 2014; Ramamurti, 2012), notwithstanding the idea that "global and industry effects are still dominated by the country effects in emerging markets in contrast to developed markets" (Phylaktis & Xia, 2006: 459). While certain industry types are clearly associated with different emerging markets (e.g. manufacturing in China, IT in India, agriculture and mining in Brazil), we nonetheless expect that we can learn from variation by industry type across our twelve-country sample. In Table 15.1, we see how the relative identification of capabilities varies by industry, broken out into high-tech, low-tech, and service sectors. Our sample of firms had a relatively even breakout across industries, with

Table 15.1 *Breakout of capabilities by industry*

	High-tech (22 firms)	Low-tech (26 firms)	Service (24 firms)	Total responses (72 firms)
Understanding local customer needs	18	19	19	56
Relationship capabilities	13	15	19	47
General sales capabilities	11	21	14	46
Local product/service adaptation	12	16	18	46
Ability to develop resources internally	14	14	17	45
Research & development	15	12	10	37
Product manufacture	15	16	6	37
Soft skills	9	8	18	35
Supply chain management	8	19	5	32
Production management	10	15	7	32
Adjusting to poor infrastructure	9	14	9	32
Hard skills	8	10	13	31
Resource identification	10	11	9	30
Cross-cultural management	8	9	12	29
Ability to purchase product inputs	8	14	6	28
Political and negotiating capabilities	6	8	13	27
Entrepreneurship	7	6	13	26

22 high-tech firms, 26 low-tech firms, and 24 service firms. However, the importance of the different capabilities was not as evenly distributed. While three of the most frequently indicated capabilities (understanding local customer needs, relationship capabilities, and local product/service adaptation) seemed to apply relatively evenly across all industries, other capabilities seemed to be relevant more within certain industry types. We examine some of these now.

Research and development (R&D) was disproportionately identified by the high-tech firms (15 out of 22, i.e. 68 percent) versus the low-tech (12 of 26) and service (10 of 24) firms. Since high-tech firms rely to a much greater degree on having advanced technology, is rapidly changing in many industries, strong R&D capabilities seem essential (Helfat, 1997). These firms would also be most likely to rely on the internal development method of upgrading capabilities, which would require R&D. R&D may be less important in low-tech and service industries, where competition is not necessarily based on being at the highest technology level but rather on other factors, like process innovation (Davenport, 2013) and cost innovation (Zeng & Williamson, 2007), suggesting the need for lower-level capability development methods.

However, even in other industries, there was still evidence of a drive to develop higher-value products. For example, the CEO of China's car seat manufacturer Baby First, a company that would be classified as low-tech, noted the need to continually innovate to accommodate changes in consumer expectations and needs, and new technologies in cars (Chapter 3):

Maybe in 10 years nobody will drive a car. The key point is that there may not be a product called "car seat." However, we still have a need to protect kids during travel. Maybe something will come out completely new, but we will not call it a car. People still need to travel, and when people are traveling, the kids need to be protected. Maybe we can do such a kind of service. That should be done step by step. First, we need to make all our products smart. At least they can connect our products to smartphones or cars or others that may be coming soon.

In another example from China, an executive from Chervon, a global leader in outdoor power tools and lawn equipment, notes that their R&D team is constantly working to improve its capabilities:

We work with renowned design companies to help us develop products directly. Second, we ask our team, and when we work with pioneers or opinion leaders, we learn from how they work. We even learn how to observe users and how they use tools. We learn how to brainstorm ideas, how to generate ideas, how to filter out better ideas, test ideas in different ways, and then define products (Chapter 3).

Supply chain management was disproportionately associated with the low-tech firms in our sample, among which 19 out of 26 identified this capability as strategic, compared to less than half of high-tech firms and less than a quarter of service firms. The low-tech products made by many of our sample companies often depend on inputs from other companies and sometimes serve as inputs to others as well as being part of global supply chains (Gereffi, Humphrey, & Sturgeon, 2005). Since these goods tend to compete based on low prices, having an efficient supply makes sense in order to ensure cost efficiency as well as innovation (Gereffi, 1999). This capability seems most consistent with the integration of capabilities through alliances and the incorporation of capabilities through acquisition, two of the methods of gaining capabilities (Capron and Mitchell, 2012; Wang & Zajac, 2007), discussed in Chapter 2, to the extent that these methods allow firms to connect with capabilities at other stages of the supply chain. For example, supply chain management was noted as an important strategic capability by Colombian firm Sempertex, which manufactures rubber and latex products (Chapter 12). To better address concerns at the back end of the company's value chain, Sempertex established a distribution center, which enables the company to dispatch on the same day product orders received before noon (Endeavour Colombia, 2016). On the input side of the value chain, supply chain management is also very important in terms of their access to latex, as the company acquires over 3,000 tons of latex every year from suppliers in Guatemala and Colombia.

While less identified with services, supply chain management was nonetheless identified as important in the retail sector. For example, Sportmaster in Kazakhstan has striven to create fast merchandising and a more agile supply network in order to successfully match offers across all the markets where it operates and to deliver merchandise more efficiently (Chapter 8). To accomplish this, the firm created its own distribution centers across the countries where it operates, with the largest and most central one being located in Moscow, which supplies the whole CIS region. The usage of a combination of main hubs and then redistribution to other countries has proved to be efficient for the company in terms of developing scale economies and maintaining quality control.

General sales capabilities were also disproportionately identified with low-tech firms, with 21 out of the 26 firms identifying this capability as strategic. This compares to 11 out of 22 high-tech firms and 14 out of 24 service firms. As low-tech firms tend to produce less differentiated goods, having strong general sales capabilities would seem important for them. These capabilities would seemingly be relatively more applicable to firms at lower development levels within the four-I framework, who are relying on their abilities to exploit existing capabilities as opposed to developing new ones.

Several examples from Peru (Chapter 14) illustrate the importance of marketing, sales, and control of the traditional distribution channel as crucial strategic capabilities. Yobel uses its access to 700,000 points of sales across Latin America in order to be attractive to foreign multinationals. Alicorp has developed rapid vertical and horizontal market coverage of its products as well, which are strengthened by the company's ability to create valuable brands. Cantol uses its distribution capacity and associated connections to traditional hardware stores in Peru to attract international vendors. Finally, Deltron became the preferred distributor of internal computer parts and peripherals in Peru through access to traditional distribution channels.

Soft skills: among the service firms in our sample, 18 out of 24 reported soft skills as an important strategic capability, versus 9 out of 22 for high-tech firms and 8 out of 26 for low-tech firms. Service firms are more difficult to place within the four-I framework, particularly when they are considered collectively as a group as we have done here to keep the industry sectors relatively similar in sample sizes. Firms involved in high-tech consulting, such as Globant of Argentina, or providing medical services, such as Dr.Consulta of Brazil, differ significantly from service firms such as Kidzania of Mexico, which runs children's play centers, or Sanpower of China, which is involved in retail. These differences highlight how some services, often known as credence services (Emons, 2001) are difficult to evaluate even after being performed, while others are based on a more definable experience. Nonetheless, services certainly involve a much higher degree of connection with the local environment, often even involving the customer directly in the process of service development (Boddewyn, Halbrich, & Perry, 1986; Dunning, 1989). Soft skills would thus appear to be crucial to service delivery.

Among firms noting this strategic capability is Vidanta, a Mexican hotel, golf course, and urban development chain with facilities in the country's main touristic sites (Chapter 13). The firm claims that its soft skills have been a strong force in firm growth, as they have aided the firm in adapting to Mexico's poor infrastructure (Instituto Nacional del Emprendedor, 2016). In particular, Vidanta is effective at matching resources and alliance opportunities with the company's relationships and political capabilities, allowing Vidanta to provide a high-quality service.

Entrepreneurship was also disproportionately noted as a strategic capability by service firms, with 13 of 24 service firms reporting this versus only 7 high-tech firms and 6 low-tech firms. As in the case of soft skills, service firms are difficult to place in the four-I framework of capability development with respect to entrepreneurship due to the wide variety of service types. However, services often require developing creative ways to interact with the host country environment (Oliver, 1997; Martin, 2014; Peng, 2002), particularly given the direct interaction that service firms have with their customers (Boddewyn et al., 1986). It may therefore not be surprising that entrepreneurship is a capability strongly identified by these firms as strategic (Hitt, Ireland, Camp, & Sexton, 2001; Ireland, Hitt & Simon, 2003).

The Brazilian company Dr.Consulta (see Chapter 10) exemplifies the importance of entrepreneurship in emerging market settings where service industries are often underdeveloped. In this case, the firm has developed a new business model to address health service needs for those on very low incomes, who are not being adequately served by existing services. To start the business, the firm relied on key capacities of entrepreneurship and innovation to develop affordable ways to address this market segment.

Ability to develop resources internally was identified as a strategic capability by 17 out of the 24 service firms in our sample, versus 14 low-tech and 14 high-tech firms. Given the nature of services and the types of resources they may be assumed to need, the relatively stronger association with internal resource development was an unexpected result. However, this may also be a function of the difficulty of establishing services in many emerging markets and the specific needs of some of the exceptional firms in our sample. For example, to adequately deliver the services they provide, firms providing healthcare such as Dr.Consulta in Brazil or Farmacias Similares in Mexico would need to develop resources associated with the medical field. Similarly, Argentinean technology services company Globant would need specific technology resources to deliver its services.

Multinationality Differences

It seems logical that the degree of multinationality would affect the types of strategic capabilities needed by emerging market firms. Multinationality has been associated with firm performance in both developed (Contractor, Kundu & Hsu, 2003; Lu & Beamish, 2001) and emerging market contexts (Cuervo-Cazurra, Ciravegna, Melgarejo & Lopez, 2018; Geleilate et al., 2016). Moreover, multinational firms often need different and additional capabilities beyond those needed in their domestic home market contexts (Buckley & Casson, 1976; Dunning, 1977; Hymer, 1976; Johanson & Vahlne, 1977), many of which are commonly lacking in emerging markets, such as international management capabilities (Cuervo-Cazurra, Newburry & Park, 2016) that enable firms to manage the differences across countries (Ambos & Haksanson, 2014; Ghemawat, 2001; Kogut, 1985). Thus we would expect differences in the strategic capabilities reported based on the level of multinationality of an emerging market firm. In our sample, we have a division between multinational corporations (MNCs, 43 firms), exporters (22 firms), and firms that focus purely on their domestic markets (7 firms). Table 15.2 presents a breakout of the relative identification of capabilities based on a firm's degree of multinationality, i.e., whether it only operates domestically, exports, or is an MNC. In the remainder of this section, we highlight some differences in the relative capabilities reported in each of these three categories, starting with domestic firms and proceeding to exporters and then MNCs.

Supply chain management: among our purely domestic firms, supply chain management was easily the most consistently identified strategic capability. Out of 7 purely domestic firms, 6 identified supply chain management as a strategic capability, compared to less than half of the firms in both our exporter and MNC sub-samples. Looking at their placement in the four-I capability development framework, purely domestic firms would generally rely on more basic capability methods, such as imitation and integration with partners. This result seems consistent with the framework

Table 15.2 *Breakout of capabilities by multinationality*

	Purely domestic (7 firms)	Exporter (22 firms)	Multinational (43 firms)	Total responses (72 firms)
Understanding local customer needs	6	17	33	56
Relationship capabilities	4	16	27	47
General sales capabilities	4	13	29	46
Local product/service adaptation	4	13	29	46
Ability to develop resources internally	4	14	27	45
Research & development	2	10	25	37
Product manufacture	2	14	21	37
Soft skills	4	10	21	35
Supply chain management	6	8	18	32
Production management	2	11	19	32
Adjusting to poor infrastructure	3	7	22	32
Hard skills	4	5	22	31
Cross-cultural management	2	5	22	29
Ability to purchase product inputs	4	8	16	28
Political and negotiating capabilities	4	6	17	27
Entrepreneurship	2	5	19	26
Resource identification	4	7	19	3

because supply chain management is less focused on developing new capabilities, and more on efficiently managing current ones.

As noted in Chapter 14, Peruvian computer hardware wholesaler Deltron has built its business model around its procurement capabilities. The firm has developed a strong international network of suppliers around the globe to purchase computer hardware and has developed capabilities to deal with this foreign supplier network efficiently . Similarly, Indian textile firm Gokaldas Exports relies heavily on its strategic capability in supply chain management to source raw materials from third-party vendors (Chapter 4). The company's location in India has an advantage due to its strong knowledge of and relationships with local textile mills. Proximity to suppliers allows the firm to develop better understanding of the technical capabilities of different vendors, while also affording advantages in raw-material pricing and short delivery times. As Gokaldas's major customers are in the United States and Europe, transportation costs and time to the customer are also important factors in their supply chain management. Gokaldas does its best to reduce transportation costs and time through a mix of different modes of transport and logistics partners.

Relationship capabilities: while important all around, relationship capabilities were particularly crucial to exporters, with 16 of 22 export firms (73 percent) indicating this as a strategic capability versus 4 out of 7 domestic firms and 27 of 43 MNCs. Relationships are important for all types of firms. However, emerging market firms that rely solely on exporting would most likely be focused on exploiting current advantages in host markets. They may be missing the potential to explore markets to develop new advantages (Cantwell & Mudambi, 2005; Solomon, 2005) given that they have not invested in significant capabilities in these host markets as a basis to create new opportunities. This suggests that they are at lower development stages and that relationships may be particularly important for these firms. For example, Chilean winery Casas del Toqui knows that producing a premium product is not enough to be competitive in international wine markets (see Chapter 11). Relationship capabilities are important for establishing long-term relationships with both distributors and buyers. To build these, Casas del Toqui participates actively in international wine fairs. The top management team, including the company president and owner, sell potential buyers not only on their wines' premium quality but also on the mystique surrounding it. Casas del Toqui uses different strategies to develop a "story" behind its products, including emphasizing the family nature of the boutique winemaker as well as the company's eco-friendly practices.

The owners of Polish game-maker Granna (see Chapter 7) similarly emphasize that relationships with distributors are essential for the company's growth in foreign markets, with their local partners providing knowledge and access to sales channels. In each market, Granna grants one distributor exclusive rights to its games. The local distributor takes responsibility for sales and marketing activities in their local market, while Granna offers assistance with game selection, necessary adaptations (translation of instructions and packaging text as well as culturally relevant modifications), organizing transport, and preparation of promotional materials in the local language. To maintain good local relationships, the company offers its partners the option of placing their logo on the packaging, even with small orders.

Production management: being able to efficiently and effectively manage production operations was also more important to exporters (11 out of 22 companies) and MNCs (19 out of 43), than for domestic firms (2 out of 7). Both exporters and MNCs need to compete again host country firms in the markets where they are selling their goods (Hymer, 1976). This suggests that they will face greater competitive pressures than a domestic firm competing only in its home market, as they will need to overcome the liability of foreignness (Zaheer, 1995) and other sources of disadvantages

(Cuervo-Cazurra, Maloney & Manrakhan, 2007) in host markets. This will put pressure on their production management processes to be efficient. The slightly greater importance identified by exporters in relationship to MNCs could reflect the fact that MNCs are more likely to have advanced to the point where they are competing based on internally developed capabilities. Thus they are less likely to compete solely on low cost and production efficiency.

Emblematic of the benefits of production management to both exporters and MNCs, initially, Argentina's San Miguel emphasized its production capabilities, focusing on volume and efficiency in growing and sourcing produce at quality standards consistent with premium export markets (Chapter 9). However, the company's internationalization did not take off until it decided to focus on citrus fruit and professionalized its management. San Miguel's chief marketing officer noted that "Our products cost about USD 20 cents per kilo in their place of origin and are worth more than USD 5 per kilo in their destination market. This applies to citrus fruit but can be extended to other products as well. Our challenge is to understand in what parts of the value chain we can be successful and in what parts we should not operate." Thus the company is using production management techniques in assessing how to capture rents from an optimal product range and vertical integration.

Brazil shoe manufacturer Grendene (Chapter 10) also uses highly developed production management skills in the company's vertically integrated production processes. In making their shoes, they control all stages of production, starting with manufacturing polyvinyl chloride and ethylene vinyl acetate, the main inputs for plastic injection in the company's shoe manufacturing processes. The firm also creates its own shoe molds, which allows it even greater manufacturing flexibility. Grendene launches about 1,000 new products every year, with a capability to produce 250 million pairs of shoes per year entirely in Brazil, and produces about 1 percent of the global total production for injected plastic footwear.

General sales capabilities: looking specifically at the capabilities relatively identified as being strategic by MNCs, general sales capabilities stood out as particularly important, being identified as strategic by 29 out of the 43 MNCs in our sample, versus only 4 out of 7 domestic firms and 13 out of 22 exporters. This result may reflect that multinationals are operating outside of their home markets, where they may need to focus on sales versus stronger competition than they face in their emerging home markets. Given less brand recognition and limited reputational capital (Cuervo-Cazurra et al., 2016), particularly when investing outside their home region, the need to demonstrate sales capabilities may be relatively more important for these firms. Given the regional nature of most firms' investment strategies (Rugman & Verbeke, 2004; 2008), MNCs' multinationality may be a positive factor in more local investments (Borda et al., 2016), as firms are more likely to be known in neighboring countries.

One of the exporters' stories is particularly interesting. While Bodega Lagarde's proprietary vineyards date back to 1906, and preservation of their historical winery that was built in 1897 allows the company to emphasize tradition in the company's brand, the Argentinian winery's innovations allow it to maintain a connection with customers (see Chapter 9). Bodega Lagarde was the first Latin American producer to plant nontraditional grape varieties such as Viognier and Moscato Bianco. Bodega Lagarde was also early to diversify into estate tourism, and the company opened a restaurant where local cuisine accompanies its wines. More recently, the company introduced sparkling and organic wines. The company CEO observes: "We have our core products, such as our Malbec wines, which drive our business. However, to keep wine critics, influencers on social media, and distributors interested, we need to develop new product lines and present novelties. We present the stories behind each of our wines and need to tell different stories to audiences in different markets."

Cross-cultural management capabilities were identified as strategic by 22 out of the 43 MNCs in our sample, versus only 2 out of 7 domestic firms and 5 out of 22 exporting firms. The strategic importance of cross-cultural management capabilities (Earley & Ang, 2003; Thomas & Peterson, 2016) may be a direct function of the fact that multinationals operate outside their home country, essentially forcing them to manage in a cross-cultural environment that requires particular skills (Collings, Scullion, & Caligiuri, 2019). This is also a capability that emerging market firms have been known to struggle with due to limited available human capital with international management training in most emerging markets (Cuervo-Cazurra et al., 2016).

While the fact of MNCs needing cross-cultural management capabilities is not surprising, the case of the one domestic firm also needing these capabilities is interesting. Peruvian firm Deltron, which operates in the computer industry, has a business model focused around strong procurement capabilities (see Chapter 14). While purely a domestic firm in terms of its operations and sales, Deltron has nonetheless built an international network of computer hardware suppliers in the United States, China, and around the globe. To efficiently deal with this foreign supplier network, the company has had to develop the cross-cultural managerial capabilities needed to understand and negotiate with different suppliers from multiple countries.

Home Country Differences

We also explored differences in identified strategic capabilities across countries and regions. The country of origin has been shown to be an important predictor of many facets related to the strategies of firms (Cuervo-Cazurra, 2011; Cuervo-Cazurra, Luo, Ramamurti & Ang, 2018; Luo & Wang, 2012; Sethi & Elango, 1999; Yiu, Lau & Bruton, 2007; Sethi & Elango, 1999). As such, it should also influence the capabilities that company leaders identify as strategic. These are presented in Table 15.3.

Understanding local customer needs: looking at Table 15.3, it is readily visible that understanding local customer needs is a highly identified characteristic in all six Latin American countries in our study, with five or more companies indicating this in each country. Aguilera, Ciravegna, Cuervo-Cazurra & Gonzalez-Perez (2017), Vassolo, De Castro, and Gomez-Mejia (2011) and Cuervo-Cazurra (2008; 2016), among others, note the many commonalities across Latin America in terms of factors such as colonial history, common language (Spanish or Portuguese), common religion (Roman Catholic), similar experiences with the "lost decade" of the 1980s and market liberalizations in the 1990s, etc. These common experiences may be influential in this common result across Latin American countries. By contrast, this capability is indicated in less than half of the companies examined in China, India, and Poland, although those in Kazakhstan, Russia, and South Africa align with Latin American companies in identifying this capability as strategic. As noted earlier in this chapter, while important to all firms, understanding local customer needs may be particularly important to firms from countries at lower to middle development levels, which would generally be the case for most Latin American companies.

One Latin American company that identified the importance of understanding local customer needs is Colombian coffee maker Colcafé (Chapter 12). To increase sales in the Japanese market, the company needed to understand the requirements and expectations of the Japanese coffee market in terms of quality and volume. In response to this information, the company developed products crafted specifically for Japan (and the broader Asian market) including unique blends and specialized packaging designed for smaller households with less storage space.

Relationship capabilities: it is interesting that China scores lower than any other country in terms of identifying the importance of relationship capabilities, with only one company in the sample naming this as a strategic capability. This is particularly striking given the importance of *guanxi* to business relationships in China (Chen et al., 2017; Luo, Huang &

Table 15.3 *Breakout of capabilities by country*

Capability	Argentina (7)	Brazil (6)	Chile (7)	Colombia (7)	Mexico (7)	Peru (6)	China (8)	India (4)	Kazakhstan (5)	Poland (6)	Russia (5)	South Africa (4)	Total Responses (72)
Understanding local customer needs	7	6	7	5	6	6	3	1	5	2	5	3	56
Relationship capabilities	3	6	6	5	6	3	1	2	5	6	0	4	47
General sales capabilities	3	6	7	2	4	6	4	1	5	0	4	4	46
Local product/service adaptation	2	6	3	4	4	4	4	3	4	6	3	3	46
Ability to develop resources internally	6	6	2	4	5	3	2	4	5	2	3	3	45
Research & development	2	5	2	2	4	3	5	2	5	4	2	1	37
Product manufacture	4	3	2	2	5	5	3	3	3	0	4	3	37
Supply chain management	4	3	3	4	1	5	3	3	3	0	1	2	32
Soft skills	1	6	5	4	5	2	0	3	3	0	3	3	35
Production management	4	5	2		4	4	2	4	3	1	1	2	32
Adjusting to poor infrastructure	5	3	1	2	5	5	1	4	4	1	0	1	32
Hard skills	1	5	5	2	3	1	0	2	5	0	3	4	31
Cross-cultural management	3	4	0	2	3	3	3	2	4	1	3	1	29
Resource identification	4	6	1	1	3	2	1	2	2	1	3	4	30
Ability to purchase product inputs	4	1	2	3	4	2	4	3	3	0	0	2	28
Entrepreneurship	2	4	2	2	4	0	0	3	3	2	2	2	26
Political and negotiating capabilities	2	6	2	0	5	2	3	1	4	0	0	2	27

Wang, 2012; Park & Luo, 2001). While unexpected, this may reflect that China as a country and its companies have progressed to the point where they are focused on internal development as a capability development method, versus other capability development methods that are more dependent upon relationships with other parties. Other firms operating in countries at lower development stages still appear to rely on relationships relatively more. This result is also consistent with a study of relational favoritism, which found "that Brazilian and Chinese managers perceived more negative consequences of relational favoritism than did American managers – even though the Brazilians and the Chinese perceived stronger particularistic cultural norms in their countries than Americans did in the United States" (Chen et al., 2017: 63).

South Africa provided strong examples of how relationship capabilities are needed with respect to a company's many stakeholders. For example, a South-Africa-based investment banking manager noted the importance of relationships with government stakeholders, stating: "We think it is important to have good personal relationships with [government] stakeholders, so both our chief executives and other senior members in the country, we will encourage them to have good relationships with people in the presidency and the various ministries, the central bank, state-owned enterprises, etc. and we will also encourage people from the broader group when they visit the country to take the time to meet with government stakeholders and establish relationships" (Chapter 5).

A commercial executive of a South African agribusiness company noted the importance of supplier relationships: "So we do encourage local development [of suppliers] as an extension of our investment. ... I think for that part you need to be very close to your suppliers because you know, you don't fight these days on an individual product level, you fight on the value chain level" (Chapter 5). Of course, customer relationships are also important. As a Nigeria-based operations manager of a South African bank noted: "because we are client-centric, we are not just developing products and just say take it this is what we have for you and everything. We actually look at the needs of those customers ... so if we want to introduce a new product and improve our processes and everything it has to be from a client's point of view" (Chapter 5).

Research and development: consistent with their relatively advanced development levels, R&D capabilities were reported as being more important in Brazil (5 of 7 firms), China (5 of 8 firms), Poland (4 of 6 firms), and Mexico (4 of 7 firms). These countries are also commonly more associated with high-tech firms, where R&D capabilities might be in greater demand. As noted in the four-I framework (Chapter 2), the overall capability of internal development is most prominent among relatively more advanced economies. Firms from these economies would naturally need greater R&D capabilities to achieve this internal development goal, which is certainly reflected in our results.

Chervon in China is an exemplar of a firm that has used R&D capabilities to consistently raise its technology standards throughout the company's transition from original equipment manufacturer to original design manufacturer (Chapter 3). Chervon's R&D team works constantly to improve its capabilities. For example, when the team cooperates with a big foreign design team, it focuses on learning to improve its own operations (see the quotation from a Chervon executive in the section on home country differences earlier in the chapter).

Political and negotiating capabilities were prominent only in the two large Latin American countries: Brazil (all 6 firms) and Mexico (5 of 7 firms). Since 2008, Brazilian firms have operated in a particularly turbulent political and economic environment (see Chapter 10), which certainly explains the identification of this capability by all the Brazilian firms in our sample. In the context of the overall economic and political crises facing Brazil, firms have often found themselves in periods of retrenchment, and divestment of foreign operations has become a strategic topic on the agendas of many Brazilian firms.

Mexican firm Farmacias Similares provides an example of a company in an industry where political and negotiating capabilities might be particularly important (Chapter 13). Farmacias Similares has grown organically, preferring to expand to geographic locations with similar cultures to Mexico's, and using alliances when advantageous to over overcome differences in regulations and other market characteristics. Pharmaceutical regulations differ by country: for example, in Chile locating a pharmacy and a doctor's office next to each other is prohibited, a standard practice of the company in other countries.

15.3   Summary and Conclusion

In this chapter, we integrated the insights obtained from the interviews conducted with business leaders across twelve emerging markets in five continents to understand better which capabilities leaders in emerging market multinationals identify as being strategically important. In doing so, we examined which capabilities appear to be commonly assessed as being strategic across our study contexts, and which ones varied by company level of multinationality, industry, and country of origin.

Looking across the various capabilities identified by the senior managers in our study, our results suggest that the strategic capabilities needed by emerging market firms to be successful outside their home markets occur at multiple levels. These include management-level capabilities, firm-level capabilities, industry-level capabilities, and home-country capabilities. These capabilities influence a firm's ability both to internationalize and to be successful, which often have reinforcing influences on each other. Being able to sustain high performance is a key factor in the success of emerging market firms (Park, Zhou and Ungson, 2013). We have also noted that these capability levels tend to be interconnected. For example, management-level abilities to understand local customer needs certainly reinforce firm-level capabilities in local product/service adaptation. Similarly, certain home country capabilities such as greater R&D capabilities are partially associated with firms in these countries tending toward industries where R&D is more important to success.

Managerial-level capabilities: Looking specifically at the different levels, understanding local customer needs was the most widely identified strategic capability among the emerging market firm leaders in our study. This managerial-level capability was perceived as essential across industries and levels of multinationality. There was some interesting variation by country, however. The capability was universally identified as important across all of the six Latin American countries in the study, while being indicated in only three other countries (Kazakhstan, Russia, and South Africa). Our second most identified strategic capability, relationship capabilities, also occurs at the managerial level and was shown to be commonly identified across industries and levels of multinationality. There was some slight variation among countries in this capability, with a particularly low score in China being most notable. While this seems to contradict the highly reported use of *guanxi* in China, the result may reflect the level of development of Chinese firms, leading the country to focus on internal development of capabilities, where relationships may be less important.

Firm-level capabilities: as noted earlier, there is a high interconnection between managerial- and firm-level capabilities. For example, local product/service adaptation requires multiple managerial capabilities to achieve. Similarly, developing resources internally is dependent upon the supporting skills to do so.

Industry-level capabilities: certain capabilities were also highly related to particular industries. For example, R&D capabilities were highly associated with high-tech industries, where competition may be based on differentiation as opposed to cost. By contrast, supply chain management was identified more frequently among low-tech firms. As low-tech may be more likely to compete based on cost, having an efficient supply chain may be important for efficiency in production and distribution processes.

Home country influences. We also noted differences based on firms' home countries. Some of these were naturally associated with certain industries being more prominent in a particular country. For example, firms from more developed home countries were more likely to be involved in high-tech industries that required R&D capabilities. We also noted that the Latin American countries, in particular, had a strong propensity as a region to identify understanding local customer needs as a strategic capability.

As noted throughout the chapter, the various capabilities occurring at multiple levels (see Figure 15.3) create the conditions necessary for emerging market firms to complete successfully both in their home markets and as they expand into foreign countries. They specifically create the ability to internationalize, which further influences a firm's performance. This progression may not necessarily occur in a linear fashion due to difficulties particularly at the early phases of internationalization (see, Cuervo-Cazurra, Newburry & Park, 2016).

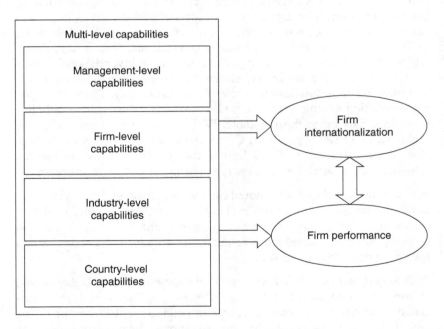

Figure 15.3 Summary of strategic capability levels

At the start of this book, we noted how merging market firms have become increasingly influential in the global economy, impressing managers and academics alike. Many have become large multinationals dominating their industries, effectively competing against long-time incumbents from advanced economies (Cuervo-Cazurra & Ramamurti, 2014; Guillén & García-Canal, 2012a; Khanna & Palepu, 2010; Ramamurti & Singh, 2009; Williamson et al., 2013). However, surprisingly little attention has been devoted to how these firms have become internationally competitive. In this book, we have attempted to address this deficiency and to analyze the development of strategic capabilities of firms from emerging markets to achieve international competitiveness (Williamson et al., 2013), especially before firms become multinationals. We have aimed to provide a better understanding of how firms manage the twin challenges of upgrading capabilities to international levels while operating in emerging economies.

Overall, through our examination, we have developed insights into the specific capabilities that CEOs and top managers of emerging market firms consider strategically important, based on a sample obtained from 72 companies in twelve countries across five continents. We believe our collective efforts have provided insights that will be valuable for practitioners, along with guidance for academics to aid in further understanding the important phenomenon of emerging market firms and the capabilities that allow them to succeed in the global economic arena.

Bibliography

Abernathy, W. J., & Utterback, J. 1978. Patterns of industrial innovation. *Technological Review*, 807, 40–47.

African Development Bank, Organisation for Economic Co-operation and Development & United Nations Development Programme. 2017. *African Economic Outlook 2017: Entrepreneurship and Industrialisation*, www.afdb.org/fileadmin/uploads/afdb/Documents/Publications/AEO_2017_Report_Full_English.pdf.

Ageeva, N. 2002. *Handbook of Competition and Competitiveness*. Kurgan: Kurgan State University. [Агеева Н. Справочник по конкуренции и конкурентоспособности.]

Aggarwal, R., & Agmon, T. 1990. The international success of developing country firms: Role of government-directed comparative advantage. *Management International Review*, 30, 163–180.

Aguiar, M., Azevedo, D., Becerra, J., et al. 2018. Why multilatinas hold the key to Latin America's economic future. Boston Consulting Group, https://image-srcbk.bcg.com/Images/BCG-Why-Multilatinas-Hold-the-Key-to-Latin-Americas-Economic-Future-Mar-2018_tcm50-186904.pdf.

Aguilera, R., Ciravegna, L., Cuervo-Cazurra, A., & Gonzalez-Perez, M. A. 2017. Multilatinas and the internationalization of Latin American firms. *Journal of World Business*, 52(4), 447–460.

Air Astana. 2017. *Annual Report*, https://airastana.com/Portals/2/About-Us/Corporate-Governance/Annual-Reports/Annual-Reports-en/Annual_Report_2017_EN.pdf.

Ajai, O. 2015. Failure of Africa-to-Africa internationalization: Key factors and lessons, in I. Adeleye, K. Ibeh, A. Kinotu, & L. White (eds.), *The Changing Dynamics of International Business in Africa*, 148–168. London, UK: Palgrave Macmillan.

Akimova, I. 2000. Development of market orientation and competitiveness of Ukrainian firms. *European Journal of Marketing*, 34(9/10), 1128–1148.

Al-Aali, A., & Teece, D. 2014. International entrepreneurship and the theory of the (long-lived) international firm: A capability perspective. *Entrepreneurship Theory and Practice*, 38(1), 95–116.

Alden, C., & Schoeman, M. 2015. South Africa's symbolic hegemony in Africa. *International Politics*, 52(2), 239–254.

Alicorp. 2000. *Annual Report*.

Alicorp. 2015. *Company Annual Report*, www.alicorp.com.pe/media/PDF/reporte-alicorp-2015_06Kl3z8_bDKHZ0u.pdf.

Alicorp. 2019. *Corporate Presentation*, May, http://docplayer.net/168978462-Corporate-presentation-may-2019.html.

Alkanova, O., & Smirnova, M. 2014. Marketing in emerging markets: Approaches to the definition and direction of research. *Russian Management Journal*, 12(1), 95–108. [Алканова О., Смирнова М. Маркетинг на развивающихся рынках: Подходы к определению и направления исследований. Российский журнал менеджмента.]

Ambos, B. and Håkanson, L., 2014. The concept of distance in international management research. *Journal of International Management*, 20(1), 1–7.

Ambos, T. C., Ambos, B., & Schlegelmilch, B. B. 2006. Learning from foreign subsidiaries: An empirical investigation of headquarters' benefits from reverse knowledge transfers. *International Business Review*, 15(3), 294–312.

América Economía. 2017. *Ránking Multilatinas 2016*, https://rankings.americae conomia.com/2016/multilatinas/.

Amit, R., & Schoemaker, P. J. 1993. Strategic assets and organizational rent. *Strategic Management Journal*, 14(1), 33–46.

Amsden, A. H., & Chu, W. W. 2003. *Beyond Late Development: Taiwan's Upgrading Policies*. Cambridge, MA: MIT Press.

Anderson, B., & López, A. 2008. La victoria del Dr. Simi. *Expansión*, December 8, http://expansion.mx/expansion/articulo-de-portada/2008/11/26/la-callada-vic toria-del-dr-simi.

Andersson, U., Björkman, I., & Forsgren, M. 2005. Managing subsidiary knowledge creation: The effect of control mechanisms on subsidiary local embeddedness. *International Business Review*, 14(5), 521–538.

Andersson, U., Forsgren, M., & Holm, U. 2002. The strategic impact of external networks: Subsidiary performance and competence development in the multinational corporation. *Strategic Management Journal*, 23(11), 979–996.

Anseel, F., Lievens, F., & Schollaert, E. 2009. Reflection as a strategy to enhance task performance after feedback. *Organizational Behavior and Human Decision Processes*, 110(1), 23–35.

Antons, D., Declerck, M., Diener, K., Koch, I., & Piller, F. T. 2017. Assessing the not-invented-here syndrome: Development and validation of implicit and explicit measurements. *Journal of Organizational Behavior*, 38(8), 1227–1245.

Awate, S., Larsen, M. M., & Mudambi, R. 2012. EMNE catch-up strategies in the wind turbine industry: Is there a trade-off between output and innovation capabilities? *Global Strategy Journal*, 2(3), 205–223.

Azoev, G. 1996. *Competition: Analysis, Strategy and Practice*. Moscow: Center for Economics and Marketing. [Азоев Г. Конкуренция: Анализ, стратегия и практика.]

Azoev, G., & Chelenkov, A. 2000. *Firm Competitive Advantage*. Moscow: Novosti. [Азоев Г., Челенков А. Конкурентное преимущество фирмы.]

Bain, J. S. 1956. *Barriers to New Competition*. Cambridge: Harvard University Press.

Baker, T. & Nelson, R. E. 2005. Creating something from nothing: Resource construction through entrepreneurial bricolage. *Administrative Science Quarterly*, 503, 329–366.

Banco de la República de Colombia. 2019. Flujos de inversión extranjera directa, www.banrep.gov.co/es/inversion-directa.

Banda, G., Mugwagwa, J., Kale, D., & Ndomondo-Sigonda, M. 2016. Pharmaceutical standards in Africa: The road to improvement and their role in technological capability upgrading, in M. Mackintosh, G. Banda, W. Wamae, & P. Tibandebage (eds.), *Making Medicines in Africa*, 224–242. Basingstoke, UK: Palgrave Macmillan.

Barinov, V., & Sinelnikov, A. 2000. Development of the organization in a competitive environment. *Management in Russia and Abroad*, 6, 3–13. [Баринов В., Синельников А. Развитие организации в конкурентной среде. Менеджмент в России и за рубежом.]

Barkema, H. G., Boll. J. H., & Pennings, M. 1996. Foreign entry, cultural barriers, and learning. *Strategic Management Journal*, 17(2), 151–166.

Barnard, H., & Luiz, J. M. 2018. Escape FDI and the dynamics of a cumulative process of institutional misalignment and contestation: Stress, strain and failure. *Journal of World Business*, 53(5), 605–619.

Barnard, H., Cuervo-Cazurra, A., & Manning, S. 2017. Africa business research as a laboratory for theory-building: Extreme conditions, new phenomena, and alternative paradigms of social relationships. *Management and Organization Review*, 13(3), 467–495.

Barney, J. 1991. Firm resources and sustained competitive advantage. *Journal of Management*, 17(1), 99–120.

Barney, J. B. 1999. How a firm's capabilities affect boundary decisions. *Sloan Management Review*, 40(3), 137–146.

Bartels, F. L., Napolitano, F., & Tissi, N. E. 2014. FDI in sub-Saharan Africa: A longitudinal perspective on location-specific factors (2003–2010). *International Business Review*, 23(3), 516–529.

Bartlett, C. A., & Ghoshal, S. 1989. *Managing Across Borders: The Transnational Solution*. London, UK: Century Business.

Battisti, G., & Stoneman, P. 2010. How innovative are UK firms? Evidence from the fourth UK community innovation survey on synergies between technological and organizational innovations. *British Journal of Management*, 21(1), 187–206.

BBC Country Profiles. 2018. Kazakhstan country profile, www.bbc.com/news/world-asia-pacific-15263826.

Becker-Ritterspach, F., & Bruche, G. 2012. Capability creation and internationalization with business group embeddedness: The case of Tata Motors in passenger cars. *European Management Journal*, 30(3), 232–247.

Belka, M. 2013. *How Poland's EU Membership Helped Transform Its Economy*. Group of Thirty Occasional Paper 38. Washington, DC: Group of Thirty.

Belticos. (n.d.). Belticos, Tu especialista en bebidas, http://frutiqueko.com.mx/contacto/.

Belticos. 2013. Video institucional Belticos, www.youtube.com/watch?v=UCvvYgqWSh8.

Belticos. 2016. Belticos 2016, www.youtube.com/watch?v=jqP3t6TVzwo.

Berkowitz, B., Ramkolowan, Y., Stern, M., Venter, F., & Webb, M. 2012. *The Role of South African Business in Africa: South African Outward Investment – Final Report*, November 20. Pretoria, South Africa, and London, UK: TNS Research Surveys and DNA Economics, http://new.nedlac.org.za/wp-content/uploads/2014/10/RegionalInvestmentDevelopment20Nov2012.pdf.

Besley, T., & Burgess, R. 2004. Can labour regulation hinder economic performance? Evidence from India. *Quarterly Journal of Economics*, 119(1), 91–134, https://doi.org/10.1162/003355304772839533.

Bgashev, M. 2012. *Strategic Management*. Saratov: Saratov State University. [Бгашев М. Стратегический менеджмент.]

Biocon. 2018. *Annual Report*, www.biocon.com/docs/Biocon_Annual_Report_2018.pdf.

Birasnav, M. 2014. Knowledge management and organizational performance in the service industry: The role of transformational leadership beyond the effects of transactional leadership. *Journal of Business Research*, 67(8), 1622–1629.

Bisang, R. 1998. La estructura y dinámica de los conglomerados económicos en Argentina, in W. Péres (ed.), *Grandes empresas y grupos industriales latinoamericanos*, 81–150. Mexico City, Mexico: Siglo Vientiuno Editores.

Bisang, R., Fuchs, M., & Kosacoff, B. 1992. *Internacionalización y desarrollo industrial: Inversiones externas directas de empresas industriales argentinas*. Documento de Trabajo 43. Buenos Aires, Argentina: CEPAL.

Black, J., & Boal, K. 1994. Strategic resources: Traits, configurations and paths to sustainable competitive advantage. *Strategic Management Journal*, 15, 131–148.

Blackstone, E. A., & Fuhr, J. P. 2013. The economics of biosimilars. *American Health & Drug Benefits*, 6(8), 469–478, www.ncbi.nlm.nih.gov/pmc/articles/PMC4031732/pdf/ahdb-06-469.pdf.

Bloomberg. 2018a. *Industrial Conglomerates: Company Overview of AVIC International Holding Corporation*, March 5, www.bloomberg.com/research/stocks/private/snapshot.asp?privcapId=5480121.

Bloomberg. 2018b. *Industrial Conglomerates: Company Overview of Chervon Holding Limited*, May 20, www.bloomberg.com/research/stocks/private/snapshot.asp?privcapId=22399165.

Boddewyn, J. J., Halbrich, M. B., & Perry, A. C. 1986. Service multinationals: Conceptualisation, measurement and theory. *Journal of International Business Studies*, 17(3), 41–57.

Bogdanowicz, M. S., & Bailey, E. K. 2002. The value of knowledge and the values of the new knowledge worker: Generation X in the new economy. *Journal of European Industrial Training*, 26(2/3/4), 125–129.

Borda, A., Newburry, W., Teegen, H., et al. 2017. Looking for a service opening: Building reputation by leveraging international activities and host country context. *Journal of World Business*, 52(4), 503–517.

Bruton, G. D., Lau C. N., & Ob łlój, K. 2014. Institutions, resources, and firm strategies: A comparative analysis of entrepreneurial firms in three transitional economies. *European Journal of International Management*, 8(6), 697–720.

Bruton, H. J. 1998. A reconsideration of import substitution. *Journal of Economic Literature*, 36(2), 903–936.

Buckley, P. J. and Casson, M., 2016. *The Future of the Multinational Enterprise.* Springer.

Burcharth, A. L. D. A., & Fosfuri, A. 2014. Not invented here: How institutionalized socialization practices affect the formation of negative attitudes toward external knowledge. *Industrial and Corporate Change,* 24(2), 281–305.

Burgess, S. M., & Steenkamp, J. B. E. 2006. Marketing renaissance: How research in emerging markets advances marketing science and practice. *International Journal of Research in Marketing,* 23(4), 337–356.

Business Daily. 2017. SA's Tiger Brands to focus on home market after Africa review, www.businessdailyafrica.com/corporate/companies/Tiger-Brands-foc us-home-market-afterreview-/4003102-3941742-53v3fe/index.html.

Calixto, C. V. 2013. *Estratégias de internacionalização das empresas calçadistas brasileiras.* Masters Degree dissertation, Universidade do Vale do Rio dos Sinos, Brazil, www.repositorio.jesuita.org.br/bitstream/handle/UNISINOS/46 75/CyntiaCalixto.pdf;sequence=1.

Campins, M. 2015. Modalidades de internacionalización de dos empresas farmacéuticas argentinas en perspectiva histórica: Los casos Bagó y Sidus. *Apuntes: Revista de ciencias sociales,* 42(76), 95–136.

Cantwell, J., & Mudambi, R. 2005. MNE competence-creating subsidiary mandates. *Strategic Management Journal,* 26(12), 1109–1128.

Capelleras, J.-L., & Rabetino, R. 2008. Individual, organizational and environmental determinants of new firm employment growth: Evidence from Latin America. *International Entrepreneurship and Management Journal,* 4(1), 79–99.

Capelleras, J.-L., Contin-Pilart, I., Martin-Sanchez, V., & Larraza-Kintana, M. 2013. The influence of individual perceptions and the urban/rural environment on nascent entrepreneurship. *Investigaciones Regionales,* 26 (May), 97–113.

Capron, L., & Mitchell, W., 2012. *Build, Borrow, or Buy: Solving the Growth Dilemma.* Boston, MA: Harvard Business School Publishing.

Casanova, L., & Miroux, A. 2016. *Emerging Market Multinationals Report (EMR) 2016: The China Surge.* Ithaca, NY: Emerging Markets Institute, S. C. Johnson School of Management, Cornell University.

Celano Gómez, C. 2018. Luis Pagani: El "golosinero" que conquistó 120 países. *Fortuna,* November 20, https://fortuna.perfil.com/2018-11-20-201247-luis-pagani-el-golosinero-que-conquisto-120-paises/.

Celis, F. 2016. El Doctor Simi domina mercado de farmacias en México. *Forbes México,* September 27, www.forbes.com.mx/el-doctor-simi-domina-el-mercado-de-farmacias-en-mexico/.

Cervantes, M. 2018. MultiMexicans in information technology: Binbit and Softtek, in A. Cuervo-Cazurra & M. Montoya (eds.), *Mexican Multinationals: How to Build Multinationals in Emerging Markets,* 545–581. Cambridge, UK: Cambridge University Press.

Chang, S. J. 1995. International expansion strategy of Japanese firms: Capability building through sequential entry. *Academy of Management Journal,* 38(2), 383–407.

Chen, C. C., Gaspar, J. P., Friedman, R., et al. 2017. Paradoxical relationships between cultural norms of particularism and attitudes toward relational favoritism: A cultural reflectivity perspective. *Journal of Business Ethics,* 145(1), 63–79.

Chena, C., & Huang, J. 2009. Strategic human resource practices and innovation performance: The mediating role of knowledge management capacity. *Journal of Business Research*, 62(1), 104–114.

Cheng, M. Y., Lin, J. Y., Hsiao, T., & Lin, T. W. 2010. Invested resource, intellectual capital, and corporate performance. *Journal of Intellectual Capital*, 11(4), 433–455.

Chittoor, R., Sarkar, M., Ray, S., & Aulakh, P. S. 2009. Third-world copycats to emerging multinationals: Institutional changes and organizational transformation in the Indian pharmaceutical industry. *Organization Science*, 20(1), 187–205.

Chowdhury, S., Schulz, E., Milner, M., & Van De Voort, D. 2014. Core employee based human capital and revenue productivity in small firms: An empirical investigation. *Journal of Business Research*, 67(11), 2473–2479.

Churchill, N. C., & Mullins, J. W. 2001. How fast can your company afford to grow? *Harvard Business Review*, 79(5), 135–166.

CIA [US Central Intelligence Agency]. 2017. *The World Factbook*, www.cia.gov/library/publications/resources/the-world-factbook/index.html.

CIA. 2018. *The World Factbook*, www.cia.gov/library/publications/resources/the-world-factbook/index.html.

Ciabuschi, F., Dellestrand, H., & Martín, O. M. 2011. Internal embeddedness, headquarters involvement, and innovation importance in multinational enterprises. *Journal of Management Studies*, 48(7), 1612–1639.

Ciabuschi, F., Kong, L., & Su, C. 2017. Knowledge sourcing from advanced markets subsidiaries: Political embeddedness and reverse knowledge transfer barriers in emerging-market multinationals. *Industrial and Corporate Change*, 26(2), 311–332.

Ciszewska-Mlinarič, M. 2016. Foreign market knowledge and SMEs' international performance: Moderating effects of strategic intent and time-to-internationalization. *Entrepreneurial Business and Economics Review*, 4(4), 51–66.

Ciszewska-Mlinarič, M., Obłój, K., & Wasowska, A. 2018. Internationalisation choices of Polish firms during the post-socialism transition period: The role of institutional conditions at firm's foundation. *Business History*, 60(4), 562–600.

Ciszewska-Mlinarič, M., Wójcik, P., & Obłój, K. 2019. Learning dynamics of rapidly internationalizing venture: Beyond the early stage of international growth in a CEE context. *Journal of Business Research*, DOI:https://doi.org/10.1016/j.jbusres.2019.03.002.

Clark, D. 2016. *Alibaba: The House That Jack Ma Built*. New York, NY: Harper Collins.

Clover Group. (n.d.). Geographic footprint: Our reach, www.clover.co.za/about/geographic-footprint/.

Cohen, W. M., & Levinthal, D. A. 1990. Absorptive capacity: A new perspective on learning and innovation. *Administrative Science Quarterly*, 35(1), 128–152.

Collings, D. G., Scullion, H. & Caligiuri P. (eds.). 2019. *Global Talent Management*. London: Routledge.

Collins, D. 1994. How valuable are organizational capabilities? *Strategic Management Journal*, 15 (winter special issue), 143–152.

Colpan, A. M., Hikino, T. and Lincoln, J.R. eds., 2010. *The Oxford Handbook of Business Groups*. Oxford University Press.

Contractor, F. J., & Lorange, P. 1988. *Cooperative Strategies in International Business*. Lexington, MA: Lexington Books.

Contractor, F. J., Kundu, S., & Hsu, C. 2003. A three-stage theory of international expansion: The link between multinationality and performance in the service sector. *Journal of International Business Studies*, 34(1), 5–18.

Contractor, F. J., Lahiri, S., Elango, B., & Kundu, S. K. 2014. Institutional, cultural and industry related determinants of ownership choices in emerging market FDI acquisitions. *International Business Review*, 23(5), 931–941.

Contreras, L. 2013. Un imperio entre metales y aceite. *Forbes México*, May 1, www.forbes.com.mx/un-imperio-entre-metales-y-aceites-interlub/.

Correa, A., Acosta, M., Gonzalez, A. L., & Medina, U. 2003. Size, age and activity sector on the growth of the small and medium firm size. *Small Business Economics*, 21, 289–307.

Craze, M. 2016. Alicorp's Nicovita rolling out technology to Latin America shrimp farmers, *Undercurrent News*, December 1, www.undercurrentnews.com/2016/12/01/alicorps-nicovita-rolling-out-technology-to-latin-america-shrimp-farmers/.

Crunchbase. 2018. Globant, www.crunchbase.com/organization/globant.

Cuervo-Cazurra, A. 2008. The multinationalization of developing country MNEs: The case of Multilatinas. *Journal of International Management*, 14(2), 138–154.

Cuervo-Cazurra, A. 2011. Global strategy and global business environment: The direct and indirect influences of the home country on a firm's global strategy. *Global Strategy Journal*, 1(3–4), 382–386.

Cuervo-Cazurra, A. 2012. Extending theory by analyzing developing country multinational companies: Solving the Goldilocks debate. *Global Strategy Journal*, 2(3), 153–167.

Cuervo-Cazurra, A. 2016. Multilatinas as sources of new research insights: The learning and escape drivers of international expansion, *Journal of Business Research*, 69(6), 1963–1972.

Cuervo-Cazurra, A., & Genc, M. 2008. Transforming disadvantages into advantages: Developing-country MNEs in the least developed countries. *Journal of international Business Studies*, 39(6), 957–979.

Cuervo-Cazurra, A., & Ramamurti, R. (eds.). 2014. *Understanding Multinationals from Emerging Markets*. Cambridge, UK: Cambridge University Press.

Cuervo-Cazurra, A., & Ramamurti, R. 2017. Home country underdevelopment and internationalization. *Competitiveness Review*, 27(3), 217–230.

Cuervo-Cazurra, A., Carneiro, J., Finchelstein, D., et al. 2019. Uncommoditizing strategies by emerging market firms, *Multinational Business Review*, 27(2), 141–177.

Cuervo-Cazurra, A., Ciravegna, L., Melgarejo, M. and Lopez, L., 2018. Home country uncertainty and the internationalization-performance relationship: Building an uncertainty management capability. *Journal of World Business*, 53(2), 209–221.

Cuervo-Cazurra, A., Luo, Y., Ramamurti, R., & Ang, S. H. 2018. The impact of the home country on internationalization. *Journal of World Business*, 53(5), 593–604.

Cuervo-Cazurra, A., Maloney, M. M. and Manrakhan, S., 2007. Causes of the difficulties in internationalization. *Journal of International Business Studies*, 38 (5), 709–725.

Cuervo-Cazurra, A., Narula, R., & Un, C. A. 2015. Internationalization motives: sell more, buy better, upgrade and escape. *Multinational Business Review*, 23(1), 25–35.

Cuervo-Cazurra, A., Newburry, W., & Park, S. 2016. *Emerging Market Multinationals: Managing Operational Challenges for Sustained International Growth*. Cambridge, UK: Cambridge University Press.

Cui, L., Hu, H. W., Li, S. and Meyer, K. E., 2018. Corporate political connections in global strategy. *Global Strategy Journal*, 8(3), 379–398.

Davenport, T. H., 1993. *Process Innovation: Reengineering Work Through Information Technology*. Harvard Business Press.

Davidsson, P., Achtenhagen, L., & Naldi, L. 2006. What do we know about small firm growth? In S. C. Parker (ed.), *The Life Cycle of Entrepreneurial Ventures*, 361–398. New York, NY: Springer Science & Business Media.

Day, G. 1994. The capabilities of market-driven organizations. *Journal of Marketing*, 58(4), 37–52.

De Villa, M. 2016. From Multilatina to Global Latina: Unveiling the corporate-level international strategy choices of Grupo Nutresa. *AD-minister*, 29(2), 23–57.

De Villa, M., Rajwani, T., & Lawton, T. 2015. Market entry modes in a multipolar world: Untangling the moderating effect of the political environment. *International Business Review*, 24(3), 419–429.

Del Sol, P., & Kogan, J. 2007. Regional competitive advantage based on pioneering economic reforms: The case of Chilean FDI. *Journal of International Business Studies*, 38, 901–927.

Demirbag, M. and Yaprak, A. eds., 2015. *Handbook of Emerging Market Multinational Corporations*. Edward Elgar Publishing.

Dengis, J., & Dengis, M. F. 2006. *Argentine Wine: A Practical Handbook*. Buenos Aires, Argentina: Albatros.

Denis, J. E., & Depelteau, D. 1985. Market knowledge, diversification and export expansion. *Journal of International Business Studies*, 16(3), 77–89.

Dierickx, I., & Cool, K. 1989. Asset stock accumulation and sustainability of competitive advantage. *Management Science*, 35(12), 1504–1511.

Dinero. 1997. Abriendo puertas. *Dinero*, September 1, www.dinero.com/edicion-impresa/negocios/articulo/abriendo-puertas/17025.

Dinero. 2016. Top of Mind: Las marcas más recordadas por los colombianos. *Dinero*, April 28, www.dinero.com/edicion-impresa/caratula/articulo/top-of-mind-las-marcas-mas-recordadas-por-los-colombianos/222929.

Dinero. 2017a. Grupo Bios, el nuevo gigante de la agroindustria. *Dinero*, April 27, www.dinero.com/edicion-impresa/negocios/articulo/grupo-bios-nueva-asociacion-que-compite-en-agroindustria/244539.

Dinero. 2017b. Las 5000 empresas más grandes de Colombia. *Dinero*, July 20, www.dinero.com/edicion-impresa/caratula/articulo/5000-empresas-mas-grandes-de-colombia-2017/247787.

Dollar, D. 2007. Poverty, inequality, and social disparities during China's economic reform. *World Bank Documents & Reports*, http://documents.worldbank.org/curated/en/182041468241155669/Poverty-inequality-and-social-disparities-during-Chinas-economic-reform.

Dosi, G., Nelson, R., & Winter, S. 2000. *The Nature and Dynamics of Organizational Capabilities*. New York, NY: Oxford University Press.

Doz, Y. L., Santos, J., & Williamson, P. J. 2001. *From Global to Metanational: How Companies Win in the Knowledge Economy*. Boston, MA: Harvard Business School Publishing.

Dr.Consulta. 2017. Dr.Consulta website, www.drconsulta.com.

Dunning, J. H. 1956/1998. *American Investment in British Manufacturing Industry*. New York, NY: Taylor & Francis US.

Dunning, J. H. 1981. Explaining the international direct investment position of countries: Towards a dynamic or developmental approach. *Weltwirtschaftliches Archiv*, 117, 30–64.

Dunning, J. H. 1989. Multinational enterprises and the growth of services. *Service Industries Journal*, 9(1), 5–39.

Dutta, S., Narasimhan, O., & Rajiv, S. 2005. Conceptualizing and measuring capabilities: Methodology and empirical application. *Strategic Management Journal*, 26, 277–285.

Dyer, J. H., 1996. Specialized supplier networks as a source of competitive advantage: Evidence from the auto industry. *Strategic Management Journal*, 17 (4), 271–291.

Earley, P. C. and Ang, S., 2003. *Cultural Intelligence: Individual Interactions across Cultures*. Stanford University Press.

ECLAC [United Nations Economic Commission for Latin America and the Caribbean]. 2017a. *Economic Survey of Latin America and the Caribbean*. Santiago de Chile: UN-ECLAC.

ECLAC. 2017b. *Foreign Direct Investment in Latin America and the Caribbean*. Santiago de Chile: UN-ECLAC.

Ecolab. (n.d.). Nalco Champion: Our history, www.ecolab.com/nalco-champion/about/our-history.

Edwards, S. 1995. *Crisis and Reform in Latin America: From Despair to Hope*. New York, NY: Oxford University Press.

Eifert, B., Gelb, A., & Ramachandran, V. 2008. The cost of doing business in Africa: Evidence from enterprise survey data. *World Development*, 36(9), 1531–1546.

Eisenhardt, K. M., & Graebner, M. E. 2007. Theory building from cases: Opportunities and challenges. *Academy of Management Journal*, 50(1), 25–32.

Eisenhardt, K. M. and Martin, J. A., 2000. Dynamic capabilities: What are they? *Strategic Management Journal*, 21(10–11), 1105–1121.

Elbehri, A., Hertel, T., & Martin, W. 2003. Estimating the impact of WTO and domestic reforms on the indian cotton and textile sectors: A general-equilibrium approach. *Review of Development Economics*, 7, 343–359, doi:10.1111/1467-9361.00195.

El Colombiano. 2016. Sempertex innova en fiestas para exportar a 70 países. *El Colombiano*, February 9, www.elcolombiano.com/negocios/globos-que-export a-sempertex-con-innovacion-DD3566216.

El Heraldo. 2016. Sempertex entra al mercado del Sudeste Asiático. *El Heraldo*, December 1, www.elheraldo.co/economia/sempertex-entra-al-mercado-del-s ureste-asiatico-241129.

EMIS. 2017a. Colcafé Business Report, EMIS Professional database, www.emis .com/php/company-profile/CO/Industria_Colombiana_De_Cafe_SAS_Que_ Podra_Utilizar_Para_Todos_Sus_Efectos_La_Denominacion__Colcafe_SA S__es_1198692.html.

EMIS. 2017b. Sempertex de Colombia Business Report, EMIS Professional database, www.emis.com/php/company-profile/CO/Sempertex_De_Colombi a_SA_es_1213202.html.

Emons, W. 2001. Credence goods monopolists. *International Journal of Industrial Organization*, 19, 375–389.

Endeavor Colombia. 2016. *Inspire: Historias de quienes han construido empresa en donde otros no veían oportunidades*. Bogota, Colombia: Endeavor Colombia.

Erisman, P. 2015. *Alibaba's World: How a Remarkable Chinese Company is Changing the Face of Global Business*. Basingstoke, UK: Palgrave Macmillan.

Ernst and Young. 2014. *EY's Attractiveness Survey, Africa 2014: Executing Growth*, http://mb.cision.com/Public/1179/9588229/b0664e1207a65aa4.pdf.

Ernst and Young. 2017. *EY's Attractiveness Program, Africa May 2017: Connectivity Redefined*, https://ukgcc.com.gh/wp-content/uploads/2017/06/ey-africa-attractiveness-report.pdf.

Escalante, J. 2017. Fabricación de maquinaria minera: Resemin, https://gestion.pe/ especial/50-ideas-de-negocios/noticias/rumbo-llegar-al-centro-tierra-noticia-1992855.

Escalante, J. 2017. Fabricación de maquinaria minera: Resemin, https://gestion.pe/ especial/50-ideas-de-negocios/noticias/rumbo-llegar-al-centro-tierra-noticia-1992855.

Estrin, S., Meyer, K. E. & Pelletier, A., 2018. Emerging Economy MNEs: How does home country munificence matter? *Journal of World Business*, 53(4), 514–528.

Euromonitor. 2019. Colombia Country Profile, Euromonitor Passport database, May 24, www.portal.euromonitor.com/portal/Analysis/Tab.

EXIM Bank. 2014. Outward direct investment from India: Trends, objectives and policy perspectives. EXIM Bank Occasional Paper No. 165, www.exim bankindia.in/Assets/Dynamic/PDF/Publication-Resources/ResearchPapers/5fi le.pdf.

Expansión. 2016. Entrevista con Daniel Chávez Morán, fundador de Grupo Vidanta (interview), www.youtube.com/watch?v=R5R6KJ7hcU.

Export.gov. 2017a. Peru Market Overview, www.export.gov/apex/article2?id=P eru-Market-Overview.

Export.gov. 2017b. Peru Market Challenges, www.export.gov/article?id=Peru-Market-Challenges.

Fanem. 2017. Fanem website, www.fanem.com.br.

Farley, J. U., & Deshpandé, R. 2006. Charting the evolution of Russian firms from Soviet "producer orientation" to contemporary "market orientation". *Journal of Global Marketing*, 19(2), 7–26.

Farmacias Similares. 2011. Farmacias Similares: Todo lo que debes saber, www .youtube.com/watch?v=L-Amn6jN9t0.

Fatkhutdinov, R. 2005. *Management of Organization Competitiveness*. Moscow: EKSMO. [Фатхутдинов Р. Управление конкурентоспособностью органи зации.]

Finchelstein, D. 2017. The role of the state in the internationalization of Latin American firms. *Journal of World Business*, 54(2), 578–590.

Finchelstein, D. 2018. Social embedding of the corporation: Family conglomerates around the world, in C. May & A. Nolke (eds.), *Handbook of the International Political Economy of the Corporation*. Cheltenham, UK: Edward Elgar.

Fischer, B., Lago, U., & Liu, F. 2013. *Reinventing Giants: How Chinese Global Competitor Haier has Changed the Way Big Companies Transform*. San Francisco, CA: Jossey-Bass.

Fleury, A., & Fleury, M. T. 2011. *Brazilian Multinationals: Competences for Internationalization*. Cambridge, UK: Cambridge University Press.

Fleury, A., Fleury, M. T., & Borini, F. M. 2013. The Brazilian multinationals' approaches to innovation. *Journal of International Management*, 19, 260–275.

Forbes. (n.d.). WEG. *Global 2000: The World's Largest Public Companies*, www .forbes.com/companies/weg/#742aa884c900.

Forbes. 2017. El emprendimiento que México necesita, Xavier López Ancona, https://youtu.be/iZfG2gHAbZk.

Forbes. 2019. The world's largest public companies, www.forbes.com/global2000/ list/#tab:overall.

Fortune. 2019. Global 500, http://fortune.com/global500/list/.

Fosu, A. K. 2015. Growth, inequality and poverty in sub-Saharan Africa: Recent progress in a global context. *Oxford Development Studies*, 43(1), 44–59.

Franco, M., & Haase, H. 2010. Failure factors in small and medium-sized enterprises: Qualitative study from an attributional perspective. *International Entrepreneurship and Management Journal*, 6(4), 503–521.

Fuentes-Berain, R. 2007. *Oro gris: Zambrano, la gesta de CEMEX y la globalizacion en Mexico*. Madrid, Spain: Aguilar.

FundingUniverse. (n.d.). Ecolab Inc. history, www.fundinguniverse.com/com pany-histories/ecolab-inc-history/.

Furman, J. L., Porter, M. E., & Stern, S., 2002. The determinants of national innovative capacity. *Research Policy*, 31(6), 899–933.

Gallo Machado, G. 2008. Guarne fábrica de dientes para el mundo. *El Colombiano*, July 19, www.elcolombiano.com/historico/guarne_fabrica_diente s_para_el_mundo-KREC_6729.

Galunic, D. C., & Eisenhardt, K. M. 1994. Renewing the strategy–structure–performance paradigm. *Research in Organizational Behavior*, 16, 215–255.

Galunic, D. C., & Rodan, S. 1998. Resource combinations in the firm: Knowledge structures and the potential for Schumpeterian innovation. *Strategic Management Journal*, 1912, 1193–1201.

Games, D. 2013. Failure in Nigeria is often due to poor business strategies. *How We Made It in Africa*, November 12, www.howwemadeitinafrica.com/failure-in-nigeria-is-often-due-to-poor-business-strategies/.

Gammeltoft, P., Barnard, H., & Madhok, A. 2010. Emerging multinationals: Outward foreign direct investment from emerging and developing economies. *Journal of International Management*, 16(2), 95–194.

Gartner. 2018. Cool Vendors 2018: Technologies and business come together to solve hard problems. Gartner Trend Insight Report, www.gartner.com/en/doc/3879512-cool-vendors-2018-technologies-and-business-come-together-to-solve-hard-problems-a-gartner-trend-insight-report.

Gazprom. (n.d.). Website, www.gazprom-mt.com/Pages/default.aspx.

Ge, Y., Lai, H., & Zhu, S. C. 2015. Multinational price premium. *Journal of Development Economics*, 115, 181–199.

Geleilate, J.-M. G., Magnusson, P., Parente, R. C., & Alvarado-Vargas, M. J. 2016. Home country institutional effects on the multinationality–performance relationship: A comparison between emerging and developed market multinationals. *Journal of International Management*, 22, 380–402.

Gereffi, G., 1999. International trade and industrial upgrading in the apparel commodity chain. *Journal of International Economics*, 48(1), 37–70.

Gereffi, G., Humphrey, J. and Sturgeon, T., 2005. The governance of global value chains. *Review of International Political Economy*, 12(1), 78–104.

Gestion. 2013. Alicorp sale del negocio de alimentos para mascotas. *Gestion*, 4 December, https://gestion.pe/impresa/alicorp-sale-negocio-alimentos-mascotas-54091-noticia/.

Ghemawat, P. 1986. Sustainable advantage, *Harvard Business Review*, September, 53–58.

Ghemawat, P. 2001. Distance still matters. *Harvard Business Review*, 79(8), 137–147.

Ghemawat, P., & Khanna, T. 1998. The nature of diversified business groups: A research design and two case studies. *Journal of Industrial Economics*, 46, 35–61.

Gibb, A., & Davies, L. 1990. In pursuit of frameworks for the development of growth models of the small business. *International Small Business Journal*, 9(1), 15–31.

Global Edge. 2017. Peru: Economy, https://globaledge.msu.edu/countries/peru/economy.

Global Standards. 2012. Belticos – En el ramo alimenticio, calidad e inocuidad: ¡Es todo! www.youtube.com/watch?v=Q2ZrNPfk5ss.

Godinho, R. 2011. *O filho da crise*. São Paulo, Brazil: Matrix.

Gokaldas Exports. 2018. *Annual Report 2016–2017*, www.moneycontrol.com/annual-report/gokaldasexport/directors-report/GE05.

Golden, P. A., Doney, P. M., Johnson, D. M., & Smith, J. R. 1995. The dynamics of a marketing orientation in transition economies: A study of Russian firms. *Journal of International Marketing*, 3(2), 29–49.

Gomez, C., & Gonzalez-Perez, M. A. 2015. Internationalization of video-game studios from emerging markets: A Colombian case study based on an activity-based view, in W. Newburry & M. A. Gonzalez-Perez (eds.), *International Business in Latin America: Innovation, Geography and Internationalization*, 140–155. Basingstoke, UK: Palgrave Macmillan.

Gonzalez-Perez, M. A., & Velez-Ocampo, J. 2014. Targeting their own region: Internationalisation trends of Colombian multinational companies. *European Business Review*, 26(6), 531–555.

Gorynia, M., Nowak, J., Trąpczyński, P., & Wolniak, R. 2014. The internationalization of Polish firms: Evidence from a qualitative study of FDI behaviour, in M. T. T. Thai & E. Turkina (eds.), *Internationalization of Firms from Economies in Transition: The Effects of Politico-economic Paradigm Shift*, 39–66. Cheltenham, UK: Edward Elgar.

Götz, M., & Jankowska, B. 2018. Outward foreign direct investment by Polish state-owned multinational enterprises: Is "stateness" an asset or a burden? *Post-Communist Economies*, 30(2), 216–237.

Govindarajan, V., & Ramamurti, R. 2011. Reverse innovation, emerging markets, and global strategy. *Global Strategy Journal*, 1(3–4), 191–205.

Grant, R. M. 1991. The resource-based theory of competitive advantage: Implications for strategy formulation. *California Management Review*, 333, 114–135.

Greenley, G. E. 1995. Forms of market orientation in UK firms. *Journal of Management Studies*, 32(1), 47–66.

Grendene. 2017. Grendene website, www.grendene.com.br.

Grosse, R. and Meyer, K. E. (eds.). 2019. *The Oxford Handbook of Management in Emerging Markets*. Oxford University Press.

Grove, A. S. 1996. *Only the Paranoid Survive: How to Exploit the Crisis Points That Challenge Every Company*. New York, NY: Random House.

Grupo Bios SAS. 2017. Informe de Gestión de la Junta Directiva y el Presidente de Grupo Empresarial Bios SAS a la Asamblea General Ordinaria de Accionistas de 2016, www.grupobios.co/Portals/0/Documentos/Informe-Fundaci%C3%B3nGB-2017.pdf.

Grupo Elektra. (n.d.). Estrategia, www.grupoelektra.com.mx/es/estrategia.

Grupo Elektra. 2017a. Company overview, www.gruposalinas.com/images/Eljk Eng.pdf.

Grupo Elektra. 2017b. *Reporte Anual 2016*, www.grupoelektra.com.mx/Docum ents/ES/Downloads/Grupo-Elektra-Informe-Anual-2016.pdf.

Grupo Nutresa. 2013. Excelentes resultados en 2012, www.gruponutresa.com/wp-content/uploads/2016/02/comunicado_asamblea.pdf.

Grupo Nutresa. 2014. Grupo Nutresa crea "Oriental Coffee Alliance" un JV con Mitsubishi Corporation para la comercialización de productos de café, www.gruponutresa.com/noticias/grupo-nutresa-crea-oriental-coffee-alliance-un-jv-con-mitsubishi-corporation-para-la-comercializacion-de-productos-de-cafe/.

Grupo Nutresa. 2016. *Integrated Report 2016*, http://2016report.gruponutresa.com/.

Grupo Vidanta. 2015. Grupo Vidanta: Una historia de éxito aún en construcción, www.youtube.com/watch?v=98rm_eo0vRY.

Gubbi, S., Aulakh, P. S., Ray, S., Sarkar, M. B., & Chittoor, R. 2010. Do international acquisitions by emerging-economy firms create shareholder value? The case of Indian firms. *Journal of International Business Studies*, 41(3), 397–416.

Güemes-Castorena, D., & Díaz, J. A. 2014. A Mexican Edutainment business model: KidZania. *Emerald Emerging Markets Case Studies*, 3(5), 1–14.

Guesalaga, R., Gabrielsson, M., Rogers, B., Ryals, L., & Cuevas, J. 2018. Which resources and capabilities underpin strategic key account management? *Industrial Marketing Management*, 75, 160–172.

Guillén, M. F., & García-Canal, E. 2009. The American model of the multinational firm and the "new" multinationals from emerging economies. *Academy of Management Perspectives*, 23(2), 23–35.

Guillén, M. F. and García-Canal, E., 2012. *Emerging Markets Rule: Growth Strategies of the New Global Giants*. McGraw Hill Professional.

Gurkov, I., & Saidov, Z. 2017. Current strategic actions of Russian manufacturing subsidiaries of Western multinational corporations. *Journal of East–West Business*, 23(2), 171–193.

Guseva, N. 2016. Innovating cultural synergy in French–Russian collaboration: Building a puzzle from cultural diversity. In I. N. Dubina & E. G. Carayannis (eds.), *Creativity, Innovation, and Entrepreneurship Across Cultures: Theory and Practices*, 121–134. New York, NY: Springer Science and Business Media.

Guseva, N. 2017. Russia. In R. Carney & S. Park (eds.), *Emerging Market Multinationals: Navigating an Uncertain World*, 32–34. Shanghai, China: CEIBS.

Guseva, N., & Rebiazina, V. In press. How to build strategic capabilities in emerging market firms: The case of Russia, in E. Yasin (ed.), *Proceedings of the XX April International Academic Conference on Economic and Social Development*. Moscow, Russia: HSE.

Helfat, C. E. 1997. Know-how and asset complementarity and dynamic capability accumulation: The case of R&D. *Strategic Management Journal*, 18(5), 339–360.

Helfat, C. E. and Peteraf, M. A., 2003. The dynamic resource-based view: Capability lifecycles. *Strategic Management Journal*, 24(10), 997–1010.

Heritage Foundation. 2020. 2020 Index of Economic Freedom, www.heritage .org/index/.

Hermans, M. 2003. *Small and Medium-Sized Enterprises' Restructuring in a Context of Transition: A Shared Process – Inter-player Effects on Efficient Boundary Choice in the Argentine Manufacturing Sector*. Estudios y Perspectivas series. Buenos Aires, Argentina: UN/ECLAC.

Hernandez, E., & Guillén, M. F. 2018. What's theoretically novel about emerging-market multinationals? *Journal of International Business Studies*, 49(1), 24–33, doi:10.1057/s41267-017-0131-7.

Hernández Bonilla, J. M. 2017. "Hay que garantizar la seguridad alimentaria": Presidente Grupo Bios. *El Espectador*, April 27, www.elespectador.com/econo mia/hay-que-garantizar-la-seguridad-alimentaria-presidente-de-grupo-bios-ar ticulo-691303.

Hitt, M. A., Ireland, R. D., & Hoskisson, R. E. 1999. *Strategic Management: Competitiveness and Globalization*. Cincinnati, OH: South-Western College Publishing.

Hitt, M. A., Ireland, R. D., Camp, S. M. and Sexton, D. L., 2001. Strategic entrepreneurship: Entrepreneurial strategies for wealth creation. *Strategic Management Journal*, 22(6–7), 479–491.

Hobday, M. 1994. Technological learning in Singapore: A test case of leapfrogging. *Journal of Development Studies*, 30(4), 831–858.

Hobday, M., & Rush, H. 2007. Upgrading the technological capabilities of foreign transnational subsidiaries in developing countries: The case of electronics in Thailand. *Research Policy*, 36(9), 1335–1356.

Hofstede Insights. 2016. Mexico – Geert Hofstede, www.hofstede-insights.com/country/mexico/.

Hoskisson, R. E., Eden, L., Lau, S. M., & Wright, M. 2000. Strategy in emerging economies. *Academy of Management Journal*, 43(3), 249–267.

Hu, Y., & Hao, Y. 2017. *Haier Purpose: The Real Story of China's First Global Super Company*. Oxford, UK: Infinite Ideas.

Hubbard, G., Pocknee, G., & Taylor, G. 1996. *Practical Australian Strategy*. Sydney, Australia: Prentice Hall Australia.

Hunter, R. J., & Ryan, L. V. 2001. A transitional analysis of the Polish economy: After fifteen years, still a "work in progress". *Global Economy Journal*, 5(2), 1–19.

Hymer, S. H. 1960/1976. *The International Operations of National Firms: A Study of Direct Foreign Investment*. Cambridge, MA: MIT Press.

IFAD [International Fund for Agricultural Development]. 2013. *Smallholders, Food Security, and the Environment*, www.ifad.org/documents/10180/666cac24-14b6-43c2-876d-9c2d1f01d5dd.

IGDA Colombia. 2017. *Directorio*, https://igda.org/chapters/colombia/.

IMF [International Monetary Fund]. 2005. *The First Ten Years After Apartheid: An Overview of the South African Economy*, www.imf.org/external/pubs/nft/200 6/soafrica/eng/pasoafr/pasoafr.pdf.

IMF. 2017. *Sub-Saharan Africa Regional Economic Outlook: Fiscal Adjustment and Economic Diversification*, www.imf.org/en/Publications/REO/SSA/Issues/2017/10/19/sreo1017.

IMF. 2018a. Consumer Price Indexes, December, https://data.imf.org/regular .aspx?key=61015892.

IMF. 2018b. Data and statistics, March, www.imf.org/en/data.

IMF. 2018c. *World Economic Outlook: Database – WEO Groups and Aggregates Information*, www.imf.org/external/pubs/ft/weo/2018/02/weodata/groups .htm.

INEGI [Instituto Nacional de Estadística y Geografía] [Mexico]. 2010. *Censo de población y vivienda 2010*, www.beta.inegi.org.mx/proyectos/ccpv/2010/.

INEGI. 2018. *Encuesta intercensal 2015*, www.beta.inegi.org.mx/temas/estructura/default.html.

Informa Colombia. 2017. Informe Comercial Grupo BIOS SAS, www.einforma .co/servlet/app/portal/ENTP/prod/LISTA_EMPRESAS/razonsocial/bios.

Ingham, B. 1995. *Economics and Development*. Maidenhead, UK: McGraw-Hill.

Instituto Nacional del Emprendedor [Mexico]. 2016. Daniel Chávez Grupo Vidanta, www.youtube.com/watch?v=QFktiDHBQcI.

Integration. 2017. Integration website, www.integrationconsulting.com.

Interlub Group. 2016a. Interlub website, www.interlub.com/.

Interlub Group. 2016b. Interlub video corporativo 2015, www.youtube.com/watch?v=QqsDM8OM_UA.

Ireland, R. D., Hitt, M. A. and Sirmon, D. G., 2003. A model of strategic entrepreneurship: The construct and its dimensions. *Journal of Management*, 29(6), 963–989.

Itami, H., & Roehl, T. W. 1987. *Mobilizing Invisible Assets*. Cambridge, MA: Harvard University Press.

Johanson, J., & Vahlne, J.-E. 1977. The internationalization process of the firm: A model of knowledge development and increasing foreign market commitments. *Journal of International Business Studies*, 8(1), 23–32.

Johanson, J., & Vahlne, J.-E. 2009. The Uppsala internationalization process model revisited: From liability of foreignness to liability of outsidership. *Journal of International Business Studies*, 40(9), 1411–1431.

Kak, A., & Sushil, H. 2002. Sustainable competitive advantage with core competence: A review. *Global Journal of Flexible Systems Management*, 3(4), 23–38.

Kallumal, M., Philip, D. A., & Gurung, H. M. 2016. *Revenue (Foreign Exchange) Implications of the Outward Foreign Direct Investment: A Case of Indian Firm Level Investments*. New Delhi, India: Centre for WTO Studies.

Kantor, D. 2017. Investigación exclusiva: El ranking de las 100 empresas de mayor reputación de la Argentina. *Clarín*, November 12, www.clarin.com/economia/ranking-100-empresas-mayor-reputacion-argentina_0_BJylFuQyM.html.

Katz, J., & Kosacoff, B. 1989. El proceso de industrialización en la Argentina: Evolución, retroceso y prospectiva. Buenos Aires, Argentina: CEPAL.

Keijzers, G. 2002. The transition to the sustainable enterprise. *Journal of Cleaner Production*, 10(4), 349–359.

Keogh, W., & Evans, G. 1999. Strategies for growth and the barriers faced by new technology-based SMEs. *Journal of Small Business and Enterprise Development*, 5 (4), 337–350.

Khanna, T. and Palepu, K. G., 2010. *Winning in Emerging Markets: A Road Map for Strategy and Execution*. Boston, MA: Harvard Business Press.

Kirezieva, K., Luning, P. A., Jacxsens, L., et al. 2015. Factors affecting the status of food safety management systems in the global fresh produce chain. *Food Control*, 52, 85–97.

Kiruga, M. 2016. Conquering Africa: What the story of South African firms in Kenya – and Nigeria – teaches those looking for riches. *Mail & Guardian Africa*, January 3.

Kogut, B. 1985. Designing global strategies: Profiting from operational flexibility. *Sloan Management Review*, 27(1), 27–38.

Kogut, B., & Zander, U. 1992. Knowledge of the firm, combinative capabilities, and the replication of technology. *Organization Science*, 3(3), 383–397.

Kosacoff, B., & Ramos, A. 2010. Tres fases de la internacionalización de las empresas industriales argentinasuna historia de pioneros, incursiones y fragilidad *Universia Business Review*, 25, 56–75.

Kriauciunas, A., & Kale, P. 2006. The impact of socialist imprinting and search on resource change: A study of firms in Lithuania. *Strategic Management Journal*, 27(7), 659–679.

Kumaraswamy, A., Mudambi, R., Saranga, H., & Tripathy, A. 2012. Catch-up strategies in the Indian auto components industry: Domestic firms' responses to market liberalization. *Journal of International Business Studies*, 43(4), 368–395.

Kussaga, J. B., Jacxsens, L., Tiisekwa, B. P., & Luning, P. A. 2014. Food safety management systems performance in African food processing companies: A review of deficiencies and possible improvement strategies. *Journal of the Science of Food and Agriculture*, 94(11), 2154–2169.

Latin Trade. 2017. Top 500 mayores multilatinas por ventas. *Latin Trade*, Second Quarter 2017, www.latintrade.com/wp-content/uploads/2018/07/Latin-Trade-Magazine-2T-2018-SPA.pdf.

Lau, C. M., & Bruton, G. D. 2008. FDI in China: What we know and what we need to study next. *Academy of Management Perspectives*, 22(4), 30–44.

Legiscomex. 2017a. Colcafé Exports, September 19. Legiscomex database, www.legiscomex.com/ReporteDetallado/IndexEstadisticas/.

Legiscomex. 2017b. Sempertex de Colombia Exports, September 19. Legiscomex www.legiscomex.com/ReporteDetallado/IndexEstadisticas/.

Lemus, D., Montoya, M., & Cervantes, M. 2015. Los parques científicos tecnológicos como espacios para la innovación: Evidencias del centro del software en Guadalajara. *Intersticios Sociales*, 9, https://papers.ssrn.com/sol3/paper s.cfm?abstract_id=2549891.

Lessard, D. and Lucea, R., 2009. Embracing risk as a core competence: The case of CEMEX. *Journal of International Management*, 15(3), 296–305.

Lessard, D. R., Lucea, R. and Vives, L., 2013. Building your company's capabilities through global expansion. *MIT Sloan Management Review*, 54(2), 61–67.

Li, J. T. 1995. Foreign entry and survival: Effects of strategic choices on performance in international markets. *Strategic Management Journal*, 16(5), 333–351.

Library of Congress. 2006. Country Profile: Kazakhstan, www.loc.gov/rr/frd/cs/profiles/Kazakhstan-new.pdf.

Lishchuk, A. 2014. Evolution of the theory of competitiveness and competitive advantages: Concept of value networks. *Problems of the Modern Economy*, 4(52), 172–176. [Лищук А. Эволюция теории конкурентоспособности и конкурентных преимуществ: Становление концепции сетей ценности. Проблемы современной экономики.]

London, T., & Hart, S. L. 2004. Reinventing strategies for emerging markets: Beyond the transnational model. *Journal of International Business Studies*, 35(5), 350–370.

Lu, J. W., & Beamish, P. W. 2001. The internationalization and performance of SMEs. *Strategic Management Journal*, 22(6/7), 565–586.

Luna, F. 1994. *Breve historia de los argentinos*. Buenos Aires, Argentina: Planeta / Espejo de la Argentina.

Luo, Y., 2000. Dynamic capabilities in international expansion. *Journal of World Business*, 35(4), 355–378.

Luo, Y., & Rui, H. 2009. An ambidexterity perspective toward multinational enterprises from emerging economies. *Academy of Management Perspectives*, 23(4), 49–70.

Luo, Y., & Tung, R. L. 2007. International expansion of emerging market enterprises: A springboard perspective. *Journal of International Business Studies*, 38(38), 481–498.

Luo, Y. and Wang, S. L., 2012. Foreign direct investment strategies by developing country multinationals: A diagnostic model for home country effects. *Global Strategy Journal*, 2(3), 244–261.

Luo, Y., Huang, Y. and Wang, S. L., 2012. Guanxi and organizational performance: A meta-analysis. *Management and Organization Review*, 8(1), 139–172.

Luo, Y., Sun, J., & Wang, S. L. 2011. Emerging economy copycats: Capability, environment, and strategy. *Academy of Management Perspectives*, 25(2), 37–56.

Luo, Y., Xue, Q., & Han, B. 2010. How emerging market governments promote outward FDI: Experience from China. *Journal of World Business*, 45(1), 68–79.

Macher, J. T., & Mayo, J. W. 2015. Influencing public policymaking: Firm-, industry-, and country-level determinants. *Strategic Management Journal*, 36 (13), 2021–2038.

Madhok, A., & Keyhani, M. 2012. Acquisitions as entrepreneurship: Asymmetries, opportunities and the internationalization of multinationals from emerging economies. *Global Strategy Journal*, 2, 26–40.

Manzoni, C. 2018. Marcelo Siano: "Arcor es un grupo que está acostumbrado a la transformación." *La Nacion*, September 12, www.lanacion.com.ar/econo mia/marcelo-siano-arcor-es-grupo-esta-acostumbrado-nid2171025.

Marin, A., & Bell, M. 2006. Technology spillovers from foreign direct investment (FDI): The active role of MNC subsidiaries in Argentina in the 1990s. *Journal of Development Studies*, 42(4), 678–697.

Martin, X., 2014. Institutional advantage. *Global Strategy Journal*, 4(1), 55–69.

Martínez Álvarez, C. B. 2016. China–Kazakhstan energy relations between 1997 and 2012. *Journal of International Affairs*, January 1, https://jia.sipa.columbia .edu/china-kazakhstan-energy-relations-1997-2012.

Mateu, A. M., & Stein, S. (eds.). 2008. *El vino y sus revoluciones: Una antología histórica sobre el desarrollo de la industria vitivinícola argentina*. Mendoza, Argentina: EDIUNC.

McEvily, S., & Chakravarthy, B. 2002. The persistence of knowledge-based advantage: An empirical test for product performance and technological knowledge. *Strategic Management Journal*, 23(4), 285–305.

McGrath, R. G., Tsai, M., Venkataraman, S., & Macmillan, I. C. 1996. Innovation, competitive advantage, and rent. *Management Science*, 42, 389–403.

Melo, G. 2010. *Reconfiguração dos recursos ao longo do processo de internacionalização de empresas: Um estudo de caso na WEG SA*. Masters Degree dissertation, Universidade Federal do Rio Grande do Sul, Brazil.

Mercadotecnia FE Economía. 2016. Modelo de negocio Víctor González Torres, www.youtube.com/watch?v=YQdoplTU-3U.

Meyer, K. E. 2014. Process perspectives on the growth of emerging economy multinationals, in A. Cuervo-Cazurra & R. Ramamurti (eds.), *Understanding Multinationals from Emerging Markets*, 169–194. Cambridge, UK: Cambridge University Press.

Meyer, K. E., & Sinani, E. 2009. When and where does foreign direct investment generate positive spillovers? A meta-analysis. *Journal of International Business Studies*, 40(7), 1075–1094.

Meyer, K. E., Mudambi, R., & Narula, R. 2011. Multinational enterprises and local contexts: The opportunities and challenges of multiple embeddedness. *Journal of Management Studies*, 48(2), 235–252.

Meyer, M., Lang, N., Baise, N., et al. 2018. Meet the 2018 global challengers. Boston Consulting Group, www.bcg.com/publications/2018/global-challen gers-2018.aspx.

Mezias, J. M. 2002. Identifying liabilities of foreignness and strategies to minimize their effects: The case of labor lawsuit judgments in the United States. *Strategic Management Journal*, 23(3), 229–244.

Miller, D., & Shamsie, J. 1996. The resource-based view of the firm in two environments: The Hollywood film studios from 1936 to 1965. *Academy of Management Journal*, 39, 519–543.

Moiseeva, N. 2007. *Strategic Management of a Touristic Company*. Moscow: Finance and Statistics. [Моисеева Н. Стратегическое управление туристской фирмой.]

Molina, O., Olivari, J., & Pietrobelli, C. 2016. Global value chains in the Peruvian mining sector, Inter-American Development Bank, https://publications.iadb .org/bitstream/handle/11319/7895/Global-Value-Chains-in-the-Peruvian-Mi ning-Sector.pdf?sequence=1.

Moneyweb. 2015. Clover prowling Africa for "gems". March 24, www.money web.co.za/news/companies-and-deals/clover-prowling-africa-for-gems/.

Montalvo, R., & Daspro, E. 2018. MultiMexicans in the entertainment industry: KidZania and Cinépolis, in A. Cuervo-Cazurra and M. Montoya (eds.), *Mexican Multinationals: How to Build Multinationals in Emerging Markets*, 494–521. Cambridge, UK: Cambridge University Press.

Montoya, M., & Alcaraz, J. 2018. MultiMexicans: An overview, in A. Cuervo-Cazurra and M. Montoya (eds.), *Mexican Multinationals: How to Build Multinationals in Emerging Markets*, 29–58. Cambridge, UK: Cambridge University Press.

Montoya, M., Vázquez, M. E., & López, M. A. 2018. MultiMexicans in the retail industry: Elektra and Coppel, in A. Cuervo-Cazurra and M. Montoya (eds.), *Mexican Multinationals: How to Build Multinationals in Emerging Markets*, 418–441. Cambridge, UK: Cambridge University Press.

Moraes, J. 2004. *A trajetória de crescimento da WEG: A folga de recursos humanos como propulsora do crescimento da firma*. Masters Degree dissertation, Universidade Federal do Rio de Janeiro, Brazil.

Mostafa, G., & Mahmood, M. 2018. Eurasian Economic Union: Evolution, challenges and possible future directions. *Journal of Eurasian Studies*, 9(2), 163–172.

Narula, R. 2012. Do we need different frameworks to explain infant MNEs from developing countries? *Global Strategy Journal*, 2(3), 188–204.

National Treasury, Republic of South Africa. 2013. Website annexure to the 2013 Budget Review: Gateway to Africa and other reforms, www.treasury.gov.za/do cuments/national%20budget/2013/review/Annexure%20W3.pdf.

NBP [National Bank of Poland]. 2017. Zagraniczne inwestycje bezpośrednie w Polsce i polskie inwestycje bezpośrednie za granicą w 2016 roku [Foreign direct investments in Poland and Polish direct investments abroad in 2016], www.nbp.pl/publikacje/ib_raporty/raport_ib_2016.pdf.

Nell, P. C., & Ambos, B. 2013. Parenting advantage in the MNC: An embeddedness perspective on the value added by headquarters. *Strategic Management Journal*, 34(9), 1086–1103.

Nelson, R. R., & Pack, H. 1999. The Asian miracle and modern growth theory. *Economic Journal*, 109(457), 416–436.

Nelson, R. R., & Rosenberg, N. 1993. Technical innovation and national systems, in R. R. Nelson (ed.), *National Innovation Systems: A Comparative Analysis*, 3–21. Oxford, UK: Oxford University Press.

Neoris. 2014. Neoris: ¿Sabias que ... ? www.youtube.com/watch?time_continue=23&v=2CzmEgLLyVw.

Neoris. 2015. Neoris: ¿Quiénes somos? www.youtube.com/watch?time_continue=27&v=5vZ3Cs5Euxk.

Neoris. 2016. Reporte global, www.neoris.com/files/NEORISGlobalReport/2016/online_es/#p=1.

New Stetic. 2017. Historical overview, www.newstetic.com/newstetic/nosotros/resena-historica.

Newburry, W. 2010. Reputation and supportive behavior: Moderating impacts of foreignness, industry and local exposure. *Corporate Reputation Review*, 12(4), 388–405.

Newburry, W., & Yakova, N. 2006. Standardization preferences: A function of national culture, work interdependence and local embeddedness. *Journal of International Business Studies*, 37(1), 44–60.

Nonsoque, J. C. 2017. La compañía colombiana Brainz lleva sus videojuegos a 160 países. *La República*, August 17, www.larepublica.co/internet-economy/la-compania-colombiana-brainz-lleva-sus-videojuegos-a-160-paises-2538589.

North, D. C. 1991. Institutions. *Journal of Economic Perspectives*, 5(1), 97–112.

North-West University and Columbia Center on Sustainable Investment. 2016. An original ranking of South Africa's global players for 2013–2015, http://ccsi.columbia.edu/files/2013/10/EMGP-South-Africa-Report-2016-FINAL.pdf.

Notimex. 2017. Parques Kidzania en Estados Unidos requerirán inversión de 105 mdd. *20 minutos*, April 9, www.20minutos.com.mx/noticia/207888/0/parques-kidzania-en-estados-unidos-requeriran-inversion-de-105-mdd/.

Nowiński, W. 2017. International acquisitions by Polish MNEs: Value creation or destruction? *European Business Review*, 29(2), 205–218.

NTMX Agencia. 2017. Generó la industria del entretenimiento ingresos por 22.8 mil mdd en México. *El Sol de México*, February 23, www.elsoldemexico.com.mx/finanzas/Generó-la-industria-del-entretenimiento-ingresos-por-22.8-mil-mdd-en-México-215592.html?pollResult=249362.

Obłój, T., Obłój, K., & Pratt, M. 2010. Dominant logic and entrepreneurial firms performance in a transitional economy. *Entrepreneurship Theory and Practice*, 34 (1), 151–170.

Ocean Unite. (n.d.). Pre-empting Russia's year of ecology, www.oceanunite.org/round-up/pre-empting-russias-year-ecology/.

OEC. 2014. Which countries import computer parts and accessories? https://atlas.media.mit.edu/en/visualize/tree_map/sitc/import/show/all/7599/2014/.

OECD. (n.d.). OECD data: FDI stocks, https://data.oecd.org/fdi/fdi-stocks.htm.

OECD. 2017. *Argentina: Multi-dimensional Economic Survey*. Paris, France: OECD.

O'Gorman, C. 2001. The sustainability of growth on small and medium-sized enterprises. *International Journal of Entrepreneurial Behavior & Research*, 7(2), 60–75.

Oliver, C. 1997. Sustainable competitive advantage: Combining institutional and resource based views. *Strategic Management Journal*, 18(9), 697–713.

Osei-Assibey, E. 2009. Financial exclusion: What drives supply and demand for basic financial services in Ghana? *Savings and Development*, 33(3), 207–238.

Osores, C. 2015. *Valoración de la Empresa Alicorp S.A.A.* Masters Degree dissertation, Universidad Pacífico, Peru, http://repositorio.up.edu.pe/bitstream/handle/11354/1127/C%C3%A9sar_Tesis_maestria_2015.pdf.

Park, S. H. and Luo, Y., 2001. Guanxi and organizational dynamics: Organizational networking in Chinese firms. *Strategic Management Journal*, 22(5), 455–477.

Park, S. H., Zhou, N., & Ungson, G. 2013. *Rough Diamonds: The Four Traits of Successful Breakout Enterprises in BRIC Countries*. San Francisco, CA: Jossey-Bass/Wiley.

Patrakhina, T. 2015. Strategic potential of the organization: Russian and foreign approaches. *Young Scientist*, 6, 442–444. [Патрахина Т. Стратегический потенциал организации: Российский и зарубежный подходы. Молодой ученый.]

Pedersen, T., & Shaver, J. 2011. Internationalization revisited: The big step hypothesis. *Global Strategic Journal*, 1(3–4), 263–274.

Peng, M. W., 2002. Towards an institution-based view of business strategy. *Asia Pacific Journal of Management*, 19(2–3), 251–267.

Peng, M. W., 2003. Institutional transitions and strategic choices. *Academy of Management Review*, 28(2), 275–296.

Peng, M. W., 2012. The global strategy of emerging multinationals from China. *Global Strategy Journal*, 2(2), 97–107.

Penrose, E. 1959. *The Theory of the Growth of the Firm*. New York, NY: Oxford University Press.

Péres, W. (ed.). 1998. *Grandes empresas y grupos indstriales latinoamericanos: Expansión y desafíos en la era de la apertura y la globalización*. Mexico City, Mexico: Siglo Vientiuno Editores.

Phylaktis, K., & Xia, L. 2006. Sources of firms' industry and country effects in emerging markets. *Journal of International Money and Finance*, 25, 459–475.

Piekkari, R., Welch, C., & Paavilainen, E. 2009. The case study as disciplinary convention: Evidence from international business journals. *Organizational Research Methods*, 12(3), 567–589.

Portafolio. 2011. Sigue creciendo la inversión colombiana en el exterior, July 18, www.portafolio.co/economia/finanzas/sigue-creciendo-inversion-colombiana-exterior-134536.

Portafolio. 2012. 10 movidas empresariales del 2012, December 24, www.porta folio.co/negocios/empresas/conozca-10-movidas-empresariales-2012-colom bia-112498.

Portafolio. 2014. Auge de empresas colombianas que invierten en el exterior, July 9, www.portafolio.co/negocios/empresas/auge-empresas-colombianas-inv ierten-exterior-52758.

Portafolio. 2017. Grupo Bios: La apuesta es actor clave en agroindustria, April 27, www.portafolio.co/negocios/empresas/grupo-bios-la-apuesta-es-ser-actor-clav e-en-agroindustria-505351.

Porter, M. E. 1980. *Competitive Strategy: Techniques for Analyzing Industries and Competitors*. New York: Simon and Schuster.

Porter, M. E. 1985. *Competitive Advantage*. New York, NY: Free Press.

Porter, M. E. 1998. Clusters and the new economics of competition. *Harvard Business Review*, 76(6), 77–90.

Prahalad, C. K., & Doz, Y. 1987. *The Multinational Mission: Balancing Local Demands and Global Vision*. New York, NY: Free Press.

Prashantham, S., & Young, S. 2011. Post-entry speed of international new ventures. *Entrepreneurship Theory and Practice*, 35(2), 275–292.

Ramamurti, R. 2012. What is really different about emerging market multinationals? *Global Strategy Journal*, 2(1), 41–47.

Ramamurti, R., & Singh, J. V. (eds.). 2009. *Emerging Multinationals from Emerging Markets*. New York, NY: Cambridge University Press.

Ramasamy, B., Yeung, M., & Laforet, S. 2012. China's outward foreign direct investment: Location choice and firm ownership. *Journal of World Business*, 47 (1), 17–25.

Ramsey, J. R., de Magalhães, A. F., Forteza, J. H., & Junior, J. F. 2010. International value creation: An alternative model for Latin American multinationals. *GCG: Revista de globalización, competitividad y gobernabilidad*, 4(3), 62–83.

Razo, C., & Calderón, A. 2010. Chile's outward FDI and its policy context. Columbia FDI Profiles, March 12. New York, NY: Vale Columbia Center on Sustainable International Investment.

Richard-Jorba, R. 2006. Formación, crisis y reorientaciones de la vitivinicultura en Mendoza y San Juan, 1970–2000. Aportes para el estudio del sector en la Argentina. *Boletín geográfico*, 28, 79–122.

RMB Global Markets. 2017. *Where to Invest in Africa:*, 2016/2017 edn., www .rmb.co.za/globalmarkets/wtiia2017/contactForm.html.

Rock, M., Murphy, J. T., Rasiah, R., van Seters, P., & Managi, S. 2009. A hard slog, not a leap frog: Globalization and sustainability transitions in developing Asia. *Technological Forecasting and Social Change*, 76(2), 241–254.

Rodengen, J. L. 2009. *The History of Embraer*. Fort Lauderdale, FL: Write Stuff Enterprises.

Roersen, M. J., Kraaijenbrink, J., & Groen, A. J. 2013. Marketing ignorance and the validity of Narver and Slater's MKTOR scale in high-tech Russian firms. *Journal of Product Innovation Management*, 30(3), 545–559.

Roldán, A. 2015. Colcafé: Una empresa colombiana con alto reconocimiento en el mundo del café industrializado, in O. Morales, A. Roldán, & J. Kim (eds.), *Casos exitosos de empresas latinoamericanas en Asia*. Cuajimalpa de Morelos, Mexico: Cengage Learning Editores.

Rosenberg, N. 1994. *Exploring the Black Box*. New York, NY: Cambridge University Press.

Rossi, L. 2015. Como a WEG se tornou a empresa do ano de Melhores e Maiores. *Exame*, August 19, http://exame.abril.com.br/revista-exame/o-motor-do-cresci mento/.

Rowe, A. J., Mason, R. O., Dickel, K. E., et al. 1994. *Strategic Management: A Methodological Approach*, 4th edn. Reading, MA: Addison-Wesley.

Rugman, A. M. 2014. Subsidiary specific advantages and multiple embedded-ness in multinational enterprises. *Academy of Multinational Enterprises*, 7, 1–8.

Rugman, A. M., & Verbeke, A. 2004. A perspective on regional and global strategies of multinational enterprises. *Journal of International Business Studies*, 35(1), 3–18.

Rugman, A. M., & Verbeke, A. 2008. A new perspective on the regional and global strategies of MNE service firms. *Management International Review*, 48, 397–411.

Rumelt, R. P. 1982. Diversification strategy and profitability. *Strategic Management Journal*, 3(4), 359–369.

Russo, J. 2012. Emerging markets, emerging opportunities, www.nielsen.com/ wp-content/uploads/sites/3/2019/04/Emerging-Markets-Global-Forces-Whit e-Paper-Mar-2012.pdf.

Saa, J. 2013. El cerebro detrás de Brainz. Apps.co, October 23, https://apps.co/ comunicaciones/noticias/el-cerebro-detras-de-brainz/.

Safiullin, N., & Safiullin, L. 2008. *Competitiveness: Theory and Methodology*. Kazan: Center for Innovative Technologies. [Сафиуллин Н., Сафиуллин Л. Конкурентоспособность: Теория и методология.]

Sainz, A. 2004. Farmacias Similares anuncia su ingreso al mercado local, www .lanacion.com.ar/economia/llega-una-nueva-cadena-mexicana-de-farmacias-nid608955.

Santiso, J. 2008. The emergence of Latin multinationals. *CEPAL Review*, 95, 7–30.

Sapienza, H. J., Autio, E., George, G., & Zahra, S. A. 2006. A capabilities perspective on the effects of early internationalization on firm survival and growth. *Academy of Management Review*, 31(4), 914–933.

Sarith, M. 2004. *Competitiveness: Multilevel Analysis*. Moscow: Sinistor. [Саритх М. Конкурентоспособность: Многоуровневый анализ.]

Sauvant, K. (ed.). 2009. *The Rise of Transnational Corporations from Emerging Markets: Threat or Opportunity?* Northampton, MA: Edward Elgar.

Schwalb, M. M., & Casafranca, J. C., 2000. *Casos ganadores de los Premios MAX/ EFFIE*, http://repositorio.up.edu.pe/bitstream/handle/11354/74/AE37.pdf? sequence=1.

Selznick, P. 1957. *Leadership in Administration.* New York, NY: Harper.

Sethi, S. P., & Elango, B. 1999. The influence of "country of origin" on multinational corporation global strategy: A conceptual framework. *Journal of International Management,* 5(4), 285–298.

Seyhan, M., Ayas, S., Sonmez, U., & Uğurlu, Ö. Y. 2017. The relationship between strategic capabilities and competitive performance: The moderating role of internal cooperation. *International Journal of Academic Research in Economics and Management Sciences,* 6(1), 146–161.

Shane, S. 2000. Prior knowledge and the discovery of entrepreneurial opportunities. *Organization Science,* 11, 448–469.

Sheth, J. N. 2011. Impact of emerging markets on marketing: Rethinking existing perspectives and practices. *Journal of Marketing,* 75 (4), 166–182.

Shinkle, G. A., & Kriauciunas, A. P. 2012. The impact of current and founding institutions on strength of competitive aspirations in transition economies. *Strategic Management Journal,* 33(4), 448–458.

Slay, B. 1994. *The Polish Economy.* Princeton, NJ: Princeton University Press.

Smallbone, D., Leig, R., & North, D. 1995. The characteristics and strategies of high growth SMEs. *International Journal of Entrepreneurial Behavior & Research,* 1(3), 44–62.

Smirnova, M., Naudé, P., Henneberg, S. C., Mouzas, S., & Kouchtch, S. P. 2011. The impact of market orientation on the development of relational capabilities and performance outcomes: The case of Russian industrial firms. *Industrial Marketing Management,* 40(1), 44–53.

Smirnova, M. M., Rebiazina, V. A., & Khomich, S. G. 2017. When does innovation collaboration pay off? The role of relational learning and the timing of collaboration. *Industrial Marketing Management,* 74, 126–137.

Smith, P. B. S., Torres, C., Leong, C.-H., et al. 2012. Are indigenous approaches to achieving influence in business organizations distinctive? A comparative study of guanxi, wasta, jeitinho, svyazi and pulling strings. *International Journal of Human Resource Management,* 23(2), 333–348.

Sol, P., & Kogan, J. 2007. Regional competitive advantage based on pioneering economic reforms: The case of Chilean FDI. *Journal of International Business Studies,* 38, 901–927.

Song, M., & Montoya-Weiss, M. 2001. The effect of perceived technological uncertainty on Japanese new product development. *Academy of Management Journal,* 44(1), 61–80.

Song, X., & Parry, M. 1997. A cross-national comparative study of new product development processes: Japan and the United States. *Journal of Marketing,* 61 (2), 1–18.

Spanos, Y., & Lioukas, S. 2001. An examination into the causal logic of rent generation: Contrasting Porter's competitive strategy framework and the resource-based perspective. *Strategic Management Journal,* 22(10), 907–934.

Stalk, G., Evans, P., & Shulman, L. 1992. Competing on capabilities: The new rules of corporate strategy. *Harvard Business Review,* 70(2), 57–69.

Statista. 2018. Digital Market Outlook: Apparel worldwide.

Stefanini. 2017. Stefanini website, www.stefanini.com.

Steiner, R., & Vallejo, H. 2010. Economic history, 1819–1999, in R. A. Hudson (ed.), *Colombia, a Country Study*, 141–207. Washington, DC: Library of Congress.

Tallman, S. and Yip, G. S., 2009 Strategy and the Multinational Enterprise. In Rugman, A. (ed.). *The Oxford Handbook of International Business*. Oxford University Press.

Tanus, A., Salinas, R., Peña, E., & Yong, G. 2008. Diversas intervenciones en la inauguración de la planta ensambladora de motocicletas Italika. Transcript of presentation, Presidencia de la República, Toluca, Mexico, September 10.

Teece, D. J. 2007. Explicating dynamic capabilities: The nature and microfoundations of (sustainable) enterprise performance. *Strategic Management Journal*, 28(13), 1319–1350.

Teece, D. J. 2014. A dynamic capabilities-based entrepreneurial theory of the multinational enterprise. *Journal of International Business Studies*, 45(1), 8–37.

Teece, D. J., Pisano, G. and Shuen, A., 1997. Dynamic capabilities and strategic management. *Strategic Management Journal*, 18(7), 509–533.

Thite, M., Wilkinson, A., & Budhwar, P. 2016. *Emerging Indian Multinationals: Strategic Players in a Multipolar World*. Oxford, UK: Oxford University Press.

Tian, T., & Wu, C. 2015. *The Huawei Story*. Thousand Oaks, CA: Sage.

Titan Company. (n.d.). About us [web page], www.titancompany.in/about-us.

Tomlinson, B. R. 1993. *The New Cambridge History of India*. Cambridge, UK: Cambridge University Press.

Transparency International. 2018. *Corruption Perceptions Index*, www.transparency.org/cpi2018.

Trąpczynski, P., & Gorynia, M. 2017. A double-edged sword? The moderating effects of control on firm capabilities and institutional distance in explaining foreign affiliate performance. *International Business Review*, 26(4), 697–709.

Treid. 2017. Treid website, www.treid.co.

Tse, E. 2015. *China's Disruptors: How Alibaba, Xiaomi, Tencent, and Other Companies are Changing the Rules of Business*. New York, NY: Portfolio/Penguin.

UNCTAD [United Nations Conference on Trade and Development]. (n.d.). *UNCTADStat Reports*, https://unctadstat.unctad.org/wds/ReportFolders/repo rtFolders.aspx?sCS_referer=&sCS_ChosenLang=en.

UNCTAD. 2006. *World Investment Report 2006 – FDI from Developing and Transition Economies: Implications for Development*, https://unctad.org/en/docs/ wir2006_en.pdf.

UNCTAD. 2013. *World Investment Report 2013 – Global Value Chains: Investment and Trade for Development*, https://unctad.org/en/PublicationsLibrary/wi r2013_en.pdf.

UNCTAD. 2014. *World Investment Report 2014 – Investing in the SDGs: An Action Plan*, https://unctad.org/en/PublicationsLibrary/wir2014_en.pdf.

UNCTAD. 2015a. UNCTADStat, https://unctadstat.unctad.org/wds/ReportF olders/reportFolders.aspx.

UNCTAD. 2015b. *World Investment Report 2015 – Reforming International Investment Governance*, http://unctad.org/en/PublicationsLibrary/wir2015_en.pdf.

UNCTAD. 2016. *World Investment Report 2016 – Investor Nationality: Policy Challenges*, https://unctad.org/en/PublicationsLibrary/wir2016_en.pdf.

UNCTAD. 2017a. UNCTADStat, http://unctadstat.unctad.org/wds/ReportFol ders/reportFolders.aspx.

UNCTAD. 2017b. *World Investment Report 2017 – Investment and the Digital Economy.* http://unctad.org/en/PublicationsLibrary/wir2017_en.pdf.

UNCTAD. 2018. Foreign direct investment flows and stock, https://unctadstat .unctad.org/wds/ReportFolders/reportFolders.aspx.

UNCTAD. 2019a. UNCTADStat, https://unctadstat.unctad.org/wds/Report Folders/reportFolders.aspx?sCS_ChosenLang=en.

UNCTAD. 2019b. World Investment Report: Annex Tables, https://unctad.org/ en/Pages/DIAE/World%20Investment%20Report/Annex-Tables.aspx.

Unger, J., Rauch, A., Frese, M., & Rosenbousch, N. 2011. Human capital and entrepreneurial success: A meta-analytical review. *Journal of Business Venturing,* 26, 341–358.

Value Stocks. (n.d.). NALCO history, https://stock-financials.valuestocks.in/en/ nalco-company-history.

Vassolo, R. S., De Castro, J. O., & Gomez-Mejia, L. R. 2011. Managing in Latin America: Common issues and a research agenda, *Academy of Management Perspectives,* 25(4), 22–36.

Velez-Ocampo, J., & Gonzalez-Perez, M. A. 2015. International expansion of Colombian firms: Understanding their emergence in foreign markets. *Cuadernos de administración,* 51(2), 189–215.

Verhoef, G. 2016. *Latecomer Challenge: African Multinationals from the Periphery.* ERSA Research Brief, https://econrsa.org/system/files/publications/research_ briefs/research_brief_61.pdf

Vijande, M. L., Pérez, M. J., González, L. I., & Casielles, R. V. 2005. Organisational learning and market orientation: Interface and effects on performance. *Industrial Marketing Management,* 34(3), 187–202.

Villafaña, M. 2017. Interview with Miguel Montoya, September 25.

Villaseñor, T. 2017. Mesón de la Misericordia recibe premio de Fundación Simi. *El Informador,* July 28, www.informador.com.mx/jalisco/2017/732383/6/meso n-de-la-misericordia-recibe-premio-de-fundacion-simi.htm.

Von Hippel, E. 1988. *The Sources of Innovation.* New York, NY: Oxford University Press.

Vorozhbit, O. 2008. Competitive advantages in the system of competitive relations within organizations. *Economic Sciences,* 3(40), 258–261. [Ворожбит О. Конкурентные преимущества в системе конкурентных отношений организации. Экономические науки.]

Wach, K. 2017. Exploring the role of ownership in international entrepreneurship: How does ownership affect internationalisation of Polish firms? *Entrepreneurial Business and Economics Review,* 5(4), 205–224.

Wang, L. and Zajac, E. J., 2007. Alliance or acquisition? A dyadic perspective on interfirm resource combinations. *Strategic Management Journal,* 28(13), 1291–1317.

Wang, S. 2014. *Capability Upgrading by Emerging Economy Enterprises.* PhD thesis, University of Miami, USA.

Wang, S., & Cuervo-Cazurra, A. 2017. Overcoming human capital voids in underdeveloped countries. *Global Strategy Journal,* 7(1), 36–57.

Wang, S. L., Luo, Y., Lu, X., Sun, J., & Maksimov, V. 2014. Autonomy delegation to foreign subsidiaries: An enabling mechanism for emerging market multinationals. *Journal of International Business Studies*, 45(2), 111–130.

Wąsowska, A., Obłój, K., & Ciszewska-Mlinarič, M. 2016. Virtuous and vicious learning cycles in the internationalization of emerging market firms. *European Journal of International Management*, 10(1), 105–125.

Weg. 2017. Weg website, www.weg.net.

Wernerfelt, B., 1984. A resource-based view of the firm. *Strategic Management Journal*, 5(2), 171–180.

Williamson, P., Ramamurti, R., Fleury, A., & Fleury, M. T. (eds). 2013. *Competitive Advantages of Emerging Country Multinationals*. Cambridge, UK: Cambridge University Press.

Winter, S. 2000. The satisficing principle in capability learning. *Strategic Management Journal*, 21, 981–996.

Wong, K. Y. 2005. Critical success factors for implementing knowledge management in small and medium enterprises. *Industrial Management & Data Systems*, 105(3), 261–279.

World Bank. (n.d.). *Doing Business*, www.doingbusiness.org.

World Bank. 2017. World Development Indicators, https://openknowledge.worldbank.org/handle/10986/26447.

World Bank. 2018a. The World Bank in Kazakhstan: Country snapshot, http://pubdocs.worldbank.org/en/684001524140579949/Kazakhstan-Snapshot-Spring2018.pdf.

World Bank. 2018b. World Development Indicators, https://databank.worldbank.org/reports.aspx?source=world-development-indicators.

World Bank. 2018c. Inflation, GDP deflator – Argentina, https://data.worldbank.org/indicator/NY.GDP.DEFL.KD.ZG?locations=AR.

World Bank. 2019a. *Doing Business 2019: Training for Reform*. World Bank, https://openknowledge.worldbank.org/handle/10986/30438.

World Bank. 2019b. Foreign direct investment, net outflows (BoP, current US $) – China, https://data.worldbank.org/indicator/BM.KLT.DINV.CD.WD?end=2017&locations=CN&start=1982&view=chart.

World Bank. 2019c. Unemployment, total – South Africa, https://data.worldbank.org/indicator/SL.UEM.TOTL.NE.ZS?locations=ZA&most_recent_year_desc=false.

World Bank Group. 2017. *Global Investment Competitiveness Report 2017/2018: Foreign Investor Perspectives and Policy Implications*. Washington, DC: World Bank.

World Economic Forum. (n.d.). *Global Competitiveness Reports*, www.weforum.org.

World Economic Forum. 2009. *Global Competitiveness Report*, www.weforum.org/reports/global-competitiveness-report-2009-2010.

Worldometer. (n.d.). Russia population (live), www.worldometers.info/world-population/russia-population/.

Wright, M., Filatotchev, I., Hoskisson, R. E., & Peng, M. W. 2005. Strategy research in emerging economies: Challenging the conventional wisdom. *Journal of Management Studies*, 42(1), 1–33.

Wrona, T., & Trąpczynski, P. 2012. Re-explaining international entry modes: Interaction and moderating effects on entry modes of pharmaceutical companies into transition economies. *European Management Journal*, 30(4), 295–315.

Yamin, M., & Andersson, U. 2011. Subsidiary importance in the MNC: What role does internal embeddedness play? *International Business Review*, 20(2), 151–162.

Yang, C., Marlow, P., & Lu, C. 2009. Assessing resources, logistics service capabilities, innovation capabilities, and the performance of container shipping services in Taiwan. *International Journal of Production Economics*, 122(1), 4–20.

Yang, S. 2016. *The Huawei Way: Lessons from an International Tech Giant on Driving Growth by Focusing on Never-Ending Innovation.* New York, NY: McGraw-Hill.

Yergin, D., & Stanislaw, J. 2002. *The Commanding Heights: The Battle for the World Economy.* New York, NY: Simon and Schuster.

Yi, J. J., & Ye, S. X. 2013. *The Haier Way: The Making of a Chinese Business Leader and a Global Brand.* Dumont, NJ: Homa & Sekey.

Yin, R. K. 2009. *Case Study Research, Design and Method*, 4th edn. London, UK, and Thousand Oaks, CA: Sage.

Yip, G. S. 2000. *Asian Advantage: Key Strategies for Winning in the Asia-Pacific Region (Updated Edition – After the Crisis).* Cambridge, MA: Perseus.

Yiu, D. W., Lau, C. and Bruton, G. D., 2007. International venturing by emerging economy firms: The effects of firm capabilities, home country networks, and corporate entrepreneurship. *Journal of International Business Studies*, 38(4), 519–540.

Zaheer, S. 1995. Overcoming the liability of foreignness. *Academy of Management Journal*, 38(2), 341–363.

Zahra, S. A., Ireland, R. D., & Hitt, M. A. 2000. International expansion by new venture firms: International diversity, mode of market entry, technological learning, and performance. *Academy of Management Journal*, 43(5), 925–950.

Zanni, P. 2013. *O processo de internacionalização de empresas de serviços profissionais: O caso da integration consultoria.* Doctoral dissertation, Escola de Administração de Empresas de São Paulo, Fundação Getulio Vargas, Brazil.

Zeng, M. and Williamson, P. J., 2007. *Dragons at Your Door: How Chinese Cost Innovation Is Disrupting Global Competition.* Boston, MA: Harvard Business School Press.

Zhang, J., & He, X. 2014. Economic nationalism and foreign acquisition completion: The case of China. *International Business Review*, 23(1), 212–227.

Zhang, J., Zhou, C., & Ebbers, H. 2011. Completion of Chinese overseas acquisitions: Institutional perspectives and evidence. *International Business Review*, 20(2), 226–238.

Zhao, H., & Luo, Y. 2005. Antecedents of knowledge sharing with peer subsidiaries in other countries: A perspective from subsidiary managers in a foreign emerging market. *Management International Review*, 45(1), 71–97.

Zhao, M. 2006. Conducting R&D in countries with weak intellectual property rights protection. *Management Science*, 52(8), 1185–1199.

Zhao, Y., Lu, Y., & Wang, X. 2013. Organizational unlearning and organizational relearning: A dynamic process of knowledge management. *Journal of Knowledge Management*, 17(6), 902–912.

Index

Acevedo, Jose Maria, 303, 304
Advantech (China), 58–61
Africa. *See also* South Africa; *specific countries*
  multinational enterprises in, 101
    emerging, 101
  South African MNEs in, operations of, 110
Air Astana (Kazakhstan), 190–194
  international expansion of, 191, 192
  international partnerships, 191
  national context for, 193–194
Akimov, Alexey, 200, 202
Alibaba, 1
Alicorp (Peru), 347–350
  distribution network for, 348
  international expansion of, 349
ALTO (Chile), 267–269, 285
  business model of, 267
  internationalization of, 267
  organizational structure of, 269
  research and development strategies, 268–269
"Anti-offshore" law, Russia, 127–129
Aplisens (Poland), 163–167
  internationalization of, 165–166, 191–192
  subsidiaries, 166
Arcor (Argentina), 228–230
  globalization strategies of, 229
  product diversification strategies, 228–229
  strategic capabilities of, 229–230
  vertical integration strategies for, 230
Argentina
  economic context for, 207–211
    under Convertibility Law, 209
    import substitution industrialization policies, 208, 212, 224–225
    after Industrial Revolution, 207
    of international business, 207–211
    in international economy, 209–211

  key economic indicators, 210
  openness of markets, 208–211
  protectionism, 208–211
  emerging market multinational enterprises in, 207–208
  foreign direct investment in, 207
    in Grupo ASSA, 220
    in Grupo Bagó, 223
  national firms in, internationalization of, 211
    analysis of, 233–234
    Arcor, 228–230
    Bodega Lagarde, 215–218
    Citricola San Miguel, 218–220
    company profiles for, 213
    financial information for, 213
    firm-level dynamics, 211
    Globant, 225–228
    Grupo ASSA, 220–223
    Grupo Bagó, 223–225
    Grupo Mirgor, 211–215
    under Industrial Promotion Laws, 215
  strategic capabilities, of national firms in, 232
    Arcor, 229–230
    Bodega Lagarde, 216–218
    Citricola San Miguel, 219–220
    client-oriented marketing capabilities, 231
    cross-cultural management capabilities, 222
    entrepreneurship capabilities, 222
    Globant, 227–228
    Grupo ASSA, 221–223
    Grupo Bagó, 224–225
    Grupo Mirgor, 214–215
    managerial capabilities, 225
    marketing-driven capabilities, 217
    organizational capabilities, 211
    production and operations capabilities, 229–230, 231

production capabilities, 214–215, 217, 219–220
research and development capabilities, 224–225
technological capabilities, 208, 227
Audioteka (Poland), 172–174
domestic market, 172
international expansion of, 173–174
AVIC International Holding Company (China), 46–51
Azevedo, Guilherme, 251

B2B models. *See* business-to-business models
Baby First (China), 61–62
as original design manufacturer, 61–62
as original equipment manufacturer, 61–62
banking industry, in Kazakhstan
under banking laws, 202
lack of transparency for, 189
Bartelle, Alexander Grendene, 249
BBVA (Peru), 337
BeitGroup (Chile), 277–280, 284
internationalization of, 278–280
Belmont, Eduardo, 353
Belmont, Fernando, 353
Belmont, Jorge, 353
Belticos (Mexico), 322–324
certification processes for, 322–323
as low-tech firm, 324
Biocon (India), 87–90
biosimilars, production of, 87–89
collaboration with other pharmaceutical firms, 90
human resources at, 89
research and development at, 89
Bodega Lagarde (Argentina), 215–218
international distribution strategies, 217
vertical integration strategies, 216
BPO portfolio. *See* business process outsourcing portfolio
Brainz (Colombia), 301–303
restructuring of, 302
Brazil
economic context of, 235–236
emerging multinational enterprises in. *See also* strategic capabilities
emergence of, 236–238
foreign direct investment in
inward, 237
outward, 236–238
strategic capabilities for EMNEs in, 238, 254, 256. *See also* WEG

country-of-origin effects, 257
Dr.Consulta, 251–253
Fanem, 242–244, 253–256
Grendene, 249–251, 256–257
Integration, 246–249
management-related capabilities, 236
marketing capabilities, 236, 257
market-related capabilities, 236
production capabilities, 257
Stefanini, 244–246, 256–257
technological capabilities, 236
business acumen, 110–113, 120
evolving, 112–113
foundational, 111–112
business process outsourcing (BPO) portfolio, 245
business-to-business (B2B) models, 352
ByTerg (Russia), 142–144
collaboration with Chinese manufacturers, 142
strategic capabilities of, 142–144

Cadavid, Mateo Jaramillo, 294
Canepa, Raul, Jr., 340–341, 342
Canepa, Raul, Sr., 340
Cantol/Canepa Business Group (Peru), 340–342
distribution network, 341
capability maturity model (CMM), 245
Caputo, Antonio, 212
Caputo, Jose Luis, 212
Caputo, Nicolas, 212
Cardoso, Renato, 251
Carrera, Alejandro, 214
Casas del Toqui (Chile), 275–277, 283–284
CEMEX (Mexico), 1
certification processes, 266–267
Belticos, 322–323
Interlub, 318
Chandavarkar, Arun, 89
Chervon (China), 51–54
original design manufacturer, 53
original equipment manufacturer, 51
research and development for, 53–54
Chile
economic growth in, GDP rates, 262
economic outlook, 259–262
concentration of exports, 259–260
national firms in, strategic capabilities of, 281
ALTO, 267–269, 285
BeitGroup, 277–280, 284
Casas del Toqui, 275–277, 283–284

Chile (cont.)
client-relationship capabilities,
267–268
cross-cultural management
capabilities, 283
customer relationship management
capabilities, 274
Derco, 273–275
design capabilities, 278–279
distribution capabilities, 270, 279–280
eClass, 265–267
Forus, 271–273
Kunstmann, 269–271, 284
manufacturing capabilities, 270–271
methodological approach to, 262–263
networking capabilities, 268
political capabilities, 275
relationship capabilities, 283
research and development capabilities,
268–269, 283
outward foreign direct investment in,
258, 260–262, 280–282
China, People's Republic of
ByTerg and, collaboration with manufacturers in, 142
Cultural Revolution in, 43
dimensions of strategic capabilities
innovation capabilities, 60
research and development capabilities,
53, 64
economic growth in, 39
administrative and policy measures for,
43–44
internationalization of, 46–51,
56–57, 64
economic outlook for, 43–46
from 1979 to 1997, 43–44
from 1998 to 2018, 44–46
FDI in
inward, 39
outward, 39, 46
GDP, 39
growth rates for, 44, 45
total merchandise exports, 48
Great Leap Forward in, 43
historical background of, 43–46
industrialization of, 39
MNCs in, 39–43, 54–57. See also specific
companies
high-tech, 46–51, 58–61, 64–66
low-tech, 51–54, 57–58, 61–62
"One Belt, One Road" policy in, 46
-pening-up policy in, 43
strategic capabilities in
for Advantech, 58–61

for AVIC International Holding
Company, 46–51
for Baby First, 61–62
for Chervon, 51–54
for Higer, 62–64
for Sanpower, 54–57
for ShangGong Group, 64–66
for Siwei-Johnson, 57–58
TCS iON in, 81
Citricola San Miguel (Argentina), 218–220
strategic capabilities of, 219–220
Clover Industries (South Africa), 108
CMM. See Capability Maturity Model
Colcafé (Colombia), 296–297
internationalization of, 296
in Japan, international trade partnerships
in, 296, 297
collaborations and partnerships
Air Astana, 191
between Biocon and other
pharmaceutical firms, 90
for economic growth, in Kazakhstan, 187
Granna, and, with foreign distributors,
176–177
Lolimsa, 343–344
between TCS iON and other MNCs, 82
Colombia
capability development, for EMNEs,
289–290, 305–306
Brainz, 301–303
Colcafé, 296–297
comparative analysis of, 305–308
financial data in, 290–292
Grupo Bios, 292–294
Haceb, 303–305
Mattelsa, 294–295
networks for, identification of, 289
New Stetic, 300–301
Sempertex, 298–300
dimensions of strategic capabilities in
knowledge development capabilities,
294–295
marketing-related capabilities,
305–307
networking capabilities, 289
organizational capabilities, 293
production capabilities, 297
relational capabilities, 297, 299,
305–307
research and development capabilities,
295, 298–299
sales capabilities, 297
economic outlook, 287–289
import substitution industrialization
policies, 300

macroeconomic data, 287
outward foreign direct investment in,
    288–289
Community Innovation Survey, 110
competition, economic
  in emerging markets
    diversity in levels of competition, 11
    for local firms, 11
  for Kamaz, 198
    Chinese manufacturers as, 199
  in Kazakhstan, between national
    firms, 206
  for Prochem, 179
  among Russian multinational
    corporations, 130–131
  TCS iON and, 85–86
Convertibility Law, Argentina, 209
cross-cultural management
  capabilities, 374
cultural model reinforcement program, in
    Mexico, 326
Cultural Revolution, in China, 43
customer embedding, in South Africa
    MNEs, 118

D'Angelo, Francisco, 353–355
Deltron (Peru), 350–352
  business-to-business models, 352
Deng Xiaoping, 43
Derco (Chile), 273–275
  government intervention factors, 275
  product diversification, 274
  subsidiary relationships with, 275
distribution networks
  for Alicorp, 348
  for Bodega Lagarde, 217
  for Cantol/Canepa Business Group,
    341
  for Kamaz, 199
  for Kunstmann, 270
diversification of products. See product
    diversification
Dr.Consulta (Brazil), 251–253
  IT capabilities, 252–253

EAUE. See Eurasian Economic Union
eClass (Chile), 265–267
  certification processes, 266–267
  organizational culture of, 266
Ecolab (Russia), 144–147
  in emerging markets, 147
  localization strategies for, 145
  mergers and acquisitions strategies, 146
  research and development strategies,
    145–146

economic competition. See competition
economic growth
  in Chile, 262
  in China, 39
    administrative and policy measures for,
      43–44
    internationalization of, 46–51,
      56–57, 64
  in India, 71
  in Kazakhstan
    GDP, 186–187
    stabilization of, 188
    through strategic partnerships, 187
  in Peru, 338
    GDP and, 339
  in Poland
    "big step hypothesis" for, 156
    five pillars of, 159
    limited resources as factor for, 155–156
    "shock therapy" for, 155
  in Russia, 125
    GDP in, 125
Elektra (Mexico), 329–331
  international expansion of, 330
embeddedness, in South Africa MNEs,
    113–118
  intra-MNE, 113–114
  local, 115, 122
  parent-subsidiary, 114
  regulator, 115–117
  subsidiary-subsidiary, 115
  supplier, 117
Embraer, 1
emerging markets. See also strategic
    capabilities; upgrading of strategic
    capabilities; specific companies; specific
    countries
  access to skilled workers in, 11
  competition in
    diversity in levels of, 11
    for local firms, 11
  Ecolab in, 147
  FDI models, 12–15, 19
  global leaders from, 12–26
    legacy brands, 26
  publicly traded firms, 17–18
  infrastructure challenges in, 11
  intellectual property protections in, 11
  local firms in, economic competition
    against global firms, 11
  in Poland, 180–185
emerging multinational enterprises
    (EMNEs), 101
employee management, in garment
    manufacturing industry, 78

entrepreneurship capabilities, 369–370
EU. *See* European Union
Eurasian Economic Union (EAUE), 188
European Union (EU), Poland accession
    to, 159, 165–166
exports
    from Chile, 259–260
    from China, 48
    from Kazakhstan
        by Tsesna-Astyk in, 204–205
    from Mexico, 310
    from Poland
        Granna, 177–178
        Prochem, 179

Fabre, André, 329
Fabre, Kid, 329
Falkowski, Ewa, 175–176
Falkowski, Konrad, 175–176
Fanem (Brazil), 242–244
    international expansion strategies,
        242–244, 253–256
    product diversification, 244
Farmacias Similares (Mexico), 326–327
    cultural model reinforcement program
        in, 326
    international expansion of, 326
FDI. *See* foreign direct investment
firm-level capabilities, 379
food and beverage production and
        distribution
    in Argentina, 218–220, 228–230
    in Chile, 269–271
        Casas del Toqui, 275–277
food production and distribution, in
        Argentina, 218–220, 228–230
foreign direct investment (FDI). *See also*
        inward foreign direct investment;
        outward foreign direct investment
    in Argentina, 207
    in Grupo ASSA, 220
    in Grupo Bagó, 223
    in Brazil
        inward, 237
        outward, 236–238
    in global emerging markets, 12–15, 19
    IMF countries and, 13, 37
    in India, 72–73
        outward, 72–73
    in Mexico, 311–314
    in Peru, 358
    in Poland
        outward, 155, 162
        trends in, 159
    in Russia, 126–129

under "Anti-offshore" law, 127–129
    inward, 126–127
    outward, 126–129
    recipients of, 129
    in South Africa, 103–106
        inward FDI, 103, 104
        outward FDI, 103, 105, 106
    UNCTAD and, 12–15, 19
Forus (Chile), 271–273
    business model for, 272–273
    internationalization of, 272–273
    vertical integration strategies, 273

Ganapathi, S., 80
garment manufacturing industry
    fragmentation in, 79–80
    global economic impact of, 79–80
    in India, 77–80
        employee management in, 78
        under Multi-Fibre Agreement, 77
        negative publicity about, 79
        production planning in, 78–79
Gazprom Marketing & Trading (GM&T)
        (Russia), 138–142
    global expansion of, 140–141
GDP. *See* gross domestic product
general sales capabilities, 363–365, 368,
        373–374
globalization. *See also* internationalization
    of Arcor, 229
    of multinational enterprises, in India, 73
Globant (Argentina), 225–228
    IT services, 226–227
    strategic capabilities of, 227–228
GM&T. *See* Gazprom Marketing &
        Trading
Gokaldas Exports (India), 77–80
Gomez, Francisco, 296–297
González, Alejandro, 302
Granna (Poland), 175–178
    collaborations with foreign distributors,
        176–177
    exports by, revenue generation through,
        177–178
    international expansion of, 176
    product diversification, 177
Great Leap Forward, in China, 43
Gref, German, 202
Grendene (Brazil), 249–251, 256–257
    product development, 249–250
    vertical integration strategies, 250
gross domestic product (GDP)
    of China, 39
        growth rates for, 44, 45
    of Kazakhstan, 186–187

of Mexico, 310
of Peru, 339
of Poland, 157, 159
of Russia, 125
of South Africa, 102
Grupo ASSA (Argentina), 220–223
    foreign direct investment in, 220
    strategic capabilities of, 221–223
Grupo Bagó (Argentina), 223–225
    foreign direct investment in, 223
    under import substitution
        industrialization policies,
        224–225
    international expansion of, 225
Grupo Bios (Colombia), 292–294
    commodity management, 293
    product diversity, 292
Grupo Mirgor (Argentina), 211–215
    product diversification, 214
    strategic capabilities of, development of,
        214–215

Haceb (Colombia), 303–305
    internationalization of, 304–305
Haier, 1
health management firms, Dr.Consulta,
    251–253
Higer (China), 62–64
high-tech MNCs
    in China, 46–51, 58–61, 64–66
    in Mexico, 315–316
Huawei, 1
human capital development, by Sberbank,
    201–202
human resources issues, Biocon,
    89

IFDI. See inward foreign direct investment
IMF. See International Monetary Fund
imitation method, for upgrading of strategic
    capabilities, 29–30
import substitution industrialization (ISI)
    policies
    in Argentina, 208, 212, 224–225
    in Colombia, 300
imports
    from Mexico, 310
    Polish, 159
incorporation methods
    innovation as element of, 31–32
    for upgrading of strategic capabilities,
        31–33
India
    demographics for, 73
    dimensions of strategic capabilities

    adjusting to poor infrastructure
        capabilities, 96
    design capabilities, 80, 99
    entrepreneurial capabilities, 71, 96
    hi-tech capabilities, 75–76
    internal resource development cap-
        abilities, 96
    manufacturing capabilities, 71, 80, 89
    marketing capabilities, 97
    political and negotiating capabil-
        ities, 96
    product/service capabilities, 97
    research and development capabilities,
        89, 93
    sourcing capabilities, 80
    strategic capabilities, 73
    economic growth in, 71
    economic outlook for, 71–76
    foreign direct investment in, 72–73
        outward, 72–73
    garment manufacturing industry in,
        77–80
    employee management in, 78
    under Multi-Fibre Agreement, 77
    negative publicity about, 79
    production planning in, 78–79
    multinational enterprises in, 71–72. See
        also Tata Consultancy Services iON;
        specific companies
    Biocon, 87–90
    case studies, 74, 98–100
    globalization of, 73
    Gokaldas Exports, 77–80
    interviews about, 76–77
    during licensing era, 75–76
    Titan, 90–96
    state-owned enterprises in, 73–75
    strategic capabilities in, for firms
    analysis of, 96–98
    modes of acquisition, 98
    summary of, 96
Industrial Promotion Laws, Argentina, 215
Industrial Revolution, Argentina, 207
industry-level capabilities, 379
information technology (IT) companies
    Dr.Consulta, 252–253
    Globant, 226–227
    Neoris, 320–322
    Sportmaster, 194
    Stefanini, 244–245
    TCS iON and, 81
Integration (Brazil), 246–249
    international expansion of, 247–248
integration method, for upgrading of
    strategic capabilities, 30–31

intellectual property (IP), in emerging
    markets, protections in, 11
Interlub (Mexico), 316–320
    certification strategies, 318
    internationalization of, 319
    product development by, 319
internal development method, for
    upgrading of strategic capabilities,
    33–34
international finance service firms, 107
International Monetary Fund (IMF), FDI
    and, 13, 37
internationalization, of firms
    in Brazil
        Integration, 247–248
        WEG, 239–240
    in Chile
        ALTO, 267
        BeitGroup, 278–280
        Forus, 272–273
        Kunstmann, 269–270
    in Colombia
        Colcafé, 296
        Haceb, 304–305
    in India
        TCS iON, 81–83
        Titan, 91–92
    in Kazakhstan, 206
        Sberbank, 200
        Tsesna-Astyk, 204
    in Mexico
        Elektra, 330
        Farmacias Similares, 326
        Interlub, 319
        KidZania, 328
    in Peru
        Alicorp, 349
        Lolimsa, 344
        Yobel, 353–354
    in Poland, 165–166
        Aplisens, 165–166
        Granna, 176
    in Russia
        Ecolab, 147
        Gazprom Marketing & Trading,
            140–141
        SIBUR, 137–138
intra-MNE embeddedness, in South Africa
    MNEs, 113–114
inward foreign direct investment (IFDI), 13
    in Brazil, 237
    in China, 39
    in Russia, 126–127
    in South Africa, 103, 104
IP. See intellectual property

ISI policies. See import substitution
    industrialization policies
IT. See information technology

Jadue, Álvaro, 277–278
Jadue, Jorge, 277–278
Japan, Colcafé in, international trade
    partners with, 296, 297

Kamaz (Kazakhstan), 197–199
    distribution network for, expansion
        of, 199
    global economic competition for, 198
        Chinese manufacturers as, 199
    maintenance system in, integration
        of, 199
    product development, 198
Kazakhstan
    banking sector in, lack of transparency
        for, 189
        under banking laws, 202
    dimensions of strategic capabilities, in
        MNCs
        brand capabilities, 198, 204
        brand management capabilities, 195
        distribution and service network
            capabilities, 199
        distribution capabilities, 197
        engineering capabilities, 198
        management of regulatory
            relationships capabilities, 202
        manufacturing capabilities, 197,
            198, 204
        marketing capabilities, 197, 204
        technical capabilities, 195
        technology capabilities, 201
    economic growth of
        GDP, 186–187
        stabilization of, 188
        through strategic partnerships, 187
    economic profile of, 186–189
        foreign assets, 188
        lack of diversification in, 188
        socioeconomic indicators, 187
    in Eurasian Economic Union, 188
    national firms in
        Air Astana, 190–194
        domestic competition between, 206
        Elektra, 329–331
        internationalization of, 206
        Kamaz, 197–199
        Sberbank, 199–203
        Sportmaster, 194–197
        Tsesna-Astyk, 203–205
        types of, 190

outward foreign direct investment in,
    188–189
KidZania (Mexico), 327–329
    internationalization of, 328
Kooptech Cinema (Poland), 174–175
    research and development by, 175
Krzanowski, Adam, 167
Krzanowski, Jerzy, 167
Kunstmann (Chile), 269–271, 284
    distribution networks for, 270
    internationalization of, 269–270
Kunstmann, Armin, 269, 270

legacy brands, 26
licensing
    in India, 75–76
    in India, for multinational enterprises,
        75–76
Liendo, Rolando, 342–343
local embeddedness, in South Africa
        MNEs, 115, 122
local product capabilities, 363–365
Lolimsa (Peru), 342–345
    international partnerships with,
        343–344
    internationalization of, 344
    research and development by, 343
    under WIPO agreements, 343
Longquan Pan, 51
Lopez, Abraham, 342–343
low-tech MNCs
    in China, 51–54, 57–58, 61–62
    in Mexico, 315–316
        Belticos, 324

M&A. See mergers and acquisitions
maintenance systems, for Kamaz, 199
management-related capabilities, 379
    in Brazil, 236
marketing capabilities, for Brazil EMNEs,
        236, 257
Martinez, Ezaquiel, 342–343
Mattelsa (Colombia), 294–295
    research and development for, 294–295
    target marketing by, 295
mergers and acquisitions (M&A)
    for Ecolab, 146
    Nowy Styl and, 169–170
    for Sanpower, 56–57
    for Sberbank, 202–203
Mexico
    developing capabilities, for EMNEs, 315
        Belticos, 322–324
        CEMEX, 1
        comparative analysis of, 331–336

Elektra, 329–331
Farmacias Similares, 326–327
for high-tech firms, 315–316
Interlub, 316–320
KidZania, 327–329
for low-tech firms, 315–316, 324
Neoris, 320–322
operations management capabilities,
    334–335
product management capabilities,
    331–333, 334
relationship capabilities, 331–333
resources in, 332
service capabilities, 334
for service firms, 315–316
Vidanta, 324–325
dimensions of strategic capabilities, 332
    adaptability to global needs
        capabilities, 335
    general sales capabilities, 330
    local product adaptation
        capabilities, 327
    location capabilities, 324
    outstanding human resources
        capabilities, 335
    political capabilities, 324, 325,
        327, 331
    production capabilities, 320
    production management capabilities,
        333, 334–335
    product/service capabilities, 334
    relationship capabilities, 320, 322,
        324, 325, 328–329, 333
    understanding of clients' needs
        capabilities, 335
economic context for, 310–315
    export of goods, 310
    import of goods, 310
    proximity to USA as factor for, 311
    by sector, 313–315
    small and medium enterprises, 310
economic growth, GDP and, 310
foreign direct investment, 311–314
    in international companies, 312–313
    outward, 312–313
Migoya, Martin, 228
Mittal, Arcelor, 72
Mittal, Lakshmi, 72
MNCs. See multinational corporations
MNEs. See multinational enterprises
Montoya, Santiago Peidrahíta, 292
Multi-Fibre Agreement, in garment
        manufacturing industry, 77
multinational corporations (MNCs).
        See also specific countries

multinational corporations (cont.)
    in China, 39–43, 54–57. *See also specific
        companies*
    high-tech MNCs, 46–51, 58–61,
        64–66
    low-tech MNCs, 51–54, 57–58, 61–62
    TCS iON partnerships with, 82
multinational enterprises (MNEs) *See also
        specific countries, specific companies*
    in Africa, 101
        emerging MNEs, 101
    in India. *See* India

Nedbank Group (South Africa), 108
Neoris (Mexico), as IT firm, 320–322
New Stetic (Colombia), 300–301
    import substitution industrialization
        policies, 300
    product diversification, 301
Nigeria, 114
Nowy Styl (Poland), 167–171, 185
    domestic market for, growth in, 168
    global expansion of, 168–169
        into Ukraine, 168–169
    mergers and acquisition and, 169–170
    product diversification, 169

ODM. *See* original design manufacturer
OEM. *See* original equipment manufacturer
OFDI. *See* outward foreign direct
        investment
"One Belt, One Road" policy, in China, 46
opening-up policy, in China, 43
operations management capabilities, in
        Mexican EMNEs, 334–335
original design manufacturer (ODM)
    Baby First, 61–62
    Chervon, 53
original equipment manufacturer (OEM)
    Baby First, 61–62
    Chervon, 51, 53
outward foreign direct investment (OFDI),
        13–15, 16
    in Argentina, 207–208
    in Brazil, 236–238
    in Chile, 258, 260–262, 280–282
    in China, 39
    in Colombia, 288–289
    in India, 72–73
    in Kazakhstan, 188–189
    in Mexico, 312–313
    in Panama, 285
    in Poland, 155, 162
    in Russia, 126–129
    in South Africa, 103, 105, 106

Padilla, Pedro, 330–331
Panama, outward foreign direct investment
        in, 285
parent–subsidiary embeddedness, in South
        Africa MNEs, 114
partnerships. *See* collaborations and
        partnerships
People's Republic of China. *See* China,
        People's Republic of
Pereira, Jose Angel, 216
Peru
    economic context for, 338–339, 358
        trade agreements in, 338
    economic growth in, 338
        GDP and, 339
    foreign direct investment in, 358
    strategic capabilities, in multinational
        corporations
        Alicorp, 347–350
        BBVA, 337
        brand management capabilities,
            348–349
        Cantol/Canepa Business Group,
            340–342
        competitive capabilities, 340–341
        cross-cultural management
            capabilities, 344, 346
        Deltron, 350–352
        Lolimsa, 342–345
        managerial capabilities, 346, 351, 357
        manufacturing capabilities, 355–357
        marketing capabilities, 341
        operational capabilities, 346
        procurement capabilities, 351, 352
        product and services capabilities, 357
        product management capabilities, 341
        relational capabilities, 344
        research and development capabilities,
            341, 344, 347, 357
        Resemin Group, 345–347
        supply chain management capabilities,
            355–357
        Yobel, 352–355
Pescarmona, Luis Menotti, 216
Pescarmona, Sofia, 216
Pliauzer, Rallys, 223–224
Pogodina, Daria, 147, 148
Poland
    dimensions of strategic capabilities, 182
        business modeling capabilities, 174
        customer service capabilities, 175
        design capabilities, 170
        games development capabilities, 175
        local responsiveness capabilities, 156
        management capabilities, 156

managing external environments
    capabilities, 181
marketing capabilities, 181
obtaining resources capabilities, 181
operations and management
    capabilities, 181
product and technology
    capabilities, 166
product development capabilities, 167,
    171, 177–178
products/services capabilities, 181
relational capabilities, 168, 169, 174,
    177–178
research and development capabilities,
    171, 175
economic growth in
"big step hypothesis" for, 156
five pillars of, 159
limited resources as factor for, 155–156
"shock therapy" for, 155
economic profile of, 155–157
after accession to EU, 159,
    165–166
during Communist regime, 155
exports as part of, 157, 162
GDP, 157, 159
imports as part of, 159
institutional characteristics of,
    160–161
international trade, 159
political transition (1989–2017) as
    factor in, 158–162
foreign direct investment in
outward, 155, 162
trends in, 159
national firms in, 156
Aplisens, 163–167
Audioteka, 172–174
Granna, 175–178
internationalization of, 165–166
Kooptech Cinema, 174–175
Nowy Styl, 167–171, 185
political system influenced by,
    160–161
Prochem, 178–180
strategic capabilities for, 180–185
political system in
national firms impacted by, 160–161
transition of (1989–2017) as factor in,
    158–162
political and negotiating capabilities, 378
private label development, 195
Prochem (Poland), 178–180
domestic market for, 179–180
export of services, 179

international contracts, 178–179
international economic competition
    for, 179
product development
by Grendene, 249–250
by Interlub, 319
by Kamaz, 198
by Resemin Group, 347
by Sberbank, 201
product diversification
Arcor, 228–229
Derco, 274
Fanem, 244
Granna, 177
Grupo Mirgor, 214
New Stetic, 301
Nowy Styl, 169
product management capabilities, 372–373
in Mexican EMNEs, 331–333, 334
production capabilities, for Brazil
    EMNEs, 257
protectionism, in Argentina economy,
    208–211
Prudnikov, Andrey, 142–143

Quispe, Nestor, 350

Ramos, Patricia, 269
R&D. See research and development
regulator embedding, in South Africa
    MNEs, 115–117
relationship capabilities, 362–363, 372,
    375–377
in Mexican EMNEs, 331–333
research and development (R&D),
    366–367, 377–378
for ALTO, 268–269
at Biocon, 89
at Chervon, 53–54
in Chile, for national firms, 283
in Colombia, Sempertex, 298–299
for Ecolab, 145–146
by Kooptech Cinema, 175
Lolimsa, 343
in Peru MNCs, 357
by Resemin Group, 345–346
by Sportmaster, 195
Resemin Group (Peru), 345–347
product development by, 347
research and development by, 345–346
Russia
economic growth in, 125
    GDP in, 125
economic profile, 125–129
    trade partners, 126

Russia (cont.)
  foreign direct investment in, 126–129
    under "Anti-offshore" law, 127–129
    inward, 126–127
    outward, 126–129
    recipients of, 129
  multinational corporations in, 124–125.
    See also specific companies
    ByTerg, 142–144
    competitiveness of, 130–131
    dynamic capabilities of, 131
    Ecolab, 144–147
    economic profiles of, 134
    foreign assets of, 128
    Gazprom Marketing & Trading,
      138–142
    low transparency of, 129
    political sanctions against, 141–142
    SIBUR, 136, 137–138
    Swilar, 147–149
    trade partners with, 126
  strategic capabilities, of MNCs in,
    124–125
    customer orientation capabilities,
      143–144
    definition of, 153
    diversification capabilities, 145–146
    general sales capabilities, 151–153
    identification of, 150
    innovative capabilities, 142–143,
      145–146
    market knowledge capabilities,
      143–144
    marketing-related capabilities, 131
    mergers and acquisitions
      capabilities, 146
    obtaining resources capabilities,
      151–153
    organizational capabilities, 130
    reliability of equipment
      capabilities, 143
    research and development
      capabilities, 146
    service capabilities, 143
    skills capabilities, 151–153
    specialist capabilities, 144
    sustainability capabilities, 145–146
Salinas, Richard, 330–331
Sanpower (China), 54–57
  mergers and acquisition for, 56–57
Sberbank (Kazakhstan), 199–203
  human capital development, 201–202
  international markets for, 200
  mergers and acquisitions for, 202–203
  product development by, 201

technological capabilities, 201
Schmid, Tobias, 147
Schmidt, Arthur, 242
Schneider, Georg, 147
Sempertex (Colombia), 298–300
  research and development for, 298–299
  supply chain management, 299
  upgrading of production
    technologies, 298
service adaptation capabilities, 363–365
service capabilities, in Mexican
    EMNEs, 334
Serzaliyev, Marat, 198
ShangGong Group (SGG) (China), 64–66
Shaw, Kiran Mazumdar, 87, 89
Shishkina, Larisa, 145–147
"shock therapy," for economic growth in
    Poland, 155
Siberian-Ural Petrochemical and Gas
    Company (SIBUR) (Russia),
    133–138
  business model for, 136
  global partnerships with, 136
  internationalization through expansion,
    137–138
SIBUR. *See* Siberian-Ural Petrochemical
    and Gas Company
Siwei-Johnson (China), 57–58
skilled workers
  access to, 11
  at TCS iON, assessment of skills for,
    83–85
small and medium enterprises (SMEs), in
    Mexico, 310
SOEs. *See* state-owned enterprises
soft skills capabilities, 368–369
South Africa
  economic outlook, 102–106
    apartheid legacy as influence on, 102
    selected indicators for, 103
  foreign direct investment in, 103–106
    inward, 103, 104
    outward, 103, 105, 106
  GDP in, 102
  International Finance service firms
    in, 107
  multinational enterprises in, 101–102,
    122–123. *See also* strategic
    capabilities; *specific companies*
    analysis of, 120–122
    case studies for, 106–107
    Clover Industries, 108
    establishment of, 106
    evidence for, 109
    Nedbank Group, 108

Standard Bank Group, 107–108
Tiger Brands, 108–109
strategic capabilities, for MNEs,
    109–120, 121
  business acumen capabilities, 109,
    110–113, 120
  in Community Innovation Survey
    hierarchy, 110
  customer embedding, 118
  embeddedness, 113–118. See also
    specific topics
  evolving business acumen, 112–113
  foundational business acumen,
    111–112
  intra-MNE embeddedness
    capabilities, 109, 113–114
  leapfrogging, 113
  local embeddedness capabilities, 109,
    115, 122
  parent–subsidiary embeddedness, 114
  regulator embedding, 115–117
  subsidiaries and, 121–122
  subsidiary–subsidiary
    embeddedness, 115
  supplier embedding, 117
  in wider Africa, operations of, 110
Sportmaster (Kazakhstan), 194–197
  IT development, 194
  private label development, 195
  research and development by, 195
Srougi, Thomas, 252
Standard Bank Group (South Africa),
    107–108
Starukhin, Vsevolod, 136–137
state-owned enterprises (SOEs), in India,
    73–75
Stefanini (Brazil), 244–246, 256–257
  business process outsourcing
    portfolio, 245
  Capability Maturity Model for, 245
  as IT company, 244–245
strategic capabilities. See also upgrading of
    strategic capabilities; specific
    companies
  ability to develop resources internally
    capabilities, 363–365
  in Argentina. See Argentina
  in Chile. See Chile
  in China. See China
  cross-cultural management
    capabilities, 374
  development of, 2
  dynamic capabilities, of Russian
    MNCs, 131
  firm-level capabilities, 379

general sales capabilities, 363–365, 368,
    373–374
home country differences, 375–378, 380
in India
  analysis of, 96–98
  modes of acquisition, 98
  summary of, 96
industry differences in, 365–370
  for entrepreneurship, 369–370
  soft skills, 368–369
  supply chain management, 367–368
industry-level capabilities, 379
local product capabilities, 363–365
management-related, 379
  in Brazil, 236
marketing capabilities, for Brazil
    EMNEs, 236, 257
market-related capabilities, for Brazil
    EMNEs, 236
multinationality differences in, 370–374
national context as factor in, 2–3
operations management capabilities, in
    Mexican EMNEs, 334–335
for Polish national firms, 180–185
political and negotiating
    capabilities, 378
product management capabilities,
    372–373
  in Mexican EMNEs, 331–333, 334
production capabilities, for Brazil
    EMNEs, 257
relationship capabilities, 331–333,
    362–363, 372, 375–377
research and development, 366–367,
    377–378
research methodology for, 3–8
  company list, 7–8
  data collection in, 4
  potential capabilities in, 5
in Russia. See Russia
service adaptation capabilities, 363–365
service capabilities, in Mexican
    EMNEs, 334
in South Africa. See South Africa
summary of, 380
supply chain management, 367–368,
    370–371
technological capabilities, in
    Kazakhstan, 201
theoretical approach to, 1–3
  organization in, 3–10
understanding local customer needs
    capabilities, 360–362, 375
usage patterns for, 360–365
by value chain segment, 364

424   Index

subsidiaries
   for Derco, 275
   in South Africa MNEs, 121–122
   parent–subsidiary embeddedness
      in, 114
   subsidiary–subsidiary
      embeddedness, 115
   Swilar and, 147
subsidiary–subsidiary embeddedness, in
   South Africa MNEs, 115
supplier embedding, in South Africa
   MNEs, 117
supply chain management capabilities,
   367–368, 370–371
   in Colombia EMNEs, 299
Swilar (Russia), 147–149
   strategic resources for, 148–149
   subsidiaries and, 147

Tata Consultancy Services iON (TCS iON)
      (India)
   in China, 81
   economic competition, 85–86
   globalization of, through expansion, 81–83
   IT services, 81
   in local markets, 86
   organizational structure, 85–86
   partnerships with other MNCs, 82
   skills assessment by, for workers, 83–85
   tax reporting, in Kazakhstan, 196
TCS iON. See Tata Consultancy
      Services iON
technological capabilities, for Brazil
      EMNEs, 236
Tencent, 1
Tiger Brands (South Africa), 108–109
Titan (India), 90–96
   capital requirements, 93–94
   economic competition for, 93
   internationalization of, 91–92
   manufacturing strength, 91
   market factors for, size of, 94–95
   research and development by, 92–93
trade partners
   for Polish national firms, 159
   with Russian MNCs, 126
transparency, for Russian multinational
      corporations, 129
Tsesna-Astyk (Kazakhstan), 203–205
   distribution structure, 203–204
   exports, 204–205
   international expansion of, 204
   market selection, 204–205

Ukraine, Nowy Styl in, 168–169
UNCTAD. See United Nations Conference
      on Trade and Development
understanding local customer needs
      capabilities, 360–362, 375
United Nations Conference on Trade
      and Development (UNCTAD),
      19, 37
United States of America (USA),
      Mexican economic context
      influenced by, 311
upgrading of strategic capabilities, in
      emerging markets, 26–37
   definition of, 101
   development stages in, of firms, 29
   as dynamic process, 29, 36
   methods for, 11
      frequency of, 29
      imitation, 29–30
      incorporation, 31–33
      integration, 30–31
      internal development, 33–34
USA. See United States of America

Valencia, Andres, 304
Valenzuela, James, 345
value chain segments, 364
Vazquez, Roberto, 212
vertical integration strategies
   Arcor, 230
   Bodega Lagarde, 216
   Forus, 273
   Grendene, 250
Vidanta (Mexico), 324–325
Virobyan, Yuri, 139–140

WEG (Brazil), 239–242
   internationalization of, 239–240,
      253–256
      in Chinese markets, 240–241
      in local markets, 241
Willi, Guillermo, 227, 228
wine production, in Argentina, 215–218
World Intellectual Property Organization
      (WIPO), 343, 357

Xi Jinping, 46
Xiaomi, 1

Yobel (Peru), 352–355
   international expansion of, 353–354

Zevallos, Oscar, 350–351

CPSIA information can be obtained
at www.ICGtesting.com
Printed in the USA
BVHW040952131020
590913BV00012B/250